T0327689

Industrial Eden

Industrial Eden

A CHINESE CAPITALIST VISION

BRETT SHEEHAN

 Harvard University Press

Cambridge, Massachusetts
London, England
2015

Library of Congress Cataloging-in-Publication Data

Sheehan, Brett, 1960–
  Industrial Eden : a Chinese capitalist vision / Brett Sheehan.
    pages cm
  Includes bibliographical references and index.
  ISBN 978-0-674-96760-1 (alk. paper)
  1. Industries—China—History—20th century. 2. Industrial policy—
China—History—20th century. 3. Businessmen—China—History—20th
century. 4. Capitalism—China—History—20th century. 5. China—
Economic conditions—1912–1949. 6. China—Politics and government—
1912–1949. 7. China—History—Republic, 1912–1949. I. Title.
  HC427.8.S45 2015
  338.092'251—dc23   2014035333

For the family that keeps me sane, especially:
    my mother SHIRLEEN NEU,
    my wife YIYU JIANG, *and*
    my sons, KEVIN *and* ANGEL

Contents

Industrial Eden

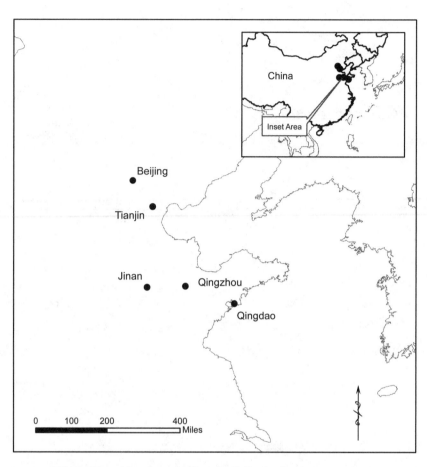

MAP 1   North China cities where the Song family lived or had business operations.

Introduction

IN THE LATE 1870s a seven-year-old poor peasant boy named Song Chuandian left his home in central Shandong to go to school in another village. Details remain murky, but it must have been a boarding school because his family had to prepare food for him to take. Song Chuandian's departure was unusual because at this particular time and place, education was hard to come by, especially for poor illiterate peasants. Both his father and mother were Christians, a fact that already set Song Chuandian apart from the majority of his neighbors; perhaps he was used to feeling different. It is likely that the school he attended had some relation to the British Baptist mission based in that area of Shandong because a few years later he moved on from the village school to attend the newly established middle and high school at the mission compound in the county capital of Qingzhou. His father went along with him to work as a laborer at the mission to pay for his tuition. Mission school educations, apparently, did not come free.[1]

As the boy left for school that first time he could not have imagined the wrenching change and tumultuous events in which he and his family would participate. This book tells the story of Song Chuandian, and even more so the story of his son Song Feiqing, their transformation into businessmen, their eventual crowning as "capitalists" as that term became current, their relations, sometimes confrontations, with five successive and mutually hostile authoritarian regimes that ruled North China in the twentieth century, and Song Feiqing's mission to use industry to transform society, to create an "Industrial Eden." In short, this is a book about capitalists and authoritarianism in twentieth-century China.

"Industrial Eden" is the phrase I have coined to describe a particular vision of business developed by Song Feiqing and others amid the chaos that was China in the first half of the twentieth century. In the present digital age "industry" sounds slightly old-fashioned and a bit grimy, but for many in China during the first half of the twentieth century, industry held the promise of economic development, national strength, modernity, and even beauty. To some, industry was just a path to personal wealth, either as a vehicle for investment or a source from which to extract resources. For many, however, industry had a redemptive quality. The frustrated British Baptist missionaries in late nineteenth-century Qingzhou turned to handicraft industry to relieve the grinding poverty of their parishioners. By the 1920s and 1930s, many industrialists like Song Feiqing saw industry as the means to save China from the depredations of imperialism, to deliver society from backwardness, and to drive toward a utopian modernity. It is this utopian aspect, and the Christian background of the Song family, that makes "Eden" an apt modifier for this particular vision of industrial development, thus "Industrial Eden." Song Feiqing was not alone in seeing industry as socially, culturally, and politically transformative, so I use "Industrial Eden" both to refer specifically to his Christian-tinged vision and more generally to refer to any redemptive industrial experiments of the time in China and abroad.

I call Song Feiqing's Industrial Eden a "capitalist" vision because in the late 1940s Communists and other leftists labeled him a capitalist and that is what he has been called by most Chinese commentators ever since. "Capitalism," however, was and is a problematic concept.[2] Some scholars approach capitalism as simply the existence of private enterprise.[3] If the operation of private business served as a rough proxy for capitalism, then the severe limitations on the freedom of private businesses to operate in China were also limitations on capitalism. Throughout the first half of the twentieth century, private businesspeople like the Songs were subject to extortion and potential confiscation from a series of five more or less rapacious authoritarian governments, each one increasingly interested in building state-run, rather than private, economies. Other scholars see distribution of goods and services through free markets as the key element to capitalism.[4] From this standpoint, the Songs did not operate in a fully capitalist system, nor did they seem to want to. They welcomed protective tariffs and profitable monopolies whenever possible. Still other scholars see capitalism as including democracy in some manner. Early thinkers ranging from Barrington Moore to Josef Schumpeter have argued for a close relationship between capitalism and democracy.[5] Bruce Scott argues that a necessary component of capitalism is indirect governance of the economy through a regime that is accountable to political markets, usually through democracy.[6] In spite of having some local elected bodies, China was not a functioning democracy at the time, so this aspect of capitalism was also lacking. By any of these measures—private business, free markets, and democracy—China was not fully capitalist at this time. Thus the members of the Song family were essentially capitalists without capitalism.

Song family business relations with five successive authoritarian regimes and Song Feiqing's utopian "Industrial Eden" capitalist vision provide the two threads that serve as the organizational principle of this book. Although these two threads intertwine, Chapters 1, 2, 4, 6, and 7 deal primarily with business relations to the five regimes and Chapters 3, 5, and 8 discuss the Industrial Eden vision.

By following the Songs across five regimes, this book traverses the governmental changes that often make up the beginning and ending points of books and articles on modern China. Following the Song family across these political divides provides an opportunity both to see how businesspeople interacted with a variety of authoritarian governments and to understand the experiences of Chinese whose lives did not begin or end with each new government. Each of those regime changes, however, offered a unique set of challenges in terms of finding sources. I have cast my net widely, using family papers, missionary archives, corporate records, government documents, diplomatic correspondence, newspapers, magazines, recorded oral histories, novels, and interviews, among others. Toward the end of her life, Song Feiqing's widow, Li Jingfang, made copious notes about the family's history. One of Song Feiqing's trusted lieutenants, Shi Shaodong, even drafted a memoir that was never published. In addition, Song Feiqing's daughter Roberta Sung (Song Yunzhang) wrote a biography of her father, which collected many stories from family and friends. Li Jingfang's notes, Shi Shaodong's memoir, and Roberta Sung's book served as especially important sources, though they were only three among thousands.

This book makes four major arguments. First, the experiences of the Song family provide new evidence to address an old question about the impact of imperialism on the Chinese economy. From the beginning, the Songs' business grew in intimate contact with the world trading systems, cultural production, and political regimes of imperialism. The story of the Songs shows that imperialism brought both opportunities—such as education, new products, markets, and modes of production—and challenges—such as fierce competitors and an ever-shifting and often dangerous political landscape—to Chinese businesspeople. From the standpoint of the Songs it is impossible to label imperialism as strictly good or bad, but I argue that it is clear that the impact of imperialism was uneven and often arbitrary in its effects for the Chinese economy. Second, the story of the Songs adds to the growing body of evidence that there is no single, culturally determined set of Chinese business practices. The Songs engaged in pragmatic and eclectic business practices that had hallmarks of both foreign influence and Chinese culture. At the same time, under Song Feiqing, pragmatism coexisted in uneasy tension with a utopian vision of the firm as a vehicle to reshape Chinese society. Here, too, Song Feiqing took an eclectic approach in developing his brand of utopian, visionary pragmatism and drew widely on both foreign and domestic sources of influence. Third, control over the narrative of the place of business in society became both a business strategy and a political tool tinged with moral and patriotic concerns. During the lifetimes of Song Chuandian and Song Feiqing, and for decades after, the Songs, their employees, and a host of political figures struggled over control of the narrative of the Song family businesses. Analysis of this shifting narrative shows that "capitalist" was a term that intruded into Song Feiqing's life in the 1940s and that was used as a label to try to oversimplify and essentialize his role as a businessperson in society. For Song supporters and opponents alike, capitalism and business were judged by moral standards as much as by financial success. Fourth and finally, the authoritarian governments that ruled North China over the course of the twentieth century varied widely with each other and in their relations with business, but a common thread shows that over time Chinese states and businesspeople alike came to accept and expect an increasingly intrusive government role in business. There was no fetishization, or even discussion, of free markets on either side. Although state intervention became accepted as normal, it was often chaotic, arbitrary, and venal. The result was simultaneous mutual interdependence and mutual suspicion between North China's authoritarian states and private business.

The Song Family and Imperialism

Although the Songs came from a relatively remote part of Shandong, their lives became inextricably intertwined with the global forces of imperialism as early as the 1870s when Song Chuandian left home for school for the first time to study at British missionary schools. Much of the literature on the economic impact of imperialism on China is both outdated and inconclusive.[7] Sherman Cochran's more recent work has rejected the question of whether imperialism was good or bad and has looked at the ways that Chinese businesses have become active agents in the creation of modern consumer culture.[8] For the Songs, European imperialism brought the missionaries who made possible the family's escape from rural poverty, but who also left many others relatively untouched. The gospel of development they preached launched the Song family on the road to wealth, but did little to transform the Shandong countryside.

At the same time, European and then Japanese imperialism created a world trading system that reshaped business opportunities through both trade and the spread of a new consumer culture based on foreign products and industrial production. This trading system brought both opportunities and challenges. Song Chuandian made a fortune in handicraft consumer products when he used cheap Chinese labor to produce hairnets for export, but when Song Feiqing tried industrial-style production to manufacture knitting yarn for domestic Chinese consumption in the 1930s as a way to be both modern (read "foreign") and patriotic at the same time, he succeeded at competing with foreign producers only with tariff protection and tax subsidies from the Nationalist government. When foreign competitors relocated plants to China after 1936, Song found it difficult to compete with these foreign-labeled and Chinese-produced goods. Subsequently, with the Japanese invasion of China, Song Feiqing faced the long arm of imperialism more directly. War and the Japanese occupation created business opportunities and threats that often came together in no predictable pattern. Song's Dongya Corporation survived, and often thrived, during the war by taking advantage of the "economy of things" created by infla-tion and Japanese attempts at economic control. In the "economy of things," individuals preferred goods, virtually any goods, in lieu of money. Song Feiqing and his managers proved themselves masters at adapting to this new economic environment. After the Japanese surrender in 1945, China's monetary problems continued, and the situation was made even more prob-lematic by renewed foreign competition and chaotic foreign exchange mar-kets. Formal imperialism may have ended in China, but Chinese business-people were still tied to an international economic system outside of their control. Communist victory in 1949 promised a state strong enough to sta-bilize China's place in the international economy, but when Song Feiqing became disillusioned with the new regime, he and his family found refuge of a sort in that last bastion of Western imperialism in China: the British colony of Hong Kong.

In short, Song Feiqing and his father more or less adeptly used, borrowed from, adapted to, and rejected Western and Japanese imperialism, de-pending on both pragmatic interests and personal preferences.

The Song Family and Chinese Business Practices

The eclectic business practices used by Song Feiqing and his father add to existing evidence that Chinese businesspeople were not necessarily tied by cultural constraints in the conduct of their operations.[9] Tellingly, culture has been used at different times to explain both the failures and successes of Chinese business.[10] Divergent opinions can be found in virtually every aspect of study of culture's impact on Chinese business, including whether Chinese businesspeople can be classified as "true" entrepreneurs, a debate on the cultural propensity for preferring quick profits over long-term in-vestment, the use of particularistic networks, and the primacy of the family-owned firm.[11] The latter two, particularism and the family-owned firm, are those characteristics most often associated with Chinese business. Li Chun has gone so far as to say that on the one hand, "the idea that mem-bers of the public would be invited to join one's business and share in its control and profits was indeed repugnant. On the other hand, the notion that one's money be put into the pocket of some strangers for them to run a business was just as unthinkable."[12] In a classic article, Siu-lun Wong allowed for a greater range of activity, but he still proposed that "the essence of Chinese economic organization is familism." He defined three aspects of Chinese economic familism, "the preferential recruitment and promotion of kinsmen within a firm," "how superiors and subordinates interact in a company," and "ownership and control of business assets by the family."[13]

The empirical scholarship shows significant variation across space and time in the way networks operate as well as in business form, which ranged from family-owned and lineage firms to partnerships with clear division between ownership and management, and successful adoption of the Western limited-liability corporation.[14] Since much of the scholarship that argues for the importance of particularistic networks and family firms derives from a skewed sample focused primarily on business operations among the Chinese diaspora, it is possible that scholars merely saw the effects of the sojourning environment rather than a particular cultural legacy.[15] Arif Dirlik questions the very process of representing Chinese capitalism "in terms of unchanging values associated with an abstract Chineseness."[16] In any case, the growing literature on business in late Qing and republican-period China shows both indigenous variation and examples of successful adaptation of many Western business practices.[17]

The evidence from Song family businesses joins this growing chorus. From the early days of making hairnets for export in rural Shandong, to manufacturing knitting yarn and then gunnysacks in Tianjin in the 1930s and 1940s, Song family business practices were pragmatic and drew eclectically from both Chinese and international influences. Sometimes the Songs used particularistic networks such as family, friends, and native-place compatriots to find investors and employees. They also managed their employees with a paternalism often associated with Confucianism, but there is no reason to label such phenomena as exclusively Chinese. In studying the United States, Philip Scranton identified a kind of "familiar paternalism," where owners relied on native-place networks, "individually dispensed rewards and punishments, and 'knew their hands by name, pressed their souls toward church or chapel, commanded their political allegiance, and rewarded the virtue of the diligent, devout, deserving few.'"[18] Other Song management practices were conscious foreign adoptions, such as seeking investment from strangers and using impersonal and highly technical management methods.

Most famously, Song Feiqing developed his vision that eclectically mixed Confucian paternalism and Chinese nationalism with Western Christianity, "scientific" management, hygienic practice, consumer capitalism, industrialism, and modern discipline.[19] Outside of the factory, Song Feiqing and his company promoted a "modern" consumer culture, which claimed to be based on scientific principles. Within the Dongya factory, Industrial Eden included a broad range of employee welfare policies. Such employee welfare policies, inspired in part by foreign example, were not unknown in China in the 1920s and 1930s, but only spread rapidly during World War II in state-owned enterprises in areas controlled by the Nationalist government.[20] Although Dongya was a private company operating in Japanese-occupied China, it nonetheless adopted a similar range of policies including education, social activities, housing, and health care. Accounts of the Dongya Corporation published in the 1930s and 1940s, as well as histories written after about 1980, focus on the benevolent and enlightened nature of these policies.[21] Here I show how fragile Industrial Eden really was. Rather than a shared utopian vision that bound management and employees together in pursuit of a disciplined and productive modernity, it was at least in part the purchase of temporary loyalty by generous welfare policies paid for by wartime profiteering. Under the strains of post–World War II inflation, any sense of unity and shared purpose between management and labor collapsed at the Dongya Corporation. I also show how Industrial Eden employee welfare policies were mixed with a militaristic commitment to discipline, regulation, measurement, and hygiene.[22] One of the factory's management slogans called for "Christian spirit and *military* discipline" (emphasis added). This disciplinary dark side of employee welfare eerily complemented many of the militarist, fascist, and Leninist visions of the authoritarians who strove to rule China at the time.[23]

The Song Family and Narratives of Capitalist Morality

As capitalists without capitalism, Song Chuandian and Song Feiqing lived at a time when there was little agreement about the role of business and businesspeople in society. Song Chuandian used his business success to launch a career in politics, making himself a capitalist-politician, but the vagaries of warlord politics ended his political career and almost destroyed his business. By the 1930s, Song Feiqing tried to wrap his business operations in the protective cocoon of his Industrial Eden vision. He presented his business enterprise as a positive transformative force in the nation and society. To borrow Karl Gerth's words, Song portrayed himself as one of the "exemplars of a new nationalistic ethic of consumption and production."[24] By promoting the social and patriotic roles of his company he received publicity for his products, and support from the Nationalist state which had economic development goals to strengthen China. My argument here goes well beyond the relationship between patriotism and production, however, because the evidence here shows that the discussion of National Products was only part of a larger moral debate on the nature of business. Song Feiqing also staked a claim to the moral high ground by promoting modernity outside of the factory and by instituting a series of policies inside the factory to see to the welfare of his employees. His success at holding that moral high ground eventually came to be judged as part of a debate on the nature of capitalism.

For most of their lives as businesspeople, the Songs themselves did not seem to worry about whether they were capitalists or whether they worked within a capitalist system.[25] As used in the sources I examined, "capitalism" was not a well-defined type of economic or even political-economic activity. "Capitalism" did not presume any particular combination or type of ownership, market, or business-state relations. Instead, it was a constantly shifting category through which businesspeople, workers, and politicians came to construct their understanding of the world.

The notion of the capitalist and the implied tension between labor and capital began appearing in relation to Song Feiqing during the Japanese Occupation of World War II. The lyrics of a new company song extolled mutual benefit for both capital and labor. By implication, this lyric points to the existence of anticapitalist rhetoric, perhaps by Japanese military figures, many of whom detested capitalism. By the late 1940s the growing strength of the Communist Party and its program of labor agitation in cities like Tianjin brought the word "capitalist" to the fore in the public discourse as a pejorative term. By 1947 Song Feiqing was responding to the negative meaning of the term in lectures to Dongya employees. Most famously, Song Feiqing took issue with the growing negative connotations of capitalism by writing his essay "Labor and Capital Are on the Same Side" (Laofang jiushi zifang). For a brief moment, Song Feiqing thought he had a chance at defining "capitalism" in a way that would embrace both capital and labor in peaceful coexistence, but the labor strife at Dongya in the postwar period made clear this was mostly wishful thinking on his part.' In the end his conceptualization was overwhelmed by the growing power of a Communist state hostile to private business and willing to wield the label of "capitalist" to wrest control of the narrative and implement state control over both business and labor.

Later, in the period of Maoist rule from 1949 to the late 1970s, state legitimacy rested in part on the ability to undermine China's capitalist past, especially the redemptive foundations of the Industrial Eden vision. Except for a brief relaxation in the early 1960s, "capitalist" became a term used to label and dismiss anyone associated with the management of private business. The capitalist was the other against which heroic narratives of Communist and worker struggles could be painted. Beginning in the 1980s, however, there was a complete reversal and the capitalist became a potential model of heroic national strength. Song Feiqing's utopianism made him particularly prominent as both a target of criticism and a model of enlightened economic behavior.

Throughout the twentieth century and into the twenty-first, for critics and supporters alike, however, evaluation of capitalism focused on the social and political goals of a business, not financial success. Public discussions of business, the narrative the Songs tried so hard to control, had profoundly moral overtones. These morally-charged discussions derived in part from the need to justify private business in the face of intrusive authoritarian states.

The Song Family and Authoritarian Governments

Song Feiqing and his father operated their businesses under five successive authoritarian regimes, defined here as systems "in which a leader or small group exercises power without formal limits."[26] The Song family operated under these regimes from about 1915 to the 1950s, and subsequently the Song legacy was subject to interpretation and reinterpretation by the fifth of those regimes, the Communists, over the course of more than another half a century.

The question of authoritarian governments has loomed large in the scholarship on Chinese business, especially for the dynastic period prior to the
fall of the Qing dynasty in 1911. For that period, some scholars see the private sector as dwarfed by and insignificant compared to the state, some see
a symbiotic relationship between business and the state, and some see a
vibrant private sector isolated from and potentially hostile to the state.[27]
Specific case studies from the Qing period show examples of all three patterns as well as some that fell in between. State-business interaction varied
from industry to industry, from location to location, and from time to time.
Sometimes there was wary cooperation, sometimes interdependence, and
sometimes relative autonomy.[28] Turning to the republican period, studies
of business show a diverse pattern of interaction, but there are fewer examples of the relative autonomy exercised by some businesses under the
Qing. In her seminal study of the Chinese bourgeoisie during the warlord
and Nationalist periods, Marie-Claire Bergère finds that business was not
strong enough to oppose the state or to develop without state help.[29] For
the period of Nationalist rule in the 1930s, Parks Coble identifies the Nationalists as a predatory state, whereas Linsun Cheng sees considerable
room for private dynamism in the banking industry.[30] In contrast to Cheng,
I have argued that the demands of trust as a framework forced the banking
industry and the state into an uneasy mutual dependence followed by outright state predation by the mid-1930s.[31] Turning to the wartime period,
Morris L. Bian sees the emergence (or perhaps reemergence) of state
dominance of business as part of mobilization for war in the Nationalist-
controlled areas, while in occupied Shanghai Parks Coble sees savvy businesspeople hedging their bets under the onslaught of Japanese confiscation
and Nationalist war requisitioning.[32] Business in the postwar and early
Maoist periods has received very little attention in the scholarly literature,
but new studies of the choices businesspeople made under early Communist rule also show a range of variation from cooperation to opposition.[33]
    Showing similar range, the relations of Song family businesses to the
five governments under which they operated show everything from state
dominance to mutual hostility, though that hostility never precluded cooperation at some level. For the most part, the Song family was subject to
political processes over which they had little influence. Although at times,
the Songs made a bid for active participation in politics—Song Chuandian

ran for election to the Shandong provincial assembly, and his son, Song Feiqing, received nomination to run for the National Assembly under the Nationalists in 1946 and appointment to the People's Consultative Conference under the Communists in 1950—neither father nor son proved able to translate political participation into long-term power. In spite of that lack of power, the Songs conducted business under the warlords who stamped out the last remnants of China's post-dynastic democratic experiments, the Nationalists who ruled as a single party and often exhibited hostility to private business, the Japanese occupation regime, which sent the Nationalists into retreat and tried to subsume large parts of China and Chinese business into the Japanese empire, the Nationalists who came back after Japanese surrender and who during the war had turned increasingly to state ownership and direction of economic activity, and the Communist Party, which was ideologically opposed to private business but initially needed business allies to build the Chinese economy. Over the first half of the twentieth century, these five regimes fomented revolution, went to war with each other, invaded, and struggled to build viable states. Amid that turmoil, each presented the Song family with different challenges and opportunities. Remarkably, in spite of some ups and downs, the Song family landed on its feet after each regime change and established good relations with every incoming government. Relations deteriorated after Song Feiqing left China in 1950, and the Communist state used him and his family as examples of the evils of capitalism, but by the 1980s, the Song legacy was on its feet again as he became a poster boy for enlightened capitalism during the post-Mao period.

Following the Song family across all five regimes, it is clear that their experiences confirmed the growing impression that regimes became increasingly intrusive in society and the economy over the course of the first half of the twentieth century.[34] At the same time, in a lesser-known story, businesspeople such as Song Feiqing expected a great deal from the state and continued to do so even as government became more intrusive and sometimes more hostile to private business. Even a utopian and visionary businessperson such as Song Feiqing took a pragmatic approach to the political environments in which he functioned. In his own words, "If you stay away from 'government,' you don't have any other place to go, it's hard to get ahead; if you get the least close to 'government,' it's hard to be a [moral] person."[35] In reality he usually chose involvement with the state. As with much of the world in the twentieth century, the visible hand of the state in the economy became a norm in China.[36]

The visible hands of the five regimes that ruled North China in the first half of the twentieth century took a variety of forms but can be classified generally as leaning toward one or more of three models: the laissez-faire free-market state, the developmental state (which has both socialist and capitalist manifestations), and the extractive state. In truth the laissez-faire free-market model was virtually absent except perhaps for a brief time in a few places during the early warlord period of the late 1910s. In contrast, the early twentieth century was a time of growth for developmental states all over the world and in China as well. A developmental state takes an active hand in planning and allocating resources to achieve specific economic goals and thus contrasts with states that allow, or encourage, allocation of resources through markets. The classic example of the developmental state is the Marxist (or Stalinist or Maoist) state where private property is limited or nonexistent and the state controls the means of production. In addition to the Marxist state, Chalmers Johnson has asserted that there exists an alternative kind of "capitalist" developmental state.[37] Hugo Radice has noted that the capitalist developmental state "in contrast to the conventionally polar models of liberal free-market capitalism and the state-socialist planned economy . . . is seen as a distinctive political economy that combines elements of market and plan."[38] Following Chalmers Johnson's model, Yu-shan Wu explains the four constituent elements of the developmental state—state autonomy, developmental consensus, bureaucratic penetration into society, and industrial policy suited to world markets.[39] In contrast to both the socialist and capitalist versions of the developmental state, scholars point to the extractive or predatory state, which extracts "at the expense of society, undercutting development even in the narrow sense of capital accumulation."[40]

In recent decades, inspired in part by the post–World War II success of the East Asian economies, the developmental state literature has become so influential that one reference book on political philosophy raises the "successes of capitalist development engineered by authoritarian regimes in East Asia" as an important exception to the normal correlation of capitalism with democracy.[41] The story of the Song family provides new evidence for the analysis of Chinese capitalists and developmental or predatory authoritarian governments over the course of the twentieth century. In reality, most of the regimes under which the Song family conducted its business operations combined elements of both development and extraction. Bruce Cumings has noted that "states appropriate the market and firms appropriate the state, in a political range from conflict of interest to consensus," and the story of the Song family shows a variety of phenomena along that range.[42] Importantly, although classifying regimes as more or less developmental or predatory is a useful starting point in studying relations with the authoritarian regimes under which the Songs operated their businesses, it obscures the messy and arbitrary nature of business-state relations of the time. Authoritarianism did not necessarily mean efficiency, or even unity, in rule. Thus sometimes the Songs looked to the state for official developmental policies to help business, but just as often they dealt with states through the "back door," ex officio channels that often involved bribery and deal making made possible by the chaotic, arbitrary, and venal nature of the states that ruled North China. The use of extralegal channels to deal with the agents of authoritarian states is reminiscent of the kind of "adaptive informal institutions" Kellee Tsai describes in China after the post-Mao reforms.[43] The experience of the Song family indicates, however, that such channels were less stable, less institutionalized, and less functional in the ever-shifting political landscape before 1949.

In sum, the story of Song family interactions with these five regimes tells two stories, one of a general increase in state direction of the economy over time mirrored by increasing expectations of the state from businesspeople and one of wide variation and messiness within that general trend. In the short run, states ruled and the Songs made money, but in the long run, the combined effects of these two stories did not produce either effective states or viable businesses. As politicians of all stripes dreamed of invincible and well-regulated states and as Song Feiqing dreamed of a profitable and orderly business firm, the endless mobilization of people and resources in the name of industrialization and national strength led to the chaos of endless war and disputes over scarce resources. The middle managers employed by state builders proved quick to compromise their loyalty to their regimes, either to line their own pockets or to engage in crisis management and enable survival in an uncertain world. Constant political conflict led the agents of mobilizing states to pursue victory at all costs. In search of consistency and conformity, they created disparity and inequality. In search of economic growth, they undermined production. At the same time, China's participation in global consumer culture died under the on-slaught of the demands from states for mobilization of resources for war, and later for socialist construction, which inexorably moved the economic center of gravity away from society and toward state needs.

Amid this constant chaos, the story of Song Chuandian and Song Feiqing showed that idealistic businesspeople compromised too and often accepted bad deals from the state in lieu of destruction. At the end of his life, a bat-tered and broken Song Feiqing was left with little more than his idealism, his belief in an Industrial Eden that could transform society. He never ac-cepted the fact that his own Industrial Eden had hit its peak when financed by war profiteering. In reality, however, the idea of redemptive and uto-pian industrialization promised much, but delivered little. Development plans by British Baptist missionaries in Qingzhou in the late nineteenth century failed to transform the Shandong countryside, though they cer-tainly transformed the lives of the Song family. Likewise, Song Feiqing's utopian vision failed to strengthen the Chinese state, transform society, pro-tect him from labor unrest, or even ensure the survival of the company as a private enterprise. Redemption through industrialization remained elusive.

More important, however, Song Chuandian's and Song Feiqing's actions showed the resilience and flexibility of businesspeople in dealing with their environment and with the uncertainty that plagued their world.[44] They re-mained locked in an uneasy and suspicious interdependence with the au-thoritarian states that ruled North China. In spite of increasing state power and increasing state interference, the states that ruled China re-mained at least partially as dependent on the Songs' private business as those businesses remained dependent on states. Even after 1949 when the Song family lost control of its business, the Communist state relied on the Songs' legacy to justify both socialist construction and, later, market reforms. The story of the Songs and their legacy shows that Chinese business was neither a natural ally of democracy nor a completely willing handmaiden of authoritarianism.

1 The Warlord State and the Capitalist-Politician

WHEN SONG CHUANDIAN left his village to go to school, the Qing dynasty (1644–1911) still ruled China.[1] Of the same generation as the late Qing revolutionaries who would advocate overthrow of the Qing, over the course of his life Song Chuandian saw the fall of the Qing dynasty, the establishment of a republic in its place, and then the disintegration of that republic into regional and local warlord rule.[2] Warlord China from approximately 1916 to 1928 witnessed both economic vitality in certain sectors and a concurrent breakdown of the national political system.[3] On the surface, the ever-escalating civil wars—at the rate of about one war every two years—the predatory military governments, the lack of the rule of law, and the constantly changing political regimes created an inhospitable environment for business. Nonetheless, some businesses did grow and prosper.

Small rural businesspeople like Song Chuandian at the start of his career could operate in a laissez-faire space out of the extractive reach of the warlord governments. As time went on, warlord governments became more predatory and Song's business grew to substantial proportions, but he used political position to protect and promote his business interests until a regime change in 1928 ruined him. The story of the Song family's rise and fall from the early part of the twentieth century to 1928 shows both the resilience of business amid uncertainty as well as its ultimate weakness when faced with coercive political power. To understand this story, though, it is necessary to go back to the 1870s and 1880s and investigate the conditions in which the Song family first turned to business as a profession.

The Gospel of Economic Development

Song Chuandian came from the Song Family Village (Songwangzhuang), where even in the year 2000 mud-thatched houses gave the appearance of a sleepy place that time forgot. Nestled among rolling hills spotted with wheat fields, the Song Family Village is in the mountainous southwest part of Qingzhou (formerly Yidu) County in central Shandong Province. This part of the county "was barren and the people poor," according to an observer in 1919.[4] Hills around the Song Family Village were too steep for extensive fields, so many peasants relied on products from the mountains such as firewood for their livelihoods.[5] In this barren and hilly landscape, the village is still so insignificant that it does not appear on the county map a century later in the 1989 local gazetteer.[6]

At the end of the nineteenth century, the Song Family Village was a half day's walk to the Qingzhou county seat, which itself was a three-day ride—by the relatively exalted means of riding a horse—from the provincial capital of Jinan.[7] Qingdao, Shandong's largest commercial city, was twice as far. Shanghai was a twelve-day journey, partly by boat.[8] From the standpoint of geography, the residents of Song Family Village did not seem to have a propitious position for upward social mobility.

Yet appearances can be deceiving. Isolated and poor, the Song Family Village nonetheless lay in, or at least near, the path of wrenching changes that transformed Shandong Province in the nineteenth and twentieth centuries. The commercial core of Shandong Province had previously been west of the provincial capital, Jinan, among towns along the Grand Canal, which connected North and South China. In the nineteenth century, environmental degradation and a shift in the locus of commerce away from this center to the coasts left a backwater where the economy previously thrived.[9] Rising coastal cities such as Qingdao, where Germany established the beachhead of its imperialist project in China, became Shandong's new economic centers. The Song Family Village lay between the old declining western part of the province and the new rising east. As these changes were taking place, in the 1870s and 1880s, agents of new opportunities arrived not just in the county seat of Qingzhou, but in rural areas such as the Song Family Village as well. New commercial opportunities came in the form of British Baptist missionaries who arrived on horseback, on foot, and on sedan chair. Confronted by the poverty of central Shandong where rural people "built their own houses, made their own bricks, [and] ground and [ate] their own [grain]," these missionaries eventually turned themselves to the task of bettering the lives of locals with a kind of gospel of economic development.[10]

Barred by the Qing dynasty from living in the provincial capital of Jinan during the nineteenth century, foreign missionaries took up residence in various Shandong county seats.[11] Most centers of missionary activity, such as Chifu and Weihai, were near the coast, but some hardy souls penetrated places in Shandong's rather unwelcoming interior such as Qingzhou County. Qingzhou's county seat was a medium-sized city which also served as the prefectural seat overseeing administration of eleven counties. By the 1870s an agreement between American Presbyterians and British Baptists placed Qingzhou in the latter's sphere of activity.[12] Qingzhou was as far into the interior of Shandong Province as protestant missionaries ventured during the nineteenth century. In fact, one missionary later noted that journeying southwest from Qingzhou, "one might travel all the way to [Hankou] [in central China, a distance of about five hundred miles] without meeting a single mission station."[13] As its pioneer in interior Shandong the British Baptist Missionary Society (BMS) dispatched Timothy Richard. After arriving in Qingzhou in 1875, he noted that the city "possessed an Islamic theological college, two mosques, Buddhist and Taoist temples, and an abundance of new religious sects."[14] Richard advocated an approach that focused on converting elites, teaching science and technology, and providing opportunities for the poor, thus making himself vulnerable to criticisms of working for social change rather than teaching the gospel. During the famine in Shandong in the late 1870s, Richard established an orphanage for boys that taught "occupations, so that the boys, who ranged from twelve to eighteen years of age, could earn their living."[15] Richard was soon posted to Shanxi and replaced in Qingzhou by Alfred Jones who shared many of Richard's ideas. Both of them were on the forefront of the so-called social gospel movement, which would become popular with some Protestants in the West in the 1880s and 1890s.[16]

Locals called Jones "foreign devil," so in order to blend in and gain acceptance, he adopted a Chinese style of dress, including growing the long braid, or queue, worn by Chinese men.[17] His unorthodox appearance may have helped him in the eyes of wary Chinese, but his future in-laws, American protestant missionaries in a coastal Shandong city, disapproved.[18] Western missionaries enjoyed some privileges, of course. For local travel, "where there are roads [missionaries] have mule-litters, carts & barrows, but where there are NO ROADS [they] are carried in sedan chairs, protected thoroughly from the sun."[19]

In Song Family Village, poor peasants like the Song family had no such luxury. They walked everywhere. Song Chuandian's father, Song Guangxu had been left an orphan by the age of eleven; he herded sheep, worked for relatives, and collected firewood in the mountains for sale in the county seat.[20] At the age of twenty-two, his relatives found him a bride, a woman from a nearby village who might have been a Christian protestant.[21] If she was protestant, she was one of very few. Even a decade after her marriage, the BMS mission in Qingzhou counted only "1,094 members, scattered over 63 stations."[22] If she was Christian, it would help explain how, in spite of their poverty, they sent their first son, Song Chuandian away to a Christian-sponsored rural school around the age of seven. By 1886 the BMS had eight schools attached to its village stations "where some 80 boys study both native and Christian books."[23]

The fact that such schools existed at all defied the directives of the BMS in Britain, whose members saw little need for secular education. Alfred Jones encountered fierce opposition when he decided to go beyond village schools and proposed turning the Qingzhou county seat orphanage Timothy Richard had founded into a "good *school* on a small pointed well directed base, to act as a promoter of scientific knowledge—a melter of supersticion [*sic*]. . . . It is a right handmaid to a church *in* heathen land."[24] The China subcommittee of the BMS argued that missionary resources would be better spent on "ecumenical extension." On leave in England, Jones made a personal appeal to members of the society and asked for sympathy for "peculiar forms of work necessitated by our peculiar—our most peculiar circumstances. . . . If our work is not to be suicidal, if we are not going to set class against class and breed sedition over again, then Literary, Official, and Educational work must be begun."[25] Eventually Jones prevailed and returned to China with a BMS blessing for a new school in 1884.[26]

Perhaps drawn to Jones, a number of like-minded missionaries would make their way to Qingzhou over the final years of the nineteenth century.

By 1885 there were a total of seven Western missionaries, including J. S. Whitewright who founded the Whitewright Institute and Museum, because "we know that a little natural science is able to kill a great deal of superstition, and to set men enquiring—in a word, to waken men into mental activity."[27] In addition to Whitewright, the BMS also sent Samuel Couling and his wife to oversee the new county seat school. Samuel Couling became an accomplished sinologist who was one of the first Westerners to collect the earliest known forms of Chinese writing, oracle bones, and who in 1917 published *The Encyclopaedia Sinica*, which became a standard English-language reference work on China. He would also later become "joint author of *The History of Shanghai* and editor of the *New China Review*."[28] Mrs. Couling's presence derived from a specific strategy conceived by Alfred Jones to convert Chinese women to Christianity.[29] In addition to requesting a married couple like the Coulings, Jones also requested two "unmarried female missionaries to work among the women."[30]

The Coulings arrived in Qingzhou in March of 1886, and in 1887 opened a boys' school where "a select number of boys from the village schools may in addition to a good Chinese education learn something of western mathematics and the cultural sciences, and receive that moral training which it is so difficult for them to get at home."[31] One of their first students was none other than Song Chuandian. Song arrived in the Qingzhou county seat with his father who worked as a laborer in the mission compound, while his son, and later his other children, attended school.[32] Song Guangxu had to work to offset the cost of his children's education because the school was run on a shoestring and required more contributions from families than most missionary schools in North China.[33]

In the early 1890s, about five years after Song Chuandian started school in the Qingzhou county seat, Alfred Jones and Samuel Couling became obsessed with finding new economic opportunities to alleviate the poverty they perceived as the number one problem in rural Shandong. Couling was particularly qualified in this respect because he had been "brought up to business [and] . . . was for years engaged on the Correspondence of a London Insurance Office."[34] On leave in Scotland in 1891, Couling spent much of his time visiting local congregations saying that "*in addition* to the spiritual loss—of heaven or of the soul, the Chinese were also in this life of all men most miserable; because lack of Christianity implies lack of all those material benefits which come to English people as *indirect* results of Christianity."[35] Alfred Jones who had himself spent time in the woolen trade before becoming a missionary was another enthusiastic supporter of developing the rural Chinese economy. On leave in England in 1891 he wrote, "I see the people starving while we are teaching to them. Giving them money does not fill the bill. Giving them the Gospel even does not fill their stomachs nor lighten the load of work that weights down moral progress." Like Couling, he believed in a causal link between Christianity and prosperity. Elsewhere he wrote that "our Christians . . . in China have a good many longings. One is not only to taste the good word of God but to reach forward to some of the promises of the life that now is. They see there is a social state dependent on and going with Christianity vastly superior to that they are in. Political reform would of course be what they desire in the ultimate, but meanwhile some way to relieve social pressure on the individual would be the next most acceptable thing. . . . They know we western have the power by device plus labor to increase wealth as they could not."[36] Ultimately Jones advocated for a complete reform of Chinese social, political, and economic structures, though in the short run he looked only for incremental change in economic opportunities.

Couling and Jones engaged in fuzzy thinking regarding the relationship between Christianity and prosperity. Both argued that Britain's material wealth stemmed from its Christian faith. The causality in this line of argument travels from Christian belief as the basis to material wealth as the result. Yet both Couling and Jones believed that material progress, increased wealth, should be introduced to China even if the Chinese did not believe in Christianity. Although in theory they saw prosperity as an outgrowth of Christianity, in practice they saw the causal link between Christianity and prosperity as mutually reinforcing. In their minds, it was essentially impossible to have one without the other. It is also interesting to note that they focused on broad-based economic development, and not generating income for mission needs. The Catholic Church in the Yangzi River valley had long-established workshops to print books and carve images, as well as investments in real estate and shipping, though Jones, predictably unsympathetic to anything Catholic, dismissed their efforts because their work focused solely on church needs and did not extend into the larger society.[37] Thus, Jones and Couling preached a gospel of economic development intended to transform Chinese society. The missionaries wracked their brains for enterprises that could be introduced to rural Shandong.

Jones dismissed the idea of big factories in rural China and instead proposed use of low-level technology, which he felt was more appropriate to the Chinese situation. Still on leave in Scotland in 1891, Couling wrote a long letter to Jones discussing possible business ventures. He had apparently already trained one Chinese convert to make soap, but his pupil had left the business and Couling lost his investment. Couling listed the criteria for evaluating businesses and placed anything that could increase agricultural production first. Second, he listed manufactured goods, which could be exported to wealthy nations in order to take advantage of cheap Chinese labor. Third, he advocated any process that could cheapen the cost of living for Chinese themselves, such as spinning wheels. Fourth, he looked for new products that could be either exported or sold in the interior of China itself. In this category he rejected papermaking, because the Chinese already made the best paper in the world, and electroplating, which was too dangerous. Candles were a good idea, but rural Chinese had a very limited supply of animal fat because they killed few animals. Dying and fastening of color on cotton goods seemed quite practicable, and he thought that a church savings bank was a good idea but worried that only a dozen or so members of the church had anything to save at all. Finally, in a postscript to his letter, Couling noted that, while home in Scotland, his wife had learned to make pillow lace and hoped to introduce its production to Shandong. Couling concluded that lace making required only simple materials, labor, and patience, plus lace was light so had very minimal freight charges. Cautiously, he predicted that "it may go."[38] Little did he know then, but the lace making he casually mentioned in a postscript would become the most successful venture that grew out of the BMS gospel of economic development in Qingzhou.

The Coulings also had other models on which to draw. American protestant "missionaries commonly ran actual businesses in which they employed impoverished women from the church who needed support."[39] Close to home nearby in Shandong the American Presbyterian missionary George S. Hays, "in charge of the boys' school in [Chifu], taught his pupils how to preserve fruits and vegetables. Mrs. Hays learned the Swiss method of making torchon lace, and then taught the art to a number of Chinese women. The initial outlay for a pillow and a set of bobbins was so small that lace-making rapidly became a home industry. . . . This handsome lace was so well made and so cheap that large quantities were exported."[40] In 1895, James McMullan and his wife took over the Presbyterian industrial operations in Chifu.[41] The Coulings almost certainly knew both the Hays and McMullan families, and they most certainly read the *Chinese Recorder*, the English-language Protestant missionary journal of record in China, where the McMullans published reports on their industrial work in 1899, 1902, and 1914.[42] Like Couling and Jones, McMullan also preached a gospel of economic development. In 1914 he would write, "There is no reason why industrial training or enterprises may not be as valuable an auxiliary to mission work as educational or medical work.[43]

In spite of the similarities with some American Presbyterians in Shandong about the role of the church in promoting economic opportunity, the gospel of economic development preached by Couling and Jones did not necessarily represent the majority view among British Baptists. Although, they communicated their ideas in outreach to local congregations in Britain, Jones did not dare to bring the idea of introducing new small industries before the BMS China subcommittee. Instead he appealed directly to the secretary of the BMS, saying, "Oh what a grand thing it would be if we could give these people new ways of getting a few more shillings a month, something that would turn the scale between misery & comfort, something that would lift them beyond low grinding care, give their souls a chance to expand."[44] His appeal did not succeed immediately, and by February of 1892, Jones complained that the BMS still had not assigned someone to work on the "Industry question."[45]

Little remains in the historical record to tell what became of the Qingzhou mission's plans to found small-scale industries, but there are a few tantalizing hints. One source points to Jones's "schemes for the improvement of the silk worm and spinning industries, in the homes of . . . Christians."[46] In another, apparently separate venture, Alfred Jones spent two and a half years in Zouping, another Shandong city, overseeing the construction of equipment for an unspecified industry, which he then shipped back to Qingzhou in mid-1895.[47] After fleeing to Japan to escape the Boxer Uprising, Jones wrote that both Qingzhou mechanical plants burned during the violence.[48]

In the end, in spite of this apparently substantial mechanical infrastructure, Alfred Jones's and Samuel Couling's industrial enterprises apparently left little noticeable impact on either the Qingzhou economy or the lives of Christian converts. Mrs. Couling's lace-making business, in contrast, which did not take two and a half years of machinery preparations and which had composed only a brief postscript in Couling's plans, proved extraordinarily successful. Song Chuandian played a key role in that success.

From Teacher to Capitalist

When the young Song Chuandian arrived at the county seat school sometime in the mid-1880s, Alfred Jones and the Coulings had not yet turned their attention to the "industrial question." Education at the school combined Western subjects such as science and mathematics, with study of the traditional Chinese canon. Surprisingly the school offered no classes in English.[49] Instead, the Coulings hired a member of the local literati to teach the Chinese classics. Song Chuandian, however, was such a good student that the Coulings relented and taught him the English language.[50] A brilliant student, by the age of seventeen Song Chuandian began teaching physics and mathematics at the school, earning enough money to help fund the education of his younger brothers and sisters.[51] He would later edit a textbook on chemistry.[52]

Education was a growth industry in Shandong during the heady years of reform and revolutionary tumult at the turn of the twentieth century. Song Chuandian's Western-style education made him one of a few thustrained Chinese individuals in Qingzhou at a time when demand for his skills was ready to explode. The British Baptists added a girls' school in 1897.[53] Five years later, local Chinese officials sponsored a Western-style school. Song Chuandian taught there, dividing his days between mornings at the BMS school and afternoons at the Chinese school. He became locally known for riding a bicycle, one of the first in Qingzhou, back and forth between the two locations. In 1905 he became principal of the higher-level primary school founded by the local county magistrate, and later he served as chairman of the county education association.[54] In 1907 he taught for a while at the precursor to Shandong Christian University where one of his faculty colleagues was Henry W. Luce, father of the man who would found the *Time-Life* publishing empire.[55]

In spite of the opportunities provided by this growth, Song Chuandian did not remain an educator for long. The coming of the railroad to Qingzhou in 1904 pulled the county seat more tightly toward Shandong's business centers. The Qingdao-Jinan (Jiaoji) railway ran straight through the Qingzhou county seat. The three-day horseback ride to the provincial capital, Jinan, now took only four and a half hours by train. Qingdao to the east could be reached in seven hours.[56] The railroad placed the Qingzhou county seat, and its rural hinterland, squarely in the middle of east-west trade along the Shandong Peninsula, and closer to China's major north-south rail axis, the Tianjin-Qingpu (Jinpu) railway, which ran through Jinan as it linked North China with the Yangzi River valley.

Mrs. Couling's lace-making business apparently grew apace during this time as well. The Presbyterian missionary James McMullan listed it as one of three lace-making missions in 1902.[57] In 1908 the BMS transferred Samuel Couling to Shanxi Province to work.[58] The Coulings looked to Song Chuandian, one of their favorites whom they called godson, to take over their business operation.[59] Song Chuandian found three other partners to invest, and they began the Dechang Lace Company (Dechang huabian zhuang). Few reliable details about the lace-making operation remain, but all accounts stress the fact that the business was small. One former employee recalled that working capital was so scarce that the company virtually limped by day to day.[60] Dechang's operations did not really take off until its owners added a new consumer product for the American and European markets: hairnets.

It is unclear now exactly when Dechang added hairnets to its product lineup. Li Jingfang, Song Chuandian's daughter-in-law, indicates—probably correctly—that it was around 1916. The boom in hairnet fashion reached its peak in the West during World War I, before declining with the popularity of bobbed hair in the 1920s.[61] Likewise, several sources show that the Presbyterian James McMullan was heavily involved in the hairnet business, but none of the McMullans' writings through 1914 mentioned hairnets.[62] Made of real human hair to match the hair of the wearer, hairnets had to be laboriously knotted by hand, inspected and tied into bundles. The

Dechang Lace Company took advantage of the large pool of cheap labor in central Shandong and began producing hairnets in large quantities.

Production ran on a putting-out basis. Dechang Lace Company, now renamed the Dechang Hairnet Company, received the hair of American and European women from abroad, divided it into bundles and sent them to thousands of households in the Shandong countryside. According to one estimate, as many as 15,000 households were making hairnets for Dechang.[63] In the villages near the Qingzhou county seat, nearly everyone made hairnets for the company.[64] Later Song Chuandian, or perhaps his oldest son, Song Feiqing, developed a chemical method for stripping the dark color from Chinese hair and dying it red, brunette, gray, and blond to match the hair color of American and European customers.[65] With this method, Dechang purchased hair domestically in China and reduced costs of production significantly. Lessons in chemistry at the BMS school in Qingzhou, or the lessons given his similarly trained son, literally paid off.

By all accounts the operation had few frills.[66] Dechang used middlemen to distribute hair and collect hairnets from rural households.[67] In many cases, women and children did the work. One worker later recalled that he began making hairnets at about the age of nine, in 1919. "Dechang took the purchased hair, sorted it, washed it and dyed it brunette, gray, blond, and black. It was sorted into strands, twelve of which made a bunch. Twelve bunches made a pack (one pack was 144 strands). Then it was distributed for work. . . . The three brothers in our family all knotted [hairnets]."[68] Another worker who began making hairnets as a young girl recalled that in one day she could make twenty-four hairnets and receive 960 copper coins, or something less than half a yuan in wages.[69] Accounts of wages paid and costs of production differ. A longtime Song family employee remembered that Dechang paid a price closer to 1,200–2,000 copper coins for twenty-four hairnets, but it is possible this estimate included the cost of middlemen.[70] A foreign scholar commenting on the Shandong hairnet industry in general stated that "Hair-nets are made in the homes for from fifteen to twenty cents a dozen, the rate depending on the demand of the market."[71] This jibes with the female employee's estimate of about half a yuan for two dozen.

In truth, though the work was undoubtedly hard and the hours interminable, Chinese in the Shandong countryside had few opportunities to earn monetary income. At about the same time, skilled factory workers only earned about twenty yuan per month in Jinan.[72] Skilled construction workers such as masons or stonecutters earned fifty to seventy cents a day.[73] A manager who worked for the Song family later remembered that in one household in his village "the elders knotted hair, and the youngsters wove hairnets. Neighbors said if you walked by there in the evening you could hear the sound of money clanging. At New Year's, the daughter and daughter-in-law both got new sets of clothes . . . one household could make twenty to thirty yuan per month."[74]

In addition to the thousands of men, women, and children in villages who made the hairnets, Dechang established facilities in Qingzhou to inspect and package hairnets for shipping. The company progressively moved to larger and larger buildings. One worker who started as a boy of about eleven or twelve in about 1920 or 1921 remembers an operation with sixty to seventy people.[75] This was likely one of two locations. At one time Dechang had a factory workshop for male workers, while female workers operated out of Song Chuandian's house.[76] By 1924 Dechang had expanded into a courtyard of about ten to twenty thousand square meters where several hundred employees, both male and female, worked in a building of about three thousand square meters.[77]

Shandong had no shortage of workers willing to labor. Population growth and periodic famines had increased pressure on rural livelihoods across China. Some rural Shandong people responded by emigrating. More than ten million people moved to Manchuria permanently in the years from 1900 to 1925, and Shandong was favorite recruiting ground for soldiers and overseas laborers.[78] For those who stayed home, employment at Dechang was a viable option for survival. A worker named Gao Xinzhai later recalled that he left school at the age of eleven, and because his family farm could not produce enough to eat for more than two months of the year, he went to work at Dechang at the age of thirteen, courtesy of a family introduction. Workers, at least male workers, lived in dormitories at the factory site and ate food prepared by a factory cook. They slept in bunk beds, ten to a room.[79] More than one former worker remembers eating flatbread, a traditional Shandong staple, contaminated with chicken feces.[80] Hours were long. By one account the workday started at 5:30 in the morning and did not end until 9:00 at night with an hour for lunch and half an hour each for breakfast and dinner. Workers toiled seven days a week with the exception of Sunday mornings when they attended the Qingzhou Baptist service en masse.[81] Dechang did provide some medical services and employees could line up to see doctors who visited the factory.[82]

In the space of about five years, hairnets provided the engine to build a commercial empire first in and around Qingzhou and then throughout Shandong. Estimates of profits earned from the export of hairnets vary from a low of a half yuan to a high of one yuan per gross (144 hairnets).[83] Even at the low end of the spectrum, hairnets generated astounding profits. At a minimum, Dechang produced five hundred to a thousand gross of hairnets each month.[84] At a half yuan per gross, the low end of estimates, profits after expenses would have been 250–500 yuan per month, a fortune in rural Shandong. Other sources place production much higher, approximately 300,000 gross per year, or nearly 1,000 gross per day. This higher level of production is more consistent with the number of households and factory employees said to be working at peak production times.[85] At those levels, profits would have been approximately 25,000 yuan, or about U.S.$10,000, per month, a fortune anywhere in the world in the 1920s. Regardless of the actual figure, there is no doubt that the hairnet business was extremely good. A 1919 guide to Qingzhou noted that of all the city's industries, Dechang was especially prosperous.[86]

With such high profits, control of the Dechang Hairnet Company became a matter of considerable importance. When Song Chuandian took the lace-making business over from the Coulings, three other investors joined him. He played the most important role from the beginning; he invested two fifths of the capital and they each invested one fifth.[87] As the business grew, so did Song Chuandian's control. One by one, he bought out, or perhaps forced out, each of the other partners.[88] Although reliable details are sketchy, it is clear that Song kept management pretty close to himself.[89]

As the money rolled in, Song Chuandian quickly diversified his investments. Soon he also had a match factory, soap company, and warehouse in the Qingzhou county seat. So many rural people depended on his business for income that someone said with hyperbole that he was the "guide of the people's livelihoods" (*minshengzhuyi de xiandao*). Rumors spread that he was worth a million yuan and that he could go to any big city in China and afford his own house rather than needing a hotel.[90] His reputation was such that even the records of the BMS in London noted that one of their local church members developed a business into a "great concern."[91] It is impossible to know how much money he made, but his second-oldest son, Song Yuhan, later wrote that in one of his better years Song Chuandian made a half million silver dollars, an astounding sum for the time.[92]

As the business grew, Dechang opened branch offices in a number of cities around Shandong. Eventually, by the early 1920s, although operations continued in the Qingzhou county seat, which had become a bustling city, Song Chuandian decided to move the headquarters of the company to Jinan.[93] Since both the east-west and north-south railroad lines crossed in Jinan, it was even better situated for trade than Qingzhou. In addition, although the Baptist missionaries had made Qingzhou an early center of Western-style education, it had been left behind in the first decade of the twentieth century when Shandong's British Baptists and American Presbyterians decided to locate Shandong Christian University first in Wei County and then in Jinan.[94] By 1917 even the Whitewright Institute and Museum had transferred to Jinan from Qingzhou, leaving the latter nothing more than an ordinary mission station.[95]

At the time Song Chuandian moved there, Jinan was in the midst of a small economic boom. Although much of Shandong's economic growth in the early part of the twentieth century focused on the coastal city of Qingdao, Japanese occupation of the German-built city caused numbers of merchants to move from the coast to Jinan, making it "more prosperous every day."[96] Like many Chinese cities at the time, Jinan had an older, primarily Chinese section and a newer area where foreigners and Chinese lived and worked. In the older section, the city's streets were, "for the most part, narrow, roughly paved with cobblestones, and poorly drained." In fact, "The density of population [was] greater than that of Peking . . . [averaging] 50,000 [people] to the square mile." The streets bustled with rickshaws, sedan chairs, bicycles, and carts.[97] Although the richest people in and around Jinan were "salt merchants [working under state monopoly] followed by the descendants of officials," there was also a growing class of private businesspeople who were mostly immigrants to the city.[98] The main merchant groups came from Zhangqiu, Licheng, Shouguang, and Huantai, thus making the Songs something of outsiders in the city.[99]

Jinan's boomtown nature was evident. As late as 1919, Jinan had no cars
at all, but by 1920, "one or two important persons drove around town."[100]
In 1922 an American traveler passing through Jinan observed that the
smokestacks of factories—mostly flour mills—stood where "ten or fifteen
years ago little more than graves grew."[101] There were also two match factories, one cotton mill, and a beet sugar mill and alcohol factory.[102] In addition to this bourgeoning industrial sector, Jinan served as a collection
and distribution center for commodities, "chiefly food grains, cotton, and
peanuts" for North China.[103] The city also stood "as a subordinate distributing center for Shanghai and [Tianjin]" for imports.[104] "Petroleum products, machinery, cotton goods, cigarettes, lumber, and sundry goods" composed the chief foreign imports.[105] "Secondary lines of trade included rural
handicraft products such as silk, in all its semi-processed and finished forms,
straw braid, and cotton cloth."[106] Similar to many Chinese cities, Jinan contained large numbers of male sojourners. Men outnumbered women by
50,000 to 60,000 in the early 1920s.[107] Most of them were between the ages
of fifteen and twenty-five, indicating the existence of a large pool of sojourning male labor. Additionally, 70,000 or more girls and women worked
at home.[108]

Thus when Song Chuandian decided to move the Dechang headquarters to Jinan in 1922, he found there a small and crowded city with a large
sojourning population of male businesspeople and laborers, a small but
growing industrial base, some regional trade, and some handicraft production as well. Although operations continued back in Qingzhou, Dechang
set up a shop to inspect and package hairnets in Jinan, where it initially
hired three hundred plus women workers.[109] Soon, feeling cramped in
rented quarters, Dechang bought forty *mu* (about six and a half acres) of
land in the foreign section of Jinan where it built "a three-story building,
a staff dormitory, and a cafeteria . . . the number of women workers expanded to 1,000 plus."[110] At that time, Jinan only had around forty firms
that employed more than twenty people each.[111] Dechang stood as one of
the largest businesses in the city.

Song changed the name of the company from the Dechang Hairnet
Company to the Dechang Foreign Trade Company (Dechang Yanghang),
though the official English name was Sung Chuan Tien & Co. (see
Figure 1.1). The name change reflected a dramatic expansion in the com-

HAIRNETS, CHINESE CARPETS & RUGS

HEAD OFFICE: TSINANFU

SUNG CHUAN TIEN & CO.

(World's Largest Manufacturers of Hairnets)

TSINANFU, SHANTUNG, CHINA.

Other Exports	*Imports*
Ground Nuts	Piece Goods, cotton & woolen
Raw Silk	Novelties
Cotton	Motors
Cotton Cuttings	Bicycles
Ferric Oxide	Accessories

Import Offers invited from Manufacturers in all countries.

REFERENCES:

Equitable Eastern Banking Corporation, Shanghai.

International Trade Developer, Shanghai.

Commercial and Credit Information Bureau, Shanghai.

National Trading Company, Chicago.

Balm Hill & Sons, Ltd., Nottingham.

BRANCHES AT:

SHANGHAI—TSINGCHOWFU

WEIHSIEN—WUTINGFU

———

CABLE Add. "SUCHTIENCO"

BENTLEY'S CODE.

FIGURE 1.1 Advertisement for the Sung Chuan Tien & Co., showing its huge headquarters building. In *The Comacrib Commercial Directory of China*, vol. 2, *1926*. Shanghai: Commercial Credit and Information Bureau, 1926.

pany's range of business activities. In addition to hairnets, the company produced and sold carpets, exported commodities such as nuts, silk, cotton, and ferric oxide, and imported finished goods like cotton piece goods, novelties, motors, and bicycles. It had branches in four other Shandong cities, including Qingzhou, of course, and in the treaty port of Tianjin on the coast north of Shandong.[112] By 1928, Song Chuandian had bought out his last partner, and this large and growing company became his sole proprietorship.[113]

Dechang was only one of several firms in Jinan that inspected and exported hairnets.[114] In addition to private rivals, the government used prison labor to make some hairnets.[115] In the face of such fierce competition, Dechang emerged as a leader in the hairnet business in part because of its ability to use talented employees. Dechang had a reputation for undermining other firms by using high wages to hire their most skilled workers away as soon as they finished their apprenticeships. One former worker who had made the move from another hairnet manufacturer to Dechang later recalled that "Jinan had a lot of hairnet companies at that time, but under pressure from Dechang, they all went out of business, only Dechang made a lot of money."[116]

As the company expanded in the early 1920s, business practices improved over the rough-and-ready operation back in Qingzhou. Even the most critical accounts of Song Chuandian's business practices admit that his management had a humanitarian side. "Rather than use pressure on his employees, he used small favors to get them to work harder . . . [there were] no fines for the first time late, workers who were asleep would be tapped on the shoulder to wake up, sometimes [the company] would make bean soup to give workers to eat, if it rained or snowed and workers couldn't go home, they could stay in the factory, [and] worker wages were slightly higher than in competing factories."[117] Dechang provided meals for workers that were essentially the same as those for management staff, but with fewer dishes. One worker who had followed Song Chuandian from Qingzhou to Jinan later recalled that "in Jinan, life was a little better than in [Qingzhou]. After work you could go out and have fun."[118]

Although Dechang paid relatively high wages for regular workers, the company also saved money by relying heavily on apprentice labor. Apprentices composed as many as six hundred of the one thousand or so workers at Dechang in Jinan.[119] Apprenticeship contracts ran for three years and included food, housing, and personal services such as haircuts. After the end of the apprenticeship, wages would be determined by the high or low level of skill.[120] Apprentices received only nominal pay during their three-year contracts. Accounts from former apprentices vary, but earnings ranged somewhere between a low of less than one and a high of five yuan per month.[121] One former apprentice remembered receiving beatings.[122]

Discipline in general was strict. "In each work room there were tables for ten people, two supervisors and eight workers. The supervisors would sit at each end with four workers on each side. At work no one was allowed to talk freely. There was one bathroom pass for each table so two people couldn't go to the bathroom at the same time." As well, "in each work room there was a male bookkeeper and a woman overseer [referred to as 'teacher']" who assigned work and kept track of the distribution and collection of hairnets from work tables.[123] As in Qingzhou, on Sundays, company staff led the workers to church for a service.[124] In spite of this strict discipline, though, over the years the Song family built up a reservoir of loyal employees drawn mostly from the Shandong countryside. Many of these employees began work in Qingzhou and then followed the family to Jinan.[125]

From Businessman to Politician

Song Chuandian's decision to move to Jinan, the provincial capital, derived in part from his entrance into Shandong politics when he was elected to the provincial assembly in 1921. As the business expanded, Song Chuandian spent less and less time managing it and more and more time in political affairs. It is hard to know when his interest in politics began. One Song family managerial employee later claimed that Song Chuandian had actually joined the Tongmenghui, a revolutionary anti-Qing dynasty society organized by Sun Yat-sen, in the years before the 1911 revolution. This employee even claimed that the Qing government arrested Song and agreed to his release only under pressure from British missionaries.[126] If true, Song's involvement with the Tongmenghui gave him impeccable revolutionary and progressive credentials for a career in republican-period electoral politics. Even if not true, Song's early work in education in Qingzhou placed him in local political circles as early as the first decade of the twentieth century.

At the time of his assembly election, however, the early promise of republican electoral government in Shandong, as elsewhere in China, had been under assault by a variety of militarists for almost a decade. In Jinan the provincial assembly "became progressively weaker and more corrupt after [Yuan Shikai, then president of China] successfully suppressed the parliament and the assemblies in 1914."[127] After Yuan Shikai's death in 1916, various regional and local warlords divided China into satrapies, often provinces, and fought wars with each other every couple of years. By the 1920s authoritarian provincial governments led by warlords dominated China's political scene. Elected officials, such as assembly members like Song Chuandian, had to continually negotiate and maneuver within the framework created by warlords and their demands for funds to finance their armies. There was a general air of corruption and one foreign observer noted that "everyone in China seems to expect officials to hold on to some of the money that passes through their hands."[128] Like elsewhere in China, warlord politics in Shandong Province had more than a hint of corruption and Machiavellian maneuver.

Japanese imperialism in Shandong complicated politics in the province even more. At the start of World War I, Japan seized the German-built city of Qingdao on the Shandong coast and the Qingdao-Jinan railroad. In Qingdao the Japanese enlarged the harbor and wharves, built warehouses and a new section of the business district, gave streets Japanese names, and replaced Germans schools with Japanese schools. In addition to inheriting German mining rights in Shandong, the Japanese "took over the telegraph line paralleling the railroad and soon established radio transmitters at [Qingdao] and [Jinan]." The Japanese also moved to exert their influence at the other end of the railway in Jinan. They established a garrison there in 1914, and Japanese businesspeople became a force in the city. Finally in return for a series of loans, the nominal government of China in Beijing agreed in 1918 to "recognize Japan as the rightful claimant to Germany's leasehold rights in [Shandong]." When this agreement became public during the negotiations over the Treaty of Versailles in May of 1919, Chinese students took to the streets in protest and anti-Japanese activities sprang up in cities all over China. The aftermath of those protests set the stage for Song Chuandian's entry into Shandong's provincial politics.[129]

At the time of Song Chuandian's election to the provincial assembly, Shandong's military governor Tian Zhongyu dominated the province. Tian took power in 1920 after the previous military strongman failed to suppress anti-Japanese activity with enough enthusiasm. In the 1910s and early 1920s, the warlord in control of Shandong needed three things: some tie to the nominal national government in Beijing, control of the Fifth Division of the army, which garrisoned the province, and control of provincial revenues.[130] Tian Zhongyu had come up through the ranks of the army, serving in a variety of positions in North China and Manchuria, and he had close ties to factions in Beijing, especially the pro-Japanese Anfu clique that dominated Beijing politics at the time. He took command of the Fifth Division in order to ensure military control of Shandong and then began maneuvers to dominate the provincial assembly so he could get access to the funds needed to pay his soldiers.

Politics remained tumultuous all over China in the aftermath of the anti-Japanese agitation of 1919, and the pro-Japanese Beijing government soon fell, replaced by the so-called Zhili (for Zhili Province, modern-day Hebei) faction. In spite of the fall of his national patrons, Tian Zhongyu played republican politics adeptly. He managed to stay out of the fighting, keep his post as military governor, and switch allegiance to the Zhili faction. He did resign his concurrent position as civil governor and accepted a succession of appointed civil governors with close ties to the Zhili faction, but, at least for the moment, he remained generally in control of Shandong. At the same time, Tian Zhongyu had to navigate the vicious politics surrounding the settlement of the "Shandong question"—continued debates about Japan's role in Shandong Province. In 1919 Woodrow Wilson and the Japanese foreign minister, Uchida, came to an understanding that the leasehold of Jiaozhou Bay, including the city of Qingdao, and the Qingdao-Jinan railway would be returned to China.[131] Negotiations over exact terms of the return, and who in China would benefit from taking control of Japanese assets, took four years and included side negotiations at the Washington Conference of 1921.

With the change in factional control of the nominal national government in Beijing and the continued negotiations about return of some Japanese economic interests to Chinese hands, the Shandong provincial assembly roiled in turmoil. As in the previous assembly election in 1918, "large-scale fraud and open vote-buying" marked the 1921 election. Divisions ran so deep that the newly elected assembly contested the selection of an assembly president for more than a year. Tian Zhongyu still leaned toward Anfu-clique politics at the time and his candidate faced opposition as too pro-Japanese. Afraid of losing a vote, Tian even sent soldiers to surround the assembly and disrupt the election procedures.[132] This military intervention aborted the elections, and two months later nearly ten thousand people gathered at a park in Jinan to call for Tian Zhongyu's resignation.[133]

During the year from January 1922 to January 1923, the Shandong assembly remained without a president. As long as Tian Zhongyu exercised power, the conflict continued. In the fall of 1922 a new Zhili-affiliated civil governor, Xiong Bingqi, took office.[134] Under his supervision, the assembly held another election on 8 January 1923.[135] Two factions of Jinan local notables each put up candidates. A group made up primarily of merchants nominated a man named Chen Luanshu.[136] The second faction, often identified as a "gentry" faction, nominated Song Chuandian.[137] Interestingly, both candidates came from Qingzhou and, like Song Chuandian, Chen Luanshu had been active in education circles in Qingzhou during the early twentieth century.[138] It is almost certain they knew each other previously and the bad blood between them may have started back in Qingzhou. As the two contested the position, prices for votes ranged from 3,000 to 5,000 yuan apiece.[139] Using his tremendous wealth, Song Chuandian emerged victorious. Accounts vary, but most agree Song spent something in the neighborhood of 200,000 yuan on the election.[140] The assembly elected Chen Luanshu vice president.

Resolution of the selection of assembly president did not end the year-long conflict among assembly members. In fact, it created a flurry of activity as various assemblymen moved to challenge the legality of the election on the technical grounds that Song Chuandian had illegally called the 1923 session an extension of the 1922 session or that reelection of some assemblymen in the interim required rescission of Song's election and a new ballot. Appeals to the Interior Ministry in Beijing for legal rulings in the first half of 1923 achieved no satisfaction for the complainants and Song remained leader of the assembly.[141]

Conventional wisdom has concluded that the Shandong provincial assembly failed to "enact any meaningful legislation" during the time before and during Song Chuandian's presidency.[142] Unfortunately, few records are available from the assembly itself. The question remains, however, why would Song Chuandian be willing to spend a large fortune on one election? History has been unkind in judging him. Most accounts portray him as an assembly president lining his own pockets. Various rumors exist about his actions as well. Some say that the civil governor Xiong Bingqi gave Song Chuandian 180,000 yuan to reimburse his expenses in buying votes, that Song asked the Jinan-Qingdao railway to ship products for Dechang for free or at reduced rates, and that he received fees for making recommendations on appointments to official positions.[143] Even a member of the Song family later recalled that applicants paid Song Chuandian as much as 10,000 yuan for appointment as magistrate to a large county, or as little as 5,000 yuan for a small one.[144]

All of this may be true, but we will probably never know. We do know that government-granted monopolies were common in Jinan during the republican period.[145] Song took advantage of such a monopoly at least once. In 1922 a famine relief organization built a number of roads in Shandong in order to supply rural areas. Afterward, the roads saw very little traffic, so Song Chuandian invested 50,000 yuan (and convinced a group of assemblymen to invest another 100,000) to form a long-distance bus company in that part of Shandong. Their company got the rights to use the roads without paying tolls to the government.[146] Utilizing his connections in Christian circles, he recruited an officer from the Jinan YMCA to run it. The bus company had six midsize vans, which could seat nine people, and nine large buses, which could seat twenty-one. According to its former manager the bus company generated a tidy profit of 5,000 to 10,000 yuan per week.[147] Even though there is little doubt that Song Chuandian could not have received the rights to create such a company without his position in the Shandong provincial government, there is no evidence that this enterprise represented a particularly corrupt use of government resources.

More important to the assessment of Song's career in government, there is substantial evidence that Song Chuandian had an active and serious political agenda. In 1921 he founded a short-lived newspaper.[148] In addition, a few days after he took office in 1923, he cabled the nominal central government in Beijing to present "eight accusations of inappropriate conduct" against Tian Zhongyu.[149] As was common practice at the time for such telegrams, the newspapers published the text, making it as much an act to influence public opinion as one to urge the central government to launch an investigation.[150] Most of Song's accusations had to do with Tian's misuse of public funds for military expenditures, and Tian Zhongyu responded in twelve pages of excruciating detail. Tian impugned Song's motives by stating that these kinds of accusations were typical of the works of "party" (read "elected") activists, that Song had only recently been elected as assembly president, and that someone of his status should "speak carefully."[151]

Two months after this exchange, Song Chuandian turned his attention to Japan's relations with China when he led a rally of twenty thousand people at a Jinan park to demand the Chinese government withdraw concessions given to Japan in 1915.[152] Later that year Song Chuandian launched a new campaign to criticize the way the central government handled disposition of public assets in the formerly Japanese-controlled Qingdao. On 4 September he sent a cable on behalf of the Shandong provincial assembly to the cabinet and Treasury in Beijing protesting newspaper reports about the sale of assets in Qingdao. The telegram stated in part, "the people of Shandong swear that they will not accept [this sale] and this assembly is an organ of the people with rights and responsibilities. We ask the central [government] to cancel this contract in order to put the suspicions of the people at rest."[153] Interestingly, in spite of their recent conflict over the assembly presidential election, both Song Chuandian and Chen Luanshu signed the telegram. The Interior Ministry responded that the newspaper report was untrue.[154] Not mollified, a second newspaper report prompted the Shandong provincial assembly to send a second cable about the use of Qingdao assets as collateral for loans. This time, they stepped up the rhetoric claiming that the people of Shandong have "sworn to die rather than accept" the situation.[155] In response the Interior Ministry sent a confidential telegram to Xiong Bingqi, Shandong's civil governor, telling him that the newspaper reports were merely rumors and asking him to communicate this to the assembly to avoid misunderstanding.[156] Rather than deal with elected officials, the Interior Ministry appealed to the appointed civil governor in Shandong to use his influence to quiet the assemblymen. In the end, Song Chuandian and the provincial assembly had little influence over the disposition of Japanese assets, and the Zhili faction in power in Beijing proved adept at steering economic benefits in Shandong to itself and its supporters. "The local Shantung leadership was soundly defeated by a combination of Peking bureaucrats and Japanese interests."[157]

While the conflict between Tian Zhongyu and the Shandong provincial assembly, led by Song Chuandian, continued, the vagaries of warlord politics intervened to put additional pressure on Tian. In May of 1923, renegade soldiers in Shandong stopped a special train on the Jinpu railway. They kidnapped about two hundred people including more than thirty Westerners. The kidnapping became a major international incident and, in the end, the Beijing government paid off the renegade soldiers who released their captives. In October the Foreign Ministry called Tian to Beijing theoretically for the celebration of the 10 October anniversary of the republic and the inauguration of Cao Kun, a leader of the Zhili faction, as president.[158] In truth, Tian Zhongyu had run out of support, and Zheng Shiqi, head of the Fifth Division, replaced him at the end of October.[159] Zheng never had Tian's stature as a leader, and the civil governor Xiong Bingqi became the most powerful political figure in Shandong.

Song Chuandian had spent his first year as assembly president actively promoting a political agenda against Tian Zhongyu, against Japanese imperialism, and against distributing Japanese assets in Shandong to Zhili faction purposes. His rhetoric called on populist themes by emphasizing the elected nature of the assembly in unspoken contrast to the appointed governorships. He appeared fearless in the face of the most controversial issues of the day confronting both domestic military power and foreign imperialism; however, at the end of 1923 with Tian Zhongyu out of the way, much of the steam seemed to go out of Song Chuandian's political agenda. His appearance in the historical records becomes only sporadic for the next five years. Although the activities of the provincial assembly certainly continued, he seemed to retreat from the center of the controversial issues of the day.

This decline in political activism probably derived from a number of factors. For example, Tian Zhongyu's departure left the assembly without an obvious local target; final resolution of the disposal of Japanese assets left the assembly licking its wounds. Most important, warlord politics once again changed the political map of North China and the constellation of power in Shandong. In 1924 the Zhili faction lost a war with the Fengtian faction (based in Manchuria) and the infamous Zhang Zongchang, sometimes called the "dog meat general," took power as Shandong military governor in May 1925. As David Buck has noted, "it was not until [Zhang Zongchang] became military governor in 1925 that the full force of warlordism descended upon [Jinan]."[160]

Zhang Zongchang had tried to take over Shandong during the first Zhili-Fengtian war of 1922 when he landed four thousand troops in the province, but the Fifth Division beat him back and he retreated until the Zhili faction lost the second Zhili-Fengtian war of 1924. After Xiong Bingqi, bereft of patrons at the national level, left, Zhang Zongchang moved to claim Shandong again. He visited Jinan in February 1925 and his reputation for "personal brutality and venery led provincial leaders to offer him $200,000 [yuan] to leave the province, but the money only made him all the more eager to stay." He "took his post on 7 May 1925, arriving with his harem and his feared White Russian soldiers. Making his presence felt at once, he declared martial law. . . . During the first six months of [Zhang's] governorship, [Jinan's] schools stood closed because they didn't have enough money to operate."[161] He promptly moved in his own troops and relocated the Fifth Division outside of the province.

When Zhang arrived, the economy in Jinan was already suffering from the results of the return of Qingdao to Chinese control. "Many Chinese firms, especially those from [Tianjin] and Shanghai, shifted their [Shandong] operations from [Jinan] to the more convenient and more pleasant coastal city." The situation became worse when Zhang began a series of vicious extractions from Jinan's already stressed business community. Commerce slowed because Zhang "closed the [Qingdao-Jinan] railroad to regular traffic in order to use it to deploy his troops around the province." He also "printed huge amounts of unsupported paper money . . . [and] collected twenty-three different kinds of merchandise taxes in [Jinan], with ruinous effects on commerce."[162] Among other depredations, he confiscated most of the vehicles from Song Chuandian's bus company leaving only seven broken-down vehicles with which to limp along. The bus company manager had heard that Zhang offered Song 50,000 yuan in compensation, but there is no confirmation of this fact.[163] "By early 1928 most commerce and business in [Jinan] had come to a halt, but this did not matter to [Zhang

Zongchang]. With another season of military campaigning ahead, he needed more money. He began to confiscate bank reserves outright, and a great many commercial interests simply closed their doors." Famine during the winter of 1927–28 exacerbated the situation and an estimated one million people left Shandong for Manchuria that year.[164]

In many ways Zhang Zongchang serves as the archetype of the warlord. Venal, capricious, colorful, ruthless, Zhang treated Shandong as his personal property. Elected officials in Shandong kept their heads low and displayed none of the willingness to confront Zhang that they had shown against Tian Zhongyu. Zhang did not allow election of a new provincial assembly at the end of its term, so Song Chuandian and his colleagues continued at their posts. During this period Song Chuandian served in a series of ceremonial posts, including vice-director of a company set up to manage funds donated to redeem the debt owed to Japan for the Jinan-Qingdao railway and vice-chairman of the Shandong chapter of the International Red Cross.[165] It is also possible that Song found ways to profit under Zhang Zongchang's rule. Later critics claimed that Zhang allowed him to make the appointments and receive bribes for ten-plus county heads.[166] Song's political agenda, however, made little progress, and by the late 1920s the appearance of the Nationalist Party on the Chinese political horizon ended Song's political career.

In 1926 the Chinese Nationalist Party, most identified in the West with the figure of Chiang Kai-shek, left its base on China's southern coast to begin a "Northern Expedition" intended to destroy the warlords, unite China militarily, and fight the power of foreign imperialism. As the Northern Expedition neared Shandong in 1927, the Japanese government announced that it would dispatch troops to the province to protect its interests. Although turned back in fighting with Chinese forces, the Northern Expedition returned in 1928, as did Japanese troops. That year the Nationalists succeeded in routing Zhang Zongchang and his allies, and in taking Jinan, but then clashed with Japanese troops in the city. After a year of negotiation, the Japanese turned Jinan over to the Nationalists, who declared Song Chuandian one of the criminals of the Zhang Zongchang regime and issued orders for Song's arrest and confiscation of his property.[167]

In one version of the story, Song Chuandian's old rival Chen Luanshu convinced the Nationalists to declare Song a criminal because back in 1925

Song had sent a cable in his capacity as president of the provincial assembly to welcome Zhang. Later, when Zhang entered Shandong, Song led a party of assembly members to act as a reception committee.[168] While such personal animosity might have played a role in Song Chuandian's fall, purges of the members of previous regimes were standard procedure in warlord China.[169] In addition, Song might have been hampered by his Christian faith and his close ties with Europeans in China. The 1920s saw growth in anti-Christian movements all over China, many of them fomented by Nationalist Party members.[170] As early as 1922 "Christian missions were denounced, not just as tools of foreign influence, but in specifically Marxist-Leninist terms as handmaidens of the forces of capitalist imperialism." After the Nationalists took power in Shandong, the BMS closed its schools due to Nationalist policies on secular curricula.[171]

In any case, with a warrant out for his arrest and confiscation of his property, Song Chuandian and most of his family fled to safety in the foreign concessions in Tianjin.[172] The Nationalist government froze Song's assets in Shandong and shut down Dechang's operations. Song Chuandian's journey from poor peasant to educator to businessman to politician ended.

Doing Business in Warlord China

Imperialism arrived in Qingzhou in Shandong Province in the decades after about 1870 in the form of Baptist missionaries, new forms of education, connections to world markets, and a foreign-built railroad, but these phenomena worked unevenly and even arbitrarily. British Baptist missionaries chose one county seat as their locus of operations and not another. The particular missionaries included people such as Alfred Jones and Samuel Couling who developed their "gospel of economic development" through their experiences in the Shandong countryside. One bright young boy received an education from these missionaries while other intelligent boys and girls did not. Lace making, intended to give churchwomen a little income, provided an avenue to a major export business. The railroad went through Qingzhou and not another city.

Imperialism unquestionably had a transformative effect on Song Chuandian and the lives of a number of village residents, especially those of his children, brothers and sisters, nephews and nieces. All received good educations and virtually all left the village to live and work in cities. Other villagers may have left to work for Dechang in Qingzhou or Jinan never to return, but the same developments—missionaries, schools, export industries, railroads—that made Song's rise possible left many others behind. By all indications, the village Song Chuandian left as a child had been little transformed. In fact, as warlord rule became particularly chaotic in the 1920s, some of the new opportunities closed down. Even the Qingzhou county seat, which had been a prosperous and dynamic place in the 1910s, remained only a shell of its former self. By 1929 Qingzhou "struck a visiting BMS deputation as like 'a dead city,' controlled by bandits, with almost all BMS work closed."[173]

Given the opportunities with which he was provided, Song Chuandian's achievement depended on an international market in consumer goods, over which he had little control, and successful management of a business, where he proved to be a master. Many of his management techniques were consistent with common Chinese business practices of the late nineteenth and early twentieth centuries. Dechang began as a partnership, perhaps necessary because he personally had limited capital, then Song gradually eliminated his partners and made it into a family firm. Both partnerships and family firms were common at the time. He also staffed his business with family members and compatriots from his home village and county, showing use of particularistic networks commonly associated with Chinese business. At the same time, he also put to work his knowledge of foreign chemistry to dye hair and he took his employees to Christian services every Sunday. Song Chuandian's management mixed both the Chinese and the foreign.

Already in Jinan, many of the management practices that Song Chuandian's son Song Feiqing would later implement were present in embryonic form. Management was very paternalistic; Song Chuandian combined strict discipline with care for workers and benefits such as meals, housing, and haircuts. Although there is no record showing that Song Chuandian believed that business could transform society outside of the factory, his British Baptist mentors certainly thought so. In any case, within the factory Song did try to transform his employees' moral worldview by taking them to weekly church services.

Song Chuandian went from rags to riches during a time of political chaos, but he did not despair of the uncertainty that characterized the social, political, and economic realms within which he worked. As David Buck has remarked about politics at this time and place, "Frequent sudden changes in warlords made any kind of economic prediction difficult."[174] Song Chuandian's life showed, however, that unpredictability did not prevent economic success. A rapacious political system did not deter him or others. As Buck observes, many businesspeople were "willing to work with any Chinese regime in [Jinan] which would profit their own interests."[175] With a mix of idealism and pragmatism he persisted in taking advantage of opportunities regardless of the difficulties and dangers.

In many ways Song Chuandian lived a life of contradictions. His use of child labor and imposition of strict discipline and long workdays make him appear as a robber-baron businessman. Yet, his ability to channel significant income to rural households, payment of high wages, and relatively good treatment of employees make him seem like a positive force for development. One telling of his life showed a man trained in Western science and certainly influenced by the gospel of economic development preached by Alfred Jones and Samuel Couling. From this perspective, Song Chuandian's life looked like an obvious lesson in the benefits of Western liberal capitalism. Businessman, Christian (Protestant, for those who follow Weber's theories on the relationship between religion and capitalism), patriot, champion of elected officials in the face of militarism, in many ways Song appeared to be the ideal democratic capitalist in the Western mode. On closer inspection, however, his disregard for the legalities of electoral politics, corruption, and willingness to cooperate with authoritarian regimes pointed to a less liberal kind of businessman and less democratic kind of politician.

His fight with the warlord Tian Zhongyu in 1923 could be written either as a stand for electoral representation and republican form of government against authoritarian militarism or as pursuit of power and factional conflict by any means available. His ability to stand up to Tian Zhongyu made him look strong, while his impotence in the face of Zhang Zongchang's ravages made him look weak. His business in hairnets made him look like a businessman of the private sphere and his bus company made him look like a man dependent on state policies. The difficulty in reconciling the extremes of these interpretations points to the need for a different approach to explanation of the significance of his activities. In the end Song Chuandian's life teaches us that easy categories such as "liberal democrat," "capitalist," or "authoritarian" do not easily contain the complexities, the contraditions, and the cognitive dissonance present in one remarkable life. For Song Chuandian, politics and business did not occupy separate, easily distinguished realms. Instead the mutual interactions between business and politics existed and could be used, exploited, or avoided as possible depending on circumstances and personal goals.

Song Chuandian did not live long enough after his flight from Shandong to rebuild the family fortune. That job fell to his oldest son, Song Feiqing, whose ability to turn a bad situation good, to persevere in the face of adversity, to invest in spite of tremendous uncertainty, and to advocate an idealistic kind of business not inconsistent with the gospel of development would be both assisted and sorely tested in the coming decades by a frequently changing series of four more authoritarian regimes.

2 The Prewar Nationalists' Uncertain Developmental State

THE SONG FAMILY'S downfall in Shandong came as part of the incorpora-
tion of North China into the Nationalist regime, which had high goals in
terms of centralization of power and economic control, but at the same time
it was riven by internal conflict and a tenuous hold on national power.[1] One
of the great divides within the movement came in regard to economic policy.
Chiang Kai-shek preferred an economy of heavy industry tuned to the
needs of the military, while the Wang Jingwei faction focused on engineering a centralized economy with enough autarky to resist Japanese
imperialism.[2]

By the early 1930s when Song Feiqing launched the Dongya Corporation, the two sides shared power in an uneasy coalition that launched a "National Products Movement" to jump-start domestic industrialization and
reduce reliance on foreign imports. Parks Coble has argued that Nationalist "efforts to assist and develop China's industry and commerce were neither systematic nor of significant magnitude. The conferences and native-
goods campaigns were intended chiefly to improve public relations. The
regulations were largely window-dressing reforms."[3] From a slightly different angle, Karl Gerth sees the "National Products" Campaign as partly
a movement of the people, though he leaves open the possibility of direction or manipulation by the state.[4] The evidence from Song Feiqing's
Dongya Corporation agrees with Coble on the lack of systematic efforts
by the state to promote national products, but it also shows that policies—
such as tax breaks and reduced shipping charges—were effective in individual cases, though applied in an arbitrary manner. At the same time, the
evidence here shows less public support for national products than posited

by Gerth. The Dongya Corporation competed on price as much or more than on its designation as a national products company. Its customers quickly turned back to imported products when Dongya could not undercut the prices of its foreign competitors.

Of course the National Products Campaign was only part of the world in which the Dongya Corporation functioned. Dongya struggled between implementing a vision of scientific, hygienic modernity and surviving in a dog-eat-dog environment of ruthless international competition and domestic political uncertainty. The imprint of imperialism is everywhere in this formulation. Many of the ideas of modernity promoted by the Songs, including science, hygiene, and consumer culture all came from the West, but at the same time, the family had to compete with better-capitalized foreign companies in a domestic environment made unstable in part by imperialism itself. In dealing with this volatile and dangerous environment, the Song family showed resilience and adaptability. Their business activities drew on a wide range of repertoires that paradoxically mixed personalism and simultaneous efforts to institutionalize control to limit the power of personal networks. At the same time, their dealings with the government showed the divided nature of the regime, which at times acted like an autonomous and predatory political movement, especially in its early years, at times exhibited the characteristics of warlordism, and, at times, implemented the policies of a developmental state, though at best an uncertain one.

New Generation, Old Politics?

At first, imposition of the Nationalist regime in North China meant disaster for the Song family, whose assets were frozen in Shandong while family members fled to the offices of the Dechang branch within the safety of the French concession in the treaty port of Tianjin. Concessions were mini, quasi-colonies under the control of foreign countries, granted by treaty, and located in the centers of some Chinese cities. Originally, Tianjin had hosted nine foreign concessions, but by the 1930s most of these had been returned to Chinese authority. Four concessions remained, three on the south bank of the Hai River administered by Japan, France, and Britain respectively and one on the north bank, the Italian concession (see Map 2).

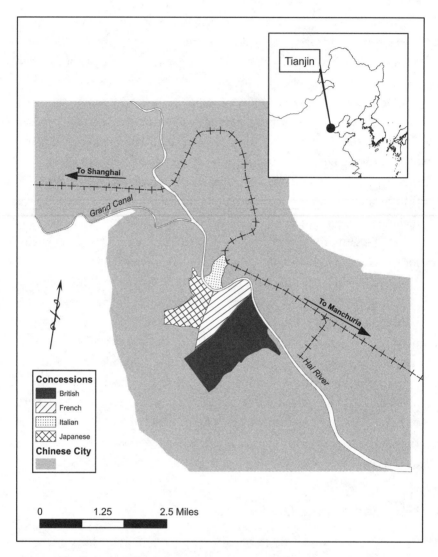

MAP 2 Tianjin in the 1930s.

As more Song relatives arrived from Shandong, living conditions became cramped.[5] For two or three years, the family scrambled to make a new start and this struggle demonstrated the close reliance of business on political patronage during the early years of the Nationalist regime. In some ways, in spite of the imposition of the new Nationalist Party-army regime, warlord politics continued as usual in North China.

Song Chuandian fell ill shortly after arriving in Tianjin, and the family business began to depend more and more on the abilities of his oldest son, Song Feiqing, whose upbringing had exposed him to a broad range of experiences. He was born in Song Family Village in 1899, but spent most of his early life in the cities and towns where his father worked. Feiqing's parents had provided him with the best possible education. He attended primary school in Jinan with Henry Luce, the son of missionaries and future founder of *Time* magazine. Then he went back to Qingzhou to the missionary school where, he would later recall, "during vacations I would often go to rural households to spread the gospel. I was very courageous."[6] In 1912, after the fall of the Qing dynasty, Feiqing went to middle school in Shanghai and attended Huiwen High School in Beijing in 1914, where three years later in 1917 he started at Yanjing University.[7] In short, by the age of eighteen or nineteen, he had lived and studied in many places deeply connected to the educational and missionary networks of his father and mother, including Qingzhou and rural Shandong, but he had also lived in both Shanghai, China's largest and most cosmopolitan treaty port, and Beijing, the nation's capital.

Both Song Feiqing and his father came of age at a time of radical politics, but the environment in which Song Feiqing grew up was even more highly charged with new ideas. His father, as a young adult, had witnessed the agitation to reform the Qing dynasty through constitutional government and eventually the overthrow of that dynasty in 1911. Song Feiqing, in contrast, came of age at a time when intellectuals were proposing adoption of ideas ranging from anarchism to Leninism. His years in Beijing came immediately before 4 May 1919 when students demonstrated against the negotiations for the Treaty of Versailles, during which Chinese politicians agreed to turn over many of Germany's concessions in China to Japan.[8] The years before and after 1919 are often referred to as the May Fourth Movement, a time when some intellectuals came to question much of Chinese tradition and propose increasingly radical ideas for solution to China's extended political crisis. One scholar has dubbed it the "Chinese enlightenment."[9] Song Feiqing may not have actually witnessed the May Fourth demonstrations because he was back in Shandong by at least June for his marriage to Li Jingfang, another student in Beijing with whom his parents had arranged an engagement two years earlier.[10] Nonetheless, having been in school in Beijing during the years immediately prior, he would have been well aware of intellectual trends of the time.

May Fourth Beijing, however, was not the only milieu that shaped Song Feiqing. In the mid-1920s, he went to the United States, where he studied briefly at Northwestern University and where, according to one source, through the help of his father's business contacts, he toured some of the largest American industrial firms such as Ford Motor.[11] Back in China, he also may have spent about ten days in the custody of the military at the time of his father's fall from power.[12] Thus Song Feiqing had a background steeped in progressive Chinese political and social movements, in business, in Christianity, in Chinese nationalism, in rural areas, and in cities, abroad in the United States and at home in Shandong.

Song Feiqing was a member of the May Fourth generation, but students of Chinese history often associate the May Fourth Movement with intellectual, literary, and political radicalism. In Song Feiqing, we can broaden our understanding by seeing the period's influence on a businessperson. For example, as a result of his experiences, Song Feiqing had a different vision of business from that of his father. His father had taken advantage of new opportunities for international trade in growing foreign consumer markets, but he had turned to politics for influence. Song Feiqing, in contrast, while cementing relations with the state, saw business as the transformative engine China needed.

Song Feiqing preferred business based on industrial-style production and consumerism as part of a modern, hygienic, scientific, and well-regulated society. He reflected this outlook in his own well-regulated life. Every day he was up at 6:00 a.m. for exercise and Bible reading, washing up and then breakfast before arriving at work at 8:00 a.m. sharp. He tried not to be early in order not to make his employees nervous about their own arrivals. Of course, he was more than just the embodiment of modern discipline. He was known for his bad temper, he read *Romance of the Three Kingdoms* to his children every weekend, and he practiced calligraphy. He also had a wicked sense of humor. He once told his children a slightly off-color joke about a young boy who noticed that when the girl sitting next to him got up, her dress was caught between the cheeks of her buttocks. He pulled it out for her, but when he saw his father look disapproving, he stuffed the dress back in. In later years he summed up his personal philosophy in a letter he wrote on the occasion of his oldest son's marriage. The topics he addressed in the letter were health, character, study, experience, cordiality, persistence, thrift, and love of others as oneself. Thrift, in particular, stands out in consideration of his day-to-day life. He did not keep a personal car, he rented his house in Tianjin, and he prohibited his children from wearing expensive or fashionable clothing.[13] In short, he appreciated Chinese and Western cultural traditions, he tried to live the life of frugal self-discipline he preached, and his seriousness was leavened both by a quick temper and by humor.

Song Feiqing's management of the Dechang branch in Tianjin showed an interesting combination of the practical businessman and the progressive intellectual. Without its Shandong operations, the family had only the assets of the Tianjin branch of Dechang on which to rely. By one estimate, "working capital was probably not more than 50,000 yuan."[14] This was still a considerable sum at a time when unskilled laborers might earn only 20–30 yuan a month, but times had certainly changed since the period when Song Feiqing's father spent about four times that amount on his election to the assembly presidency in Shandong.

Dechang Tianjin "exported carpets, hairnets, straw hats and whips, and imported cars and wool cloth."[15] In short, Dechang sold and bought what the market would bear, and Song Feiqing traded in anything he thought would be profitable. Once he lost 10,000 yuan on a bad bet on the movement of U.S. dollars but then made the money back by selling gasoline.[16] Of all his lines of business, automobiles and automobile parts proved particularly important. The Dechang office in Tianjin operated out of an iron shed and had none of the grandeur of the confiscated Dechang headquarters in Jinan. Nonetheless, Dechang Tianjin still sold enough American-produced Federal trucks and truck products to impress Federal's president on a visit to Tianjin (see Figure 2.1).[17]

The import-export business, however lucrative, clashed with the political mood in China in the early 1930s when the new Nationalist regime's sponsorship of a National Products Campaign reached a high tide. Imports, especially, became politically fraught. In the first two months of 1930, Tianjin's major newspaper, *Dagong bao*, reported almost frenetic activity as a merchant association outlined steps to promote national products, like the use of stores devoted to domestic products. Chiang Kai-shek, the head of

FIGURE 2.1 Dechang advertisement for Federal vehicles and parts. *Dagong bao* (Tianjin), 24 January 1930.

the Nationalist regime, made a speech about the National Products Movement, and his wife appealed to the women of China to wear domestically made clothes.[18]

Dechang's New Year's message to the people of Tianjin in 1930 showed both the importance of imports to the company and the need to attempt to position the company as progressive in the political atmosphere of the time. The advertisement claimed that "transportation is the key to advancement," and of course Federal trucks could help make a step in that direction with the hope of "contributing something to society."[19] The ad is a clear attempt to portray Dechang as a patriotic company dedicated to advancing the nation in spite of the fact that it imported products.

While trading in trucks and other products, Song Feiqing longed to engage in modern industrial production organized along purportedly scientific principles. Song's interest in a "scientific" road to modernity was a common sentiment among businesspeople at the time. Wu Dingchang, a banker and rising influence in the Nationalist government, gave a speech in Tianjin in mid-1930 when he argued that China's "national shame" was not just the result of foreign imperialism and warlord predations but also included a failure to commit to science.[20] Scientific, industrial production of the kind enunciated by Wu Dingchang and desired by Song Feiqing required substantial resources, however, and without resolution of his father's political situation, it was hard for Song Feiqing to obtain the large amounts of capital needed for such a venture.

In order to resolve the problems with his family business, Song needed a political patron, but the early years of the Nationalist regime appeared quite dangerous for North China's capitalists. In Tianjin, the government had arrested and detained a group of salt merchants in a famous case of predatory extraction.[21] Fortunately, the regime later moderated its policies and about the same time Song found a patron in the figure of Han Fuju, a general and former warlord who had allied himself with the Nationalist regime at the time of the Northern Expedition.[22] The connection between Han and the Song family came about indirectly when a Song employee named Zhao Zizhen sold a truck to Han Fuju.[23] Zhao, a man from Shandong who had first been recommended to the Songs by an old friend of the family and who had worked for the Songs in Shandong before coming to Tianjin, later recalled that he personally delivered the vehicle to Han's residence in Beijing where he "showed Han the purchase order to prove that Dechang had only added four hundred yuan to the price."[24] After this initial bit of trust building, Zhao saw Han again when Han's own military patron, Feng Yuxiang, ordered 125 vehicles from Dechang. Before Dechang could deliver the cars, however, Chiang Kai-shek, the supreme military leader of the Nationalist government, got wind of the deal and had both Zhao and Song Feiqing arrested in Tianjin in order to keep the cars out of the hands of Feng Yuxiang who was plotting against Chiang. Apparently, the Nationalists had not fully abandoned their predatory methods. Shortly thereafter, Han Fuju himself changed allegiances, threw his weight behind Chiang Kai-shek and the Nationalists, and had Zhao released from prison.[25] These events apparently cemented the relationship between Han Fuju and Zhao Zizhen, and then in turn between Han and the Song family.

To the remarkable benefit of the Song family, in September of 1930 the Nationalist government transferred Han Fuju to become governor of Shandong Province. As one of his first acts in office, Han ordered the reconsideration of the cases of those who had been declared criminals two years earlier during the Nationalist consolidation of power in the province. At the end of 1930 Han sent recommendations to Chiang Kai-shek for the cancellation of arrest warrants and return of confiscated property in almost every case, including that of Song Chuandian.[26] Unfortunately Song Chuandian died in Shanghai about two weeks before the official request to cancel his arrest warrant, but apparently he already had news of the coming event before he died.[27] The family took Song Chuandian's body back to the Song Family Village for burial.[28] He had completed the journey begun when he left home for school as a young boy nearly a half century earlier.

The patronage networks of shifting military alliances made the Nationalist regime in North China look like warlordism in other clothing. In order to complete the conquest of North China the Nationalists had built a fragile coalition of their own forces and regional militarists, including Han Fuju. In January of 1929, an American diplomat counted no less than five contending military groups in Hebei Province alone.[29] Han Fuju himself had betrayed his own leader to join the Nationalists, showing that allegiances among militarists changed often. In another example, one military commander, Yan Xishan, revolted against the Nationalists and took Tianjin and its valuable customs revenues for several months in 1930.[30] In the ensuing wars four or five militarists vied for control. Zhang Xueliang, the son of the previous warlord who had controlled Manchuria, eventually took Tianjin in October and affirmed his allegiance to the Nationalist regime.[31] His brother Zhang Xueming, "a young man, entirely without experience or training in official life," became mayor of the city.[32] Even with Zhang's stated allegiance to the Nationalists, the American consul in Tianjin saw significant tension between the military-led government of the Zhang brothers and the Tianjin committee of the Nationalist Party.[33] Similarly, although Han Fuju too had pledged allegiance to the Nationalist government in Nanjing, he made Shandong virtually his own kingdom.[34] Han's warlord-like power helped make possible resolution of Song Chuandian's political situation, and it is clear that, although wary of government involvement, the Song family needed political patronage to succeed.

The Dongya Corporation and the Uncertain Developmental State

Only a month after Yan Xishan retreated from Tianjin and the Nationalists resumed control, the government convened a business and industry conference in the capital of Nanjing, where the top leaders of the regime took the podium to stress cooperation between the government and business, harmony between capital and labor, streamlining in tax regulations, improvement and reorganization of industrial associations, promotion of national resources, and confidence in the Nationalist Party.[35] Among other sectors, the economic conference of 1930 listed the wool textile industry as one of its priorities in promoting domestic production.[36] Song Feiqing may not have been taking his cue directly from the regime, but in step with government-approved trends he moved into wool textile production, specifically spinning wool knitting yarn, exactly at this time.

Wool textiles provided an obvious target for development because at the time China had only a minimal mechanized wool textile industry. Chinese efforts at developing industrial spinning and weaving of wool with foreign technology had begun in the 1870s, but with the exception of wool carpet production, which became quite successful and which included a significant amount of handwork, most woolen mills failed over the next several decades. During the First World War, Chinese industry of all sorts had a turn for the better and some efforts went to improving wool technology. Nonetheless in the 1910s and 1920s most wool textiles and all wool knitting yarn came from imports.[37] A few years earlier after he returned from America, Song Feiqing had experimented with producing wool knitting yarn in Shandong. Unfortunately, his experiment was stillborn because the equipment he ordered from a German manufacturer did not produce yarn appropriate for knitting.[38] When the Nationalists reversed his father's verdict at the end of 1930, Song revived the idea of manufacturing knitting yarn, but he faced the need for large amounts of capital to fund the purchase of state-of-the-art equipment and materials.[39]

For would-be investors, this new company was potentially a very risky business. Production of wool knitting yarn had high technical requirements, and the poor track record of mechanized wool textile companies in China over the sixty-year period from the 1870s to the 1930s, including Song Feiqing's own failure, did little to boost confidence. In spite of these risks, Song Feiqing and his colleagues and backers plowed ahead, planning and launching the Dongya Maoni Fangzhi Gufen Youxian Gongsi, or, literally, the East Asia Wool Weaving and Spinning Limited Liability Corporation. The use of the limited liability business form was unusual in China at the time, and it signaled both the desire to copy foreign business models

TABLE 2.1 Initial Large Shareholders in the Dongya Corporation, 1932 and 1934

	Invested Capital (yuan) 1932	% of Total Capital	Invested Capital (yuan) 1934	% of Total Capital
Major Investors				
Song family members	100,000	43.5	105,100	17.3
Dechang Company (Song family firm)			100,000	16.4
Han Fuju family members	50,000	21.7	70,000	11.5
Zhang Huizhong, wife of Han Fuju's subordinate Sun Tongxuan	50,000	21.7	80,000	13.1
Large Minority Shareholders				
Xu Yanshan, a Song family associate			15,000	2.5
Two military officers subordinate to Han Fuju			21,000	3.4
Yiyong Hall				
Controlled by Song family 1932				
Controlled by Zhao Zizhen after 1934	30,000	13.1	30,000	4.9
Cui Bo (unknown affiliation)			12,000	2.0
361 Smaller Shareholders			176,100	28.9
Total	230,000	100.0	609,200	100.0

Sources: Cui Shuju and Jin Yanshi, eds., "Tianjin Dongya maofang gongsi shiliao," *Tianjin lishi ziliao* 20 (8 February 1984): 9, 10; Dongya financial statements, Archives of the Dongya Corporation, 1-9-3-02. The 230,000 yuan figure for 1932 is confirmed in a profile of Dongya published in *Dagong bao,* 15 October 1933, sect. 3, p. 1. The figures here differ from Song Yunzhang and Wang Weigang, *Tade meng: Song Feiqing* (Hong Kong: Wenming), 96, which follows the recollections of Zhao Zizhen, but I accept the archival documents as more authoritative.

and the need to raise large amounts of capital. Since shareholders had no obligations to pay the company's debts they could be more willing to invest.[40] It is interesting that at the time of rising Chinese nationalism and patriotic movements to promote buying domestically produced goods, Song chose to use "East Asia" rather than "China" in the name of his company. According to former employees, he hoped eventually to export Dongya products throughout Asia, thus from the beginning he had plans to move beyond the limits of the National Products Movement.[41] The company had an official English name as well, the Oriental Wool Manufacturers, Ltd., but for brevity's sake, it will simple be referred to here as "Dongya," or the "Dongya Corporation."[42]

Dongya's capital investment initially came from four sources: the Song family, the family's new political patron Han Fuju, the wife of a military officer subordinate to Han Fuju named Zhang Huizhong, and a group of minority shareholders ranging in number from one in 1932 to several hundred in 1934 (see Table 2.1).[43]

The Song family used leftover equipment from Dechang and other money left from Song Chuandian's estate to provide about half of Dongya's initial capital.[44] In spite the family's reliance on Han Fuju for patronage, it is clear that Song Feiqing preferred not to start his new business in Shandong, which was directly in Han's control at the time. Instead, Song started Dongya in the safety of Tianjin's foreign concessions, which provided some protection from predatory militarists, even those such as Han with whom he had good relations. Song family assets alone, however, could not provide all the financing Dongya needed, and much of the rest of the company's initial investment came from Han Fuju himself, who invested in the name of his son, and Zhang Huizhong, the wife of Sun Tongxuan, one of Han's trusted subordinates.[45]

Unfortunately, available records only hint at the actual lines of power. Han Fuju's investment, in particular, raises a number of questions, both because of its importance to Dongya and because the short period of time between Song Chuandian's exoneration and Han's investment in Dongya. Did Han Fuju have ulterior motives for working to acquit Song Chuandian? Was there some sort of quid pro quo between Han and the Songs? We will never know for sure. At least three versions exist to explain Han's involvement with Dongya. In one version, Song Feiqing sends Zhao Zizhen

to convince Han to invest, in another Han is an active participant and supervisor of the founding, and in the third, Han entrusted Zhao Zizhen with
money to invest and Zhao decided to found a woolen mill.[46] Although none
of these accounts can be declared definitive, clearly the fortunes of the Song
family became intricately tied to Han's patronage at this time. In turn, Han's
personal finances and those of his associates became tied to the fortunes
of Dongya and Song Feiqing's management abilities. Indeed the initial
shareholders' meeting entrusted Song with "all matters" concerning the
company.[47]

Dongya's large minority shareholders also tell us much about the company. In 1932 Yiyong Hall held the balance of power between the Song
family on the one hand and Han Fuju and Zhang Huizhong on the other.
Conventional accounts of Dongya's founding have attributed this 30,000
yuan minority share to Zhao Zizhen, with one former employee claiming
that the minority share was a reward from the Song family for Zhao's services in connecting with Han Fuju.[48] Yiyong Hall might have belonged to
Zhao Zizhen, but he did not exercise full control. Song Feiqing's cousin,
not Zhao Zizhen, represented Yiyong Hall at Dongya's first board meeting
and first shareholder meeting in January 1933.[49] In fact, Zhao Zizhen did
not appear as representative of Yiyong Hall in the company's archival
sources until January of 1934.[50] It is possible that the Song family placed
conditions on the reward to Zhao Zizhen so the minority shareholding was
controlled by the Song family for two years before being turned over to
Zhao.[51]

If true, conditional ownership for Zhao Zizhen shows a precarious bal-
ancing act between Song family interests and Han Fuju in 1931 and 1932.
For his part, Zhao Zizhen represented Han Fuju's interests at the first shareholders' meeting in August 1931 and frequently thereafter.[52] If he also controlled the 30,000 yuan minority share, then he would have been able to
exercise full control of Dongya. With the Song family in control of his
share for the first two years, they had the majority of shares, but would
have known that majority was temporary and would end when Zhao took
over. By the time Zhao did take over in 1934, however, additional investment by the Song family through Dechang and the addition of new minority shareholders such as the Song family associate Xu Yanshan kept the
balance of power in Song hands, though Han, his associates, and Zhao

Zizhen together owned 32.4 percent of the company, enough to give them considerable weight.[53]

In terms of our understanding of Chinese business, the group of initial investors in Dongya did not conform to expected notions of capital pooled only among family members and close family friends distant from and wary of the state.[54] Nor did it fit models of liturgical governance or officially sponsored enterprises.[55] Han and his intermediaries invested in Dongya as private individuals, not as administrators of state-run enterprises. We see here the blurring of public and private interests common to the warlord period, as seen in the experiences of Song's father. Yet rather than a simple patron-client tie between Song Feiqing and Han Fuju, the role of Zhao Zizhen and other minority shareholders points to a more complex triangular, or multinodal, relationship where the major parties held limited power and each tried to balance the other by connecting with minority shareholders. Structurally, the presence of these minority shareholders made Dongya's ownership look like what Gary Hamilton calls relationship, or *guanxi*, owners, where minority shareholders link a company to other firms in the industry.[56] Here, though, some minority owners such as Zhao Zizhen and Han Fuju's associates linked Dongya to official power rather than to other firms.

When Dongya's board of directors held its first meeting in January of 1933, the rough balance of power of ownership was reflected in the composition of the company's directors. Han Fuju's representatives held three of the seven seats. Song family members held three seats as well, although one of those was a Song cousin acting in the name of Yiyong Hall, which would eventually be turned over to Zhao Zizhen. The Song associate Xu Yanshan held the seventh seat, however, which along with control of Zhao Zizhen's share, placed the majority of board members in the hands of the Song family. As with the shareholder structure, the array of directors indicated an awkward balance through the intermediation of third parties. This balance continued with Dongya's management. Song Feiqing was elected chairman of the board and president (*zong jingli*), while Zhao Zizhen was made vice president. Song Yuhan, Song Feiqing's brother, became a second vice president.[57]

From the beginning, company publications tried to take control of the narrative of the founding of the company and obscure the actual ownership structure in favor of a vision in which professional managers ran the company along scientific principles. A passage in a 1933 publication celebrating the company's one-year anniversary discussed the failure of earlier woolen mills. It stated that investment in those firms sometimes seemed "like buying lottery tickets because perhaps managers are not upright or perhaps because they are taking personal advantage of funds entrusted to them or perhaps because the shareholders are greedy."[58] In other words, the success of a firm such as Dongya depended on having trustworthy managers. Investors, in turn, would stand back and let the managers do their job. This passage could have been aimed directly at Han Fuju. Even if it was not, Dongya publications never acknowledged Han's role. A company publication in 1934 claimed that Song Feiqing gathered capital from "patriotic industrialists."[59] In 1936, Dongya's own company history emphasized the contributions of "society which trusted the company."[60] Nowhere in either source does the connection to Han Fuju or other military officers appear. In a similar vein, the company's 1934 annual report tried to present a broad base of public support by reproducing best wishes from no fewer than ninety-seven government officials, military officers, businesspeople, and well-known public figures. Han Fuju's name did not appear among them.[61]

In fact the early company charters gave later small investors more voting power than the earlier large investors. Both of the first two company charters, one issued in 1932 and a revision issued in 1933, provided for two classes of investors. In the 1933 charter, those who invested the first 300,000 yuan (including most of the investments of Han Fuju, Yiyong Hall, and the Songs themselves) received one vote for every 10,000 yuan of investment, but those who invested later, received one vote for only 1,000 yuan in investment.[62] With this provision, Han Fuju and the Song family only directly controlled about thirty plus votes. The remaining small minority shareholders, of whom there were more than three hundred by 1934, would have controlled almost three hundred votes. This provision provided an incentive for smaller investors who might otherwise have been leery of putting themselves at the mercy of either Han or the Song family.

Dongya actively solicited small shareholders, which quickly diluted the voting power of the initial investors. At a January 1934 board meeting, Song Feiqing proposed that Dongya increase invested capital to one million yuan. In an audacious plan, he suggested soliciting small investments from three thousand new shareholders to gain "attention and sympathy" from all over

China.[63] The campaign was quite successful and by the end of 1936, capital was 921,999 yuan.[64] Clearly Song aimed for a time when Dongya was not tied to any particular investor or backer.[65] Instead large numbers of small shareholders with enhanced voting rights would have trouble coordinating action and would have likely given at least tacit approval to most of Song's management decisions.

If the structure and management of Dongya intended to put as much distance as possible between Song Feiqing and his official backers, in other arenas the company actively sought close relations with the government. Since the founding of Dongya coincided with renewed interest in the National Products Movement, Dongya eagerly sought certification of its knitting yarn as a "national product."[66] The Nationalist government backed this campaign with special tax credits for domestic producers, reduced shipping costs on government-run railroads, increased tariffs on some imported items, and by a propaganda campaign encouraging the use of domestic products.

Zhao Zizhen spent months in the Nationalist capital of Nanjing trying to get the national products certification and tax exemption for Dongya. According to his later account, he first contacted a Nationalist official to whom he had sold a vehicle a few years earlier. As he made his way through the bureaucracy, Zhao gave a full set of Dongya-produced wool underwear to each official with whom he had to deal until he finally got an interview with Kong Xiangxi, then minister of industry.[67] According to Zhao's account, Kong at first refused to grant the tax exemption because the Nationalist government needed tax revenue, but finally allowed himself to be persuaded by arguments that the exemption would be good for Chinese industry. Afraid that Kong might change his mind, Zhao asked him to write a note on the spot, which he then took to the appropriate office to receive the certificate of tax exemption.[68] The picture Zhao Zizhen paints of the Nationalist bureaucracy is one of red tape and arbitrary implementation of policy based on personal connections and happenstance. Nonetheless, once certified, Dongya quickly arranged for discounted shipping on government railroads and exemption from two local taxes by the Tianjin city government.[69]

Both publically and privately, Dongya managers attributed much of the company's success to government help. In 1934, Dongya published its second annual report, thanking Zhao Zhizhen for working hard to get government help. "Fortunately, there was help from the government: the ministries of Railways, Finance, Communications, and Industry. [We] sought the agreement and investigation of various cities to prove that our products are domestic high quality wool yarn. In addition to issuing National Products certificates, [the government] reduced taxes and halved shipping rates."[70] Likewise, an internal report to the company's board of directors at about the same time stated that "this company's operations have substantially relied on the help of the government in reducing shipping rates and taxes."[71] A few years later, a letter to the Bank of Communications pointed to past government help as a mark of the company's distinction: "we have received help from your bank, all circles and special treatment from the government in excusing taxes and reducing shipping costs."[72]

In addition to tax exemptions and shipping discounts, the Nationalist regime's new tariff autonomy favored domestic production for some industries. After many years of fixed low tariffs set by the same treaties that created the treaty ports like Tianjin, the Nationalist government successfully negotiated revision of China's tariffs with the foreign powers. The first tariff revision in 1928 aimed mostly at revenue generation and had few overtones of protecting Chinese industries. In contrast, the second round of tariff revision in 1931 showed an interest in protecting and encouraging Chinese light industry, especially silk and wool textiles.[73] For imports into Tianjin, average customs taxes in 1926 were about 3.8 percent and grew to 27.2 percent by 1935.[74] In particular, the government "raised customs duties on imports of wool yarn from 5 to 10 percent in 1930 and to 12 percent in 1931." Taxes went up on the raw wool imports that Dongya needed, but not as severely as on those products with which Dongya planned to compete.[75] Also, providentially, raw wool prices were declining in the early 1930s, keeping Dongya's cost of raw materials low in spite of the small tariff increase.[76] As one of China's largest woolen mills, Dongya was in a good position to take advantage of the new tariffs. Japanese reports from the late 1930s routinely accept the narrative of tariff protection in explaining the industrial development in China in the early 1930s.[77]

In 1935, Dongya turned to the government again to lobby for favorable tariffs and a government loan. The company even sent Zhao Zizhen to Nanjing again to meet with Kong Xiangxi because the need for financing had become particularly acute.[78] Dongya had to produce and stockpile yarn throughout the summer months for sale in the fall and winter and thus had run short of cash. At the same time, competition in China's wool yarn industry had become particularly fierce and Dongya needed to improve its technology to provide competitive products. Earlier that year, the Nationalist government had taken steps to increase its grip on the Chinese economy by taking control of the Bank of China, the Bank of Communications, and three smaller banks.[79] As a result, Dongya's request for a loan from the Bank of China and Bank of Communications had become a government matter. As a precondition for making a loan, the banks conducted an investigation of Dongya's operations and discovered that the equipment the company wanted to use as collateral for the loan was outdated and overvalued. In addition, Dongya faced serious difficulty competing with better-managed and better-financed competitors.[80] Because of the delays, Kong Xiangxi, by then finance minister, intervened directly and suggested that another government bank, the National Products Bank, which had been established to support domestic production and import substitution, join with the Bank of China and the Bank of Communications in making the loan.[81] In the end, the Bank of China and the Bank of Communications, under pressure from the Finance Ministry, agreed to lend the funds by including Dongya's inventory of knitted products along with equipment as collateral.[82] At about the same time, Dongya met with representatives of six other Chinese woolen mills to plan a Wool Producers' Association in part to lobby against Japan's request to lower tariffs on wool products.[83]

Chinese Business under the Uncertain Developmental State

Song Feiqing's business activities in the 1930s show the advent of the conscious creation of a public narrative to portray business as morally beneficial. The New Year's ad for Federal vehicles in 1930 tried to portray imports as both progressive and beneficial to society. Later, obtaining National Product status for the Dongya Corporation yarn became a vital part of the company's strategy for success.

The government played many roles in Dongya's early development. Predatory confiscation of Song Chuandian's fortune almost obstructed Song

Feiqing's plans for industrial development. It is unlikely the Songs could have even founded Dongya without resolution of Song Chuandian's political situation through the help from the official and military leader Han Fuju, since much of the capital for the company came from Han and his associates. In addition to these ties to Nationalist officials, Dongya benefited enormously from import-substitution policies of the Nationalist regime. Tax breaks, discounted shipping rates, and tariffs on imported woolen goods all set the ground for Dongya's ability to compete with foreign firms. Furthermore, Dongya took advantage of financing provided by the state through state-controlled banks such as the Bank of China, Bank of Communications, and National Products Bank. It is possible to conclude, then, that the Nationalist regime was in many ways a developmental state.

The implementation of those policies, however, smacked of a kind of arbitrary personalism, which forces the conclusion that the Nationalists were at best an uncertain developmental state. Add to that uncertainty the complex relations between Dongya, the government, and its official backers like Han Fuju and even Kong Xiangxi, and perhaps it is possible to describe the Nationalists as an uncertain developmental state with warlord characteristics and occasional predatory outbursts. Nonetheless, the state contributed significantly to Dongya's ability to produce wool knitting yarn, a symbol of foreign consumer society. In fact, the state shared a vision of modernity that included the kind of urban consumerism Dongya promoted.

3 Building Eden outside the Firm with National Products and Urban Consumerism

THE CONSUMER PRODUCTS associated with Euro-American modernity were a large part of the Industrial Eden vision. As Karl Gerth has shown, however, the drive for modernity in China was in tension with the promotion of Chinese national products, and attempts to resolve that tension often rested on reshaping the role of women consumers, especially in 1934, the "Women's Year of National Products." Gerth showed how the promoters of national products tried to "destroy the attractiveness" of the urban and internationally oriented practices of consumption.[1] Song Feiqing and the Dongya Corporation also tried to shape the behaviors of consuming women, but in contrast to the national goods promoters Gerth studied, Dongya presented a vision in which Chinese-made foreign products, such as knitting yarn, allowed Chinese women consumers to be both modern and patriotic.

Dongya's marketing vision seemed to work. In the period from 1932 to 1937, the company captured about a quarter of the market share for knitting yarn in China. Close reading of the evidence, however, shows that Dongya was beginning to falter by 1936. Prior to that time, state help in terms of higher tariffs and tax reductions had allowed Dongya to sell yarn more cheaply than its foreign competitors. The decision of the Patons and Baldwins Company to avoid tariffs by manufacturing knitting yarn in China reduced Dongya's price advantage. Without that advantage, even the label of "national product" could not ensure Dongya's ability to compete with better-capitalized foreign companies.

Wool Knitting Yarn

It is hard to say when Song would have first been exposed to the wearing of wool clothes, especially hand-knitted wool clothes. Prior to the arrival of Europeans in China, references in Chinese texts about wool clothing mostly referred either to minorities and marginal peoples in mountain (sheep-raising) areas or to luxury goods. In addition textiles were woven, knotted, and felted, but there was no mention of knitting.[2] When the missionary Alfred Jones had arrived in Qingzhou, Shandong, in 1887, he remarked on the fact that "nothing woolen is to be had here—at all."[3] Of course the arrival of missionaries meant the arrival of foreign fashions as well. Although Jones adopted Chinese-style dress in his early years in Qingzhou, by the time of Song Feiqing's youth, there was a much larger missionary community, which included women who would have worn Western fashions and who likely knitted. We know for example that the McMullans, missionaries in another part of Shandong, opened a knitting school and business where they took orders for knitted underwear and other items.[4]

It is highly probable that Song Feiqing became familiar with knitting as a child from his contact with Jones and the other missionaries. In addition, wool and knitting became fashionable in cosmopolitan Chinese cities in the 1910s and 1920s at the same time that Song Feiqing's peripatetic education took him to Shanghai and Beijing. At that time, as part of what later would be called the May Fourth Movement, Chinese intellectuals founded dozens of new journals to discuss China's problems and to introduce Western ideas of modernity, including, of all things, knitting. One, the *Ladies' Journal* (*Funü zazhi*), published an article in January 1919 in its "Practical Science" section introducing wool, and especially knitted wool, as a form of scientific and "hygienic" clothing, including detailed instructions with diagrams on how to knit. Titled "Weisheng yi," which the content of the article makes clear can be translated either as "underwear" or "hygienic clothing," the article had a highly nationalist tone and implied that knitting would be one way to combat increasing wool imports from abroad, especially Japan. Ever-increasing levels of wool imports led the author to ask, "Isn't the 30,000,000 yuan lost every year [to Japanese machine-knit imports] the obligation of our women? Patriots would [knit clothing] themselves."[5] The author portrayed knitting as a social practice at the center of modern ideas of both hygiene and patriotism. Song Feiqing later made the same connections.

In fact, whether for patriotism or not, more and more Chinese women did take up knitting in the 1920s.[6] Antonia Finnane quotes a 1924 fashion feature: "Since the rise of education for girls, knitted woollen garments have become very popular. At first it was just children's socks and hats along with women's scarves, but in the past two or three years, in late autumn to early winter, women are more and more knitting woolen tops or vests as outer wear, to guard against the cold."[7] Thus Finnane notes that "the knitted jumper or cardigan helped displace the padded jacket. . . . Women of the burgeoning middle class were exposed to woollen garments as fashion items in the pages of magazines . . . which advertised the advantages of knitting and . . . depicted fashionable young women equipped with wool and needles, as though knitting belonged to the same spectrum of activities as listening to the gramophone, playing golf, or going for a drive."[8]

Chinese adoption of the practice of knitting copied the West. Song Feiqing later recalled that he had realized while in the United States that "wool knitting yarn was one of society's most common consumer products."[9] With the growth of the popularity of knitting, Chinese imports of knitting yarn increased apace with 1928 imports more than nine times those of 1920 as shown in Table 3.1.

By the time planning for Dongya began, in the early 1930s both the West and China were in the midst of a knitting boom. In the West, the combination of knitting as fashion, fueled by designers like Coco Channel in Paris, and knitting as frugality, fueled by the Great Depression, led housewives all over the world to knit as an inexpensive way of clothing themselves and their families.[10] By the mid-1930s demand for knitting yarn made up 41 percent, or 2.7 million yuan per year, of total demand for wool textiles in North China.[11] In 1930 the Shanghai pictorial *Liangyou* included knitting among pictures of the creative arts such as painting, sculpting, and photography, and in 1933 listed a new sweater for baby among other modern items of preparation for the winter such as hot water bottles and electric space heaters.[12]

In addition to its modern appeal, domestically produced knitting yarn also had patriotic overtones. When Song Feiqing had experimented with producing wool yarn back in Shandong, he planned to call his new wool

TABLE 3.1   Chinese Wool Yarn Imports, 1911–1928

Year	Yarn Imports (thousands of lbs)	% of 1911
1911	1,297	100
1912	1,277	98
1913	1,953	151
1914	1,081	83
1915	633	49
1916	569	44
1917	832	64
1918	460	35
1919	527	41
1920	856	66
1921	1,130	87
1922	1,650	127
1923	4,269	329
1924	4,115	317
1925	3,335	257
1925	3,335	257
1926	8,097	624
1927	3,903	301
1928	7,866	606

Source: Information adapted from *Shanghai minzu mao fangzhi gongye* (Beijing: Zhonghua shuju, 1963), 41, 42, 48.

yarn "Enrich the Nation" brand. He designed a label with a drawing of the Gate of Heavenly Peace in Beijing, a symbol of Chinese culture and also the place where Beijing students protested against Japan in 1919. He developed a marketing slogan that read in part, "Chinese people, Chinese money . . . Chinese material, Chinese made" (see Figure 3.1). Clearly, he wanted to link the salvation of the nation and this particular product in consumers' minds, and many of these themes reappeared later in Dongya advertising.

By the time Song Feiqing turned his hand to founding the Dongya Corporation, the sense of crisis in China was even deeper, especially with Japanese imperialist encroachment in Manchuria and North China, which put Tianjin fairly close to the firing line in the rising Sino-Japanese conflict.[13] Some parts of this conflict even played out in the streets of Tianjin. As a treaty port, Tianjin hosted a Japanese population in 1932 of approximately 6,800, more than twice the number of all Westerners combined.[14] As Japanese aggression became more and more evident, tensions between Chinese

FIGURE 3.1 "Enrich the Nation" brand yarn label reads "Chinese people, Chinese money, please use Enrich the Nation wool yarn. Chinese material, Chinese made, fair price." Courtesy of Li Yulian.

and Japanese in Tianjin ran high and resulted in an endless stream of posters and handbills, acts of intimidation, diplomatic wrangling, and sometimes even violence, which local authorities tried to keep under control.

The most visible manifestation of the Sino-Japanese conflict in Tianjin took the form of anti-Japanese boycotts sponsored by merchants, citizen groups, and the Nationalist Party from time to time, but local Chinese political authorities associated with one or another of the northern militarists more casually allied with the Nationalists usually took a dim view of such provocations.[15] Thus the city was rocked by periodic anti-Japanese mass movements sponsored by civic groups, some merchants, and some politicians, especially representatives of the Nationalist Party, and then by periodic suppression of these mass movements on behalf of other politicians associated with North China's military rulers who themselves loosely associated with the Nationalist regime.[16]

Although China's unstable political situation presented risks to Song and the other founders of Dongya, the rising tensions with Japan also fueled the National Products Campaign and antiforeign feeling in China. Just as planning for Dongya was under way, both reached fever pitch. Investors held Dongya's first shareholders' meeting on 15 August 1931 to plan the opening of the company the following year.[17] Almost exactly a month after this first shareholders' meeting, Sino-Japanese tensions reached a new high when the Japanese army seized Manchuria, the northeastern part of China abutting Japan's colony of Korea. The experience of Song Feiqing's youngest brother, Song Xianyong, showed the extent of anger in Tianjin when the next day he showed up to his primary school to find his teachers and classmates milling about while his school principal wrote an announcement denouncing the Japanese in his own blood. In Xianyong's recollection, "it was as if the sky had fallen in, the sun stopped shinning, and the air had thinned."[18] Closer to home, two months later in November, the "Tianjin Incidents" caused a four-week "mini war" when Japanese agents hired Chinese thugs to riot and attack Chinese organs of control in the Chinese-controlled portions of Tianjin.[19] This strained atmosphere reinvigorated the movement to boycott foreign imports and buy national products.

Dongya took immediate steps by promoting its yarn as a national product and writing to chambers of commerce with yarn samples and asking them to promote Butting Ram yarn in their areas as a "great patriotic contribution to the prosperity of your locality."[20] Even Dongya's brand name, Butting Ram, evoked struggle. The butting ram illustration on its logo was an aggressive symbol of strength and struggle with the ram on the left, representing the East or Asia, posed slightly higher than the ram on the right, which represented the West confronting China from across the Pacific.[21] Moreover, the Chinese for "butting ram" (*diyang* 抵羊) is actually a homophone for slightly different characters meaning "oppose the foreigners" or "oppose foreign products" (*diyang* 抵洋). Dongya prominently included the words "domestic product" in its advertising. A Dongya newspaper advertisement from 1932 shows an ancient Chinese soldier dressed for battle with a banner reading "Butting Ram Brand" and a shield with the Butting Ram logo. The text leads with the announcement of the formation of the "Domestic Products Victory Army" (Figure 3.2). Fashion, in this case knitting yarn, was shaped into a weapon of national survival.

The "national products" designation was so important, that at one point, when rumors spread in Shanghai in 1933 that Butting Ram yarn was not truly domestically produced, the Dongya Corporation offered a 10,000 yuan reward to anyone who could prove that its products were not the result of domestic production. Eventually both the Shanghai and Tianjin chambers of commerce became involved in inspecting Dongya and certifying its products as "national products."[22] The general distributor for North China was the Tianjin National Products Sales Office, with sales accounting for more than 40 percent of Dongya's revenues.[23] In one 1933 advertisement by the Tianjin National Products Sales Office, Butting Ram yarn was one of only three featured domestic brands along with a cosmetics and pencil company.[24]

FIGURE 3.2 A Butting Ram brand yarn advertisement from 1932 uses an appeal to patriotism, stressing domestic production. *Dagong bao*, 10 November 1932, section 3, p. 12.

In spite of the Nationalist government's approval of Butting Ram's status as a national product, there were indeed questions about whether or not this classification was appropriate. Dongya's application for "national products" status claims that Butting Ram yarn was made completely from domestic goods, including raw materials.[25] Likewise in a celebratory annual report published by Dongya on its first anniversary, Song Feiqing personally thanked the "compatriots who purchased Butting Ram brand yarn and who clearly understand that it is purely a national product."[26] In truth, the balance of evidence proves that Dongya quickly found that domestic wool was not appropriate for knitting yarn and the company switched to Australian wool imports for raw materials. Zhao Zizhen recalled that the coarse yarn produced from domestic wool was quickly knitted into sweaters and sold to Han Fuju for his soldiers.[27] This might have been the cause of the urgent appeals in 1933 by Dongya to hire people with expertise in knitting and weaving wool.[28] Another Dongya former employee confirmed that Dongya used imported Australian wool, and studies show most Chinese

woolen mills did as well.[29] Dongya company archives note that an employee
went to Australia in 1937 to purchase wool, though it is certainly possible
that the company purchased Australian wool before then through intermediaries.[30] Nonetheless, as late as the end of 1936 Dongya still claimed it
used only Chinese domestic wool, but this is highly unlikely.[31] With national products, as with obscuring the true ownership of the company,
Dongya executives worked from the beginning to control the public narrative of their activities.

  The "national product" designation provided only one aspect of Butting
Ram yarn's appeal. In most Dongya promotion, national salvation and modernity merged, as can be seen in a November 1933 advertisement
(Figure 3.3), which features a woman and boy. The woman wears a fashionable knitted vest over her Chinese-style dress and the boy is fully dressed
in Western-style, knitted wool clothing. Their cosmopolitan and Western
modernity is further signified by their rakish hats and a dog on a leash. In
contrast to these images of modernity, the text of the advertisement em-
phasizes the patriotic nature of the product. It reads in part, "Purchase of

FIGURE 3.3 Modernity as seen in a Butting Ram brand yarn advertisement, 1933. The
text suggests that buying the wool yarn will help strengthen the economy and, by
extension, Chinese national sovereignty. *Dagong bao*, 15 November 1933.

domestically produced wool yarn can solve all patriotic questions" and "The enormous sums which flow abroad every year for imports are our sweat and blood."

Thus Dongya focused on the promotion of knitted-wool products as a modern form of clothing that would benefit both the household and the nation. Shang Huanting, manager of the knitting department and the only female executive at the company, described the situation as follows: "Most Chinese don't pay much attention to wool garments, especially in conservative North China. People think of cotton and silk as standard and of wool as a subsidiary or luxury product." She went on to say that the solution to this problem lay "half in breaking down conservatism in order to get people to appreciate wool and half in promoting domestic products, because those who are advanced enough to appreciate wool often think of domestic products as having poor quality." In order to accomplish these goals, the Dongya Corporation directly engaged consumers in a wide variety of marketing practices that ranged from sponsoring knitting schools and knitting contests to creating print advertising campaigns using leaflets and ads in newspapers as well as periodicals.[32] Two examples of Dongya advertisements exude modernity in their art deco styling (Figure 3.4). In one, the female figure exemplifies the union of knitting and modern fashion.[33] She wears a knitted sweater while holding a ball of knitting yarn. In the other, the man seems to have no direct relationship to knitting, but his Western-style suit and fast-paced pose are both evocative of modernity. The knitting needles and balls of yarn in the corner thus become modern by association.

The Dongya Corporation also set up its own service department to handle correspondence with customers. Under the English name "Dear Young" (sounding a little like the Butting Ram brand name "Diyang" and implying youth and foreign-languaged modernity) the service department answered questions about knitting patterns, helped match colors and wools, and sold yarn by mail. In 1936, the service department corresponded with almost seven hundred customers.[34] Singer Sewing Machines had pioneered the use of sewing classes to promote sales of sewing machines in China, as well as the United States, and Dongya followed suit.[35] Dongya sponsored knitting classes that customers could attend and rewarded those who mastered the modern skill of knitting through competitions with prizes up

FIGURE 3.4 The fusion of modernity and fashion in Dongya advertising. *Left:* "Diyang Brand Domestically Produced Wool Yarn; Carried and Sold by Various Stores Nationwide." *Right:* "Diyang Brand Domestically Produced Wool Yarn." Both from *Dongya Annual*, 1934, unpaged.

to hundreds of yuan (see Figure 3.5). Dongya also started a lottery where customers could win prizes by collecting the Butting Ram logos off of yarn packages.[36]

In 1934 Dongya launched its own family magazine. Harking back to his missionary background, Song Feiqing named it the *Ark Monthly* (*Fangzhou yuekan* 方舟月刊).[37] In a later essay, Song Feiqing listed "publications" as one of the central missions of his firm (along with production and education reform).[38] For Song such publications advertised the firm's products and embodied the firm's mission to transform society. As the preface to the first edition of the *Ark Monthly* stated, "It is worth researching how to allow families to fulfill their mission of producing healthy individuals for the construction of a strong and flourishing country." Unfortunately, in the eyes of the editors of the *Ark*, "most men and women who manage families don't have clear ideas or effective methods." The Dongya Corporation and the *Ark Monthly*, however, came to the rescue by "providing training and

FIGURE 3.5   Dongya knitting class. *Dongya Annual*, 1934, unpaged.

guidance."[39] Many of the articles published in the *Ark Monthly* echoed ideas brought by foreign missionaries like those around whom Song grew up.[40] In fact, the Qingzhou missionary Samuel Couling, founder of the middle school attended by Song Feiqing, believed that missionaries had a duty to teach "the science of living—Hygiene—Sanitation etc."[41] In that first issue and over the years to come, this idea of training and guidance emphasized a vision of a scientific and modern family taking its place on the Chinese, and world, stage. Issues included articles on child rearing, relationships, household management, hygiene, and, of course, knitting. Each issue of the *Ark* contained detailed knitting patterns, instructions, and even small samples of Butting Ram yarn in the appropriate weights and colors for each pattern.

In the promotion of knitting, the editors of the *Ark Monthly* combined an earlier set of Western ideas on scientific clothing with the most modern and up-to-date women's fashions copied from patterns in Western (mostly American) women's and knitting magazines.[42] In the inaugural issue the *Ark Monthly* translated and printed a speech by the British women's advocate and family reformer Ada S. Ballin, who was presented as a cutting-edge authority even though she had died almost thirty years earlier.[43] Ballin had said, "Modern methods for taking care of infants must be made scientific. Besides nursing, sleep, bathing and temperature, the most important problem is that of clothing . . . the tender skin of those infants who wear stiff cotton clothing cannot resist the pain of being rubbed [raw]. . . . This is just the surface harm. Infants' internal organs also are unintentionally harmed by swaddling in cotton quilts and wearing stiff cotton clothing. . . . Infants' clothing should all be high-quality wool knits."[44] The message in this and other articles was clear. Wool, especially knitted wool, represented a scientific necessity for the successful management of the modern family, which was a prerequisite for China's salvation. At the same time that Dongya began publishing the *Ark Monthly*, the company's print advertising also began describing Butting Ram yarn as "scientific."[45]

Wool knits alone could not make a modern family, however. This also required relationships of mutual support between husband and wife, scientific organization and management of the household, adequate nutrition for pregnant mothers so they could give birth to strong citizens to build a strong nation, proper scientific washing of dirty clothes, proper household bookkeeping, and even scientific sex education for your children.[46] All of these and hundreds of articles on similar subjects appeared in the *Ark Monthly* in the 1930s. Each one was a testimony to the transformative social mission of the enterprise. This mission apparently struck a chord among sectors of republican-period Chinese society. In just eighteen months, circulation of the *Ark* grew from nothing to 10,500 issues per month.[47] This tremendous success led Dongya Corporation management to conclude that "the *Ark Monthly* had a huge direct effect on increasing product sales and the popularity of knitting in China."[48]

In Dongya's promotion of its knitting yarn, patriotism, modernity, and science all intersected with a gendered notion of the urban consumer. Dongya promoted the *Ark Monthly* as "a library on family problems and a good guide for modern women."[49] All of the participants in the knitting class pictured in Figure 3.5 were women. Likewise, once when a group of boy and girl students from the middle school attached to Tianjin Normal University visited Dongya, during the rest break, Shang Huanting taught the girls how to knit. There is no mention of how the boys spent their rest time, but apparently it did not involve knitting.[50] An *Ark Monthly* article

in 1937 declared, "women of the times all know how to knit."[51] The magazine echoed Nationalist propaganda as well when it published an article
on women and the New Life Movement, which stressed the "social obligations of women" as well as their "equality."[52] The "knitting housewife"
as a symbol of the good family management needed to build the nation
was not entirely without precedent in China. Textile production, and especially women's role in textile production, had been at the center of ideas
about family morality for centuries prior to the republican period.[53] Dongya
merely reshaped this ideal in the early part of the twentieth century from
spinning and weaving to knitting.

Reform of the family and modernization of women had been major issues among Chinese intellectuals since the May Fourth Movement of the
late 1910s and early 1920s. Businesspeople like Song Feiqing took up the
call. Besides Dongya, one Shanghai entrepreneur delivered a journal called
Family Weekly along with bottles of milk from his dairy. *Family Weekly* "featured articles on home management, decorating, self-improvement for
women, and marital relationships."[54] A silk clothing shop, the products of
which were clearly more in the traditional than the modern sector, sponsored its own radio show trying to position its products as part of modern
life.[55] These examples show that Song Feiqing and the Dongya Corporation's marketing program tapped into a set of powerful ideas and practices
in republican China centered around the transformative role of the enterprise in society and modern notions of consumer culture.

What Price Modernity?

By all accounts the Dongya Corporation was a great success. It was far and
away the largest Chinese producer of wool knitting yarn. One estimate
showed that Dongya accounted for 87 percent of yarn produced by Chinese companies in the first half of the 1930s.[56] Dongya's share of the total
Chinese knitting-yarn market including yarn produced by foreign companies climbed rapidly from approximately 2 percent in 1932 to a peak of
24 percent in 1935 (see Table 3.2). Imports of wool yarn and thread into
North China, where Dongya operated, decreased particularly dramatically
from 204,600 tons in 1934 to only 31,204 tons in 1936.[57] On the surface,
Song Feiqing could feel a great sense of accomplishment. Dongya was a

TABLE 3.2 Chinese Knitting-Yarn Production and Imports, 1911–1937

Year	Yarn Imports (thousands of lbs.)	Chinese Production (thousands of lbs.)	Foreign Production in China (thousands of lbs.)	Estimated Total Production (thousands of lbs.)	Dongya Corporation Production (thousands of lbs.)	Dongya Corp. Production as a % of Total Production
1911	1,297	0	0	1,297	—	—
1912	1,277	0	0	1,277	—	—
1913	1,953	0	0	1,953	—	—
1914	1,081	0	0	1,081	—	—
1915	633	0	0	633	—	—
1916	569	0	0	569	—	—
1917	832	0	0	832	—	—
1918	460	0	0	460	—	—
1919	527	0	0	527	—	—
1920	856	0	0	856	—	—
1921	1,130	0	0	1,130	—	—
1922	1,650	0	0	1,650	—	—
1923	4,269	0	0	4,269	—	—
1924	4,115	0	0	4,115	—	—
1925	3,335	0	0	3,335	—	—

1926	8,097	0	0	8,097	—	—
1927	3,903	0	0	3,903	—	—
1928	7,886	0	0	7,886	—	—
1929	?	0	0	—	—	—
1930	?	0	0	—	—	—
1931	9,159	70	0	9,229	—	—
1932	7,263	188	0	7,451	150	2.01%
1933	7,645	937	0	8,582	750	8.74%
1934	7,134	1,375	900	9,409	1,100	11.69%
1935	1,879	1,681	2,000	5,560	1,345	24.19%
1936	1,351	1,526	6,000	8,877	1,221	13.75%
1937	1,178	725	5,500	7,403	580	7.83%

Note: Chinese production estimated based on assumptions that Dongya produced approximately 80 percent of Chinese-made yarn.

Sources: Information adapted from *Shanghai minzu,* 41, 42, 48, 106; Cui Shuju and Jin Yanshi, 15, 50, 51; and *Tianjin dongya maoni fangzhi gufen youxian gongsi niankan,* 1936, unpaginated, Archives of the Dongya Corporation, 1-17-1-01, 1-17-1-06; and Yoshida, 287.

success story of Chinese business and a model of national-products-style import substitution assisted by a developmental state.

At the same time, Song had much to worry about. Dongya's 1936 annual report read: "In the few years since the founding of this company, international competition has intensified and the country's difficulties have increased, social disturbances have reached an extremely tense level. . . . In this stormy environment, advance . . . truly relies on the support of each shareholder and each friend and the enthusiastic support of all patriots."[58] This text points to three interrelated elements of the environment in which Dongya operated: international competition, the country's difficulties, and the support of patriots on whom Dongya depended for success.

In terms of competition, Dongya was not the only company that had eyed China's growing market for knitting yarn in the 1930s.[59] Companies from China, Japan, and Europe all vied for primacy. Within China, by 1934 two other companies, Xianghe and Haijing were marketing "national product" wool knitting yarn in Tianjin. Of the two, Haijing disappeared quickly, but Xianghe's Airplane (Feiji) brand provided real competition.[60] At about the same time the Zhenxing company in Shanghai began producing knitting yarn as well.[61] An internal strategy document from the Dongya Corporation dismissed these and other Chinese competitors as minor threats, but still worried that these companies "often do not pay attention to commercial morals. . . . We cannot ignore them." To counter these upstart Chinese competitors, Dongya introduced "Anti-Aircraft Gun" (Gaoshepao) brand yarn, which literally aimed with an intentional pun directly at Xianghe's Airplane brand.[62] At the same time, several well-capitalized Japanese companies pursued the Chinese wool knitting-yarn market, but most produced slightly inferior products that they sold unbranded to shops that then added local packaging and branding. In response, Dongya introduced its own line of unbranded yarn with somewhat poorer quality materials than Butting Ram.[63] Dongya's biggest competitors, however, remained European companies such as the giant Patons and Baldwins Company of Scotland.[64]

Because increased tariffs on imported yarn combined with the tax and shipping breaks from the Nationalist government gave Dongya a price advantage, Patons managers took steps to "retain our hold on the Far Eastern Market." They decided to build a large factory in Shanghai, which went into full production in 1934.[65] Not subject to the Chinese government's protective tariffs, wool yarn produced by Patons in Shanghai eroded Dongya's price advantage. At the same time, Dongya was perennially short of funds to finance expansion. In addition to the need for stopgap financing from government banks, Dongya had to rely on its old political patron Zhang Huizhong a founding investor and wife of a subordinate to Han Fuju, to finance a move to a new and larger factory complex in the British concession.[66] In contrast to Dongya's constant scramble, Patons had ample funds. As Dongya strove to reach one million yuan in total capital, Patons had capital equivalent to twenty-five million yuan, five times the total capital of all Chinese woolen mills combined.[67]

Patons's influence was omnipresent in the Chinese knitting-yarn market and even influenced Dongya's eventual takeover of its smaller Chinese competitor, the Xianghe Corporation. Dongya and Xianghe, which had extended discussions of a merger, could not come to a conclusive agreement. Although one account attributes the eventual merger agreement to the mediation of Zhang Boling, head of Tianjin's Nankai University, and a prominent Christian who would have been tied to the same missionary networks as Song Feiqing, the timing appears to have also been directly related to Patons's aggressive protection of its brand names.[68] In a series of large and sharply worded advertisements in Tianjin newspapers, Patons declared that it was bringing suit against Xianghe for brand infringement against its own Aeroplane brand yarn.[69] Less than a week after Patons's latest published accusation, Dongya and Xianghe announced their merger, Xianghe ceased to exist, and Xianghe's Airplane brand disappeared from the market.[70] For its part, Dongya itself gladly stopped producing its Anti-Aircraft brand, which did not receive the special tax treatment of its main Butting Ram brand.[71]

Even with this merger, foreign companies still produced most of the knitting yarn used in China. Patons began Chinese production in 1934, and by 1936 had recovered some of its market share, reducing Dongya's portion to approximately 14 percent in 1936 and to only 8 percent in 1937 (see Table 3.2). In the end, high tariffs on imported wool yarn did result in import substitution. The policies of the Nationalist's uncertain developmental state had worked to make production of spinning yarn a domestic industry, but it quickly came to be an industry dominated by foreign companies, not

Chinese national products producers such as Dongya. Once Patons began producing in China, tariffs disappeared as an issue and Dongya lost its price advantage. Most consumers apparently did not care if domestic production was Chinese or foreign owned.

Limits on Dongya's ability to compete are most clearly seen in the regional scope of its operations and its struggle with technical requirements. Although company managers made plans to make Dongya national, it remained primarily a regional company struggling to compete against bigger foreign rivals.[72] About half of sales were concentrated in North China.[73] The high technical requirements for knitting yarn also hampered Dongya's ability to compete. For example, in spite of its best efforts, Dongya's four-strand yarn, almost half of its production, simply did not measure up to the products produced by Patons.[74] From the beginning Dongya had been a learn-as-you-go operation. Back in the early 1930s Song was determined not to repeat the mistake of his abortive Shandong experiment when he bought the wrong machines, so he glued a sample of wool knitting yarn to the order letter to make sure the supplying company knew exactly what he wanted. In addition, Song sent his younger brother Song Yuhan (Xiafei), abroad to study textile production even as the company began operations.[75] Although Dongya hired an engineer from Shanghai to help set up the factory, Song Feiqing called on about one hundred of Shandong Dechang's most reliable long-term employees in Shandong to come to Tianjin and provide the backbone of Dongya's new workforce.[76] Although they were extremely loyal, they brought little technical expertise in spinning knitting yarn. As a result of all these problems, Dongya's yarn could not compete head-to-head in the marketplace. The company decided to have much of the four-strand yarn knitted into sweaters and sold that way. These sweaters then became collateral for the government loans needed to continue to finance Dongya's operations.[77]

If the ferociously competitive knitting-yarn market was not enough of a challenge, Dongya also had to deal with the volatile politics of North China, the "stormy environment" to which Song Feiqing referred in 1936. Evidence from the Dongya archives shows how the lack of political stability impacted the company throughout the 1930s. Reports to Dongya's shareholders in January of 1933 show how the loss of Manchuria to Japan in 1931 had eliminated a huge market for Chinese goods, how the Japanese

attack on Shanghai in early 1932 had limited sales there, and how the unrest in the Northwest made transportation difficult.[78] Then in 1933 the Japanese moved south of Manchuria into Jehol (Rehe) Province, causing the
resignation of military strongman Zhang Xueliang.[79] Dongya had to post-
pone a board of directors meeting in March of 1933 because political instability made travel difficult.[80] Signing of a truce between China and Japan
in May calmed matters, but Tianjin remained tense. In May 1933, for example, the city witnessed the arrival of more than six thousand refugees
from the fighting as well as the explosion of numerous bombs aimed at political targets.[81] Nonetheless, the Nationalist government continued to ap-
pease Japan. At the end of 1934 Zhang Ting'e replaced Wang Tao as mayor
of Tianjin because he was said to be more acceptable to the Japanese.[82] Japan
continued to demand more autonomy for North China and after another
Chinese concession in this realm, five to six thousand students marched
through Tianjin in protest while three hundred Nankai University students
took a train to the capital in Nanjing to present a petition to the government.[83] Although Song Zheyuan (no relation to Song Feiqing), another military leader, maintained uneasy stability in North China, there was constant friction and conflict with Japan.[84] Dongya remained in an uneasy
position. The year 1936 turned out to be great for knitting-yarn sales for
both Dongya and Patons and Baldwins, but in spite of the high sales and
profits, the tense political situation caused Dongya to budget very conser-
vatively for the coming year.[85]

It is possible, of course, that the growing Sino-Japanese conflict helped
Dongya, as patriots, the third and last element mentioned by Song in 1936,
supported the company. It is impossible to tell, however, how important
patriotism really was to Dongya. The company certainly included patriotic appeals in much of its advertising, but it also stressed the modernity,
convenience, warmth, practicality, and especially economical nature of
knitted wool garments. Some print advertisements did not even mention
Butting Ram's national products certificate.[86] The record on the economic
success of popular movements in China shows that money often trumps
sentiment. Over the years, popular boycotts of foreign goods inspired by
patriotism had achieved sporadic success, but often faded as initial enthusiasm for each campaign declined.[87] Even though 1933 was the "Year of National Products" and 1934, the "Women's Year of National Products," after

a bout of enthusiastic boycott activities, by January 1934 the American consul in Tianjin was reporting that the boycott "has practically ceased to exist."[88]

In addition, in North China, it became increasingly unclear how patriots were supposed to act. Song Feiqing's youngest brother, Song Xianyong, found out in the mid-1930s how hard it was to know which side you were on. It all started when a university student pedaled up on a bicycle and joined the daily soccer game of Xianyong and his middle school classmates. The bicyclist soon began teaching the youngsters about the movement to resist Japan and before they knew it the boys were distributing leaflets calling for the Chinese not to forget their national shame. Soon the boys' grade supervisor warned them not to get involved in anything "socialist." The surprised boys had no idea that their patriotic, anti-Japanese activity could be construed as socialism—involvement with which could be grounds for execution in Nationalist China.[89]

The evidence from Dongya supports a conclusion that economic considerations such as financial incentives offered to distributors and product prices were more important than patriotism in consumers' choices for Butting Ram wool knitting yarn. Dongya awarded each distribution outlet a 1.5 percent commission on sales and a bonus certificate for every two hundred pounds of yarn sold. Five bonus certificates could be exchanged for a small cash reward or for one share of Dongya Corporation stock.[90] Giving stores an equity share in the Dongya Corporation ensured that each store would have an interest in selling Butting Ram yarn, rather than other brands. In essence, the stock participation program was a cheap form of quasi-vertical integration, producing strong financial ties between sales outlets and the manufacturer without the expense of investing in factory-owned stores.[91] Dongya Corporation management estimated that within three to five years all of its sales outlets would be shareholders, "making it easy to convince them to sell our products instead of those of our competitors."[92] In its 1935 report on the woolen goods industry, the All-China Economic Commission attributed the Dongya Corporation's marketing success to the innovative nature of its distribution program, especially the stock-sharing program.[93] At the same time, Dongya competed aggressively by pricing its yarn at or beneath the prices of competitors. Company management attributed much of its success in starting the brand and competing with foreign products in 1933 to its promotion of giving away a pound of knitting yarn free for every two pounds the customer bought.[94] Likewise in early 1934, on the occasion of the company's first anniversary, Dongya offered a half pound free for every pound and a half sold.[95] At the height of the company's battle with Xianghe, Dongya deeply discounted both its Anti-Aircraft Gun and Butting Ram brands yarn through coupons.[96] Buy two pounds, get one pound free began again in August 1934.[97] A report on Tianjin's economic condition in 1935 in *Dagong bao* concluded that "Dongya's business was not particularly good last year . . . the market of its higher-end products was sluggish even though prices had been reduced."[98] The evidence indicates that the price at which consumers could purchase modernity mattered at least as much as a patriotic duty to support national products.

Building Industrial Eden under the Nationalists

For Song Feiqing, the economic mission of the corporation was tightly linked to its transformative role in society, its ability to promote Industrial Eden ideals outside of the firm itself. In the words of a training lecture given to Dongya employees: "Only when the company can provide valuable products to society can it gain profit to keep business going, enable an appropriate profit for investors, and enable workers to obtain life security. . . . In addition, the company still has a great purpose. That is the hope of the development of the enterprise, to gain a place in world industry, and get glory for the nation."[99]

In the 1930s, the Dongya Corporation implemented that mission by promoting knitting yarn as a modern consumer product with patriotic overtones. Company advertising and articles in the *Ark* linked Dongya knitting yarn with a range of practices associated with urban consumer modernity. In this vision, the knitting housewife ran a modern and hygienic household centered on the use of industrially-manufactured products. Chinese consumers could adopt modern practices and still remain patriotic by using national products such as Butting Ram knitting yarn. Any tension between foreign-inspired models of modernity and demands for Chinese nationalism went unacknowledged. Song Feiqing and other company managers produced a public narrative that painted Dongya as a shining example of a company which could help transform China, but evaluating Dongya's early years presents a mixed picture.

Most accounts of the company's growth in the 1930s point to its successes. The company did raise significant amounts of capital, even if it was still dwarfed by Patons and Baldwins. It positioned knitting yarn and the Butting Ram brand as markers of urban modernity, it established an effective distribution network, and it did sell a lot of yarn. It also made a profit, even as it consistently slashed prices in order to compete. As a company, Dongya was a scrappy and able competitor, but we should not romanticize its birth as either a story of free-market capitalism or a story of patriotic import substitution. Dongya relied heavily on official connections to raise capital and to benefit from the somewhat arbitrarily implemented import-substitution policies of the Nationalist state. Those policies, however, failed to transform Chinese industry. On the one hand, many of China's women consumers still chose to purchase the products associated with modernity from foreign companies. When Dongya's price advantage eroded, it lost market share to Patons and Baldwins and other foreign brands. On the other hand, although the Nationalist state's developmental policies helped Dongya in particular, Chinese industry as a whole still lagged behind foreign competitors. In 1936 "Japan had 841,958 wool spindles . . . while China had only around 10,000."[100] Small workshops, handicrafts, and commodity processing still dominated the Tianjin economy.[101]

Most important, we cannot ignore the rapidly changing political environment and Japan's advance into North China. As early as 1935, rumors were rife in Tianjin that the Japanese had a plan for the "economic exploitation of North China."[102] At about the same time, a Japanese military commander in China, General Tada, made a statement that envisioned North China as a "haven of peace . . . made by the Japanese for the Chinese people, and transformed into a market where Japanese and Chinese manufactured goods and other materials can circulate in freedom, stability and reciprocity."[103] In contrast to Tada's image of Chinese and Japanese goods circulating in peaceful coexistence, there is evidence to show that that Japanese military supported the primacy of Japanese industry. According to a secret plan from the Japanese garrison in Tianjin, Japanese entrance into the Tianjin market was carefully considered and meant to be coordinated with related investments in Qingdao, Shanghai, and Mongolia.[104] One

French diplomat noted in 1936 that "Japan has transformed North China into a mini colony."[105] Although Dongya valiantly fought to stand its ground in wool textiles, Tianjin's Chinese cotton manufacturers all went bankrupt and most were sold to Japanese firms. By 1937 the same French diplomat worried that the Japanese monopoly on cotton production in North China would serve both military and economic goals and that Japanese economic penetration included large purchases of land in and around Tianjin.[106] As tensions heightened companies like the city's flagship newspaper *Dagong bao* and many Chinese bank headquarters fled to the south, foreign banks reduced operations in the city, and Dongya managers worried that the cost of their financing would go up.[107] Chinese businesspeople became targets of the instability arising out of the expanding Japanese empire.

In spite of these many tensions, Song Feiqing confidently told Dongya's shareholders in March 1937 that "if the political situation remains calm, operations this year will be better than last.[108] His brother had just returned from two or three years abroad to learn about production of synthetic fibers.[109] As always, Dongya managers tried to be nimble and forward looking while they tiptoed through the political minefield of Chinese politics. Four months later, Japan invaded North China, occupied Tianjin, and presented Dongya managers with a new political regime.[110]

4 Japanese Occupation and the "Economy of Things"

IN JULY 1937 Japan invaded China and changed the political regime in Tianjin and North China once again. The war ended the course of Song Feiqing's attempt to build a successful knitting yarn company that could compete with Patons and Baldwins. It is important to remember that competition between the two companies depended on much more than their respective strength and managerial abilities. Just as Dongya had depended on the help of the policies of the Nationalist developmental state, the weakness of that state in the international environment proved to be a weakness for Dongya as well. When the Nationalists retreated to Southwest China under the onslaught of the Japanese advance, Song Feiqing and the Dongya Corporation became subject to an occupation empire that had its own developmental goals and was willing to extract resources from China and Chinese businesspeople in order to reach those goals. In the end, however, the occupation regime was crippled by disorganization, limited power, and the arbitrary exercise of authority. Surprisingly, it was these weaknesses that allowed Dongya to thrive during the first six years of the war. With foresight and quick thinking, Dongya managers became expert at participating in a new "economy of things," which provided common ground for occupiers and occupied alike. In this economy of things, the control of things—wool, knitting yarn, jute, gunnysacks, sugar, flour, machinery, land—became the key to both finding a place within the emerging military-industrial complex and taking advantage of the endemic inconsistency and corruption that riddled the occupation regime.

Early Years of the Occupation Developmental State

In spite of more than a decade of Sino-Japanese tension, the Nationalist forces in Tianjin were remarkably unprepared for the Japanese attack when it came. Within thirty-six hours after the first shot was fired on 28 July, the Japanese military firmly controlled the Chinese parts of Tianjin, but left the foreign concessions untouched.[1] In the day-and-a-half battle, Japanese artillery and aerial bombing did great damage to selected targets, but most of the city saw little of the devastation of war. After almost a decade of urban violence and increasing Japanese encroachment in North China, the Japanese invasion had finally come to Tianjin with swiftness and closely targeted destruction, though with relatively little bloodshed.

Safely ensconced in the British concession, Song Feiqing, his family, and the Dongya Corporation avoided damage during the attack. Even so, disruption from the war came at an inopportune time for Dongya. The company had just completed its "million yuan" capital campaign and management had decided to diversify its product line. To do so, they had ordered machinery to spin the thin wool thread used in cashmere clothing and the weaving of wool cloth. They had also considered the purchase of weaving machinery—especially in light of the military's demand for wool cloth—but had not yet acted.[2] As an extension of its knitting-yarn business, Dongya had even introduced a new line of knitted wool swimwear, which it heavily promoted during the hot days of summer as only half the price of foreign products.[3] Moreover, when the invasion came in early July, Dongya was just gearing up to satisfy coming demand in the fall and winter as colder weather required warm clothing. On top of that, cheap wool prices had produced heavy orders. At the time of the invasion, the company had already accepted orders for more than 1.3 million pounds of yarn, putting it on track to surpass its record set the previous year.[4]

In the first few months after the invasion, the war violently intruded on these plans. Dongya's advertising campaign that implied one's life and the nation's prosperity could be improved by switching to hygienic and domestically produced Dongya swimwear quickly gave way to crisis management. Orders declined, the war interrupted long-distance transportation, and business ground to a halt. For Dongya, 1937 was generally disastrous, though the firm did manage to eke out a little over 60,000 yuan in profit.[5]

As invasion turned to occupation, however, the Song family and the Dongya Corporation adjusted to the new reality. It turned out that the personal adjustment was more traumatic in many ways than the corporate one. Even before the war began, the family had to flee the violence of Japanese plainclothes activity more than once.[6] During the war, some members of the Song family chose to actively oppose the occupation regime. One of Song Feiqing's younger brothers, Song Xiangong, left Tianjin and died early in the war as a pilot for the Nationalist air force in Southwest China. Three of Song Feiqing's other younger siblings participated actively in anti-Japanese activities at their schools. Among them, his youngest brother, Song Xianyong, attended college at Yanjing University in Beijing in 1939. A long-time political activist, he took charge of the Yanjing University's underground "Resist Japan Corps." Unfortunately, he apparently came to the attention of the Japanese authorities in Beijing and had to flee his dormitory in the middle of the night to make his way to the coast, where he took a ship for Shanghai to find refuge.[7] As the Song family dealt with the traumas of war on a personal level, the Dongya Corporation proved adept at coping with the new environment and the shape of the occupation state's developmental policies.

At first glance, there was no place for Dongya and the Song family in the Japanese occupation state, which derived its developmental ideas from the model of an East Asian bloc where Korea, Taiwan, Manchuria, and China supplied raw materials for Japan's industrial machine and then provided markets to buy the finished goods. On the surface, there was little room for Chinese consumer products producers in this scheme, which favored Japanese industrial production. These ideas had become current in the 1930s when some Japanese saw an economic war developing in which the world would be divided into blocs.[8] In Japan's bid to establish such a bloc, occupiers and occupied, soldiers and civilians, businesspeople and artists were all expected to participate in what Louise Young has termed the "total empire" and which took on a variety of names during World War II, including the "Asia Renaissance," the "New Order in East Asia," the "Greater East Asia Co-Prosperity Sphere," and the "Sacred War."[9]

In this project, the Japanese military had very complicated relations with businesses. Powerful elements in the Japanese military had great disdain for capitalism and preferred various forms of state control, or the visible hand. At every turn, the occupation regime responded to problems with new controls, regulations, and limitations on the independence of business enterprises. At the same time, the regime allied with a number of Japanese businesses to finance the growing empire, and Chinese businesses often paid the price. The occupation regime confiscated hundreds of Chinese businesses and turned them over to Japanese companies to operate. It was unclear if there was any room at all for Chinese businesspeople to maneuver.

In the face of an occupation government committed to a Japan-centered economy, a military predilection for control, and policies favoring Japanese business, Dongya was a civilian company, publically committed to Chinese nationalism, producing goods for the urban modern consumer market, and with no apparent place in a military industrial complex. Thus, the Japanese occupation of North China seemed to set the stage for a clash between the Dongya Corporation and the occupation state, a clash between competing nationalist goals, a clash between consumer products for China and a state aimed at strengthening Japan, and a clash between private Chinese enterprise and a military-industrial complex predicated on a combination of state-directed economics and preferential treatment for Japanese business.

Nonetheless, by 1938 Dongya's business began to pick up. This upturn came in spite of the dire conclusions of one local banker, who wrote that disruptions from the war made 1938 a miserable year for Tianjin's economy.[10] Dongya had begun to demonstrate its ability to find niches within the war economy, which allowed it to outperform many other firms. Orders exceeded the company's capacity to fill them.[11] By the middle of 1938 Dongya reinstituted the night shift.[12] In fact, the outlook for yarn sales was so good that Dongya had placed more than one million yuan in deposits on raw wool orders by mid-1939. The situation in Tianjin echoed that in Shanghai where Dongya's prewar rival Patons and Baldwins had seen recovery.[13] Rivalry between the two companies became less of an issue as demand for wool yarn outstripped supply and as the occupation interrupted national markets and drove factories to sell more locally. Within two years Dongya's sales outside of North China dropped from about 50 to only 10 percent. Surprisingly, though, within North China, sales actually exceeded prewar levels.[14]

As production geared up, the biggest remaining problem was the supply of high quality Australian wool. A 1939 South Manchurian Railway survey of Tianjin's wool industry remarked that "it has been hard for Dongya . . . to find wool supplies since the 'incident' [the Japanese invasion of China]." Even mixed half and half with domestic wool, the railway researcher estimated that Dongya required over a million pounds of foreign wool each year. The researcher was well aware of the desire for autarky that drove the occupation developmental policies, and he concluded that there was a "need to quickly become independent of [foreign supplies]."[15] Thus even the affairs of private Chinese companies in the foreign concessions became tied up with regime goals early in the occupation.

Problems with wool supplies aside, Tianjin's economy gradually began to benefit from a newly privileged position in the new order. Close to other parts of the Japanese empire, such as Manchuria and Korea, and to Japan itself, Tianjin and North China received special attention for economic development.[16] International trade surged in Tianjin, while Shanghai's declined as the center of gravity of economic activity in China made a significant shift north.[17] Tianjin also received an infusion of capital as a result of the occupation. Some of that capital came from wealthy Chinese who fled the provinces with as much money as they could carry and sought shelter in the perceived safety of the foreign concessions.[18] Some of the capital came from Japanese capitalists invested under the protection of the Japanese military.[19] The results could be seen in Tianjin almost immediately. In November of 1937, just a few months after occupation began, the French consul general noted that "new factories have appeared suddenly every day for the last three months. This is not a question of modest construction, but formidable industrial cities each able to accommodate thousands of workers. . . . The Japanese population [of Tianjin] has increased from 19,000 to 35,000 in three months."[20]

Japan ruled Tianjin and the rest of North China through a complicated series of puppet government institutions, monopolistic corporations, and control boards. In truth, the Japanese military was in control. As the French consul observed, the puppet government lacked real power and had "no minister of war, finance, or foreign affairs." Instead, "these matters along with direction of communications and business [were] in the hands of the Japanese army."[21] In line with its economic goals, the Japanese military founded the North China Development Company, which focused on major industries, and the North China Transportation Company quickly followed as a means to monopolize transport.[22]

Two think tanks helped provide information and shape economic policy for the occupation regime: the South Manchurian Railway, which had performed this role for the puppet state in Manchuria, and the Koa (or Asia Renaissance) Institute (Jap., *kōain*; Chi., *xingyayuan* 興亞院; sometimes translated as the "Asia Development Board").[23] Although Kubo Toru argues that Koa Institute researchers were less ideological than those of the South Manchurian Railway, one Koa Institute researcher still described China as an "unsophisticated, animal-like nation."[24] Thus even the relatively less ideological Koa Institute researchers adhered to a vision broadly held by Japanese involved in the occupation regime. In this vision, Japan should remain technologically superior to China, China should provide resources Japan lacked, there should be self-sufficiency and independence from third-party powers, and China needed to "modernize" through introduction of scientific and orderly management.[25]

The primacy of the army and broad agreement among researchers about Japan's superiority still did not produce a well-coordinated developmental empire. The regime was multifaceted. Even the military had its own competing units, and great tensions existed among various Japanese actors as they attempted to incorporate China into the Japanese empire.[26] "The ultranationalists in the lower ranks of the army and navy displayed an intense hatred both of Communism and capitalism which they saw as corrupting forces."[27] Such military officers inclined toward government control of the economy often clashed with businesspeople who wanted a freer hand.[28] Control of the economy also appealed to those members of the Japanese elite interested in fascism who saw corporatism and an autarkic war economy as solutions to Japan's predicament.[29] Besides idealistic officers and fascists, however, the Japanese occupation force also included, in the words of one American observer, "merchants, officials, drug peddlers, prostitutes, *ronin* and big monopoly concerns."[30] More charitably, it has to be recognized also that a small army of liberal intellectuals staffed the research arms of regime organizations. Among all of these agents of the regime, some were sympathetic to the plight of ordinary Chinese, some were cruel, and some were just venal, interested only in using the war for personal gain. In short, like many states with a prominent visible hand, the occupation government of the wartime period in China had both neatly articulated claims and messy reality, both developmental policies and extractive goals.

For example, a year after the invasion, a French diplomat concluded that international trade was in chaos, as the army implemented "politics of expediency . . . without coherence," deciding one day that furs or wool cannot be exported, then the day after banning the importation of radios.[31] In another example, in September of 1938, army officers in Tianjin, a group "thirty to forty years old who have an extraordinary enterprising spirit, [are] animated by xenophobia and violent fanaticism, and given a local authority virtually without limits," issued an order for all Japanese living in the French and British concessions in Tianjin to evacuate immediately. Japanese businesspeople operating in the French and British concessions banded together and convinced cooler heads in the occupation government to rescind the order.[32]

The French and British concessions in Tianjin provided two of the largest irritants to Japanese military officers in the city. The two concessions remained relatively untouched by the war. The French and British governments continued to exercise sovereignty; communication and transportation were possible with Japanese-occupied China, with the similar "islands" of foreign sovereignty in the concessions in Shanghai, and with those parts of China still controlled by the Nationalist government. The concessions also often sheltered anti-Japanese activists and provided a space where Japanese authority was not recognized. Most important, they presented an obstacle to the implementation of the occupation government's financial policies.

Institution of a new occupation government currency and foreign exchange system proved to be one of the thorniest problems of economic control for the occupation state. The regime established a central bank and a new currency intended to be part of a "yen bloc" for trade among Japan, Taiwan, Korea, Manchuria, Mongolia-Xinjiang, and North China. Setting exchange rates among the various yen bloc currencies was difficult, and when the new system did not work smoothly, the Japanese military in China tried to purchase certain commodities such as wool and cotton at fixed prices.[33] Separately, in a telling statement, an official at the Japanese semi-official Yokohama Specie Bank bluntly told foreign diplomats, "We are conducting national politics in North China. We are masters of the country and no one can keep us from taking those measures we judge suitable. . . . We will institute foreign exchange controls and accept only those instruments which conform to the situation and Japan's interests."[34] In spite of such harsh words, problems continued. Foreign exchange controls caused huge disturbances in food supply in the region and the regime created a police force for economic affairs to control the buying and selling of food. On 9 May the Japanese consul general in Tianjin announced that he would take all necessary measures to stop price increases, monitor the actions of merchants and businesspeople, and hit them with appropriate punishment without pity.[35] Just as quickly as controls were imposed, however, loopholes would also appear. For example, almost immediately, Japanese businesses in Tianjin began marketing their services to foreign companies for a fee to help the latter avoid foreign exchange surcharges.[36]

Tianjin's concessions provided a sphere within which the old Chinese Nationalist government *fabi* (法幣) currency could circulate and where it was difficult to enforce foreign exchange controls. Chinese banks in the French and British concessions housed forty million yuan in silver reserves, which backed the Chinese Nationalist government currency and, as the French consul noted, without which "foreign exchange control would be vigorous."[37] On 15 June 1939 frustrated Japanese military officers began a blockade of the French and British concessions. For about a year, Japanese soldiers controlled all entry and exit points from these concessions as the health of the occupation-issued currency became a daily indicator of the economic success of the occupation regime in North China.[38]

The blockade presented problems for Chinese companies located in the concessions, such as Dongya, because it potentially cut off access to markets, supplies, and sometimes even workers who lived outside of the concessions. Fortuitously, the company had just received a large shipment of wool prior to the blockade.[39] In addition, the blockade was not total. Dongya still prospered and managed to move products and even machines in and out of the British concession. Even goods requiring foreign exchange could still be purchased.[40] The British firm Jardine and Matheson was able to get a permit to bring wool into the British concession in March of 1940 at the height of the blockade, though it is unknown if the wool was intended for Dongya.[41] Using wool stocks on hand and combining imported wool with domestic, Dongya maintained production, spinning just under a million pounds of yarn in 1939 and selling throughout North China in spite of the blockade. This figure was down from the more than 1.3 million pounds spun at the company's peak in 1935, but still made for respectable production, and even better profits.[42] In fact, in spite of the blockade, 1939 was Dongya's most profitable year ever.

Dongya's strength drew in part from its unique position outside of the development plans of the regime. Much of the regime's interest focused on strategic and heavy industries, and light industries such has wool textiles operated relatively independently of the state.[43] Even when Japanese founded two large woolen mills in Tianjin in May of 1939, the new factories concentrated on weaving wool cloth and carpets and left the knitting-yarn business to Dongya. In addition, Dongya was the only company in Tianjin with wool combing machinery.[44]

With declining wool stocks, however, Dongya desperately needed an additional product line and it turned to an unlikely product that would prove to be the company's lifeline for much of the next decade: gunnysacks. Through a connection with the Yongli Corporation, Dongya purchased machinery to weave jute into gunnysacks, a vital good needed for transporting mainstays of the North China economy: cement, corn, wheat, cotton, and, soybeans. The gunnysack equipment arrived in May of 1940, somehow permeating the Japanese blockade of the concessions.[45]

Shortly thereafter, negotiations between Japan and Great Britain in Tokyo finally reached fruition and the blockade of the Tianjin British and French concessions was dismantled 20 June 1940. The British and French agreed to release a certain amount of silver from Chinese bank vaults for the refugees from the flood of the previous autumn, to support the occupation currency and to allow Japanese police more freedom in investigating "anti-Japanese" elements within the concessions.[46] Most important to Japan, the occupation currency circulated more effectively in the concessions, though Dongya made some payments in old currency, some in new, and some in both.[47]

Just before resolution of the blockade crisis, establishment of a new puppet government in Nanjing under the Nationalist Party leader Wang Jingwei had prompted reorganization of the North China puppet government, which now theoretically became subservient to Nanjing. In reality, however, most of the personnel of the North China occupation regime remained unchanged and still exercised considerable autonomy from Nanjing.[48] The North China authorities instituted a new round of controls in the spring of 1940 including the expulsion of delinquent Japanese whose activities ran counter to Japanese development efforts in North China.[49] Although the occupation currency circulated more easily, neither removal of the blockade of the concessions in Tianjin, nor the reorganization of the occupation government in Beijing and Nanjing managed to maintain monetary stability. Chronic inflation proved an intractable problem, which led to an economy where things became more important than money.

The Economy of Things

Monetary uncertainty had led to a flight from money to goods as early as the last half of 1938, when many people rushed to purchase real estate or merchandise.[50] In September of 1939, there was a "lack of confidence in either new or old currency [causing people] to convert cash into goods."[51] Among common people, the culture of things became most evident with food.[52] At one point during the blockade of the concessions in February 1940, flour doubled again in price to eighteen yuan per sack—the monthly wages of a laborer.[53] Later that year after the lifting of the blockade, a shortage of building materials and an anticipated shortage of coal for the coming winter increased anxiety again.[54] Shortages continued through the end of the year and December 1940 saw increases "of from five to fifteen percent in the price of cereals, sugar and cotton cloth at Tientsin [Tianjin]." In 1941 a South Manchurian Railway researcher even admitted to a "tendency to turn money into commodities."[55]

The flight from money to commodities or other goods created an "economy of things" as shown by Dongya's experience during this time. From 1940 on, Dongya's wool purchases slowed to a trickle.[56] Yarn production followed suit. The company spun 0.43 million pounds of yarn in 1940, but only 0.17 million pounds in 1941, a huge decrease from the prior year and only a fraction of 1939 levels.[57] As wool became scarcer, though, it also became more valuable. Dongya published a report in 1941 that declared. "We have seen wool yarn go from a daily use product to a luxury product."[58] As a result, Dongya's flagship brand, Butting Ram, kept up with

Nankai University's inflation index and even grew faster than Patons and Baldwins's prices.[59] Unfortunately, by the end of 1941 the company's wool supplies had been mostly used up.[60] No matter how valuable, Dongya could not produce enough yarn to survive, thus the company's turn to gunnysacks in 1940 proved shrewd. Because of the importance of gunnysacks to transport, production remained high. In the spring of 1941, Tianjin cotton mills reduced the number of spindles in operation. "Flour mills such as Yuxing and Shoufeng found it hard to continue because rice and wheat were scarce. Only the Dongya Company's gunnysack department continued to produce goods."[61] In fact, without the gunnysack business, Dongya would have ground to a halt. Government controls limited imports of wool, and even when the company received permission from local authorities to import wool in January 1941, the company's board felt costs were too high and decided to wait.[62]

The economy of things presented an underlying reality that showed the fragility of the occupation state's development plans. For example, in the spring of 1941, a burst of either optimism or wishful thinking led the occupation regime to announce grand economic goals that included new plans for a "Greater Tianjin," which focused on developing the former Russian concession (called the "Third Special Area" at the time) across the river from the French and British concessions.[63] At the same time, the Japanese Special Military Mission took a more pessimistic view of the economy by ordering that "rice and other grains produced in North China between September 15, 1941 and August 31, 1942 . . . be placed under the control of the Japanese military authorities," in spite of the fact that the harvest outlook for 1941 was reportedly the best in years.[64] These two simultaneous announcements show how disorganized the regime truly was as the occupation government's economic program split between grand and unrealizable development goals and the need to mobilize resources in the face of a populace unable to trust the money supply.

A few months later Japan launched the Pacific phase of the war by attacking American positions at Pearl Harbor and simultaneously occupying British holdings in China, including the British concession in Tianjin. The Italian and French (soon to be Vichy French) concessions were spared as possessions of allied governments. The expansion of the war led to new rounds of economic controls in North China. Merchants were ordered to adopt fixed prices on coal, salt, cotton, cotton fabric, paper and paper articles, matches, and petroleum.[65] At the same time the regime instituted new controls on business firms to prevent "speculation, hording or refusal to sell, etc., and control of commodity transactions and the movement of goods."[66] Although a Koa Institute report in the fall of 1942 showed that price controls had brought inflation in North China under control, internal reports from the Tianjin branch of the Shanghai Commercial and Savings Bank show that prices continued to rise dramatically under the counter while goods, including basic foodstuffs, were in short supply.[67]

In spite of all the restrictions and controls, Dongya imported 100,000 pounds of wool from South America as late as January 1942.[68] With limited wool supplies, however, gunnysacks became the focus of the company. Dongya became a major military supplier as evidenced by the fact that three months before Pearl Harbor, the Japanese military placed the gunnysacks Dongya produced under a military monopoly with a price fixed in the occupation government currency (FRB) of three dollars per sack.[69] A secret report compiled by South Manchurian Railway researchers in 1942 described the monopoly system for gunnysacks and the jute from which the sacks were made. This report stated that two-thirds of all gunnysacks in China went to the military, and at that time Dongya was the only factory in China successfully manufacturing the product with domestic jute. In addition, Dongya was one of the few Chinese-owned companies officially designated by the Japanese army to purchase jute. Dongya was thus the only company that both purchased jute as part of the military supply system and manufactured bags for the military. Disapprovingly, the 1942 report concluded that this unique situation made accounting difficult, implying that the company was in a position to manipulate prices and hide profits.[70]

Business was indeed good for Dongya, though it had its ups and downs along with the North China economy and with the availability of jute supplies. Dongya's gunnysack production peaked at 1.8 million bags in 1941 and went as low as 0.78 million bags in 1942 after the attack on Pearl Harbor and the advent of the Pacific stage of the war made jute imports from India more problematic.[71] By sending representatives throughout North China, Dongya gradually located domestic supplies of jute.[72] Thus gunnysack production turned around by March of 1942 when the company reinstituted its night shift to meet large customer orders.[73] Production increased in 1943

FIGURE 4.1   Gunnysack production at Dongya. *Dongya Annual*, 1941, unpaged.

and then declined slightly in 1944 and 1945 as wartime shortages hit all areas of the Chinese economy.

Once again, as with wool knitting yarn, Dongya was in a unique position with its gunnysack business. Although there were a number of small shops that produced gunnysacks by hand or with foot-pedal-driven machines, Dongya was the only large-scale, mechanized manufacturer in North China (see Figure 4.1).[74] By 1941 when Dongya's production had shifted almost entirely from yarn to gunnysacks, profits were down but still nearly triple the highest prewar levels, even on an inflation-adjusted basis (see Figure 4.2). Profits would remain high throughout the war, though inflation took a larger and larger toll as time went on. Dongya was not alone in profiting from the war, but it was unusually successful in finding products just important enough to be vital, but not important enough to attract direct control from the authorities.[75]

In March of 1943, Dongya found another such product: medicine. A Koa Institute survey published two years previously in 1941 showed only nine factories in all of North China that manufactured Western medicine and all of them were Japanese-owned, but the chemicals needed for produc-

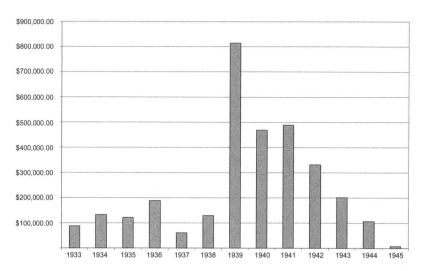

FIGURE 4.2   Dongya inflation-adjusted profit, prewar and war years. Profit figures from Archives of the Dongya Corporation, 3-5, 9-3, 8-2, 17-1, 23-2, 38-5, 42-3, 30-3 (all catalog 1), and Cui Shuju and Jin Yanshi. Nankai inflation index from Cui Shuju and Jin Yanshi.

tion were in short supply.[76] Two years after this report, Dongya management concluded that "it would be possible to gather experts and research production of all kinds of medicine. If this can be done well, there are great hopes for future development."[77] In a publicity brochure, Dongya proclaimed that the difficulties in people's livelihoods in China stemmed from the backwardness of the country's science and technology, chemicals in particular.[78] Dongya managers somehow managed to negotiate the hyperbureaucratic and control-obsessed regime. Approval to establish a chemical factory for the manufacture of medicine was received from the Tianjin government on 15 July, just three months after the Dongya board of directors initially approved the proposal.[79] Since chemicals were in extremely short supply during the war, Dongya likely used similar methods to get supplies of vitamin B and cod liver oil, among the other products it needed.[80]

The most detailed and textured account of the founding of the chemical factory comes from the manuscript left by its first manager, Shi Shaodong. Shi claims that Dongya set up its chemical factory to employ a number of scientists who were having difficulty conducting their work under wartime conditions. By coming to Dongya, they could avoid working directly for Japanese-controlled universities and research institutes, and thus could continue their own research at Dongya's expense for the duration of the war. Most were biologists, chemists, and pharmacists. Dongya constructed ten one-story buildings in the rear of its factory grounds where the scientists raised frogs, mice, and, of course, germs. Among other things, the biology departments set out on a quest to collect all the bacteria in Tianjin and North China.[81] The scientists engaged in their work with the same kind of ad hoc flexibility that marked Dongya's approach to the wartime period as a whole. Once, the daughter of a Dongya employee was admitted to the company hospital with a serious illness, and one of the factory biologists was able to grow a strain of penicillin in a dish for her treatment. In another instance, the scientists at the chemical factory perfected a method for using a bacterial solution to treat cotton stalks, which Dongya used to supplement increasingly scarce jute supplies.[82]

At a time when constraints on shipping products out of Tianjin had limited the fortunes of a number of industries, medicine was one of the few sectors that saw market activity.[83] According to Shi Shaodong, the products of the chemical division sold well, including a line of over-the-counter medicines and even some home products such as shoe polish and a balm to compete with the famous Tiger brand balm. But salaries for all the scientists and technicians were just too high to make it a profitable venture.[84] Available Dongya financial statements do not break out profitability for the chemical division, but it is worth noting that sales and income remained high throughout the war, even if they did not keep up with inflation in the final two years (see Figure 4.2). One former Dongya employee later claimed that the company only manufactured medicine for a few years before discontinuing the operation.[85]

The Dongya Corporation's transactions as part of the economy of things went well beyond manufacture of yarn, gunnysacks, and medicine. The company also bought and sold machinery, commodities like sugar, flour, and cotton, and land. In fact, in the mad rush away from money and into things, almost anything available for purchase could be an attractive investment.

Things had taken on a heightened value as soon as the invasion began. Just a few months after the Japanese invasion Dongya's equipment supplier tried to back out of its contract to supply spinning machinery for wool thread. Under wartime conditions, the terms of purchase now appeared too favorable to Dongya. Company management immediately took steps to force its supplier to come through.[86] In spite of uncertainty and the inability to ship products in the first few months of the war, the coming "culture of things" was enough to prompt Dongya management to purchase new equipment—equipment that in the end would be sold rather than used. Machinery took on such importance that by mid-1939 Dongya began copying and making new versions of its existing equipment.[87] One company technician even began work on design for wool combing machines that could process the short-haired Chinese domestic wool, though wartime conditions made the construction of this machinery impossible.[88] Later on, Dongya sold the knitting machinery for making swimwear and underwear for three and a half times the original purchase price.[89] Silk spinning and weaving machinery purchased for planned expansion in 1943 was sold the next year for 500,000 yuan, presumably at a tidy profit because the board of directors took no note of a loss.[90] In other words, during the war Dongya purchased machinery almost any time it became available, though often the equipment went unused and simply served as a store of value, a thing ownership of which was preferable to holding money.

As the war progressed, Dongya managers entertained a widening series of investment choices, though not all with success. A 1941 Dongya investment in sugar from Hong Kong became tied up in red tape after the Japanese occupation of that city.[91] A 1942 plan to purchase an oil [presumably vegetable oil] factory came to naught when it was confiscated by the Japanese military. At the same time plans went ahead to found a Dongya Bank, though nothing ever came of it.[92] Four months later, the Dongya board considered and then rejected a proposal to found an insurance company.[93] In fall 1942, the company somehow managed to purchase a shipment of scarce cotton in Shanghai.[94] In June of the next year the company satisfied its desire to diversify into insurance by investing a substantial sum in the Ping'an Insurance Company.[95] In March 1943, Dongya management simultaneously embarked on plans to expand into silk production and medicine. The former venture failed, but, as we have seen above, the latter succeeded to some extent.[96] With the exception of the insurance company and bank, all of these investments were in things, not financial assets. Things had a physical presence that must have been reassuring during times of war, and nothing had a more permanent physical presence than real estate.

Over the course of the war, Dongya undertook an ambitious program to buy land in the city of Tianjin. In August 1937, less than a month after Tianjin fell to the Japanese, when prospects for an economic recovery and return to stability remained gloomy at best, the Dongya Corporation contracted to purchase three parcels of land in the British concession.[97] By mid-1938 the company was heavily involved in the real-estate business. It rented out land, built buildings to rent, and entertained a number of attractive offers, noting that "real-estate prices for land in the foreign concessions is [now] high."[98] By 1939 property prices in the central part of the British concession had increased by 60 to 70 percent over prewar values.[99] A 1939 South Manchurian Railway report estimated the value of Dongya factory land at 400,000 yuan, almost twice the 247,526 yuan that Zhang Huizhong, one of the company's major shareholders, had paid for it just a few years earlier.[100] Concerted efforts at land purchase did not begin until 1942, however, and acquisitions really escalated in 1944. In all, the company purchased 862 *mu* (about 142 acres) of land for approximately 1.8 million yuan.[101]

The culture of things also spread to Dongya's relations with its employees. In mid-1938 the company followed the example of other Chinese and Japanese companies and began paying an inflation "meal subsidy" to all of its employees of one dime per day.[102] By mid-1939, salaries had to be raised by an average of 20 percent and monthly subsidies for food and housing were running at 15 to 20 percent.[103] By the end of 1944 salaries and subsidies were at 233 percent of prewar levels.[104] Even more important than the monetary payments that allowed workers to purchase daily necessities, Dongya also supplied many of those necessities directly. Shi Shaodong wrote that "it was possible to buy daily necessities in bulk and distribute them at cost. The company had abundant funds, if it came across cheap goods that were not needed at the moment, it could buy and store them and then distribute them." Thus "at a time when everyplace had mixed grain flours, Dongya did not have a single employee without a few bags of 'foreign' [machine-milled] flour! . . . Sometimes when I got off work and went home I would suddenly see white powder on the ground and I would think that Feiqing distributed machine-milled flour again. Before I even entered the house I would be smiling. Entering home, the entire family would happily tell me the good news. My gratitude could not be described with words."[105]

The "abundant funds" came from the huge profits gained from manufacturing wool yarn and gunnysacks combined with the profits from buying and selling machinery and commodities such as sugar. On top of those substantial streams of income, Dongya also benefited from constant increases in capital as local investors proved willing to buy Dongya shares. At the start of the war, the company's capital had just reached the million yuan mark. In the next eight years, Dongya issued new shares three more times, garnering an additional five million yuan in 1940 for expansion into the gunnysack business, another four million in 1943 for the chemical factory, and a final ten million in 1944.[106] Although the dramatically increasing amounts were partly due to inflation, there is no doubt that investors flocked to purchase shares in order to pool funds and participate through Dongya in the economy of things. The 1940 issue was limited to existing shareholders only and it was fully subscribed. Likewise in 1943, existing shareholders subscribed to all but forty-nine shares.[107]

Sometimes shareholders benefited directly from the distribution of goods in addition to dividends. In September 1944, Dongya sold its inventory of camel hair wool at cost, 35 yuan per yard, to shareholders at the rate of one-fifth of a yard for each share. Market price at the time was approximately 140 yuan per yard, so shareholders earned substantial profits on the deal.[108] Three months later, the company sold a supply of blue cotton cloth to shareholders at the rate of one yard for every two shares at a price of 35 yuan per yard.[109] In the next year, Dongya sold sugar to shareholders from the end of February through April of 1945.[110] In fact, the sale and distribution of goods under market price gave the company's stock its value both during and after the war. Large shareholders would come in trucks to get their share.[111]

Dongya was clearly awash in cash for most of the wartime period. Balance sheets do not exist for the entire period, but at the end of 1940, Dongya had nearly a half million yuan in cash, two to three times the liquidity of prewar levels.[112] Cash, however, was an unreliable store of value. Inflation, scarcity of supplies of raw materials, and lack of faith in the long-term stability of the occupation currency drove Dongya's frantic drive to buy equipment, commodities, and land.[113]

The shortages and transportation difficulties that drove the economy of things created a number of obstacles, but Dongya managers proved able to improvise endlessly. They mixed straw into the jute for the linen bags, repaired and made their own machinery, and they seemed able to move valuable commodities around China, although sometimes with difficulty.

They found wool in South America, and in March of 1945 Dongya was selling sugar to shareholders as a bonus on their investment.[114] Had the sugar tied up in Hong Kong mysteriously arrived in Tianjin?

This frenetic activity demonstrates the financial muscle of the company, but it also portrays the fragility of its prosperity. Shipments could go awry and equipment without parts eventually broke down. Also, it is important to remember that this picture of affluence did not apply to North China as a whole. At the end of 1939, when Dongya profits were at their height, the company easily found 3,500 poor children delighted to come for a company-sponsored Christmas performance. Although some of them were refugees from the flood of that autumn, the rest resided in Dongya's neighborhood, the booming wartime British concession. The happiness of these children at receiving a bag of peanut candy and a package of steamed buns served as a reminder of the economic and social environment in which the few benefited from the culture of things while the many simply tried to acquire enough things to provide food and shelter.[115]

Moreover, the facility of Dongya managers in negotiating the economy of things speaks to their abilities, but also hints at complex relations with the occupation regime, which spent so much time and effort controlling the economy. A closer look at relations between Dongya and the state during this period shows how the economy of things contributed to venality, the arbitrary exercise of power, and the hollowness of the state's plans for development. As the developmental empire foundered, businesses such as Dongya and agents of the regime participated in a complex exchange of gifts, favors, and threats.

Venality and Arbitrary Power

The economy of things that had come to dominate Dongya and the North China economy was fed by the venal and arbitrary nature of the occupation regime. The capricious nature of the regime derived in part from the policy adopted by the Japanese military in economic matters that each locality had to live on its own means (*kenchi jikatsu chūi*).[116] This policy created a lot of autonomy for lower-level military units and officials as well as space for corruption. Just a few examples of corruption would include the foreigners who routinely paid bribes to Japanese soldiers during the blockade of the British and French concessions in 1939 and 1940 to pass into or out of the Japanese-occupied parts of the city, the American firm that was forced to sell the Japanese military the bulk of three truckloads of wool at three-fifths cost in order to ship goods from Beijing to Tianjin, and the payment of two dollars occupation currency per skin by a fur dealer to a Japanese company to avoid export controls.[117]

Dongya's interaction with this occupation regime is best illustrated by the company's place in the plans for domestic jute cultivation, one of many regime priorities. As early as 1936, before the invasion of China south of the Great Wall, the Japanese implemented a special plan to grow jute in Manchuria.[118] After the invasion of North China, the occupation government included jute as one of the first products covered by export controls.[119] Chinese jute, however, was not particularly good for making gunnysacks, and most high-quality jute came from India. In order to reduce reliance on Indian supplies, the Koa Institute put together a plan to grow new kinds of jute in North China in October of 1939.[120] Efforts produced little jute, however, and in 1940 supplies were becoming so tight that the Japanese army ordered one-third of all jute coming to nearby Beijing to be limited to military use at a set price.[121] The expansion of the war at the end of 1941 further jeopardized supplies of Indian jute and forced the Japanese regime to move even more vigorously to produce adequate supplies of jute in China. Conveniently, these plans provided Dongya with the means to deal with its first serious challenge from the occupation regime.

When Japan occupied the British concession with the outbreak of the Pacific war, Dongya came directly under the purview of the occupation government for the first time. Previously, Dongya had received two letters from the puppet Tianjin city government in 1939, asking the company to move out of the foreign concessions. The company had responded by saying that moving, building a factory, and installing equipment would be very difficult in the short term, but "perhaps they could think of a way to do it gradually in order to comply with the order."[122] Such a glib response became impossible after Pearl Harbor, and Dongya faced the prospect of confiscation for the first time since the war began.

Shi Shaodong later recalled that initially after the fall of the concession the Japanese did not touch Dongya, and factory employees began to relax, thinking the Japanese would not enter private companies.[123] Then one day

Song Feiqing ordered Shi to drop everything and report for special duty. He remembered the occasion. Song Feiqing sat at his desk, carving the tip of a pencil with his fingernail (see Figure 4.3). Song finally said, "our factory is in great danger. We may have to hand it over . . . perhaps even tomorrow or the day after." Stunned, Shi listened to his superior outline a plan to keep Dongya independent. Under this plan, Dongya would offer to sponsor agricultural research on growing jute in North China to help solve the Japanese military's pending supply problems with the expected decline in imports from India. In return, the Japanese military would agree to leave Dongya alone, at least for the moment.

Song gave Shi Shaodong the task of drafting a plan to present to the Japanese military in Beijing the following day. Song insisted on strict secrecy and only one other employee was told of the assignment. The city slicker Shi knew nothing about agriculture so, taking the scholar's route, he went directly to the Commercial Press and Beijing University bookstores in the French concession. Purchasing seven or eight books, Shi went home to draft the plan in private with the assistance of one copyist. The two worked for twenty hours straight and then delivered the completed proposal to the East Station, where Song Feiqing was waiting on the train to Beijing to begin the fateful negotiations. Shi had not even had time to prepare a full budget, merely adding the note that regardless of the cost, Dongya would be able to pay for it. The proposal was not for "profit and loss," but to "enable the continued production of gunnysacks."

Song Feiqing's meeting in Beijing apparently did not go smoothly. At a tense meeting the following day in Tianjin, the senior managers of the Dongya Corporation discussed the situation. Shi's notes are cryptic, but apparently military personnel had demanded larger personal bribes than Dongya was prepared to pay. As a result, management faced the prospect of Japanese military control of the company. They decided to make one more attempt. Shi and one other executive contacted Wang Fuwu, a Chinese man who had studied in Japan, had worked in Manchuria under the Japanese-sponsored regime there, and now apparently worked for the Japanese military in Beijing. During their meeting in Beijing, Wang said that Song Feiqing had gone back on his word without realizing that this was a matter of life and death. Despite these threatening words, Dongya management eventually came to agreement with the Japanese military and the company's Beijing agricultural research station was born.

FIGURE 4.3   Song Feiqing in the office where he and Shi Shaodong met to hammer out the plan for Dongya's agricultural research department. Archives of the Dongya Corporation, undated.

As presented to the Dongya board of directors, the plan argued that various places in North China were very suitable for growing the jute appropriate for gunnysacks and this product was not only needed in Dongya's production of gunnysacks but also by society in general. Even though potential costs could reach 600,000 or 700,000 yuan, Dongya's board approved the plan ostensibly "because this matter has a close relationship to society and our company."[124] It is hard to know exactly how many details Song Feiqing presented to the board, but the phrase "a close relationship to society and our company" was clearly a nod to the rhetoric of the Industrial Eden vision and a way of obscuring that the true purpose was "bribing the regime to leave us alone." In reality implementation of the plan required more than providing the benefit of jute production to the military regime, and the responsible officials demanded bribes for themselves as well. Bribery became routine during the war period, and Song Feiqing kept a small safe on the first floor of the administration building with an off-the-books slush fund of gold and watches that he gave to Japanese visitors to Dongya without the knowledge of the company's own accounting department.[125]

In terms of the benefit of the agricultural research station to the occupation regime, it is hard to know in retrospect if bribery won the day or if the Japanese military had a true interest in promoting production of strategic crops. The truth was probably somewhere in between. It has been little studied in the English-language literature, but the Japanese occupation regime was quite interested in agriculture in China. As early as 1930, forty students a year were sent to Japan for training in rural and agricultural development to be used in China.[126] By 1943 there were twenty-two experimental agricultural stations all over North China devoted to everything from wheat to soybeans.[127] This kind of infrastructure begs the question of why the Japanese military needed the Dongya Corporation to manage such a farm if they could simply confiscate the company's assets at will.[128] Somewhere between the regime's developmental goals and the extractive desire of regime officials for bribes, space existed that allowed the Dongya Corporation to survive. Dongya executive Liu Wentian later wrote that Song Feiqing gave nearly two million yuan in antique Chinese paintings and porcelain, not to mention yarn and wool products, to the head of military supply, Major General Maekawa.[129] Was this the price of remaining an independent company? Was Maekawa Dongya's new political patron? If so, not much had changed in terms of doing business in North China since Song Chuandian had started getting state privileges such as the rights to start a long-distance bus company in Shandong or Dongya sold sweaters for use by Han Fuju's soldiers. Ties to the military arms of states seem to have been a consistent Song family strategy.

The agricultural research station and other Dongya relations with the regime were also made possible by the array of border crossers who were able and willing to negotiate between the Japanese regime and the Chinese of North China. Wang Fuwu, the Chinese man who had studied in Japan, mediated between Dongya and the upper echelons of the Japanese military apparatus. Kihara Sadamitsu, a longtime Japanese employee of Dongya, proved useful dealing with Japanese companies and bureaucrats.[130] Dongya also relied heavily on a man named Chen Xisan who had been head of the Tianjin YMCA and whose connections with the government facilitated many transactions, including the approval from the authorities to found the chemical division in 1944.[131] Eventually he became a Dongya vice president, replacing Zhao Zizhen, whose usefulness probably ended when his patron Han Fuju was executed by the Nationalist government for not resisting the Japanese during the invasion.[132] In addition, in 1942, the military required Dongya to hire a Japanese adviser named Ayama Ryūsuke.[133] At about the same time, Song Feiqing stepped down as chairman of the board in favor of longtime director Wang Yusheng, whose family had close connections with the pre-Nationalist warlord-period bureaucratic circles that supplied the pool of talent for the North China puppet government.[134] In some ways, the warlord period was still alive and well under Japanese occupation. The most important border crosser for Dongya, perhaps, was Tsujihara Yafumi, assigned by the Japanese military as assistant director of the agricultural research station under Shi Shaodong.[135] Shi later wrote that this young Japanese man "earned a lot of money, but saved Dongya a lot of bribes." In fact, Shi later portrayed him as a pretty good guy who had once saved Shi from interrogation by Japanese military police during a business trip to Baoding.[136]

The variety of positions held by these border crossers and the array of roles they played goes a long way to show the complexity of the occupation state. Some of the border crossers like Wang Fuwu, Tsujihara and even Ayama had direct connections to, and perhaps even positions in, the

Japanese military. Others developed their connections in unexpected ways. Chen Xisan relied on networks built through YMCA missionary work; Wang Yusheng was born into a family with connections to warlord-period officials. In short, connection with the regime took no one route and often had unpredictable consequences.

Similar unpredictable consequences can be seen in the ultimate fate of the agricultural research station. As the war ground on, goods became scarcer, and in August of 1943 the North China regime instituted controls on textile production by forming a fiber-control board, textile association, and a variety of other institutions. The new regulations stipulated controls on purchase and sale of all wool and jute products, with some of those products reserved for military use.[137] Up until then, "because of various reasons, the purchase of jute for gunnysack production had been centralized at the Dongya Corporation and Dongya had undertaken responsibility also for the manufacture of gunnysacks."[138] In 1944, though, the North China Jute Promotion Board (Chi., Huabei machan gaijin hui; Jap., Kahoku asasan kaishinkai) took over the job of promoting jute cultivation and controlling jute purchasing.[139] As such, jute purchase followed the general trend of other commodities such as grain and cotton, where the centralized organs of the government gradually replaced reliance on private firms.[140]

At the same time the seven largest woolen mills in North China, including the Dongya Corporation, were combined into two groups with the idea that they could share machinery. By the late war period much machinery was badly in need of repair, and the regime began confiscating some machines to cannibalize the metals for military uses. The regime's obsession with machinery became apparent a few months after organizing these cooperative groups, when the North China Textile Association prepared secret reports in excruciating detail about the maker, horsepower, and abilities of each piece of equipment owned by every woolen mill and gunnysack factory in North China. Possibly with a nod to the ever-present metal collection drives, the reports even specified which equipment was metal, which was wood, and which was part metal and part wood.[141]

It is hard to know what impact these new regulations had on Dongya. In terms of wool, the impact was probably minimal. The company spun only 3,200 pounds of wool in 1944. Gunnysack production, on the other hand, remained strong. The company manufactured almost a million gunnysacks in 1944, down from the 1.5 million the previous year, but still substantial.[142] In fact, the regulators themselves noted sheepishly that in spite of the legalistic and extensive jute regulations, only one company fell under them: Dongya.[143] One account by former Dongya managers claims that the North China Jute Cultivation and Promotion Board even ordered the arrest of four Dongya executives who only saw freedom after another round of bribery.[144]

In any case, the new regulations spelled the end of the company's agricultural research station. By all accounts, Dongya benefited by leaving the jute promotion business, and the new control organizations reported difficulties in inspecting jute production and sale.[145] The North China Fiber Control Board even listed as a success its suggestion in the spring to "issue instructions on using substitute materials such as cotton stalks and husks, jute scraps, and cattail stalks in the production of gunnysacks."[146] Of course Dongya had been using such materials for years. By 1945, the North China Political Affairs Council was asked to subsidize the North China Jute Promotion Board by more than fifteen million yuan.[147] At the same time, Dongya continued to produce gunnysacks, proving that jute was available in North China, if not plentiful, and its place in the supply chain of the military-industrial complex was safe despite the existence of new regulatory bodies. By 1945 about 70 percent of jute purchases in North China went for military use.[148]

Dongya's agricultural research station functioned from approximately June of 1942 to January of 1944, but in spite of huge costs, much of the station's activity was a show put on for the Japanese military. The model farm run by the station "looked on the outside like we had expended a lot of effort. . . . In the office, we hung up a map and a chart showing statistics on the spreading acreage of jute. These statistics were for show and far from reality. When you perform you should exaggerate anyway."[149] The school set up by the agricultural research station at an abandoned military brothel in Beijing did teach a number of Chinese students how to grow jute. Eventually, however the school's Japanese teachers were sent to the front, and the Chinese students fled their jute farms in the countryside because of the danger of being targeted by anti-Japanese guerrillas. In the end, after several years of arduous work, the personnel for the expansion of jute production "scattered to the winds, defeated and broken up." Shi Shaodong concluded, "From any vantage point, the Military Department had truly no reason to express satisfaction with Dongya's work spreading the growing of jute. But they did not have the courage to come forth and criticize. . . . The government lost a little money and private individuals made a little. Everyone involved from the top to the bottom got a share." In the shifting eddies of war priorities, the final results did not matter. Dongya had taken advantage of a key moment when such a proposal could keep the company out of trouble. When jute-promotion activity fizzled, the regime's attention was elsewhere; there were no real consequences for Dongya. The Japanese military in North China had an arbitrary and short memory.

The arbitrary and capricious nature of the wartime regime became apparent in a separate incident when two members of the Japanese military police showed up at the Dongya offices in Tianjin one day in July of 1943 and took Song Feiqing and Chen Xisan, who had been such an effective border crosser up until then, into custody for ten days.[150] The reasons for their arrest are unclear. One former Dongya employee states that Song Feiqing had refused to turn valuable equipment over to the regime.[151] This is certainly possible given the nature of the economy of things, which tied occupier and the occupied together. For ten days Song Feiqing lived in a narrow and damp jail cell with only one window. There were swarms of mosquitoes and flies. A chamber pot in the middle of the floor contributed to air so bad that "it made one want to die." Although he had cellmates, talking to them was not permitted. Yet, ever one to grab an opportunity, Song Feiqing volunteered to scrub the Japanese-style bathtub. As he later told Shi Shaodong, it gave him exercise and allowed him to have a bath every day.[152]

The process of securing Song's and Chen's release points to the endemic corruption of the occupation regime. Shi Shaodong and other Dongya employees spent ten days in endless rounds of visits, banquets, and bribery. Finally the people with "bottomless pockets" felt satiated and Song Feiqing and Chen Xisan were released with no further harm to them.[153] Remarkably, this arrest seemed to have no relation to the survival of Dongya—perhaps the moment for possible confiscation had passed the previous year, or perhaps these were simply two separate parts of the Japanese military each operating independently.

The multiplication of new control boards and monopolies, the indiscriminate arrests, and the increasing difficulty of producing goods all show how difficult wartime conditions had become by 1944 and 1945. As prices continued to rise, the regime became even more desperate for control, and the mayor of Tianjin implemented a plan to ration goods in the city.[154] In January of 1945 Dongya, ever adept at crisis management, issued new internal regulations to inform employees how to conduct themselves during air raids.[155] In February, the company announced plans to distribute flour to the poor.[156] Japan's "Sacred War" in China had reached the relatively privileged location of the former British concession in Tianjin. Nonetheless, life went on at Dongya and management even found the time to issue regulations for the rotation of employee haircuts.[157] In March the last vestige of the foreign concession system disappeared when the Japanese suspended their friendly relations with the local Vichy representatives and occupied the French consulate.[158] The paucity of documents extant in French archives for the years of 1944 and 1945 bears silent testimony to the likely Japanese efforts to burn and destroy evidence of the last desperate years of the war. Dongya, however, escaped such a fate and remained standing under Song Feiqing's control through the Japanese surrender in August 1945.

Business and War

For a businessperson in Tianjin, the war replaced the uncertain Nationalist developmental state with a disorganized, dangerous occupation state run as part of the Japanese developmental empire. Over time, this state became increasingly extractive, but that was not clear at the beginning. The war period distorted markets, created scarcity where none had existed, and made control of things such as equipment, commodities, and land the key link in political, military, and economic power. Rather than a clash between a Chinese company and a Japanese occupation, or between military and civilian mind-sets, or between state economic control and private industry, the war regime fostered an environment in which all sides participated in a common economy of things. This wartime economy of things did share some elements with the treaty-port, "urban modern/national products" consumer culture of the 1930s. In both, people endowed goods with great significance, but in wartime the frenzied flight from money into things saw goods not as barometers of modernity but as objects of stability and value in a violent and unpredictable world.

For Song Feiqing and the Dongya Corporation the key to survival, and even profit, required control of "things" just important enough to be essential to people's everyday lives or the war effort, but not so important that they invited direct Japanese control.[159] These "things" included wool and wool yarn, jute and gunnysacks, chemicals and medicine, commodities like sugar and flour, as well as hard assets like equipment and land. Dongya managers flush with cash and a little moxie took advantage of opportunities on an ad hoc basis. Specializations could be learned or specialists could be hired, but opportunity might not knock again. If you have wool, you sell wool. If you have gunnysacks, you sell gunnysacks. If you do not know how to grow jute, you buy a book. If you want a bath in jail, you volunteer to clean the bathtub. If necessary, you keep two sets of books so that the Japanese government is not completely aware of your company's operations.[160]

This ad hoc, can-do opportunism did not necessarily mean that the individuals involved had no ideology or political viewpoint. The Song family lost one member to the war and another had to flee after engaging in anti-Japanese activity. Song Feiqing left no record of his own thoughts, but Shi Shaodong and others loyal to Song Feiqing later went to considerable lengths to prove his patriotism to China. In his manuscript Shi allocated considerable space to the activities of one Zheng Fangyang who supposedly acted as go-between with "patriotic" forces, allowing Dongya to donate funds for the care of wounded Nationalist soldiers.[161] We also know that Song Feiqing traveled to the Nationalist wartime capital of Chongqing in 1939 to try to keep relations smooth with the exile government there.[162]

Political stance aside, however, the Dongya Corporation thrived for the first six years of the war. As the years passed, the institutions of the occupation developmental empire grew increasingly centralized and complex, and increasingly extractive, but control seemed to remain elusive. Most telling from Dongya's point of view, the occupation development state was disorganized and arbitrary as was seen most clearly in the personal venality that undermined the ideological discipline of the regime. Dongya survived, and even thrived, because company managers could provide products necessary for the Japanese imperialist project as well as bribes for the personal gain of regime agents. The Japanese occupiers claimed to want to build a framework for "scientific and orderly management" but administered the economy in a disorganized manner. Paradoxically, Dongya's own drive for "scientific" management and rational control reached its highest levels during the war.

5 Building Eden inside the Firm

IN FOUNDING DONGYA, Song Feiqing's ideals were part of larger movements to implement both May Fourth period and international ideals of rational, scientific, and modern industrialism within the framework of a patriotic commitment to a strong Chinese state. Dongya attempted to link modern consumer culture and national strength outside of the factory, but China's prolonged political crisis made an industrialized and modern consumer China an elusive dream. The political and economic environment lacked the stability to foster industry of the kind Song advocated, but within the Dongya Corporation his drive for Industrial Eden continued unabated and even reached its height during the Japanese occupation. In this it echoed developments taking place in state-owned factories in the Nationalist areas in the Southwest.[1] Amid the chaos and turmoil of war, Dongya aimed to become a transformative corporation able to implement at the company level that which could not happen in the economy as a whole. Borrowing eclectically from both international trends in management and more home-grown techniques, Song Feiqing and his lieutenants worked to make the corporation both a protective cocoon, a bubble, within which they tried to create an orderly, humane, and hygienic modernity in microcosm and a bold attempt to provide a model for the transformation and rebirth of all of society. In practice, such a mission required the absolute and full commitment of all of the members of the Dongya community, and Industrial Eden on the corporate level was as much about discipline and control as it was about rationality and benevolence.

Building Eden

Physically, little distinguished the Dongya Corporation from other factories or compounds in Tianjin except for a statue of the famous "butting rams" of Dongya's wool-knitting-yarn brand inside the main gate. Otherwise, Dongya presented an ordinary industrial aesthetic. For its managers, the factory's beauty lay in the company's role in production and social reform, not in architecture. There was no need to prettify the premises because of an underlying assumption regarding the essential value and worth of industry in and of itself. Views of the company celebrating that aesthetic, such as that in Figure 5.1, appear commonly in company publications. In this picture Song Feiqing, dressed as a modern industrialist in Western suit and tie, eerily looks over his creation, the transformative factory.

The various parts of the factory represented the integration of economic and social life. Inside the front gate, behind the butting rams statue, sat the main administration building beyond which lay various factory production workshops such as the washing and drying department, spinning sheds, gunnysack weaving workshop, and the wool inspection department. Besides these production areas, the factory grounds also included showers, a clinic, dormitories, and an employee cafeteria. At its heart, lay the sports fields and bleachers where communal life could be reinforced with sports competitions, performances, and celebrations.[2]

FIGURE 5.1   Song Feiqing and the Dongya factory grounds. *Dongya Annual*, 1936, unpaged.

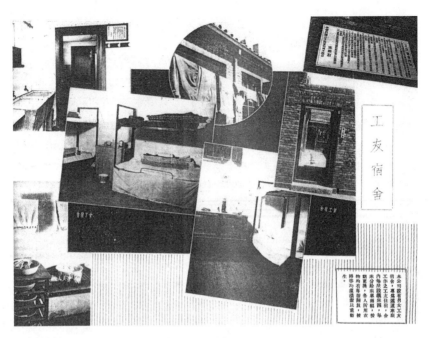

FIGURE 5.2   Montage of scenes from worker dorms. *Dongya Annual*, 1936, unpaged.

These kinds of amenities were the exception in China in the 1930s and 1940s, but they were certainly not unique. A 1936 survey of forty-nine large enterprises found that "thirty-eight provided medical facilities, and thirty-eight offered apartments and dormitories. Other services and welfare facilities included sports facilities, savings plans, schools for employees' children, recreational facilities, consumer organizations, and public dining halls."[3] The provision of welfare benefits and the attempt to create enclosed communities were hallmarks of many larger firms with claims on innovative management.[4]

The space within the factory walls provided an arena where managers could exercise control and enforce order. The pictures of the dormitories in Figure 5.2 show a desire for an orderly life among Dongya employees, who had a place for everything and who put everything in its place. Quilts are neatly folded on bunk beds, walks are swept clean, and washbasins are arranged neatly in their stand. The company constructed several men's and women's dormitories, which could accommodate several hundred employees, and dorm life was strictly regulated. According to company policy there were set times for going to sleep and waking up. Sweeping was done in rotation among employees according to a posted schedule. Enforcement of the rules came through "punishment and reward which all have set regulations and use of various kinds of prizes allows each individual to receive good results and obtain an ideal living place for enjoyable rest."[5] Having dorm facilities for workers was common for large factories at the time. Of the four major woolen mills in Tianjin, three (Manmō, Renli, and Dongya) all had at least some housing for workers, but a much higher percentage of workers lived on the factory premises at Dongya than at the other woolen mills. Manmō had only 0.69 square meters of dormitory space per worker, while Dongya had 5.86 square meters per worker.[6]

In the picture of the Dongya dormitory in Figure 5.2, laundry hanging to dry in the sun showed the commitment to cleanliness stressed in accounts of company life. A brief postwar account of benefits available to employees uses the word "hygiene" (*weisheng*) in almost every sentence, sometimes more than once in the same sentence, as in a description of the employee dormitory as a place where "hygiene facilities [bathrooms] are all appropriate in order to meet hygiene standards." The same profile also frequently used "order" (*zhixu jingran*) to refer to Dongya's appearance. In another example, description of Dongya's hair salon referred to both order and hygiene: "the room is large with seven new-style chairs and more than ten stylists. All tools are sanitized before use and equipment is complete. All employees get their hair done on schedule to ensure order and not a bit of chaos."[7] The concept of order and control even extended to rules for company memos. "All of the announcements were written in three parts with the desire that everyone could understand and implement [them] . . . (a) Content—this was the first part. Every announcement had the two characters for the title . . . (b) Reasons—this was the second part. This part stated the reasons for taking this action, its significance, public and private meaning, past failures, future prospects and results . . . (c) Method— this was the third part. It explained the method of implementation, which departments would do what, and detailed explanation of the steps."[8] Company descriptions of the employee cafeteria are similar. It was managed with the goal of "striving for hygiene, maintaining order, and economic distribution." The cafeteria itself used "the most modern and useful tables and seats. Utensils accord with conditions for hygiene. Also we publish the nutritional information about each month's food according to a doctor's direction."[9]

To maintain the order and hygiene inside the factory gates, Song Feiqing and other managers tried to seal off Dongya from contact with the corrupting and polluting forces of society as a whole. In this it was comparable to the corporate compounds built by the Bank of China as studied by Wen-hsin Yeh.[10] Similarly, in 1932 a Shenxin cotton mill manager in Wuxi in South China said, "usually it's best to completely [sever] workers from the outside world, and not permit their coming and going."[11] As a first level of protection against China's chaotic environment, Song Feiqing located the Dongya factory within first the Italian, and then later, the British concession. Within the concessions, the enclosed space of the factory was further protected and divided from the chaotic outside world by diligent gatekeepers using procedures drawn from the best methods of rational management. "No matter who you were, if you didn't have a pass, you could not even take a blade of grass out [of the Dongya factory]. Even the president and vice presidents had to have a pass to take things out. If the president and vice presidents took cars, the driver would have a pass. . . . On the other hand, things being brought in also had a system. You couldn't come in the gate without a slip. Even with a slip, the details were inquired into. Who would receive the goods? Who would inspect and weigh? Everything needed to be clear." According to Shi Shaodong, Dongya's gatekeepers enforced the rules of access so well, that one investor bought stock in the company merely because he admired the procedures. He reasoned that if the gates could be managed so rationally, the company's overall administration should be comparably impressive.[12]

The underlying principles upon which Dongya management relied combined ideas of hierarchy and filial piety from Chinese tradition, Christianity, and firm belief in the value of scientific modernity. Song Feiqing's ideas extended in part from the gospel of development preached to him as a child by the British Baptists in Qingzhou who believed that use of technology to improve people's lives was as important as belief in salvation through Jesus Christ. Song's own religious views echoed the focus on practical life problems of the gospel of development. Shi Shaodong had long conversations with Song Feiqing about religion and concluded that Song's "philosophy had other elements and these elements were not necessarily consistent with Christian thought. He firmly opposed 'Belief' [*xin*] as a phrase used for salvation. He believed in 'behavior/action' [*xing*]. Because of this he rejected the power of prayer. . . . He believed that there was only one true lord [*zhenzhu*] between heaven and earth. Buddhists, Daoists, Christians, Moslems, and [believers] in all other religions that people accepted believed in this lord, just with different names and without knowing it, so all of the conflicts between religions are foolish and unforgivable actions."[13]

Thus Song incorporated Christianity into the Dongya philosophy, but with an emphasis on universalism, behaviors, and practical results. His use of Confucianism was similar and the focus on actions can be seen in two of the most common slogans used by company management. The factory precept, known commonly in English as the "Golden Rule," conveniently came both from Confucius and from the Bible: "Do unto others as you would have them do unto you" (*ji suo bu yu wu shi yu ren*). The classical phrasing comes straight from *The Analects*, the records of the conversations between Confucius and his disciples, but also corresponds neatly to the Golden Rule from the Christian tradition.[14] This slogan appeared in key places on the factory grounds and in company publications. Also, "everybody was given a copy of the factory precept in a frame, to put at home."[15] In addition to the Golden Rule, Dongya management advocated the idea of fostering "Christian Spirit, Military Discipline" (*jidu jingshen, junshi jilü*).[16] Both slogans reflected an emphasis on behavior rather than belief. In the latter, the inclusion of the phrase "military discipline" reflected both the militarization of Chinese society, and much of the world, in the 1930s and 1940s, and also a kind of muscular moralism that characterized Dongya practices during this period. Here, too, Dongya had many similarities to the Bank of China where "at the heart of this impressively modernizing banking organization was, meanwhile, a profoundly moralistic managing philosophy, which was in full accordance with the senior leadership's neo-Confucian outlook."[17]

Besides such moralism Dongya had a profound commitment to being "scientific" in every way possible. As early as 1936, Dongya company regulations pointed to the "need to work consistently to make company operations more scientific."[18] A *Dagong bao* profile in the same year referred to management of Dongya as very scientific.[19] There was a defined form and procedure for virtually everything.[20] In line with this belief in science, the company culture made a fetish of measuring and counting things. Company publications were filled with inventive charts and graphs representing the number of shareholders, increases in company capital, the number of customer letters received, and even the ages, heights, and weights of employees. The chart pictured in Figure 5.3 was published in the company's annual report for public consumption and was only one of many such complex statistical analyses in the report. Perhaps the implication that Dongya workers were getting taller and heavier helped prove the health and strength of the company as a whole and helped demonstrate the good effects of Dongya's personnel policies.

The fetish of measurement reached its fullest extent at Dongya in the statistics department (*tongji bu*). Separate from the accounting department, which handled financial transactions, the statistics department kept track of a wide range of activities. "Every time material moved, a copy of a slip went to the statistics department. Even if an employee repaired a chair, the nails used would be reported to statistics."[21] The statistics department was

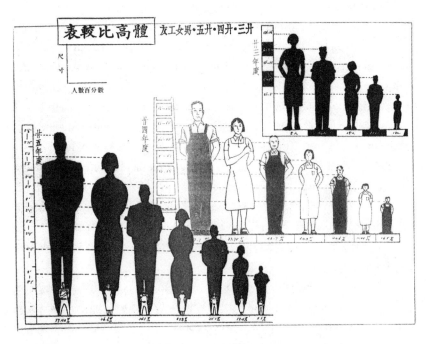

FIGURE 5.3 Worker height comparison chart for men and women, 1934–1936. *Dongya Annual*, 1936, unpaged.

especially proud of its abilities in cost accounting. The Dongya newsletter noted that three hundred engineers who visited in 1947 were surprised to hear that Dongya practiced cost accounting and thought that "this was the first instance in China."[22]

The obsession with measurement and procedure extended to Dongya's hiring practices as well. From the beginning, Dongya managers set out to be different from the smaller and more labor intensive wool textile firms, such as the carpet-making shops, which were known for giving employees long hours and low pay.[23] Dongya emphasized the youth, modernity, and enthusiasm of its employees, whom one company publication described as "young people with courage to work."[24] Indicative of the detail and planning that went into personnel issues, the manual for the personnel department ran to thirty-three pages, including numerous forms and charts. The manual began with this statement: "In hiring workers according to the needs of each department, use scientific methods to choose suitable workers."[25]

As an example, the process of hiring employees for the statistics department tells much about the goals of Dongya managers. The rigor of hiring practices went well beyond finding qualified employees and included measures for peopling Dongya's Industrial Eden with specimens fit for the company's utopian vision. In a description of hiring staff for the statistics department, Shi Shaodong notes that "Dongya wanted to train a group of naive young people who had not yet been contaminated with pollution from society, so this time applicants were limited to those who had just graduated from college." In this case, more than 1,200 applicants vied for a half dozen positions. Selection among such a large group was made by first calling the names of each applicant and watching them walk across a stage to see if they had the proper Dongya "spirit." This reduced the pool to four hundred individuals. A physical exam at the clinic was then followed by a written exam on specialized knowledge with five hundred questions, a psychological test, tests of Chinese and English, and a dexterity exercise. After two days, Dongya executives had chosen a staff of strong and "heroic" looking youths for its statistics department (Figure 5.4).[26]

Unskilled workers went through a similar rigorous hiring process as had the young college graduates who vied for positions at Dongya's statistics department. When prospective workers came to the factory, they were

FIGURE 5.4 Dongya statistics department. Archives of the Dongya Corporation, undated.

divided into groups of men and women, and an initial appraisal was made of their "external appearance, physique, temperament, and age." All of those who did not make the first cut because they were "under sixteen or over thirty, were of weak physique, or had a fierce appearance" were asked not to wait. A form made the whole process "scientific." Each potential worker was judged on five criteria: speech, manners, appearance, limbs, and dress. Each of those categories was further subdivided so that appearance, for example, was judged based on stature (fine, upright, ugly), facial skin (normal, thick, pock-marked), skin color (reddish, normal, dark), and teeth (white, yellow-black, or missing). In general, people who stood up straight, combed their hair, were neat, spoke clearly, and had no missing limbs or visible handicaps had the edge.[27] One former Dongya worker remembered the process where a group of prospective employees first had to walk around in a circle while personnel staff judged them.[28] Those who passed the initial assessment went on to stage two where job applications were filled out in groups with the help of Dongya personnel department staff. The form asked for name, gender, and native place as well as the names and ages of grandparents, parents, brothers and sisters, children, and anyone else who lived with the applicant.[29] The intrusive nature of these questions reflected both Dongya's desire to accumulate and control information as well as its paternalism. Dongya took its responsibilities seriously and the company needed to know how many dependents might need help or assistance from the company. At the bottom of the form, personnel department employees recorded the applicant's data: "weight, height, reach, lung capacity, hand strength, vision, intelligence, hand dexterity, and hand-eye coordination."

Stage three of the process tested these abilities. The manual contained detailed regulations on each test, including instruction on how the prospects were to stand or sit and be measured. There was some device to measure hand strength and men were expected to score at least thirty-five and women twenty-five. Dexterity was judged by asking them to fit small pegs into holes with one hand at a time. Unfortunately, the archives do not contain a copy of the intelligence test.[30] Gao Xinzhai, a former worker, remembered one test where employees put a wooden puzzle together in the sand. "There was a drawing, the examinees had a certain amount of time to look at it . . . [then] they asked the examinees to put it together in a fixed amount of time."[31]

Even with these stringent employment conditions, jobs at Dongya were highly prized. Unemployment was high in North China at a time when hundreds of thousands of unskilled workers migrated to Manchuria during the early years of World War II because work was difficult to find locally.[32] During the war even white-collar jobs were hard to find, partly because Japanese had taken many of the prized positions in the railroads and other government-affiliated concerns.[33] Hao Guanyi, a factory worker who began at Dongya in 1940, went through the tests three times before he was hired, but he persevered because his family was in bad circumstances. For him, "the examination [for employment] included: a vision test, [lifting] a barbell (men), blowing into a balloon, [testing] color blindness, [and] hearing." He noted that positions for women were more limited and qualified applicants had to draw straws to see who would get the job.[34] Feng Naishen, another former employee, recounted that when Dongya was first founded wages were not great, but "at that time, things were very cheap, you should be able to eat well, but we ate ordinary food."[35]

On the surface the company based its process of finding employees entirely on "scientific" analysis, but anecdotal evidence indicates that personalistic connections also served a purpose. The well-educated Song Yuzhan (no relation to Song Feiqing) went to work at Dongya through a connection between his father and Sun Tongxuan, the subordinate of Han Fuju whose wife had invested in Dongya and owned the land on which the new factory was built. Even in 1942 when Han Fuju was dead and Sun Tongxuan had fled from the Japanese to Hong Kong, these connections still counted at Dongya. Song Yuzhan recalled, "My father's classmate took care of Sun's property so he introduced me. But an introduction was not enough, you also needed talent."[36] In another indication of reliance on connections, a Dongya shareholder wrote the company and asked if shareholders could get first notification about available jobs. Company management responded that notification for all jobs would be too burdensome, but if the shareholder had someone he wanted to recommend for employment, he should do so.[37] Even Shi Shaodong admitted that hiring practices could not completely follow scientific guidelines and some employees entered Dongya because of their personal relations with Dongya executives.[38]

Those applicants judged worthy of probationary employment then received their first training lecture. The personnel manual explained that "most employees have low levels of knowledge and little experience, without proper explanation and guidance, it would be difficult for them to have results in work." This first training talk covered the nature of the work to be done, working times and punctuality, compensation, rules, and spirit. The most important rules were those regarding guarantees for employment, procedures for taking time off, smoking, fighting, and relations between men and women. Of course, the testing did not stop then, but continued through the period of probationary employment. Finally, if the prospect passed all tests, then he or she was asked to provide a guaranty and a statement of willingness. Then and only then, would he or she become an employee of the Dongya Corporation.[39]

Training and Cultivation

Training for Dongya employees did not end with the conclusion of probationary employment. In fact, continuous training (*xunlian* 訓練) and improvement were fundamental values at the Dongya Corporation. Even yarn salespeople had to come back to the factory and intern at the end of the year so they could know how yarn was made.[40] Dongya's emphasis on

training reflected larger trends within Chinese society, especially the practices of the Nationalist Party movement where training included not just
skill development, but also "indoctrination into the 'revolutionary' norms
of loyalty and obedience to the central military leadership."[41] Within the
Dongya personnel department a training group took responsibility for
training in skills, rules, and spirit. Work productivity provided a means to
test the results of skills training, an oral exam tested knowledge of rules,
and supervisors investigated "service attitude" to determine the results
of spiritual training.[42] Thus, managers tested "the work and results of
the workers as well as an individual's character and morals."[43] Of skills,
rules, and spirit, the last was possibly the most important. Song Feiqing's
American-trained brother-in-law ran the personnel department, and he adopted the body-spirit-mind formula popularized by the YMCA. He gave
primacy to spirit, and even indicated that weaknesses in spirit could lead
to illness.[44] The emphasis on spirit followed not just the YMCA, but also
the Nationalist example. Sun Yat-sen, founder of the Nationalist Party, gave
a speech in 1912 on the "spiritual training of soldiers," which was widely
printed and read during the republican period.[45] Dongya managers wanted
spiritual training to heighten interest in the work, raise spirit, cultivate morality, and cause workers to be conscientious.[46]

   The Song family had introduced employee training to teach honesty,
reliability, and skills back in the early days in Shandong. A worker named
Qie Xinyuan later recounted how he had already begun to study English
back in Qingzhou and then turned to the abacus when he followed the Song
family to Jinan.[47] In addition, employees had to attend Sunday church services. In Tianjin during the 1930s and 1940s, Dongya training was systematic and continuous. All employees were required to attend lectures as early
as 1933, only a year after Dongya began operating.[48] Former employee Hao
Guanyi recalled, "There was thought training every Friday at 7:00 for an
hour."[49] By at least 1937 Dongya began codifying training regulations and
they became more and more elaborate through the next five or six years.[50]

   Often training took the form of lectures before the assembled workers
in the bleachers by the sports fields or in the employee cafeteria. Each
training lecture was a ceremonious occasion. The workers first bowed to
the factory flag (a three-cornered flag, blue with a white edge), then bowed
to the managers who bowed in return. In the words of one training lecture,

we first bow to the factory flag. Because we work in a factory we should be respectful to the factory; the factory flag is a symbol that represents the factory. Saluting the flag is an expression of respect for the factory. As for when workers [*gongyou* 工友, literally "worker friends"] bow to the managers this also means respect for the company. Managers represent the company and lead the workers of each department in their tasks, therefore if we respect the company then we must respect its managers. . . . Because workers bow to the managers, the managers reply with a bow as well. Is this not an action that expresses mutual feelings?[51]

During the ceremony, "everyone should have a respectful attitude and stand in an orderly fashion without moving or looking left and right. Even more so [workers] should not have frivolous actions or smile because this kind [of behavior] undermines the meaning of practice and shows disrespect."[52]

Sometimes Song Feiqing himself delivered the training lectures and then his beneficence would be celebrated by the distribution of commodities to employees. Another former worker remembered that "as such, his lectures were particularly welcome."[53] The company's 1936 annual report begins with a picture of Song Feiqing lecturing to his assembled employees standing on bleachers in front of him, accompanied by the text: "In order to have progress in work and smooth operations, it is necessary to maintain a cooperative spirit, listen to the guidance of your leaders, persevere, endure hard work, put your head down and strive."[54] In the picture (Figure 5.5), Song is presented in an enlarged inset so that the photograph focuses on the faces of the attentive workers and Song appears larger than life.

Each lecture covered a different topic, and topics ranged from explaining "the goal of the company" and "the spirit of being human," to admonitions such as "don't talk back to managers," "don't bully your worker colleagues," "don't fight and argue with others," "don't incite trouble," to ethical lessons such as "why we should work hard," "why be good," and "why be nice."[55] According to one lecture, "the intention of training [was to make [employees] understand the purpose of the company and to avoid individuals misusing their energies. Also it [was] to let them know company regulations and avoid infractions. . . . After training, if [employees] make another mistake, the company would not be tolerant."[56]

FIGURE 5.5 Song Feiqing delivering a Saturday morning training lecture. *Dongya Annual*, 1936, unpaged.

Much of the Dongya training taught politeness. Hao Guanyi remembered that, "if you saw a staff member [comparable to the phrase 'white-collar employee'], you had to make a ten-degree bow, on the electric tram you should give up your seat for a staff member, in the mornings you should say good morning, if you saw a staff member while riding a bicycle, you should get off. Men and women all had to do this."[57] Feng Naishen remembered a deeper bow. "They emphasized politeness. You had to make a ninety-degree bow to the president, if you saw a staff member you had to make a ninety-degree bow, if you saw a staff member, you had to say, 'Good morning Mr. So-and-So' or 'Hello Mr. So-and-So.' You could only leave after the staff member had returned the greeting."[58] A training lecture taught, "having manners means expressing respect for others. We need to dress neatly every day. When meeting others, mutual greetings and nods should be exchanged. Superiors should receive a bow and a greeting. When asking others to do something, it is necessary to use the word 'please.' When people do something for you, you need to say 'thank you.' All of these are examples of manners."[59] Managers asked that politeness even extend to the factory's intramural sports competitions.[60]

In lecture after lecture, company managers exhorted employees to "eliminate crude language and sounds. Even more don't criticize others or say naughty things because these are often reasons for fights,"[61] and to "Pay attention to personal cleanliness, show restraint in eating and drinking, don't casually touch dirty things. These are all principles of hygiene. If an individual is conscientious in practicing [hygiene] not only will it aid in his personal health, everyone can avoid the attack of many illnesses. Isn't this the most fortunate thing?"[62]

Eventually, all of the various topics of the training lectures became subsumed under the rubric of "Dongya Spirit," which combined the principles of scientific management with Song's own Christian beliefs and Chinese Confucian ideals. In the words of Shi Shaodong, "What [was] 'Dongya Spirit'? It is not something that can precisely be explained in words. If you want to explain it briefly, then it is . . . sacrificing the small me for the big us. The Dongya precept was 'Do unto others as you would have them do unto you.' It was also 'consideration/forgiveness,' that is to say, the Confucian philosophy of 'spending a life traveling with others.'"[63] In 1945 all forty-three of the training lectures were edited into a book called *Dongya Spirit*, which ran more than four hundred pages. Each employee received a copy.[64] Company managers tested workers on their knowledge of the lectures. The evaluation of one employee read, "[he] is still not clear on the various provisions and needs to review the lectures listed below in order to accurately know them."[65]

Dongya expected its workers to be both compliant and active. An article in the company newsletter exhorted employees to set their minds on a goal and plan for advance.[66] Dedicating oneself to advancing at Dongya required commitment both during and after work hours. Another article stated that self-cultivation outside of work is the basis for advancement.[67] Thus the company placed cultivation (*xiuyang*) at the center of everyday life in a manner similar to the advocacy of *xiuyang* in *Shenghuo* magazine in the 1920s, "it was the employer's legitimate business concern—as well as his paternal duty as the teacher-master—to seek to ensure that such-and-such a young employee used his leisure time constructively."[68] To make this possible Dongya provided a host of activities and classes, which by the period of the Japanese occupation had been organized into four kinds of after-work self-cultivation: moral education, knowledge education, physical education, and group education. For moral education, the company established a "Moral Cultivation Research Society," which invited people to a lecture on morality each Sunday and also posted famous quotes at places of heavy traffic in the workplace "in order to remind and warn people of bad thoughts and bad habits." Knowledge education comprised free classes for employees on common knowledge, Chinese, the *Thousand Character Classic* (a reading primer), simple arithmetic, introductory foreign language conversation, and so on. For physical education Dongya "established all kinds of playing fields to make it easy to be active and work out, [in addition to which] there was a gentle calisthenics class divided into two classes for men and women which was taught by a specialist every day after work for about 15 minutes. In addition to this [we] had also organized basketball and volleyball teams to play in rotational practice." Group education focused on "adjustment to group life" and included "indoor games such as chess, table tennis, newspaper and magazine reading, etc."[69] Much of the implementation of this training fell to factory supervisors who worked as cultural educators for workers after shifts ended.[70]

Employee organizations ran the gamut from drama clubs (both Western-style and Peking opera), to martial arts groups, sports teams, a photography club, choir, and religious groups. Managers intended such groups to provide healthy outlets for entertainment and to promote community feeling. At the same time, they could train and strengthen individuals for their roles in Dongya's utopian modernity. Shi Shaodong wrote that participation in company sports teams could promote health, the spirit of athleticism, human feelings, and politeness. At one time the company employees fielded at least thirty different teams that engaged with each other in intramural competition.[71]

In 1939, Dongya extended its drive for improvement through education by founding its own primary school for the dependents of employees. The school's philosophy and management reflected all of the tenets of Dongya's drive to create a mini Industrial Eden. One company publication declared, "The power of a foundation of education has an extremely important status in the advancement of business." Teachers, of course, had to pass a rigorous examination process before being hired because "the knowledge, experience, appearance, habits and even every movement of elementary school teachers is closely related to the educational quality for the students." And the curriculum was based on "a scientific method to guide students and let them learn naturally." The school "lacked nothing in hygiene facilities . . . [and] there was also an exercise field where students could play basketball, volleyball, or softball." The Dongya primary school taught its students "moral ideas at every turn to correct the attitude with which they treat people and things, and trained them in methods of cultivation." To accomplish this, the company began "with the construction of a rationalized school campus environment to allow them to come into contact only with things that are rational and regulated, such as training their ability to speak, guiding their manners, managing their habits, and constraining their emotions."[72]

Dongya was able to fund the primary school because of its large wartime profits, and its construction during the occupation shows that the company's pursuit of an Industrial Eden did not slow down because of the war. Morality and self-cultivation loomed larger during the war, however, as patriotism and China's salvation no longer could be publically proclaimed as valid goals. This change can be seen in the words to the factory song. In the 1934 version, there were very simple lyrics that referred to the making of wool yarn, its sale, and the salvation of the country.[73] In 1942 Shi Shaodong wrote new lyrics to music composed by his brother who would go on to lead the Dongya choir.[74] The 1942 lyrics written at the time of the Japanese occupation did not refer to the company's economic activities at all and especially not to the salvation of China. Instead the lengthy lyrics stressed moral self-cultivation and service to society such as the line, "we want to use production to advance society . . . we want to achieve mutual benefit for capital and labor."[75] Similar to textbooks in the occupation period, the factory song excised politics in favor of morality.[76] The reference to mutual benefit for both capital and labor is particularly telling. There would be no reason to include such a lyric unless it was a response to anti-capitalist rhetoric, perhaps by anti-capitalist military figures.

Even group employee dinners had moral overtones. Song Feiqing had begun holding dinners for relations and people from Shandong who worked at the company, but sometime during the war the practice spread to include all Dongya staff (white-collar employees). As Shi Shaodong remembered, "the idea of sacrificing the small me on behalf of the big us had taken root among the workers and employees at Dongya. . . . Besides cultivating feelings among employees, the meals also had the additional use of training."[77] As time went on, the group meals became highly ritualized and each dinner began with everyone singing the factory song.[78] After everyone got their food, the Protestant minister who worked as head of the benefits department at Dongya said a blessing. In addition there was a weekly collection for a charitable cause and announcements such as births, illnesses, deaths, whose children had been accepted at college, activities of social groups, news of colleagues who were away, and so on. After the staff group dinners had been held for about a year, a workers group meal also started with 100 to 150 participants each time. The programs and methods of the worker group meals were the same as with staff, but there was no collection for charity. Once a year the president, vice presidents, and department heads served the food as thanks for a year of hard work and service. Each time Song Feiqing served, "his energy was great and his actions lively, and industrious. He liked to say to people, [we are clumsy], if there is anything in our service that is not good, please let us know. If there is anything you just cannot stand, then please get angry, beat on the plates and bowls. Today is an exception and this will not count as a violation of factory rules.' "[79]

Song Feiqing clearly intended his annual performance as a server to his employees as a model for the kind of cheerful, industrious, and selfless behavior he sought from everyone. In the vision he and other company managers promoted, going to work for Dongya was not just an economic decision, it was a moral commitment. For them, Dongya had become the real world embodiment of May Fourth ideals of self-improvement, science, and modernity. The company proudly claimed that visiting engineers had concluded that Dongya's equipment was "in accordance with modernized spirit."[80] This modernity was in turn embedded in a deeply moral set of beliefs about proper behavior, order, and hygiene. From management's perspective, the transformative corporation looked a lot like a benevolent utopia, an Eden. A Dongya publication proclaimed, "In sum, this company pays attention at all times to the hearts and bodies of employees. . . . In promoting self-cultivation we have in the same way expended a lot of energy to enable employees to not only be employees but also to be people."[81]

Paternalism and Discipline

Dongya's Industrial Eden was supremely hierarchical and paternalistic. Song Feiqing's annual stint as server at the staff group dinner was a model of behavior, not an expression of equality. The underlying premise of the Dongya system was strict paternal hierarchy and discipline. Membership in the privileged Dongya community came with responsibilities. As Song Feiqing stated in a talk at an employee banquet, "[it is] required that all of the employees strive on their own, regulate themselves, control themselves, chastise themselves [*zimian, zilü, zizhi, zize*], to the point that they could sacrifice themselves in order to allow a great project to flourish."[82] Participation in the Dongya "great project" required submission to Dongya's "scientific" forms of discipline. The company enforced the rules that governed almost every part of life at Dongya with a system of strict rewards and punishments. A native-place compatriot from Shandong, Ma Shouting, was the designated enforcer of factory rules. Using Chinese opera as a metaphor, he once joked that he "sang the villain's part" at Dongya. Ma was known for being strict and never forgiving violations of factory rules. He even used corporeal punishment with some employees.[83]

In all there were thirty rules for the management of workers during production. They ranged from "obey orders" and "come to work on time" to "don't gamble" and "don't deceive women workers or new workers." Those workers "with more than three demerits in a year will be fired."[84] Longtime Dongya employee Hao Guanyi later recalled that "workers were most afraid of losing work. If you made the smallest mistake Song Xinglin of the personnel department would call you in for a scolding. I got major demerits three times, enough to be disgraced." The first time, Hao was caught with three matches during a search in spite of the fact that smoking, or even carrying cigarettes or matches, was strictly prohibited. His appeal for leniency because of the need to support his children was ignored. Suspended from work, he reported every day only to be told that his situation was unclear. Finally, he wrote a note of repentance and found a guarantor. He was then allowed to return to work. In a fashion similar to later Communist practice, Hao had to write three such notes of repentance over the course of his career.[85] Feng Naishen remembered that the personnel department called him in for a lecture to chastise him for talking during work.[86]

Discipline was certainly strict, but there is little indication that workers lived in daily fear. Chinese researchers combed the Dongya archives and interviewed workers in the 1960s for examples of exploitative capitalist poor treatment of workers, and they only came up with about sixteen instances they felt worthy of noting. Out of about a thousand workers over a number of years, that number is hardly remarkable. Punishments for offenses usually involved suspension of work without pay for a few days or weeks.[87] The most serious poor treatment of workers they alleged came from the treatment of two women workers whose cases would become infamous after the Communist revolution. In one case, the female worker Liu Dezhong had asked for a loan to bury her husband and when Dongya managers refused, she jumped out an upper-story window and killed herself. In the second instance, the female worker Xu Wen was fired when it was discovered she had secretly wed and then become pregnant. At a later time she was re-hired on a temporary basis and was hurt in a machinery accident creating a wound from which she died.[88] Both instances were certainly tragedies. The treatment of Xu in particular showed how women had few rights under Dongya employment policies intended to limit the company's female work-force to young unmarried people. Nonetheless, there is little sense of widespread maltreatment of workers.

In addition to such flagrant rule violations, supervisors also evaluated workers for "conscientiousness." Dongya kept daily, monthly, and yearly statistics on workers' sick leave, absences, tardiness, or slowness. Workers evaluated as "conscientious" received two extra days' pay each month and those who did not miss work for a year received an extra month's wages. Pay raises and the amount of the yearly bonus also depended on conscientiousness ratings.[89]

As early as 1934, the company was trying to calculate the production of individual workers.[90] In addition, at irregular times workers would be tested on such things as their ability and speed in tying threads, the length of the knot, and the speed of changing work. Supervisors took tests as well. They had to be able to draw out diagrams of the machines, and evaluators tested the settings of the machine to see if the supervisors had properly calibrated their speed, if they produced products of desired quality. In addition to tests such as these related to production, there were other tests on general knowledge and intelligence. Employees had to put small pieces of wood together into a shape, prove their mathematical abilities, or even make suggestions for improvement. Results on these tests would be recorded and reported as evidence for promotion and raises. Those with good grades would get faster raises and those without good grades, if they were able and honest, would be promoted or given raises at the "proper time" so they would not be disappointed.[91] Staff also had to write an essay every year.[92]

Dongya management expended great effort in controlling the bodies and movements of employees. In the very early years, Dongya issued "light blue uniforms, on the back your worker number was printed in large white letters (later it was printed on the shirt pocket). . . . Because they did not know people's [names], they looked at the number and it was easy to trace mistakes. Later, the managers learned everyone's name and they changed their method."[93] Also, in every work room there were two or three passes "2 feet long and 2 inches wide, maybe 4 inches thick," which workers had to take in order to use the restroom. "Some could not wait and just urinated in the machine room."[94] At some point, Song Feiqing's brother "went to America and saw a [time] clock and brought one back for use. [It] recorded the time for the bathroom. Each worker had a card. When you left the room, you recorded the time on the card and when you came back it would record the time again. If you went to the bathroom a lot it would influence your wage and bonus."[95] During production, supervisors sat on each end of the room and could see every movement of the workers.[96]

Similar rules governed life outside of production as well. For workers who lived in the dormitory, "the lights were turned out at eight or nine o'clock and Pastor Zou, the head of benefits, made inspections. . . . [Workers who lived in the factory] could not just leave at will, but several people went out together and came back together. You couldn't be late. When you went out they recorded your names and why you were going out. If you already went out this week, then next week you couldn't go out. The personnel department also searched people when they got off work, men in one line, women in one line, one person at a time."[97] When you did leave the factory, there were regulations on proper comportment when strolling.[98] Even their health came under scrutiny. Hao Guanyi remembered that "every year or two there was a lung disease examination. If it was discovered, you were fired."[99] There were even rules, twenty of them, for employee group dinners. "Don't yell out for more food, but signal quietly," "sit according to

TABLE 5.1   Dongya Corporation 1943 Employee Stock Ownership Plan

Category of Worker	Number of Shares
Daily workers	1
Monthly workers	2
Yearly workers	3
Lower-level white-collar employees	3
Higher-level white-collar employees	5

Source: Dongya Archives, 1-42-3-06.

your place card and don't move place cards," "during dinner it is permitted to chat casually."[100]

Even when Dongya began distributing shares of company stock to employees in the 1940s, its system reinforced order, rules, and discipline.[101] The number of shares issued to an employee depended on rank and status within the company (see Table 5.1). Employees had to continue working for three years before owning their shares outright and any violation of the many company regulations during that period would result in the three-year clock being reset to zero.[102]

Separate rules governed relations between the sexes and women's behavior. A former worker stated, "Men and women could work together, but could not speak [to each other]. After we moved to the new factory, it was even stricter. Once at the old factory, [a woman worker] was hugged by a male worker. Song Feiqing saw it and hit him twice in the face without even asking his name."[103] Another worker recalled, "one winter evening at about five or six (it was already dark), a machine hurt a woman worker's hand. A male worker wrapped up her hand and was seen by [Song Feiqing] who went over and slapped the [male worker] twice."[104] In addition, women were often required to be single and/or childless.

Wei Yanying entered Dongya as a worker at the age of eighteen after she saw an advertisement stating that the company was looking for unmarried women. Although she had married at sixteen, she lied and said she was single. She later recalled,

When I was working for the personnel department, sadly I often saw women fired after giving birth who came to the personnel department to kowtow [and ask for mercy]. . . . I absolutely did not want to have a

baby, but I was married at sixteen before I entered the factory. . . . I
got pregnant for the first time in 1943 [at the age of twenty]. I was bitter
and afraid. If I gave birth, then my fate of being fired was right before
my eyes. As a result, in order to live, I thought of every possibility to
miscarry. . . . None of them succeeded. I did not want to live and went
to the wall on the side of the river four times thinking that I would
throw myself in and end it all. By the fourth month, although I wrapped
it in a wide white cloth, my stomach was getting fatter and I couldn't
hide it anymore. Then I saw an ad for a clinic . . . that would give abortions. The doctor took advantage of the situation to extort and ask for
a lot of money. I used everything I had. After the abortion, I went back
to work after only one day. But people were already suspicious. Ma
Shouting asked me if I had had an abortion. . . . I hardened myself and
said that I was sick and did not admit to the abortion. Ma Shouting
could not do anything. I went to work as usual. . . . I became pregnant
for a second time in 1944, and I took the same road again.[105]

Granted, her testimony was taken in the 1960s when the Communist government was trying to paint capitalism in a bad light, but the paternalism,
need for control, and desire to regulate women's bodies ring true.

At Dongya there was no sense that family life was separate from work
life. Company representatives even made family visits to survey their living
conditions and problems.[106] On the surface this practice sounds personalistic, but the company's tendency to count and measure still came through.
One report from the 1940s noted, among other things, that 3 percent of
workers thought the corn flour in the cafeteria was not tasty, half of male
workers ran out of money every month, 12 percent had family members
with illness, and 98 percent of women workers were friendly with each
other.[107] Dongya's interests in the private lives of workers ranged from the
trivial to crucial.

Workers did have complaints, but company records indicate that most
did not arise from excessive regulation, but from a sense of irrationality or
unfairness. Sometime in the 1940s the company produced a document to
tell supervisors how to deal with such complaints and those the company
had identified included concerns that daily workers made less money than
monthly or yearly workers and could not get promoted, that technical

workers made disproportionately more than unskilled workers, that food benefits differed for workers whose families could shop at the company co-operative and those who lived in dormitories and ate at the cafeteria for all meals, that staff members did not return the greetings of workers, and that workers from Shandong got special treatment. In general, supervisors were told to explain that the system was fair and that the company would continue to implement its policies. The report also added a moral note to talk to workers about not visiting prostitutes, gambling, or stealing.[108]

Many worker concerns stemmed from inflation, which got progressively worse in the last days of the war. The North China Textile Industry Association published recommendations for compensating and keeping workers at spinning mills. The report noted difficulties in transportation (which kept rural people from traveling to cities to work) and suggested that travel permits could be arranged with the military authorities. It suggested increasing signing bonuses, better compensation for workers, training, propaganda, and grain distribution.[109]

It should be remembered that most Dongya workers were very young. A 1933 newspaper article stated that a third of Dongya workers were children, mostly girls.[110] Although the company later ceased using child labor, in 1936 only a little more than 4 percent of women workers were in the 24–33-year-old age range. Only 2 percent of male workers were over 30. A full third of both men and women workers were in the 18–19-year-old range and half of women were 16–17.[111] This youth reflected in part the company's desire for "uncontaminated" specimens for social engineering. Most of Dongya's workers lacked permanent employment, but were hired on a daily basis giving them fewer benefits and less job security. Statistics compiled by a former Dongya accountant showed that of 1,245 workers in 1944, 88.7 percent were daily workers. Only 99 had annual contracts, and another 41 were employed on a monthly basis.[112]

Industrial Eden

In many ways Song Feiqing was a creature of his times and his generation. Many Chinese industrialists in the 1930s and 1940s adopted new and "scientific" forms of management that drew on international influences, techniques, and methods usually associated with "rational" or "scientific" management.[113] All over the world in the early part of the twentieth century managers turned to new techniques to organize economic activity. "Common to all of these strategies was a rejection of empirical methods based on practice and tradition in favor of methods developed from 'scientific principles' determined by experts. Whether applied to factory work, administration, transportation, or urban planning, these methods were expected to result in greater efficiency and productivity, which would rebound to the benefit of employers, workers, and consumers." Barbara Weinstein divides techniques of scientific management into three types. The first type, Taylorism, argued for "the simplification of tasks and the individualization of the labor force." The second, Fordism, advocated the need for workers to have "proper moral and social values and an internalized sense of discipline to perform well in the new industrial environment." Finally, a third "source of ideas that helped form the rationalization movement was the field of industrial or applied psychology . . . [where] psychologists, educators, and other professionals in Europe and the United States began advocating various 'scientific' methods of testing for job selection and orientation in the early twentieth century."[114] Song Feiqing used all three of these methods and a former Dongya executive specifically remembered that Fordism influenced Song.[115]

Mark Frazier has suggested that the provision of nonwage benefits across different regimes in China may show the influence of Confucian paternalism, but this kind of welfare capitalism had been popular in the West and there is no doubt that Dongya managers were well aware of such foreign models.[116] The Larkin Company of Buffalo, New York, for example, gave tours that "emphasized Larkin's modern scientific and production methods and praised the company's beneficence toward employees . . . such as shorter hours, better lighting, purer air and water, free noontime coffee and music, and the cordial employee relations that made the system function smoothly." Like Dongya, Larkin had an employee newsletter and employee sporting events and clubs and, more important, "it also tried to instill in employees an unquestioned work ethic as they carried out their routine daily tasks within Larkin's tightly controlled management system. 'Carrot and stick' initiatives intersected successfully to fulfill the company goals of efficiency and productivity."[117]

Although there was nothing particularly Chinese about scientific management or welfare capitalism, both resonated well with Confucian virtues and the Dongya Corporation freely combined foreign and Chinese concepts into a seamless whole. Dongya and other large Chinese companies established these kinds of "'enterprise communities' in which communal and paternalistic norms were injected into personnel departments and employee training protocols" throughout the 1930s and 1940s.[118] While the international influence on people like Song Feiqing was clear, other scholars trace the development of such enterprise communities to dependence on workplace authorities that grew out of native-place-based business organization and the effects of labor conflict that resulted from the dominance of a Communist-organized "aristocracy of labor," hence its guildlike characteristics.[119] Whatever their roots, these enterprise communities in the 1930s and 1940s helped lay the foundation for a particularly Chinese form of economic and social organization that arose in the 1950s, the work unit, or *danwei*, which combined economic production and communal living.[120]

Unlike the public-owned Communist *danwei* of the postrevolutionary period, however, Dongya was a private enterprise trying to carve out space in an increasingly state-dominated economy geared toward wartime mobilization. Was the Dongya spirit strong enough to create Eden amid the chaos of republican-period Tianjin? Did it carve out a space of safety and modernity? Did it transform the workers and staff who composed its denizens? Even the most charitable evaluation must conclude that, at best, Industrial Eden within the firm was both incomplete and under siege.

The attempts to build that protective bubble had been financed by a mix of production for China's urban consumer culture and also for the Japanese war machine. As World War II ground to an end and the Japanese finally surrendered, many at Dongya looked ahead to a chance to thrive and express the principles of Dongya spirit without the shadow of the occupation and war. The postwar period, however, would come to test sorely the precepts on which Song Feiqing founded the transformative corporation.

6 The Postwar Nationalists' Unresponsive Developmental State

AFTER JAPAN SURRENDERED in August 1945, Song Feiqing and several other industrialists headed to the Nationalist's wartime capital in Chongqing to reestablish ties with the regime there. They must have had some success currying favor with Nationalist officials because they returned to Tianjin on the same airplane as Tianjin's new mayor Zhang Ting'e.[1] One former company employee recounted that during Song's time in Chongqing, when Nationalist officials asked him what he had hoarded during the occupation, Song said, "I hoarded talent."[2] The question itself indicates great interest on the part of the Nationalists in the activities that had taken place under the Japanese occupation and it especially pointed to the state's desire to locate and allocate resources. As for Song's answer, his focus on the company's employees deflected attention from Dongya's relations with the Japanese occupation state and the "economy of things," while trumpeting the nature of Dongya as a transformative corporation, a cradle of talent, and a possible model for the postwar period.

Dongya was in a good position to take advantage of peace. The company had three potential product lines, wool yarn, gunnysacks, and medicine, and the postwar period promised to renew prospects for the kinds of urban consumer products in which Dongya specialized. Dongya had refined its systems of personnel management and discipline in a manner that managers hoped would blossom without the restrictions and chaos of war. Song Feiqing had no way of knowing that the toxic remnants of the war with Japan would combine with the stresses of civil war between the Nationalists and Communists to limit these bright prospects. From the retrospect of the postwar strife, the first six years under the Japanese occupation government would come to seem like a peaceful time of opportunity when a little bribery and something as banal as a gunnysack could keep Dongya stable and prosperous. In addition, although much of the coming strife at Dongya had roots in the postwar toxic environment, much of it also came from within the company. Under constant financial stress, the Industrial Eden built with such care proved to be partly a façade made possible by wartime prosperity.

Limping into Peace

The Japanese surrender came as a great relief to Dongya managers, who immediately began to celebrate the war's end, while they simultaneously started the process of reshaping the company's narrative to bury the war-profiteering past. In an announcement to employees on 18 August, the company declared that through eight years of bitterness and pain, "the entire body of employees had worked with one heart and struggled with their last breath to maintain everyone's livelihood. . . . Also, in this way we maintained a little of our nation's essence [*yuanqi*]." This announcement set the tone for the postwar narrative of Dongya under the occupation. Eliding the first six years of prosperity under the occupation, company managers now focused on a tale of hardship and woe in which they struggled to maintain China's national essence. The company would now, the announcement continued, "use production to help the advancement of society toward a bright future." As usual, social goals and the company's moral standing took precedence over profits in public narratives.

To celebrate, the company distributed sugar, white flour, sorghum, and coal to all of its employees.[3] The company held a celebratory event where employees marched, the Dongya choir sang, and company managers extolled the company's prospects. Decades later Shi Shaodong remembered the employees singing together as "the hearts of a thousand people bound together, love—love for the factory, love for colleagues, love for society, love for the country, great love!"[4] Two months after this celebration, advertisements featuring the full range of Dongya products, wool knitting yarn, gunnysacks, and medicine, began to appear in the newly reestablished

Dagong bao newspaper. The first ad proudly referred to Dongya's long history and large size, extolling the company's "modernized equipment and scientific management."[5] The promise of peace seemed endlessly bright.

Reality would prove much darker, however. Internal company documents showed a stark and sober assessment of Dongya's position. Song Feiqing reported to the board of directors that in all of 1945, the company had produced only 758,000 gunnysacks, half of the wartime peak in 1943, and it spun 21,000 pounds of wool yarn, a miniscule fraction of prewar production. Of all its products, only medicine saw production increases in the early postwar period, as the chemical factory founded late in the war had finally begun to ramp up operations, but even that would not last.[6] As for the modern equipment mentioned in Dongya advertising, an internal company document stated that its equipment could not compare to that of foreign companies, and "as for other aspects such as the limited number of products, limited production capacity, as well as deficiencies in management and benefits, we are less than first-rank world companies."[7]

The last line of the selection from the report quoted here is particularly telling to understand the mind-set of Dongya managers. The company's advantages in the economy of things of the wartime period had protected Dongya in many ways, and its monopoly position in jute acquisition and production of gunnysacks had provided safety and security. Dongya managers could remember their experience in the 1930s of competition with foreign companies like Patons and Baldwins, however, and they knew that without the wartime monopoly protection they would have to be able to compete with "first-rank world companies." In fact, foreign goods entered Tianjin markets rapidly during the postwar period, and Dongya managers realized that foreign-spun knitting yarn was of higher quality than their own, but sold for only two-thirds of their price.[8]

In spite of worries about aging, substandard equipment, Dongya managers proceeded to plan the creation of a first-rank world company. Under the dual assumptions that the postwar developmental state would turn to the private sector for economic revival and that the state would assist the private sector in that pursuit, Dongya drafted a plan for the Nationalist government that both justified company actions under occupation during the war and asked the government for support for a massive expansion of Dongya into a huge conglomerate. Echoing the company's announcement to employees after the Japanese surrender, the report glossed over the prosperity of the first six years of occupation and focused on hardship. "Without care for any difficulty, under the oppression of the power of the invaders, we maintained our independence, protected a little of our country's essence and besides staying alive, we moved forward a little." Looking forward to an active developmental state, the report pleaded, "At this time of national reconstruction, production is in urgent need of advance, resources in urgent need of opening up."[9] Dongya managers clearly hoped a revived Nationalist state would support the company's idealistic developmental goals.

In the environment of possibility during the early postwar period, Dongya's personnel policies proceeded as if a new era of Industrial Eden had dawned. The company rented a YMCA villa in the mountains west of Beijing and gave its employees vacations there on a rotating basis to "cultivate and build the body." Consistent with the disciplinary proclivities of the company, "the programs of the vacation were strictly set by regulation. Eating and drinking was on schedule. . . . Changing the program was prohibited as was staying lazily behind in the villa [and not partaking in group activities]." One employee came home a day early, and "Song Feiqing immediately told him to go back and come back the next day at the appointed time . . . you had to obey the regulations regardless whether things were big or small. Although it was vacation, it still had its purpose that had to be achieved." Without any sense of irony, Shi Shaodong remembered that "if everyone acted freely then that would violate the true meaning of vacation."[10]

As Dongya managers tried to put the war behind them, nagging problems remained. The Nationalist technocracy lost no time in extending its reach into newly reoccupied Tianjin. In March of 1946, the health department conducted an investigation to see if Dongya's chemical factory had complied with regulations. It is interesting to note that the letter from this low-level Nationalist functionary pointed to Dongya's profits during the war.[11] The interest of public health inspectors in Dongya's wartime profits betrays a possible, more sinister purpose in their investigation of Dongya. Perhaps any war profiteer was ripe for exploitation and the "investigation" was simply an opportunity to extort bribes. In a more direct threat, longtime Dongya backer Sun Tongxuan, former subordinate of Han Fuju and husband of Dongya shareholder and landlord Zhang Huizhong, directly accused Song Feiqing of war profiteering and collaborating.[12] According to one account, Nationalist authorities arrested Song Feiqing briefly, but Mayor Zhang Ting'e intervened and Song was released without further ado.[13] When Song Feiqing's name appeared on the list of candidates to represent the Tianjin Chamber of Commerce in the new National Assembly in March of 1946, Sun wrote a scathing letter saying Song Feiqing had a "disregard for law and morality." Sun asked that Song be arrested and punished and that his qualification for election to the National Assembly be canceled. By the time the assembly election commission received Sun's complaint, however, the election was over and Song Feiqing had not received enough votes to join the assembly. As a result the election commission simply let the matter drop.[14] Nonetheless it is clear that the intervening war years had poisoned the patronage networks that had been involved in the company's founding.

In the clear, Song Feiqing went ahead with the first steps for plans to expand Dongya into a huge conglomerate. The company called a shareholders' meeting for 30 June 1946.[15] Dongya dropped the words "woolen mill" from its name and became simply the Tianjin Dongya Enterprise Co., Ltd. (Tianjin Dongya qiye gufen youxian gongsi). In addition, Dongya increased its capital once again, this time from 20 million to 300 million yuan. In a practice that had become customary during the war, Dongya offered the new shares to existing shareholders first.[16]

The vast sum raised in this capital issue is a little misleading because of inflation, which began under the occupation regime, exploded during the last years of the war, and continued to rage when the Nationalists took over. Prices had tripled in 1943, increased by another factor of five in 1944, another factor of almost twelve times in 1945, and another factor of five again in 1946. Thus the 300 million yuan in capital represented less than seventy thousand yuan in 1937 terms. Although Dongya had increased its capital base by a factor of fifteen, it was not even keeping up with inflation. Even so, the ease with which Dongya continued to raise capital testifies to the faith that investors had in the company's ability to profit in the postwar world. It was not clear that wool knitting yarn would be the source of those profits, however, and at the end of 1946 Dongya was not producing any wool yarn because of a shortage of raw materials.[17]

At the same time, Dongya instituted a system whereby profits would be divided between worker bonuses and shareholder dividends.[18] On the surface at least, it appeared that Dongya's shareholders and workers both would benefit from the company's success, and, echoing the lyrics of the wartime company song, that capital and labor came together in cooperation under the scientific management of Dongya executives. In truth, however, the biggest threat to Dongya came from a dissatisfied labor force.

Trouble in Eden

For a company known for its benevolent treatment of employees, it seems surprising that labor unrest became Dongya's number one problem in the postwar period. There is considerable evidence that Dongya did treat its employees better than most factories in Tianjin. During the occupation, Dongya had a ten-hour day, making shifts there shorter than other woolen mills in Tianjin, and it provided lunch to its workers.[19] In the postwar period, although the data is not conclusive because of the way statistics were reported, including food, clothing, and fuel subsidies, Dongya seemed to have the highest wages out of the four largest textile firms in Tianjin.[20] When inflation eroded standards of living, however, many workers demonstrated themselves to be no more committed to Dongya and its ideals than workers at other factories.[21] One former Dongya executive attributed the unrest to the presence of large numbers of new and low-skilled workers— many hired during the good years of the war—combined with a new Nationalist-government-organized union formed by local government and party officials early in the postwar period.[22]

The new union directed the first worker dispute at Dongya in January 1946, just a few months after Japanese surrender. Workers demanded three bags of flour, three lengths of cloth, and two pairs of socks each as recompense for unfairnesses that had developed during the Japanese occupation.[23] Although the company offered workers one bag of flour and two lengths of cloth, worker protests persisted. Apparently angry and unable to operate the company as he wished, Song Feiqing submitted his resignation to Dongya's board of directors.[24] Resignations were a tried and true technique of negotiation in Chinese business, and it was unlikely that Song was ready to give up on his company so easily. Nonetheless, the situation at the factory was extremely volatile. During one confrontation, workers became violent and even beat up the official representative of the municipal government's Social Bureau.[25] In Song's absence, the board of directors quickly capitulated and agreed to worker demands after a full-scale strike.[26] Workers returned to their posts and Song Feiqing returned to Dongya, but any illusion that workers and Dongya management remained on friendly terms lay shattered.

The fallout from the strike created suspicion and tension outside and inside Dongya. The Tianjin police tried but were never able to identify the culprits who had beaten the city official. In addition, the police conducted an investigation that concluded that some of the workers who had participated in the strike were actually outside agitators.[27] Within Dongya, the new union used its victory to flex its muscles among Dongya's workers and it held back one bag of flour from every worker who had not joined the union prior to the strike.[28] This created hard feelings among workers and eventually, the union had to make concessions to the late joiners. Even with resolution of this dispute, the union betrayed nervousness about the commitment of Dongya's workforce. The union's announcement of resolution of the dispute urged union members to "put their shoulders to the grindstone, and work hard to produce for society's benefit and for the construction of the nation."[29] The union, which had stood firm in its demands only two months before, now seemed suspicious of its own membership, perhaps because worker unproductivity had driven gunnysack production to record-low levels. At the same time, the union's references to society and the nation echoed the moral nature of the public narrative of Dongya management by portraying business operations as having social and nationalist rather than financial goals.

In May of 1946, with levels of production so low Dongya could not break even, and in response to further inflation, the Dongya Corporation worked out an agreement for a cost-of-living supplement for workers and a shift from hourly wages to a piece-rate system intended to force workers to increase production. Management clearly hoped that the cost-of-living subsidy would mitigate worker concerns over moving to a piece-rate system in which workers only got paid for work completed.[30] The piece-rate system would be contentious within Dongya for some time, and after the announcement of the new pay scheme, gunnysack production at Dongya increased for only seven days before dropping below sustainable levels once again in early June.[31]

As spring turned to summer in 1946, rampant inflation created an unstable economic atmosphere and most companies in Tianjin experienced some kind of labor dispute.[32] Dongya was no exception. The union demanded increased wages and with mediation from city government bureaus, Dongya and the union came to yet another agreement on 20 June where workers received a small increase in their piece-rate pay.[33] This agreement, however, did not resolve worker dissatisfaction. A report from the Tianjin Municipal Social Bureau only ten days later noted that workers had engaged in a work slowdown and that Dongya managers had insisted they could make no further concessions.[34]

A somewhat later letter from Dongya to the Tianjin mayor asking for help outlined management's view of the situation and blamed most of the trouble on the union by claiming that "workers no longer obey the instructions of managers and sometimes use slogans 'to overthrow and uproot such-and-such a manager' . . . [including] the weaving department manager Chen Yadong [who] was forced to leave the factory several months ago and still has not returned . . . workers come and go at will during work time, laugh and talk, read, sleep . . . or everyone stops work, turns out the lights and sleeps quietly for as much as three hours." According to the company, workers had become "rude and unreasonable," and they worried about the possibility of violence. Problems had gotten so bad that production "has been very low . . . losses have been great."[35] Ever committed to scientific measurement, company management included a chart with the letter showing that Dongya had not achieved a minimum sustainable level of gunnysack production once in the five previous months.

On 5 July Dongya presented an ultimatum to workers: return to work, or there will be no July wages. Managers asked workers to consider the "company's current difficulties and the country's industrial crisis."[36] When this ultimatum did not get employees back to work, Dongya managers issued a plaintive plea for workers to return to work as normal. The request pointed out the need to compete in the international environment because "the gunnysacks of this company cannot compete with foreign goods either in quality or price." Managers even appealed to workers' sense of fairness and appreciation of Dongya's personnel policies, pointing out that in the past remuneration had been higher at Dongya than at other companies and that "all staff and workers' benefits and facilities were the best possible . . . and all were better than other factories. . . . The company and employees rely on each other like lips and teeth, 'without workers, there is no factory, without a factory, there are no workers.'"[37]

Appeals to patriotism, the demands of international competition, and reminders to workers of the benefits of the transformative corporation's Industrial Eden all fell on deaf ears. On 12 July Mayor Zhang himself visited Dongya and exhorted workers to accept the new piece rates, but his words were to no avail.[38] Rifts existed not only between management and workers, but among the workers themselves. At one point, Dongya's union leaders submitted their resignations to the city's Social Bureau because "they had been attacked" by other workers.[39] On 24 July, company management was still trying to get its employees back to work.[40] Still, Dongya's labor problems continued, as the company outlined in a letter to the mayor of Tianjin, saying they had repeatedly announced his order to return to work with no results. The mayor, Dongya managers hoped, would help in case "there is conflict or other unanticipated matters."[41]

Eventually Dongya did implement the piece-rate system and sometime in the fall of 1946 workers returned to their jobs.[42] The manager who had been driven from the factory by worker attacks returned and decades later he recalled that "the piece-rate system turned around the chaos on the production line and production became more regular. According to statistics, the original production rate was 65 percent [of capacity]. After the piece-rate method, it increased to 98 percent."[43]

Even with the strike apparently settled, Dongya managers faced enormous problems in the postwar environment. Dongya continued to struggle to get adequate supplies of wool so that yarn spinning operations could begin again. In August the Nationalist government imported eight hundred bales of Australian wool with the intent of selling it to four private factories in Tianjin and Beiping, Dongya included. But, a *Dagong bao* report concluded, at 2,400 yuan per pound, the price asked by the government was almost twice that of market prices available from foreign merchants in Tianjin who could offer wool for sale at only 1,300 yuan per pound.[44] That wool import debacle represented in concrete terms a general feeling that the Nationalist government was not dealing with its developmental responsibilities in an effective manner.

As a large, private company, Dongya had become the exception in Tianjin. The Japanese had confiscated most large industrial enterprises in the city, and at the end of the war, the Nationalist state took over those factories as enemy property. Thus by 1946 much of Tianjin industry was actually state-owned and state-run. Across China the state's National Resources Commission alone controlled over one hundred large enterprises with 172,000 employees.[45] In fact, the remnants of war shaped much of the government's economic policy. For example, even as inflation raged and the crisis became acute, an official from the Economics Ministry stated that lending from government banks could begin only when companies had completed registration procedures to prove they were not the property of the wartime puppet regimes.[46] Clearly, the Nationalist developmental state remained stalled in a mire of incompetence, financial crisis, and obsession with finding wartime collaborators with the Japanese.

To be fair, the government was not completely ineffectual. The Central Trust provided financing to allow Dongya to import wool in August of 1946 at about the same time the strike ended.[47] Dongya subsequently announced the resumption of wool yarn production in a series of advertisements in late August 1946. "Diyang brand wool yarn," the ad proclaimed, "an old friend longed for by the masses from whom it has been separated for several years."[48] The government also assisted with Dongya's public relations campaign at the end of 1946. A journal linked to the local Nationalist government featured a profile of Dongya in its initial issue in November of that year. The result was a paean to the company's scientific management and social responsibility. By then, the narrative of Dongya's history had taken a predictable form. Seeing that reliance on exports harmed China's national essence (*guojia yuanqi*), Song Feiqing founded the Dongya Corporation, which succeeded through hard work and science. At the same time, the company was as concerned about public welfare (*gongyi*) as production and profits.[49] A second profile appeared in another government-affiliated journal, the *Hebei Provincial Bank Economic Bimonthly*. This article also discussed Dongya's enlightened, scientific, and hygienic personnel policies. It ended with the statement that the company can serve as a model for the ideal Chinese light industry company. "Now with victory in the anti-Japanese war, construction of China has begun, it is deeply hoped that [Dongya] will continue to produce excellence, work for advancement, and establish a foundation for a long-term success which provides a model of industrial development."[50]

Just as the Nationalist developmental state was creaking into action with loans and positive publicity to assist Dongya, in September workers went on strike again because China Cotton (a government-run firm) and Renli Wool (a private carpet company) had both issued bonuses to their workers for the upcoming Mid-Autumn Festival.[51] On 8 September, Dongya workers sent union representatives to present demands, but managers declined saying that it was impossible to issue bonuses because of accumulated losses. The next day workers resumed their demands and Dongya agreed to pay 5,000 yuan to each worker for "moon cake expenses" for the upcoming holiday. Apparently some workers accepted this offer and collected their money, but others felt it was too little. The unsatisfied workers tried to block their colleagues from collecting bonuses and the situation became chaotic. Mediators sent by the local authorities convinced workers to calm down and go home for Mid-Autumn Festival the next day, saying that negotiations would continue after the holiday.[52]

A worker named Hao Guanyi interviewed in the 1960s, remembered it this way:

> The August Moon Festival regulations were half a *jin* of moon cakes, 1 towel, and 4 pears. That year they didn't give us things, just 5,000 yuan. 5,000 yuan couldn't buy a half *jin* of moon cakes, a towel, and 4 pears. We struck. . . . The local police chief told us to go back [home] and enjoy the festival. . . . The next day they didn't call us to work. The capitalist [Song Feiqing] asked the police, military, and military police to set up guns at the Dongya's back gate [to lock us out]. Several hundred of us went to the city government to petition. . . . Three days later, there were three announcements that the strike would be handled according to martial law. The announcement suppressed everyone's [enthusiasm] and [we] went to work.[53]

Use of the word "capitalist" to describe Song Feiqing here may refer to vocabulary Hao learned later after the Communist revolution and used in his 1964 oral history, so it may not have been used at the time. Nonetheless, the stark portrayal of conflict between labor and management is still telling of growing rifts at Dongya.

Later opinions differed on whether the police or Dongya managers ordered the lockout after the strike.[54] Either way, both Dongya and city authorities took a much harder line than in the previous two worker actions of that year. Dongya's union reported to the Municipal Social Bureau that in talks with workers Song Feiqing had been "rude and abusive" and had called for disbandment of the union.[55] In addition, city officials had infiltrated the workers and by the morning after, a report from the Three People's Principles Youth League was on Mayor Zhang's desk, claiming that "among the workers there are manipulators and schemers. They have a political cast and a list of suspects is attached."[56] At a time of rising conflict between the Nationalist and Communist parties, the phrases "manipulators and schemers" with a "political cast" were likely code for Communists or Communist sympathizers. The use of such innuendo tells us much about the toxic atmosphere in North China, where the Nationalist state blamed its enemies rather than the failure of its own developmental policies for the economic chaos of the time.

On 13 September, the combined Nationalist Party, government, and army jointly declared the Dongya strike an illegal work action. No increase in the Mid-Autumn Festival bonus was offered and the government issued a deadline by which workers had to claim it or otherwise give up their rights to any bonus at all.[57] The next day, the Tianjin police command issued the following warning: "Clearly there are unworthy people who are making trouble and scheming outside the tracks and outside the law . . . from now on elements who make trouble in factories that give rise to worker actions will be strictly punished."[58] Under the full weight of the coercive power of the state, Dongya workers fell into line and returned to work on the morning of 14 September. The extent to which the government had taken control of labor policy became clear when Dongya managers wrote the police after the strike asking how to calculate wages during the work stoppage.[59] Clearly a new era of management had dawned in the postwar period when government took an active role in everyday management of private companies.

Throughout much of the labor unrest, Song Feiqing had remained in the background and let his executives negotiate with the factory's workers and government representatives. In fact, at one point workers demanded the right to negotiate with Song Feiqing himself, but then heard news that he had gone to Beiping and disappeared.[60] They elected worker representatives to go look for him and after inquiring with many friends and family members found him in a hospital. From his hospital bed, he lectured the workers about the fact that, "during the eight years of the anti-Japanese war, the company went through many difficulties, but we made our utmost effort to take care of the living requirements of employees and workers. This is iron-clad fact and there is not a worker or employee who will deny it. . . . Everyday we set an example for society and work for the construction of the nation, and a new mission for 'Dongya Spirit.' There is nothing left of this, and it truly makes one feel depressed . . . [I'm] worn down."[61]

Song's appeal to the worker representatives rested on the moral principles of Industrial Eden. Nearly a year of worker unrest, however, showed the extent to which workers had rejected the basic tenets of Song's management philosophy. Part of the problem lay with the fact that the policies of the transformative corporation had been applied unequally among workers. At Dongya by the 1940s, Hebei natives usually outnumbered Shandong natives by about two to one among newly hired employees, but there was widespread feeling that Song Feiqing's Shandong compatriots received special treatment. The retired executive Song Yuzhan remembered that worker strife during the strikes of 1946 came primarily between groups of Shandong workers loyal to Song Feiqing and the Song family and Hebei workers who were not.[62] In fact, all but one of the thirteen suspected political agitators reported to the mayor's office by the Youth League came from Hebei or Tianjin. In addition, most did not live within the factory and thus had less access to the benevolent side of Industrial Eden.[63] In yet another line of division, workers later testified to conflict between permanent and temporary employees in their struggles for higher pay."[64] Dongya had come to rely more and more on temporary employees who did not receive the full warmth of the embrace of the transformative corporation.

Even Shandong workers were not completely loyal, however. A former executive recalled that most workers from rural areas appreciated Dongya's relatively high level of pay and benefits, but that some longtime Shandong workers had forgotten what conditions in the countryside were like. As a result, Song Feiqing would occasionally send them back to Shandong to visit so they could remember the rural poverty from which they came and thus appreciate life at Dongya.[65]

In spite of the internal tensions among workers, Song Feiqing and Dongya's other managers persevered. In September the company announced a new medicinal product from its chemical division, "Dongya Skin Balm" for curing athlete's foot and other conditions.[66] With Australian wool in short supply, Dongya introduced its "special edition" wool yarn at the end of 1946 made out of domestic wool.[67] In spite of Dongya's attempt to continue producing and selling consumer products, as 1946 came to an end, the sense of crisis in Tianjin was palpable. Prices soared, industry stagnated, and communication with much of the country was difficult because of incessant civil war between the Nationalists and Communists. A *Dagong bao* editorial called on the government to rescue Tianjin industry.[68] A report from a British diplomat noted electricity blackouts, strikes for ever-higher wages, failure of the low salaries of civil servants and educators to keep pace with the skyrocketing prices, a new harbor that lacks tugs and lighters, import and export restrictions that hamper free trade, coal shortages, incompetent government attempts to distribute coal, "communications left miraculously intact by the Japanese and equally miraculously torn to bits since the Japanese surrender and the roads, once the pride of Tientsin now becoming medieval through neglect."[69]

At the end of December, China's central bank announced a 1.7 trillion yuan loan package to rescue North China industry.[70] Nonetheless, the crisis was acute and it was clear that the government was more interested in developing the lower Yangzi region than the north. As a result, Dongya began plans to open a subsidiary in Shanghai.[71] To help workers with the unstable situation, Dongya provided employees each day with eight *jin* of coal, two *jin* of corn flour, one *jin* of millet, and one *jin* of soybeans.[72] The economy of things clearly had not died with the end of the war. In a reminder of the year's work stoppages and strikes, management docked year-end bonuses for every day workers missed over the course of the year.[73] In perhaps the clearest indication of the end of the new dawn for the transformative corporation, Dongya abandoned its policy of providing employees with vacations at the villa in the mountains near Beijing. As Shi Shaodong recalled, "The beautiful plan drafted with such arduousness disappeared without a trace just like a 'Golden Millet Dream.'"[74]

Eye of the Storm

After the turmoil of 1946, Dongya returned to some version of normalcy in the first half of 1947; however, almost every bit of good news coincided with or followed some bad news. Thus the eye of the storm makes an apt metaphor. There was only the sense of normalcy, not normalcy itself, and the raging storm impinged on that normalcy with discouraging regularity.

Part of the upturn at the beginning of 1947 came from state help when the government-run Central Trust signed a contract to provide Dongya 380 million yuan to help fund jute purchases.[75] The Nationalist state lacked a coherent program of developmental assistance, however, and the government's desperate need for revenue led to predatory behavior toward business by other parts of the regime. For example, the government tax office provided Dongya with a "voluntary" sample letter asking it to sign a pledge that company assets would guarantee the payment of taxes and any penalties for unpaid taxes. Dongya refused, but the tax office's turn to the economy of things as recourse in tax collection shows how tenuous government finances remained.[76]

Dongya began issuing a spate of publications clearly intended to put the best face possible on the company's condition. It published a song collection, which included yet a third edition of its official "Factory Song." As with earlier versions, the lyrics pointed to a vision of an Industrial Eden, but unlike the wartime version, the new lyrics once again associated industry and patriotism. One line read, "Our workers love the Dongya Corporation and unite with a fearless spirit to work hard to produce wool products and together hope for an early rebirth of China."[77] Unfortunately, it is impossible to know what workers—who had been striking only a few months earlier and who had even driven a supervisor off the factory grounds—thought when they sang such lyrics at company gatherings. Most extravagantly, the company published its first annual report since 1941 as a means of marking the name change of the company and as a celebration of the firm's fifteenth anniversary.

This publication announced a new corporate structure to the world. Dongya was now to be a multiple-product conglomerate, not just a woolen mill. Most important, in an effort to build close relations with the Nationalist regime, Dongya had made the president of the Hebei Provincial Bank,

Ji Dianchuan, the new chairman of the board. Wang Yusheng, whose connections to the politicians active in the occupation government had helped
Dongya during the war, was demoted from chairman to ordinary board
member. In a nod to the new postwar primacy of the United States, Fu
Jingbo, identified as personal adviser to the U.S. ambassador to China, became a new standing director. At the same time, Han Fuju's son remained
on the board as a sign of some continuity with old networks.[78]

Besides this new structure, however, any reader of the 1947 report could
compare this to prewar- and occupation-period publications and think that
the Industrial Eden of the developmental corporation was alive and well
at Dongya. The factory precept "do unto others as you would have them
do unto you" appeared opposite the table of contents and the factory song
came next. In perhaps a subtle reference to the strife of the previous year,
another line of lyrics read, "those who do not wait for orders but go to work
on their own are the backbone elements." There are a few references to
World War II as well. The preface by Song Feiqing describes the eight years
under Japanese occupation as a miserable time, "difficult to describe and
undesirable to recollect." In addition some Dongya employees put on a play
celebrating anti-Japanese patriotism during the war and making the company's revision of wartime history complete. Mostly, the report, as with
earlier Dongya publications, celebrated the pillars of the transformative
corporation: production of goods, scientific management, and benevolent
labor practices. As usual, the report reveled in the grimy aesthetic of industry under the assumption that industry was beautiful in its own right.
Even though yarn production had remained anemic, yarn and wool products took pride of place well before gunnysacks and medicine. In the ideal,
at least, Butting Ram yarn and modern consumer culture were still the
mainstay of the company. As well, at least a quarter of the report was devoted to employee benefits including the school for employee children, the
company clinic, dormitories, clubs, and so on. There was, for example, a
picture of the employee cafeteria with the slogan "Christian Spirit, Military Discipline" clearly visible on the far wall.[79]

A Dongya songbook published at the time of the 1947 celebration showed
how Dongya managers saw the factory's place in China and the workers'
place in the factory. It began with the national anthem and other patriotic
songs, followed by Dongya company songs, Dongya Elementary School

songs, songs used at rituals like marriage, social songs, seasonal songs, songs for cultivation, and folk songs. Among the Dongya songs, "Advance Dongya" had a typical lyric which combined the industrial aesthetic with Dongya disciplined modernity. The lyric began, "taking up our steel hammers, putting on our uniforms, we walk to the workplace. Obedience, strict adherence to regulations, life free, happy, and ideal. Everyone does his best and gives his most with a mission on his shoulders." In this vision, freedom and happiness came as a result of work, obedience, and a fully regulated life.[80]

Even if the orderly and united Dongya portrayed in these publications existed, as it did not, the economic and political environment outside of the factory remained toxic enough to poison even the best organization. Shi Shaodong recounted a humorous anecdote that showed the enormous gap between the ideals of Industrial Eden and the noxious environment of the civil war period. One day, members of the Dongya photography club went to the Tianjin railway station to photograph trains, but railway security officers figured they were Communist spies and arrested them. "No matter how they explained themselves, they couldn't dispel suspicions." No one believed that factory workers would have an interest in photography, much less in the industrial aesthetic of a train station. Finally, the workers got a call through to Dongya, which dispatched Shi to handle the matter and he used a connection at the railway to convince security of their innocence.[81]

In other examples of the toxic environment of the times, newspaper and British consular reports noted a litany of problems, especially food price increases in January ranging from 15 to 180 percent. In signs of the restless nature of the city, the government trained and deployed "a further batch of 3,000 members of the local militia," executed an official for stealing government property, and conducted house-to-house searches throughout the city looking for concealed weapons or opium. In addition, Communist activities in the interior had further interrupted railway communications. By March, the cost of living had risen another 53 percent, and the Tianjin government was strictly enforcing an 11:00 p.m. to 6:00 a.m. curfew, shooting all armed robbers and gun dealers, planning to issue identity cards, building pillboxes in the suburbs to defend the city, and dealing with refugees fleeing from the fighting with the Communists in the countryside.[82]

Under such conditions, Tianjin's workers remained understandably less than fully committed to their jobs, and Dongya's labor problems still festered. A British diplomat reported that an executive of the Dongya Corporation (Song Feiqing?) had confided that "with the same staff as he employed before the War the present output of the Mills was only about 30% of the pre-war standard." Dongya was not alone and the report went on to note other employers estimated "their output at varying levels up to 50%."[83] In February, the city government ordered Dongya to read and respond to a four-point demand from the company's union asking that workers absent the previous year be allowed to collect their 30,000 yuan cost-of-living subsidy and that workers who had been let go for "small violations" of factory rules be rehired.[84] Dongya's response gave short shrift to union demands and insisted that the company "has only had an attitude of cooperation with the union no matter how the union has acted. This company has always supported fairness and has maintained uprightness."[85]

Price increases of 50 percent during the second half of April and 93 percent in May from April continued to place pressure on the standards of living of workers. C. S. Whitamore, the British Consul General in Tianjin, reported that even when "the Social Affairs Bureau later obtained the agreement of the big flour concerns to maintain the price of flour at $80,000 per bag . . . by the end of the month a bag of flour was selling at $150,000." Industry was at a virtual standstill and "such limited funds as the authorities can spare for imports are being monopolized by the Central Trust and other similar government sponsored organisations." Tianjin residents inadvertently learned how close the Communists had come to the city when the Nationalists reported recapture of a town "only thirty miles west of Tientsin [which] has been in Communist hands for over a year."[86] *Dagong bao* reported that the Communists threatened the outskirts of Tianjin.[87] Shortages in the market and rampant inflation led to the rise of a barter economy in which even government organs took part, and one bureau agreed with the Tianjin grain merchants' guild to swap much-needed gunnysacks for grain.[88]

Even amid such chaotic conditions, Dongya tried to maintain a façade of normalcy. It began publication of a newsletter called the *Voice of Dongya* (*Dongya Sheng*) as if sheer willpower could create, or re-create, the protected and orderly space of an Industrial Eden within the walls of the factory. Some of the articles in the *Voice of Dongya* hinted at the company's troubles. One of the articles in the first issue dealt with increasing the speed of work by Dongya employees. Another article frankly acknowledged that "in the last few years we have worked hard in pursuit of scientific management, but we are obstructed by the environment and finances, so it has not been completely successful."[89] Likewise, in a clear response to the labor strife at Dongya, Song Feiqing published his famous essay "Labor and Capital Are on the Same Side" in the second issue of the newsletter.[90] Mostly, however, the *Voice of Dongya* was filled with cheerful and newsy articles celebrating the unity and cohesion of the transformative corporation. For example, in June four employees got married in Dongya's first group marriage ceremony on company premises.[91] In September there was a conversation about science and religion, and in October company employees gave a performance in honor of National Day.[92]

Dongya's celebration of its fifteenth anniversary in July presented a positively jubilant face to the public. The story of the celebration printed in *Dagong bao* showed no signs of the struggles of the factory and reported that more than a thousand guests, including famous leaders of industry, business, and finance, saw that "employees of the company were unusually happy and excited. Besides those assigned to take care of guests, employees stayed at their posts and worked as normal in preparation for guests to observe [production in process] . . . the whole body of employees . . . embroidered a flag for President Song and each vice president with 'Gongzhu Dongya' [meritorious work for Dongya] on one side."[93] This description of the anniversary celebration portrayed a close and emotional relationship between labor and management, where workers were unusually happy, both at their posts showing production in action and in presenting gifts to Song Feiqing and other Dongya executives. Close readers of the article, however, could have noticed one sign of trouble. The article noted that because of the unstable situation, Dongya could no longer sell yarn in North China and it was all shipped to the relatively more prosperous Shanghai for sale.

Scattered sources also hint that the picture of happy and industrious workers was perhaps more fiction than truth. In spite of receiving higher compensation than most textile factories in Tianjin, some Dongya workers still missed enough work over the course of 1947 to warrant a reduction in commodities issued to employees such as wool or sugar.[94] At the same time, articles published in the *Voice of Dongya* over the summer of 1947 also hinted at tensions under the surface. Two articles lectured employees that "the larger the organization, the stricter the rules," and that "obeying the law is a virtue."[95] Yet another newsletter article spoke about democracy and concluded that within the company, democracy relied on knowing one's place and in being able to govern one's own behavior.[96] In sum, skeptical readers could conclude that following rules, obeying laws, and knowing one's place were all in short supply among workers at Dongya.

In the tumultuous economic situation of the time, the relationship between Dongya and its constituents, both shareholders and employees, depended in large part on a steady flow of goods from the company. A former executive remembered that "at the time Dongya stock was valuable because it issued goods. Large shareholders would come in trucks to get their share."[97] On the occasion of the fifteenth anniversary, the company distributed wool yarn and brown sugar to each shareholder and wool yarn, brown sugar, and white flour to each employee. For shareholders this represented a substantial dividend on their investment worth about 192,000 yuan for each one hundred shares. One of Dongya's sales outlets set up shop at the factory for those shareholders who wanted to convert their yarn to cash on the spot rather than take it home.[98] In addition to these direct distributions, Dongya's participation in the ongoing economy of things extended to founding a cooperative to help employees pool funds to purchase food and other useful items.[99]

In 1947 Dongya produced just over a half million pounds of wool knitting yarn, a level not seen since 1940 and a considerable improvement over the less than seventy thousand pounds for 1946, but still a small fraction of the company's heyday in the mid-1930s.[100] If nothing else, Dongya had enough yarn to distribute some to employees and shareholders while advertising to sell some to the public.[101] Anecdotal accounts from former employees indicate that with the chaos in North China, much of the wool yarn produced was sent south to Shanghai and Guangzhou for sale. One former employee even said that about a third of the profits from these sales never made its way back to Tianjin, but was secretly sent to Hong Kong.[102] Gunnysack production surged more than 50 percent to 1.1 million bags. Nonetheless, gunnysack production was still little more than what had been achieved in 1944 at the height of the war.[103] The company had a capacity to produce 1.5 million pounds of yarn and five million gunnysacks per year.[104] In a letter to the Tianjin Customs Administration, Dongya complained of limits on imports that interfered with the purchase of materials and equipment, increases in wages and foreign exchange costs, shortages of coal and electricity, interruptions in transport, and difficulty finding financing.[105] In a hopeful move, a Nationalist government bureau met with Tianjin businesses, including Dongya, to plan an increase in exports to Southeast Asia and a campaign to remind the "people of the nation" of national products.[106] Not all government action encouraged Chinese industry, however, as when the Central Trust traded Chinese soybeans for Japanese-made wool cloth, which it then proceeded to sell in China to the outrage of Chinese woolen mills.[107] Nonetheless, the overall political situation appeared to improve. Tensions eased when Communist activity near Tianjin died down and prices leveled off over the summer.[108]

In spite of some good news, Song Feiqing remained deeply concerned. In a sermon he gave to the Dongya Protestant club, he worried about, the lack of new factories as well as stagnation among existing ones. Song proposed a hardly practical plan to "Christianize" Dongya as a solution to this economic problem, as well as to ameliorate what he saw as a general decline in morals. "Within one year the entire factory will be changed into a Christianized factory. . . . So the result of the blooming of Christian belief should be to use our belief to convert unbelievers to actively participate in our construction work for individuals and family and the world."[109] Apparently, Song felt that Christian workers would be less likely to cause trouble. As one step in this direction, Dongya placed the factory precept in huge letters on the wall of a building within the factory grounds. "Do unto others as you would have them do unto you," the company newsletter explained, was a slogan intended to "remind employees to be honest, kind, cooperative, and group-oriented."[110]

In many ways, Song's plan to Christianize Dongya was simply a restatement of the gospel of development espoused by the British Baptist missionaries back in Shandong, but rather than the amelioration of grinding poverty, which the missionaries had hoped for, Song Feiqing espoused grander goals. For him, industrialization and business enterprise could really create an Industrial Eden both at the micro level within Dongya and at the macro level within Chinese society as a whole. The publicity that Dongya received reinforced this message. A glowing profile in *Industrial Monthly* (*Gongye yuekan*) papered over more than a year of labor strife by ending with the claim that Dongya employees "express a happy spirit, move with quick movements and are stern and careful in front of the machines [they tend]. Here we feel that Chinese industry has hope for a future."[111]

Other signs of relative prosperity appeared as well. Dongya had enough yarn to distribute some of it to shareholders as a dividend in November.[112] And by the end of 1947, conditions were good enough for Dongya to increase its capital once again, this time by fifty times, from 300 million to about 15 billion yuan.[113] In deciding to increase capital, Dongya directors cited a resurgence in Chinese demand, especially in Manchuria, which had been cut off by Japanese occupation since 1931.[114] The firm even added 35 workers for a total of 880 after remaining steady at 845 for the first three quarters of the year.[115] Nonetheless, the company's labor problems still simmered beneath the surface, and continued bouts of hyperinflation, shortages of materials, and other elements of the postwar toxic environment had contaminated any sense of normalcy at Dongya.

The End Game

With the continuing crisis, Song Feiqing and his managers realized that Dongya's long-term prospects were in danger, at least in North China, so the company continued to shift activity to Shanghai.[116] Most important, Dongya set up a subsidiary outside of China's borders in the British colony of Hong Kong. Ostensibly, Dongya founded its Hong Kong subsidiary in December 1946 to purchase raw materials and machinery without the restrictions and difficulties imposed by China's unstable currency and foreign exchange.[117] In truth, Song Feiqing had sent his younger brother, Song Yuhan, to run the subsidiary, and Yuhan confided to an official in the Hong Kong colonial government that the office was not just for purchasing, but that Dongya planned to construct a full-scale factory in the colony with British-manufactured equipment.[118] The family was preparing a fallback option in case they had to abandon Tianjin. A veteran employee later recalled that Dongya insiders sent large amounts of money to Hong Kong at the time.[119] Family lore is that Song Feiqing's investment in the Hong

Kong subsidiary came from profits from his personal import and export trading.[120] Regardless of where the money came from, it was clear that Song Feiqing saw little benefit to continuing to invest in Tianjin. The Song family kept their plans secret from the public and from most Dongya employees. When *Dagong bao* reported that Song Feiqing went to England to buy machinery in November, there was no mention of the fact that the equipment was intended for a new Hong Kong factory.[121] At about the same time, or shortly thereafter, Song Feiqing sent all of his older children abroad to the United States. Only the two youngest daughters remained at home in Tianjin.[122]

At the end of 1947, the economic situation in Tianjin began to deteriorate again. Production sagged and lacking any substantive measures to spur development, the Nationalist government sponsored a production competition among Tianjin's factories.[123] Long gone were the days of the 1930s when tax breaks and tariffs, even if arbitrarily applied, promoted domestic industry, or even the days of the war when the Japanese military-industrial complex protected Dongya's monopoly position in gunnysack production. Now in the postwar period, nothing seemed to work in the face of continuing inflation and worthless currency. In an interview with *Dagong bao*, Dongya vice president Wang Xinsan explained how the lack of foreign exchange hampered business. Unable to buy wool through normal channels, the black market for foreign exchange drove the price to produce one pound of wool yarn to at least one million yuan, "but at this time when the people are poor, who can afford it?" Under these conditions, he noted, Dongya did not even dare to bring up its grand development plans. In addition, the recent capital increase to fifteen billion yuan "was not for expansion of operations, but was only a passive measure for the protection of the interests of shareholders."[124] Dongya struggled to keep wages in sync with inflation. Average monthly pay increased by a factor of ten between March and December.[125] The company paid wages half in cash and half in grain, and in December distributed overcoat wool to workers.[126] The surge in inflation came in part from worries about new Communist victories in Manchuria and northern Hebei Province. Under these conditions, Dongya and the Song family were not the only ones shifting money and activities to the south.[127] In the tight monetary situation, banks were reluctant to lend or supply foreign exchange to their customers.[128]

By January 1948, as businesspeople faced the coming Chinese New Year the sense of economic crisis in Tianjin grew. *Dagong bao* headlines screamed that industry faced a life-and-death moment. In response to the sense of crisis, Chiang Kai-shek promised help for North China, including Central Bank loans to purchase and ship food to North China to make up for food supplies cut off by Communist activities.[129] At about the same time, the mayor of Tianjin wrote to the French consulate to say that foreigners should be withdrawn from Communist areas because they were being captured and "massacred."[130] The crisis continued in March as a *Dagong bao* article pointed to both recession and the added burden of tax collection "in advance."[131]

Dongya, perhaps, was in better condition than most. Once again in time of crisis, gunnysacks became a prime commodity. The company could sell every gunnysack it produced, but shortages of jute kept it from operating at capacity.[132] In addition, Dongya continued to advertise wool yarn, indicating that it still had wool supplies.[133] Nonetheless, those supplies could not last forever, and in an interview with *Dagong bao*, Song Feiqing pointed to the continuing scarcity of new raw materials. Song Feiqing gave this interview upon his return from an extended trip abroad, and the published account made it clear that Dongya's plans to establish a factory in Hong Kong had become public. Song Feiqing denied any plans to move the company south, but did express concerns. He harbored doubts about the government-promised assistance plan for North China, especially the foreign exchange controls. His criticism of the government's bungling of the economy was surprisingly explicit, but he also said that he welcomed plans for government-controlled sales of raw materials.[134] Thus, Song's criticism did not derive from ideas that the government should stay out of the economy. Instead, he was concerned about the ineffectiveness of economic policies. As always, Song was willing to look to the developmental state for help, but that state was ineffective and unresponsive.

Apparently during his trip abroad at the end of 1947 and beginning of 1948, rumors ran rampant within Dongya about his plans. At his welcome back party, he was oddly introduced by Dongya vice president Chen Xisan with the words: "The president's trip abroad for investigation started with a decision last year in Shanghai so we did not have time to notify each of you employees." In a similar vein, Song opened his talk with the assurance that "I constantly received letters and the *Voice of Dongya* sent from the company while I was abroad, so I knew about the status of the company and employees . . . and I was constantly worried about the effect of the standard of living on each employee."[135]

In his travels, Song had gone to India, Turkey, England, and the United States and in the war-torn post–World War II world, he reserved special praise for the condition of the United States, where he saw little labor strife because "nationalism is an important part of American life which can break down class ideas." Most of his description of the United States, however, focused on America as a model of an Industrial Eden. "American public works are very developed, be it airplanes, cars, railroads, telephones, telegraphs, etc. It is all for the service of the people, and no detail is left out, it's very convenient. American life is completely mechanized, even household tasks use mechanical power to replace human power." After the paean to American industrialization, Song got to the crux of Dongya employee worries and explained, "While I was in the United States, a small factory came on the market, so I bought it and dismantled the equipment to ship to Hong Kong for installation. I plan to ship raw materials to Hong Kong in the future and make wool yarn for shipment and sale to Southeast Asia and South America, it will be very beneficial."[136]

Song Feiqing's speech at his welcome back party also included a long, moralizing section telling employees how to cope with rises in the cost of living and how to live their lives. He noted that Dongya wages were higher than most factories and suggested that "each individual should consider his or her own actions and improve his or her own life . . . you should not gamble or engage in other vices, or make meaningless expenditures. Thus you can save money, and you can cultivate your spirits." Song also used this speech to promote the Christianization of Dongya, and he lectured at length on the spirit of service as portrayed in the gospels of Jesus. "When the selfish customs of the present are swept away, then there will be hope for stability for society and the nation . . . the peacefulness, wealth and strength of America start with this influence, it comes from the close relation between the spirit of service and the state."[137] It is as if the tougher conditions became in China and for Dongya, the more utopian Song Feiqing became.

Song Feiqing summarized Dongya's condition for shareholders at their annual meeting in April 1948. "In the last year and a half, this company's woolen mill produced 500,000 pounds of wool yarn, of which 200,000 pounds was sold at preferential prices to shareholders. The gunnysack factory produced 1.1 million gunnysacks. The chemical factory is temporarily suspended because of a shortage of raw materials." He tried to allay shareholder fears about the Hong Kong subsidiary by stating that it was too difficult to ship raw materials from Hong Kong to Tianjin, so it was reasonable to set up production directly in Hong Kong.[138] In fact, not only was Dongya moving activities to Hong Kong, many Dongya shareholders were apparently doing the same thing. A month later Dongya notified shareholders that those who had money in Hong Kong could deposit it at interest in the Dongya subsidiary there as a means of financing the subsidiary's operations and giving floating capital in the British colony a place for use.[139]

Although Song Feiqing told the shareholders that "in the last year and a half, this company's employees have been at their posts and working hard," an odd talk given by Song to workers who lived in the dormitory indicated otherwise.[140] In a meeting with more than one hundred employees to announce new housing regulations, Song presented the changes as a way of improving living conditions. Among other plans, Song promised a storage room, flowers, and a bicycle rack for each courtyard in the dormitory. In his talk, however, Song threatened workers with expulsion from company housing if they did not work hard at their jobs. He announced a reduction in the number of beds to "reduce crowding" in spite of the fact that there were employees waiting to move in. Then, at the end of the meeting Song asked the gathered workers three questions: "(1) Who is willing to immediately move out of the factory? (2) Who is willing to move out within ten days? (3) Who is willing to obey [all rules] at the factory and thus not move out?" In response, "the whole group expressed willingness to obey the rules and reluctance to move out."[141] For Dongya workers, the privilege of living at the factory was evidently worth the price of obedience. Rather than creation of an Industrial Eden, Song now used withdrawal of Dongya's vaunted employee benefits explicitly to bring Dongya's recalcitrant workers in line. It seemed to work, and a month later the company newsletter reported that company dormitories were unusually orderly and quiet.[142]

Labor relations were a constant concern. Managers asked Song about how to manage workers, and the company formed "guidance committees" in the summer of 1948 to promote unity and mutual assistance among employees.[143] A month later the *Voice of Dongya* reported on the swearing-in ceremony for members of the service guidance committee, which included speeches and candle lighting.[144] A photograph from the Dongya archives shows such a ceremony with workers holding up their right hands with clenched fists as they swore to serve.[145] A retired Dongya manager remembered that the guidance committees tried to find solutions to employee problems as a means of controlling labor, and that at about the same time the company organized "Three Friend Groups" (*sanyoutuan*) as intelligence units to get news of worker attitudes and activities.[146]

Dongya workers may have needed threats and encouragement to work hard, but there were no more overt struggles. The Dongya union held an election for its officers in July of 1948 without any fuss or protest.[147] Interestingly, 6 of the 117 union representatives in the new union had been identified as agitators in the secret report by the Three People's Principles Youth League back during the strikes of 1946.[148] It is hard to know what this means. Either this new quiescent movement was less docile than it appeared on the surface or the Youth League had been hasty in its evaluation two years earlier. It is also possible that the new union represented a compromise between worker activists and more obedient employees. In any case, Song Feiqing asked the new union representatives for quiescence and cooperation and to take an active role in the moral education of workers. He stated, "Don't argue on behalf of rule violators . . . it is hoped you will help employees examine (self-criticize) their own lives. If they have bad habits or bad desires (addictions), they need to be corrected and improved. If they have good habits or other virtues, they need to be complimented to make everyone conform to the rules and in pursuit of a normal life and high character." Likewise the union needed to help management increase production based on the goal of "the good of the masses." Finally, Song reiterated the Dongya ideal that the company was like a family, and he hoped that the union leaders would not pay any attention to "outsiders," though it is unclear by 1948 if Song still worried about Nationalist Party activists or if he was more likely concerned about Communist labor organizers.[149]

In these difficult postwar years, Dongya management faced a young workforce with relatively shallow roots at the company and which had only intermittently produced the main product of the company: wool yarn. Based on available evidence from 1948, Hebei workers vastly outnumbered their Shandong counterparts, and both groups were fairly young with an average age of about thirty. Most had entered the company during the prosperous years of the early war, 1938–1942, when high prices for wool yarn and gunnysacks had made the company flush with cash.[150] Thus, few of them remembered the golden age of Dongya's rise in the wool yarn market in the 1930s. In addition, the vast majority of workers were classified as daily and had not yet risen to the monthly or yearly levels.[151]

Perhaps the youth of the employees and their relatively short time at Dongya fed part of the company's incessant drive for inspirational messages. In one such message from the *Voice of Dongya* in July 1948, the illustration depicts a muscular runner representing Dongya racing along a road that reads as the factory precept, "Do unto others as you would have them do unto you" (Figure 6.1).

With a quiescent but unproductive labor force, Dongya limped along. It produced gunnysacks with a combination of Indian and domestic jute.[152] In July 1948, the company had enough wool to distribute some to its shareholders at a preferential price and to workers for free, though it is hard to know if this was a sign of the company's relative stability or of the need to assuage shareholders and workers because of the raging inflation and instability outside of Dongya's gates.[153] The company raised the price of steamed buns it sold at preferential prices to employees who did not participate in the company meal plan and raised the price for haircuts at the company barbershop as well.[154] Two weeks later, the price of steamed buns sold to employees had tripled again.[155]

In a vain attempt to improve control over industry, the Tianjin city government separated its industrial association from that of Beiping's in May 1948. Song Feiqing was elected to the board, but this new association, like many Nationalist government initiatives, talked about increasing production, but did not seem to have any way to do so.[156] In August Song Feiqing addressed his employees for the first time after a long absence. It is not even necessary to read between the lines to see the rifts in and outside the company. First he thanked the employees for their active contributions to help refugees from the Northeast who had fled fighting between the Nationalists and Communists. Then he turned his attention to internal problems and urged the need to maintain righteousness. In the previous year he had

FIGURE 6.1   Illustration from the *Voice of Dongya* portraying the Dongya spirit. The runner's jersey reads "Dongya." The text at the top states, "Running 10,000 meters following the instructions of the factory precept." The road reads, "Do unto others as you would have them do unto you." *Dongya Sheng* 27 (1 July 1948): 3.

published his essay "Labor and Capital Are on the Same Side," and apparently anticapitalist activity had continued in Tianjin. We see here his first documented use of the term "capitalist," instead of just "capital." Song wondered, "What is a capitalist? Who is a capitalist? There are two explanations for the word 'capitalist.' (1) A small number of people who organize industry especially for their own interests and care not for the interests of others, they are called capitalists. (2) Those who depend on industry to live are also capitalists. For example, bicycle cart drivers can also be called capitalists. Ninety percent of our employees are also shareholders. . . . Who wants to overthrow whom? Creating chaos is creating chaos for whom? Is it overthrowing oneself, creating chaos for oneself?" Then Song listed the problems arising from Dongya's workforce: work slowdowns, vandalism of company property, failing to make up shifts after electrical outages, coming late and leaving early, and doing personal business on company time. According to Song, "a third of the people were running around and not at their posts. This was despicable." As always, he pleaded for cooperation in establishment of a rationalized and scientific world. He said the new guidance committees had been created "with the goal of rationalizing everyone's thoughts, habits, and living." Then, using the same technique he had several months earlier when he had threatened to reduce the number of beds in employee residences, he asked who would like Song Feiqing to go abroad to purchase wool and who would like the factory to close for two or three months due to a lack of raw materials. Finally, he asked, "All those willing to work as usual when I go abroad, please raise your hands. (Everyone raised their hand.) . . . All those not willing to work as usual, please raise your hands. (None.)"[157]

The government tried one last attempt at keeping inflation in check by floating the gold yuan and implementing a new economic policy in August. Rather than calming concerns about the currency, this move created panic. As people rushed to convert their new gold yuan for goods, Dongya limited sale of its yarn to one and a half pounds per person. Customers had been lining up at seven o'clock in the morning to buy wool.[158] This final crisis was literally visible in the appearance of the *Voice of Dongya* newsletter. In the 1 September issue, the editors announced that the rising cost of ink, paper, and printing had forced them to use a lower quality paper and they asked for their readers' forgiveness.[159] In a sign of the continuing inflationary crisis, an article noted that the company had sold flour at reduced price to employees to enable them to survive.[160] The company also sold wool overcoat material to shareholders and employees.[161] Finally, Dongya closed its two direct sales outlets because the constant rush of customers was too much to handle.[162] Merely the rumor that stores were going to sell wool yarn caused Tianjin people to gather in such numbers that the police had to disperse them.[163] As a precaution, Dongya moved all its inventory of goods within the factory gates for protection.[164]

As the economy collapsed, Dongya management implemented an odd mix of measures to manage the crisis, but also continued promoting the ideals of Industrial Eden. Inside the factory, during October, the company began a process of self-examination (using one of the same phrases Communists would later use for "self-criticism," *jiantao*) where staff were asked to report on personnel and production problems and propose resolutions.[165] On 16 October, Song Feiqing called his employees together for the second time in two months. He explained how he rushed back from his trip abroad when the government changed its monetary system. Even at this time of great emergency, he took time to compliment employees on working harder and keeping the factory and themselves clean. Then he reprimanded them for rushing to leave work at the end of shifts, not caring appropriately for company property, and not wearing their work uniforms all the time. Only 98 percent did so, and he wanted the thirty-plus employees who did not wear uniforms to change their ways. After this reprimand, Song turned his attention to the dire situation of the company, where the only raw materials available had to be purchased illegally on the black market and the sale of the company's products at the officially designated price would result in a loss. He promised to continue to distribute goods when possible, but asked employees not to expect loans from the guidance committees. Rather than monetary assistance, the guidance committee responsible for living conditions was set up to lead "employees on the path of righteousness, reform vices, use medicine, and develop common knowledge of hygiene."[166] Outside the factory inflation continued to rage.[167] Finally, on 18 October, Dongya decided to only sell its products on a barter system in exchange for other goods.[168] The same month, the Dongya employee cooperative started rationing goods: one *jin* of coal oil, two pieces of soap, three *jin* of salt per member per half month.[169]

Dongya was in full crisis mode and hunkered down to wait for some change, any change, in the political and economic environment. On 6 November, Song Feiqing once again addressed his employees, this time at a group dinner. He gave a rousing speech about maintaining character and spirit during times of danger and emergency. Among other things, he said, "I am a Christian, as a devout believer, my work here is a duty given by God. I must use all my strength at my post from beginning to end. . . . Stay at your posts. Don't be depressed, don't give up."[170] The local authorities declared martial law on 22 November 1948.[171] On 1 December, Dongya published the last issue of the *Voice of Dongya* on bad quality paper, showing the extent of shortages in Tianjin's broken economy. The newsletter editors made a valiant attempt to give an impression of normalcy. For example, the Committee for Reform of Living reported on its plans for the next year, including twelve areas where Dongya employees and their families could improve, such as going to bed and rising on schedule, using etiquette, being punctual, and working hard. Nonetheless, the civil war between the Nationalists and Communists lurked in the background. The living conditions of residents of Tianjin had deteriorated so much that Dongya had cooperated with another firm in Tianjin, Renli, to open a soup line, which was feeding 1,500 people a day. In addition, the editors published an editorial from a newspaper, the *Xinxing Bao* (which also had the name *New Star*), calling for capitalists to become aware of the need to rely on the masses.[172] This was the first indication that Dongya management was willing to consider Communist rhetoric without condemning it, and the first admission that capitalists might have the need to learn from employees.

The Unresponsive Developmental State

As the Nationalist regime in North China collapsed in the fall of 1948, a French diplomat characterized the local government as "distinguished by its dishonesty and incompetence," which in his view stemmed from the Nationalist government in Nanjing with its "regulations, controls, dirigisme, etc." He concluded thus that "without becoming Communist, the population became more and more anti-Nationalist."[173] A few months later, another French diplomat looked back at the Nationalist regime of the postwar period and described it as "a totalitarian state economy for private interests in which rigidity was made worse by incompetence and venality." In his view the incompetence of the government-controlled economy derived from the government's Central Bank, which arbitrarily set foreign exchange rates and profited from the black market, as well as from the Central Trust, the "organ of buying and selling," which picked and chose those to whom it extended favorable terms.[174]

Dongya's experiences of the postwar period confirm this conclusion, at least in part. The company struggled constantly for the foreign exchange necessary to purchase materials and only occasionally did the Central Trust enable it to succeed. The failure of the postwar Nationalist developmental state was also due, however, to the regime's inability to win the civil war with the Communists. It is hard to know if the incompetence of the regime caused its failures in the civil war or if failures in the war caused Nationalist officials to become more desperate and more incapable. At best, organs of the local government helped mediate disputes with workers and when that failed, the police proved effective at suppressing worker activism. The visible hand of state coercion came to its peak when police blocked off the factory from workers in the lockout of 1946. This kind of ad hoc intervention by the local government had none of the hallmarks of the developmental capitalist state. Most important, there was no broad social consensus and the policies did little to increase production. Instead, this was simply the visible hand of a coercive state incapable of implementing the developmental policies that Song Feiqing expected.

Not only had the postwar Nationalist state failed its developmental mission, but foreign competition made it almost impossible for Dongya wool yarn to compete in the marketplace. The formal structures of imperialism in China disappeared with the Japanese surrender, but Chinese industrialists still found themselves at a disadvantage in the world trading system. The more the company struggled, the more management clung to the desperate hope of creating an ideal transformative corporation. Continued labor unrest, however, proved that Industrial Eden only worked during the flush times of the early years of the Japanese occupation. Under the tremendous pressures of hyperinflation, however, many Dongya workers were no more or less loyal to the firm than other workers in Tianjin. Industrial Eden proved ephemeral at best.

As the Communists approached, it would remain to be seen if the coming "workers' paradise" would come any closer to the Industrial Eden ideal and if there would be any room for cooperation between the theoretically anticapitalist Communist Party and China's capitalists such as Song Feiqing.

7 The People's "New Democratic" Developmental State

THE COMMUNISTS TOOK Tianjin on 15 January 1949, less than three months after Dongya managers decided to sell goods only on barter. As with the previous Nationalist and Japanese-occupation regimes, the Chinese Communist Party (CCP) believed in industrialization, especially state-led industrialization. For a very brief time at the beginning of the regime, under the umbrella of Mao's "New Democracy" policy, Communist leaders asserted their willingness to work in concert with private firms such as the Dongya Corporation, and they even aggressively courted particular "patriotic" capitalist representatives.[1] In Tianjin, Song Feiqing and Dongya took on huge symbolic importance as one of the few large private industrial corporations left after years of war, occupation, and state-driven development. As such, both Song and Dongya were at the center of the process of determining the parameters of the New Democratic developmental state, and that process shows how the Communist regime quickly evolved away from alliance with capitalists toward a socialist developmental command state.

Early Communist Rule of Tianjin

For Song Feiqing and the Dongya Corporation, the fall of Tianjin to the Communists was a time of chaotic currency, difficulty purchasing materials after the state-decreed price freeze, and equal difficulty in refusing to sell goods in the face of "coercive buying" when "wounded soldiers came in groups and disrupted things."[2] As Communist troops approached at the end of 1948, Nationalist officials reacted with a confused mix of vows to fight to the end and rapid flight. By 8 November, French diplomats had already noted the departure of Nationalist troops. Two days later, the local Nationalist garrison published regulations permitting businesspeople in Tianjin to do business with the Communist-held areas.[3] In spite of the apparent acknowledgment of defeat in these actions, twelve days after that, Nationalist authorities declared martial law in the city. By 14 December, the Communists had cut Tianjin off from Beiping (Beijing) by land and air.[4]

Conditions for Dongya worsened. As Nationalist officials began seizing corvée labor, company management "had to plead everywhere [to be allowed to keep its workers]." With the collapse of the Nationalists, Tianjin faced the third regime change in the city in twelve years. Dongya's gunnysack business carried it through these difficult months, but the importance of the gunnysack proved a double-edged sword because the Nationalist regime simply tried to seize "200,000 Dongya gunnysacks and 200,000 *jin* of jute."[5] In spite of the danger, the company still managed to negotiate with the desperate Nationalist authorities, who eventually reduced the demand to 25,000 sacks. Dongya management felt lucky to have gotten by with giving up so little.

Even before the city fell, the Communist Party dispatched Shi Xiaodong, Shi Shaodong's brother, to talk to Song Feiqing. Shi Xiaodong delivered a message from the CCP Northern Bureau requesting Song Feiqing's cooperation under future Communist rule. Song agreed to continue running Dongya and told Shi Xiaodong about plans to move into the factory during the expected fight for Tianjin. During their conversation they discussed Song's plans for development and Song told Shi that he supported the Communist Party's "advocacy of the development of domestic industry."[6] Song clearly hoped that developmental goals would provide some common ground between business and communism.

The Dongya Corporation prepared for the coming regime change by distributing grain to employees and setting up emergency teams.[7] In December 1948, Song joined with dozens of other Tianjin notables to ask the local Nationalist authorities to either move their fight with the Communists outside of the city or simply "discontinue hostilities," in other words, surrender. They were aware of the destruction caused by the fall of Changchun to Communist forces and did not want a repeat of the carnage in Tianjin.[8]

In spite of this plea, the first day of 1949 provided occasion for a belli-cose speech by the Nationalist garrison commander in Tianjin, saying, in citing Leningrad and Stalingrad, that Tianjin would be defended house by house. By 7 January the French consul reported hearing artillery fire in the distance.[9] As Nationalist defeat became inevitable, Song Feiqing had his correspondence with Nationalist Party officials burned.[10] Encirclement of the city and the unsettled situation had caused a huge increase in food prices. One Tianjin resident noted in his diary the increase of the price of a sack of flour from 250 yuan to 1,150 yuan in three weeks.[11] In the end, the actual battle for Tianjin was anticlimactic. The Nationalists had lost the will to fight and the Communists took the city in one day. Dongya sur-vived the fight with no losses except for "one shell which landed and put a hole in the corner of the wall of the worker personnel department. No one was hurt."[12]

Compared with the chaos of the last days of Nationalist rule, initial im-pressions of the Communists were quite positive. A French diplomat re-marked that the "military is very disciplined, but amazed by modern con-veniences such as elevators."[13] Likewise, an American official with the Economic Cooperation Administration in Tianjin was favorably impressed by soldiers who "were evidently under very strict orders not to molest any-body, not to take anything, not to occupy any private properties if the owners objected. They refused gifts of every sort, the only thing they would accept being hot water or tea."[14] A Dongya executive later remembered the Communists he had met as "very young, but very nice."[15]

Day-to-day urban administration, however, posed different challenges to the Communists. Even though "the military occupation was well planned, well organized and well executed . . . the civil administration seems not nearly so well prepared. A great lack of competent administrators, execu-tives and officials is evident."[16] Such uncertainty was not entirely new to Dongya's managers who had dealt with regime changes before. The com-pany often reaped large profits from its gunnysack production at such times. The arrival of the Communist regime was different, however, because the labor strife of the preceding civil war period had set the stage for full-scale confrontation between worker activists and Dongya management.

Underground Communist Party workers among Dongya employees quickly moved to take control of the factory. In response to party calls to get the economy of Tianjin moving again, they turned on Dongya's machines and recommenced production without consideration for assured sources of raw materials. Workers also held anticapitalist demonstrations reminiscent of the worst days of the labor unrest of the civil war period.[17] Confusion reigned. The party dispatched a work team to oversee regime transition at Dongya, but within a few days, the team members submitted a self-criticism saying they had not properly listened to employee complaints.[18] Dongya was not alone, and within a month of the Communist takeover of the city, factories were besieged by worker demands for back pay, bonuses, and rehiring laid-off workers. New city officials were unwilling to suppress the workers, so industry was paralyzed.[19] At Dongya more than a hundred workers held demonstrations outside of the managerial office, yelling slogans such as "we will not continue to accept capitalist exploitation," "overthrow Song Feiqing," and "workers should be the masters of Dongya."[20] Even a Communist official acknowledged that many workers had made excessive demands in the face of capitalists' fear.[21]

A meeting of the Dongya board of directors recorded regret for the dissolution of the spirit of factory unity that had prevailed during the period of transition from Nationalist to Communist regimes. In addition to disobedient workers, the company also faced a shortage of materials and supplies.[22] Nonetheless, the company began running advertisements in the newly renamed *Jinbu ribao* (*Progressive Daily*, formerly *Dagong bao*) to sell both gunnysacks and knitting yarn.[23]

As Dongya management tried to reestablish production, Communist Party officials remained indecisive. In the words of an American observer, "the whole city of Tientsin [Tianjin] was a vacuum, as far as foreigners, foreign relations and foreign trade were concerned. . . . It should be added that Chinese industrialists, bankers and business men were gradually enveloped in almost the same sort of vacuum."[24] A Dongya manager later described the period of early Communist rule as a time of "no clear understanding of government policies"[25] In addition, the company faced a one million yuan production tax on goods used to pay employee bonuses and shareholder dividends at Chinese New Year.[26] No one seemed to know what to do.

Eventually Mayor Huang Jing did intercede at Dongya when the union representatives there realized that worker demands could bankrupt the company, but he still did not know how to treat businesspeople and refused to shake Song Feiqing's hand when they met.[27] Debates raged within the Communist Party about what to do with urban administrations, and Tianjin was an important test case of the party's ability to move beyond its rural bases. Bo Yibo, head of the CCP's Northern Bureau, worried about Tianjin's shortage of capital and raw materials, poor transportation, and the decline of foreign trade, which created a shortage of foreign exchange.[28] As the party dithered, the price of flour increased more than 500 percent in one week and a black market developed in U.S. dollars.[29]

At a meeting of top party leaders, Liu Shaoqi, the number two man in the party, advocated the development of an urban policy that would enable the smooth takeover of the Nationalists' huge state-owned industrial sector while helping private companies resume production.[30] As party leaders tried to establish a workable policy, local officials in Tianjin still demonstrated ambivalence toward capitalists. At the end of March 1949, *Progressive Daily* published a two-part article about Song Feiqing. It is impossible to know if these articles represented a publicity campaign by Dongya management, taking advantage of connections with the staff at the formerly private newspaper, or if party officials instigated the reports as part of their drive to change attitudes about capitalists. In either case, these articles would not have appeared without party approval, and they provide an illuminating look at the battle under early Communist rule to control the narrative about capitalism. In sum, the articles were a plea for unity in building a strong China under the banner of Maoist People's New Democracy. The details, however, show considerable tension in reconciling capitalists and the new regime.[31]

The articles relied heavily on giving the impression of scientific and objective investigation. The reporter devoted most of the articles to discussing wool and jute supply. Questions of politics and the role of capitalists in society opened and closed the articles, appearing as political bookends before and after this extensive discussion of supply problems and production. These opening and closing sections gave a short history of Dongya that did establish the company's credentials as a patriotic participant in the anti-Japanese national products campaign of the 1930s. Then the reporter turned to the present by noting that "the employees of the Dongya Corporation held a meeting and Song Feiqing denied he was an exploiter." The reporter then asked Song Feiqing what he thought about the party's New Democracy slogan of "Increased Production, Flourishing Economy, a Matter for Both Public and Private, Benefit to Both Labor and Capital" (*zengjia shengchan, fanrong jingji, gongsi jiangu, laozi liangli*). Song Feiqing responded ambivalently that "this principle is very good and there is no problem benefiting labor and capital. But, in the future there will be difficulties as an individual. For a lifetime I have expended money and effort, took great pains in management and accomplished certain achievements. Now I have received a label of a 'capitalist' it is truly. . . ." The reporter explained that Song could not finish his sentence because he was disturbed by these words. The article then told readers that "in truth ['capitalist'] is only a social scientific name. Under the People's New Democratic society, the capitalist class is a necessary element. In the article 'Present Conditions and Our Duty' in 'On the United Government' Chairman Mao has already made this clear. . . . [If] profits are reasonable the government will take care of you. President Song Feiqing, who has been trained in the natural sciences, can certainly understand this point." The reporter implied that science was an area of common ground that everyone shared, but ended the second article on a cautionary note with reference to the tragedy of a Dongya woman worker named Du that "should never be repeated."[32]

This very public discussion of the Dongya Corporation left a mixed impression. The newspaper praised Dongya's history of patriotism and emphasized the moderate policies of the party toward capitalists, yet at the same time, it concluded that capitalists should accept the "social scientific" basis of their class label and also be sorry for treating workers badly. Amid these contradictions, if nothing else, it was clear that Song Feiqing and the Dongya Corporation had become emblems of capitalism in Tianjin and the new China.

The Socialist Embrace of Capitalist Industrial Production

Party leaders sent Vice-Chairman Liu Shaoqi to Tianjin to see if he could make the party's urban policies work. Before leaving, Liu visited his wife's brother, Wang Guangying, who had business interests in Tianjin. Liu Shaoqi told Wang that "the war won't go on for long . . . now we need to think about how to proceed with construction [of the country]." China's new leaders were anxious to establish a direction for their own version of the industrialized developmental state. When Wang asked about joining the party, Liu Shaoqi responded by saying, "The party has lots of members and cadres, but there are very few people who understand commerce and industry. If you can wear the clothes of a businessperson and still be on the side of the party and the workers, then that would be great!"[33] Liu clearly wanted to give the impression that the party's development plans sought an alliance with business, not partification of the business world, nor businessification of the party.

As Liu Shaoqi prepared to leave for Tianjin, the CCP's Northern Bureau chief Bo Yibo reported that Tianjin party cadres were afraid they would be judged too "rightist" if they spoke moderately to capitalists, but at the same time they were reluctant to discipline workers and tell them to discontinue activism. Thus, they simply "did not express opinions about worker struggles [with capitalists]."[34] A separate report from the Tianjin party asserted that mistrust of capitalists was obstructing the return to production.[35] Liu's monthlong visit to Tianjin in April and May 1949 focused mainly on meetings with party officials and tours of state-owned factories inherited from the Nationalists, but he did give some attention to the problems of private business.[36] In fact, Dongya was one of only two private companies Liu visited while in the city.[37]

In private meetings with officials, Liu said that the party needed to "learn from its enemies."[38] To do so, lower-level party officials held a meeting with a group of Tianjin businesspeople including Song Feiqing. During this meeting Song outlined nineteen opinions about conditions in Tianjin and China and these provided the basis for discussion. Song's nineteen points demonstrated his firm belief that running industry took talent and training, and that capitalists should be able to reap the rewards of their efforts. Song acknowledged his willingness, even desire, to have government help, but was unsure how this should work under the Communist state. For example, Song stated that current state policies did not clearly define the amount of acceptable profit and that "spiritual attacks" on capitalists undermined morale. He asserted that only the board of directors empowered by the shareholders could represent capital, and he wondered that if capital and labor shared profits would they also share losses? In item twelve, in a foreshadowing of latter conflicts over ideology versus expertise, Song pointed to the difference between the masses and a small number of people with talent. He argued that "current government policies kept talented people from receiving material benefit or spiritual reward. . . . If this continues then the government will gain the masses but lose the people of talent." Finally, he concluded with support for the "freedom of belief," where he noted that foreigners would not invest in the new China if the party did not guarantee both "the freedom to believe and the freedom not to."[39] This last point seems like a not-so-veiled reference to both Communist ideology and Song's own Christian faith.

Liu Shaoqi's speeches during this visit to Tianjin have come to be known as the "Tianjin Talks," and later, in the 1960s, they would be condemned as evidence of Liu's capitalist tendencies. In 1949, however, Liu seemed truly interested in finding a formula for cooperation between the party and capitalists. In a meeting with the Tianjin party committee, Liu emphasized the need for increased economic production and he repeated the central committee's decision to unify with patriotic capitalists to build the nation. He spoke of the need to educate the working masses to take a middle road in their struggles against capitalists. "If there is only cooperation and not struggle against the patriotic capitalists, then that is rightist opportunism. If there is only struggle and no cooperation then that is leftist opportunism, but now the emphasis is on cooperation." Production was the primary goal, so he declared that working hours should remain the same, as should wages, unless they were truly too low, and then only be increased by a limited amount. Capitalists, he said, should also be free to hire and fire workers. He condemned current newspaper coverage that inappropriately attacked business.[40]

Liu called for a meeting to allow capitalists to speak fully.[41] The next day, 19 April, he invited a small number of capitalists, including Song Feiqing to a meeting. Liu told them that he felt they still did not understand the party at its base. According to one source he told Song, "Now you manage one factory. In the future you can manage two, three, or eight factories. When socialism comes, the government will issue an order and you can hand the factories over to the state or the state will purchase them. . . . Then the state will give the factories back to you to manage, you will still be president, but president of state factories. Because you are capable, the state might give you eight more factories to manage, a total of sixteen factories to manage. Your salary will not be reduced, and will even be increased, but you have to manage well!"[42] In short, he promoted a vision of the state and capitalists allied in industrial development, a vision that was not totally inconsistent with Song Feiqing's own ideas about the need for state help for business.

Liu followed up this message in a visit to the Dongya Corporation on 21 April 1949. Liu and his wife arrived in an aged limousine and spent much of the day talking with Song Feiqing and other Dongya employees. It was a leisurely visit, and his talk with workers lasted long enough for him to smoke two packs of cigarettes.[43] Most famously that day, Liu told Song Feiqing that capitalist exploitation of labor was necessary. Liu said, "'Exploitation' is not a scary word under the People's New Democratic society. How many workers do you have now?' Song replied, 'a few more than one thousand.' Liu said, 'You are exploiting too few. You can expand ten times [that number]. The more [workers] you exploit the better because that shows that the economy is developing and that has benefit for the People's New Democratic society.'"[44]

During Liu's visit to the factory, or perhaps shortly thereafter, Song Feiqing presented his plan for industrial expansion to the Communist Party. He had previously asked the Nationalist government to support his idea to build Dongya into a group of more than ten companies, but plans had died in the toxic environment of the postwar period. Now he presented the same idea to the Communists in the hope that their development policies would allow him to realize the plan he called "My Dream."[45] Song too wanted a productive alliance between a developmental state and private business.

Progressive Daily enthusiastically covered Liu Shaoqi's visit to Dongya and a subsequent exchange of letters between Song Feiqing and Liu Shaoqi. The newspaper reported that after Liu's visit, "the factory immediately decided to increase production and wrote to Liu Shaoqi outlining its plan for development." In his letter, Song Feiqing promised to add a night shift, buy wool to spin into yarn, and establish a second gunnysack factory as soon as possible. In response, Liu praised Dongya for "following the policy of benefiting both labor and capital."[46] Subsequently, in speeches to larger and larger groups of officials and workers in Tianjin, Liu Shaoqi used Song

Feiqing and Dongya as models of the cooperation of private business with the state. In one speech he said, "The Dongya Woolen Mill capitalist now exploits 1,200 people, if it could open more factories and exploit 2,000 people, 20,000 people, that would be even better. . . . No matter how you look at it, exploitation is a fact. But exploitation under certain historical conditions is progressive."[47]

Song Feiqing and the Dongya Corporation had become part of the public narrative of capitalism in Tianjin under the Communists, and company managers did their best to influence public perceptions in their favor. A few days after Liu Shaoqi's visit to Dongya, *Progressive Daily* covered a meeting between party representatives, Song Feiqing, and his workers. The newspaper reported that "the whole body of 1,100 employees with warm and happy feelings, entered the meeting place." The newspaper coverage included none of the ambivalence of a few months before. Zhang Guojun, head of the new Dongya employees' association who only three months before called for the overthrow of Song Feiqing, now praised Song Feiqing's sincerity "about development of the factory" and chastised workers who made the mistake of "thinking the patriotic capitalists are enemies." For his part, Song Feiqing dutifully "made a self-criticism about former mistakes." Then he praised the developmental policies of the People's New Democratic state: "Now this is a historic and unprecedented time of assistance to the development of industry by the government. Also, the government is prepared to make Tianjin into a national model industrial zone. Our employees should unite together and establish a large goal and recognize clearly that our duty is the movement now of China from an agricultural country to an industrial country."[48] Of course it was easy for Song to embrace the Communist Party's goal of industrialization. He had worked for the same goal most of his life.

Song Feiqing's new status as a model capitalist even received recognition from the national press. An article in *People's Daily* carried the headline, "Song Feiqing's Dream Realized." The article trumpeted the success of the alliance between the Communist Party and private capitalists. It said, "after listening to comrade Liu Shaoqi talk, [Song Feiqing] realized that capitalists have a future under the leadership of the Communist Party." The report continued with the observation that although Song had been depressed for some time, he "suddenly smiled . . . and said 'I have dreamed of developing industry for a long time, and it's finally been realized under the leadership of the Communist Party.' "[49]

There was a promise of tangible benefit from the alliance between the capitalist Song Feiqing and the Communists. A new set of Dongya worker demands at the end of August seemed paltry in comparison to earlier requests. Now workers asked for raincoats and rain boots for warehouse workers, a washbasin in some factory rooms, and more bowls and chopsticks in the employee cafeteria. Tellingly, many of the worker demands now revolved around increasing production. One workroom needed more wooden forks (used to push material through machines) and another proposed a method to repair torn threads quickly in order to avoid shutting down production.[50] In addition to a more docile labor force, the alliance between Dongya and the Communist Party also promised to support Dongya's expansion. Dongya had purchased a lot of land during the Japanese occupation period, part of the economy of things, but it was in scattered plots. Now Dongya managers reported that "the government has agreed to exchange it for a contiguous piece [of land] . . . next year construction will begin. First a factory will be built to weave jute [into gunnysacks]. Gradually, the chemical factory will also move there."[51] As a developmental measure, this land swap was eminently feasible. It did not require a huge investment on the part of the government, and it provided a benefit to Dongya that would not happen without state intervention.

As Dongya waited for the land swap, the cooperation between the state and Dongya remained mostly in the realm of public perception. As always, the company was adept at steering the narrative of its own role in society. Even before Liu Shaoqi's visit to Dongya, the company announced in a front-page advertisement in *Progressive Daily* sales of its "special edition wool yarn" made with Chinese domestic wool. Clearly the company was reinforcing the impression that it was both productive and patriotic. After Liu's visit, Dongya continued to position its public image within the People's New Democratic state. On 1 May it placed an advertisement featuring both its knitting yarn and gunnysacks under the heading "In Celebration of Labor Day." Three days later, Dongya placed a similar ad under the heading "Remembering May Fourth," the political movement to which the Communist Party traced its roots and which had had an important, but different, role in shaping Song Feiqing's youth. In July, Dongya placed an ad for

Diyang brand yarn in the Tianjin newspaper proclaiming, "Butting Ram Brand Special Edition, Economic Wool Yarn, Inexpensive—Caters to the purchasing power of the ordinary person, especially good quality—Suitable for use by workers and peasants, public officials and students!"[52] In addition to these ads, a general air of optimism began to permeate Dongya managers' public statements. One Dongya executive discussed the rosy outlook for the gunnysack business because of high demand and domestic availability of raw materials. Demand for gunnysacks in North China far outstripped supply, and the company was trying to more than double production by gearing up for shifts running day and night.[53] Meanwhile an apparently upbeat Song Feiqing, back in Tianjin from a visit to Hong Kong, "happily recounted the achievements of this trip." He announced plans to export Chinese wool in exchange for importing Australian wool and to purchase new machinery for a second gunnysack factory.[54]

Company management's internal discussions showed a marked upturn in tone as well. In the first board of directors meeting in seven months, the company decided to give shareholders a dividend of one pound of wool for every five hundred shares held at a price that was only a fraction of market value. By September of 1949, Song Feiqing reported to the board of directors that raw materials inventories were looking better and cash flow had improved.[55] In October, Dongya planned to ask the government for "U.S.$20,000–$80,000 in foreign exchange at the posted rate to import 400,000 pounds in wool ropes which could be spun into 230,000 pounds of yarn which then can be sold for 4.48 billion yuan (without counting costs of production)." Dongya managers planned to use the profit from yarn sales to purchase domestic Chinese wool for export, which would provide the foreign exchange necessary to import more Australian wool. Meanwhile, plans continued for a second gunnysack factory.[56]

Dongya celebrated the return to normalcy with an advertisement in congratulations of the founding of the People's Republic of China (see Figure 7.1). This is the first ad of the PRC period in which Dongya showed the confidence to use images other than the Butting Ram logo. Here a very nonrevolutionary woman sits quietly knitting, implying that normal life, and normal consumer culture, will continue under the new regime.

In perhaps the brightest sign yet, as the end of 1949 approached, factory management congratulated itself on finally developing a working relation-

FIGURE 7.1 A Dongya advertisement offers congratulations on the founding of the People's Republic of China and suggests for the occasion "lasting gifts" of the company's wool yarn. Tianjin Dongya Enterprise Corporation, woolen mill. *Jinbu ribao*, 2 October 1949, sect. 1, p. 4.

ship with labor. "In the factory, capital and labor are getting along well and have mutually negotiated how to proceed with various matters and decrease difficulties. This is a good phenomenon for the future and is reported to the board."[57] Publicly, *Progressive Daily* featured Dongya prominently in coverage as the first factory to implement new collective bargaining organizations in Tianjin. The Dongya labor association leader Zhang Guojun reported on the success of resolving worker complaints to a cadre meeting of the textile industry association.[58] A later Dongya management report to shareholders echoed the labor association leader's account. "At the beginning of discussions, although the two sides were somewhat halfhearted, after a few meetings, everyone began mutual discussion with true hearts to resolve problems point by point."[59]

Thus after years of striving for labor cooperation in the toxic environment of the postwar period, it was actually the Communist regime that managed to bring labor into line. Production became the common goal. Both the union and internal company accounts pointed out that the resolution of labor-capital disputes had resulted in increased production.[60] The People's New Democratic developmental state seemed to be firmly in place.

Evolution into a Socialist Developmental State

In his Tianjin talks, Liu Shaoqi had asserted that the transition to the planned economy would be slow. He wanted "dividends and profits to go up so speculative capital will leave the market and go into industry" and to "prepare to slowly move toward socialism and implementation of the planned economy . . . [so] capitalists won't feel too much pain." At one meeting with businesspeople, Liu even proclaimed that "any amount of profit is legal!"[61] On the surface it appeared as if private capitalists could continue operating for some time.

In fact, however, the position of capitalists in the new system was far from secure. The new currency system was a mess, and Dongya managers felt sure the company had lost money in 1949 even though "calculated in currency" there were perhaps "profits of People's bills of 1.14 million-plus yuan." In addition, the new regime was working through its disposition of class enemies. The government took control of the shares of Zhang Qide, a Dongya director, as well as the land owned by Sun Tongxuan's wife on which factory buildings were built. Dongya's long-term relationship with the Sun family finally came to an end. In spite of public pronouncements of optimism, the board of directors took the precautionary step of moving its meetings to Song Feiqing's house, away from prying eyes and ears at the factory. Dongya even delayed calling the annual meeting of shareholders because the regime's new company law had not yet been promulgated.[62]

Dongya quickly became enmeshed in a straitjacket of official market controls that had begun almost as soon as the Communist Party had entered Tianjin. Many of these controls came from government centralization of finance, purchasing, and distribution. In December the government stopped all loans except for working capital from the Bank of Communications, and Dongya was still waiting for financing to import Australian wool. Even after a loan was approved to import wool the next January, Dongya managers remained unsure if funds would actually be received.[63] At the same time, with considerable speed, markets for both purchase of jute and sale of gunnysacks came into government hands. Thus, even though Dongya managers had celebrated the diversity of options for purchasing jute as "democratization" of the purchasing process, at the end of 1949 a year later, democratization had turned into centralization and all purchase of jute in North China had to be made through government "unified purchase and allocation in North China."[64] Likewise, as early as March of 1950, Dongya primarily sold gunnysacks either to the government-owned Xintuo Company, or sold to the government's Bank of Communications to repay loans based on orders.[65] Sales of both gunnysacks and yarn to private customers would completely end by late 1951.[66]

The restrictions on finance, especially limited availability of foreign exchange, particularly hampered Dongya because of the need to import wool. Dongya did manage to produce 700,000-plus pounds of wool yarn in 1949 by using domestic wool in its "special edition" yarn, but since stores in China still held inventories of foreign-produced wool yarn left over from the pre-revolutionary period, Butting Ram special edition yarn could not compete, even if sold at a loss. Dongya temporarily suspended production of wool yarn until the remaining foreign products disappeared from the market. Dongya also suspended operations of its chemical factory. Once again, the company came to rely entirely on gunnysacks for survival. Here, too, the company's plan to build a second factory had stalled "because there were a lot of unexpected difficulties."[67] Among other things, the city government never fulfilled its promise to swap the land needed to build the factory.

In March 1950, company managers apologized to shareholders, saying that there had been no cash profits for two years and that year-end cash had been distributed in bonuses to employees "according to the policy of benefit for both capital and labor." Instead of a cash dividend, Dongya gave each shareholder one pound of special edition wool yarn for every five thousand shares. At least one shareholder was angry enough to write a complaint that the red color in the wool yarn had bled. Company managers

explained that the quality of dyes available in China had declined.[68] In spite
of these disappointing results, the shareholders reelected Song Feiqing and
those other board members who had not been declared enemies of the
people.[69]

That same month, Dongya's cash crunch worsened because of tax levies
combined with pressure to purchase public bonds. Of the latter, Dongya
agreed to buy "a total of 78,000 shares. Company subsidiaries in other locations agreed to purchase as well. In Beijing the company was asked to
buy 23,000 shares, but because of economic ability we could not agree."
Because its cash was limited, in the end Dongya had to rely on high-interest
loans from banks to pay for the bonds.[70]

As cash remained tight, Dongya also began negotiating bank loans to
fund its purchase of sorely needed jute.[71] In debt both for the purchase of
government bonds and for stockpiling raw materials, Dongya was at the
mercy of the government-controlled banking system. In October 1950, the
People's Bank notified Dongya that it would temporarily withdraw the company's loan because "it had the mission of shrinking loans throughout
China." Dongya's operations had become subject to macro-economic policy
adjustments by the new regime. In order to make jute purchases, Dongya
presold as-yet-unproduced gunnysacks. By the end of October the company had presold 160,000 gunnysacks. It had also used up its entire stock
of Australian wool and most of its wool yarn stocks had been sold.[72] Although the cash flow problem eventually eased, the combination of pressure to financially support the government and reliance on the banking
system had made Dongya very vulnerable to state interference.

During this period, Song Feiqing made two trips to Hong Kong. The
first came shortly after Liu Shaoqi's visit to Tianjin. At that time, an ebul-
lient Song went to Hong Kong purportedly to purchase raw materials and
new machinery. His embrace of the People's New Democratic development
state seemed to be such that he even asked each Dongya staff member to
read a progressive book while he was gone. Song himself prepared to read
Das Kapital on board the ship to Hong Kong, and he told his staff that he
would give them exams on their progressive education when he got back.[73]
A somewhat less optimistic Song Feiqing received permission for another
visit about a year later in May 1950, ostensibly for the same reasons as before. This time, he stayed in Hong Kong and two months later a loyal em-

ployee escorted Song's wife and two youngest daughters on a harrowing journey south where they managed to cross the border into Hong Kong as well.[74] Song Feiqing never returned to mainland China, but he remained in sporadic contact with Dongya. For example, in July he cabled Tianjin, "asking for leave for a time because he is ill with very low blood pressure." The Dongya board of directors cabled in reply, "asking him politely to return north to recuperate and lead the company's operations." Three months later, Song sent word again that he was "still recuperating from low blood pressure in Hong Kong and still could not return."[75]

Back in Tianjin Dongya managers ran the company without their boss, and the company began to thrive under Communist rule. Profits returned and gunnysack production soared. Dongya produced 1.2 million gunnysacks in 1949 and more than doubled that in 1950. By the end of 1951, production had increased to almost 3.5 million sacks.[76] Management focused almost entirely on production because strategic decisions no longer remained in company hands. For example, pressure to provide financial support for government projects became greater and greater. At the end of 1950, as the "Resist America, Aid North Korea" campaign took off, Tianjin's industries heeded the call to mobilization. On 31 November local industrialists and merchants held a "Mammoth Demonstration . . . in Connexion with the Anti-America and Aiding Korea Movement." Dongya's own vice president Wang Xinsan, who served as chairman of the textiles trade association, "acted as commanding officer of the directing department for the parade."[77] Five days later a quarter of a million people in Tianjin celebrated the "liberation" of Pyong Yang.[78] Accordingly, Dongya established its own "Resist America, Aid North Korea" branch committee, which put on a performance at the Big China Theater. The committee asked members of the board of directors to purchase tickets in advance in order to complete this "donation."[79] Tellingly, the committee used the word *wancheng* 完成, as in "complete a duty," to refer to the donation. By the summer of 1951, the company began making regular donations. In response to the call by the "Resist America, Aid North Korea" committee, Dongya donated two airplanes in June of a value of 3 billion.[80] In addition, Dongya also received pressure to exceed expectations. In November, when management saw that other large corporations donated enough money to purchase a plane for the war in Korea, Dongya donated yet another plane itself.[81]

By the end of 1950, gunnysack production at Dongya was operating smoothly. Dongya vice president Chen Xisan reported to the board that "it is possible that [we] will be able to pay back the bank loan next March when it comes due." In addition, Dongya had jute stocks adequate to enable ten more months of production. Under the pressure of taxes and donations, cash remained tight, but the company "presold goods through next March in order to prepare funds for year-end expenses and for shareholder dividends and bonuses." The year 1950 turned out to be very lucrative with profits over eight billion yuan.[82] By mid-1951 management reported to the board a return on investment of 13 percent as a result of state-set pricing that favored Dongya.[83]

As the government took control of Dongya's supplier markets and distribution channels, it also instituted controls on production quantities and work methods—with all efforts placed toward increasing production. By May of 1951 Dongya was operating under target production levels set by the government and it had adopted some of what would come to be hallmark Communist strategies, such as a production competition run by the union. Rather than making investment decisions, much of the board of directors' discussions became devoted to adjusting piece rates to be more equitable, beginning a system of labor (health) insurance, and reporting shareholders who were war traitors or bureaucratic capitalists (allied with the Nationalists).[84] The board increasingly adopted the language and attitude of Communist dirigisme. In July of 1951 management reported to a meeting of shareholders that "with great help from the people's government and with the development of international socialism and warm advancement of patriotism to resist America and aid North Korea and protect the nation with a production competition, this company's gunnysack production has increased greatly and has broken all existing records." They attributed the production increase to the awakening of the political consciousness of all employees "under the leadership of Chairman Mao and the Communist Party. The union has led a competition to expand production and recently held a patriotic production competition."[85] In November the city issued an ordinance on work and resting times with a schedule as follows: "7:00—arise; 7:30—eat; 8:00–9:00—political study; 9:00–12:00—time in office or at work; 12:00–1:00—eat and rest; 1:00–5:00—work; 6:00–7:00—free time; 7:00–9:00—political study; 10:00—sleep."[86] It sounded just like the rules of Dongya's own Industrial Eden except that the direction now came from the state and the Dongya spirit was now replaced by devotion to the party. In October 1951, managers proudly reported to the board that they had exceeded their production goal for gunnysacks by 5.21 percent. The next month production in excess of quota was 7.6 percent.[87] Rather than setting priorities, the Dongya board was now driven to meet and to exceed government-set goals.

The change at Dongya could be seen no more clearly than in April 1951 when the board finally dealt with Song Feiqing's absence. Accepting the fact that Song Feiqing would not return, the board of directors gingerly approached the matter as necessary because "criticism in the newspapers and inquiries from the government" had forced the issue. After a long discussion, the board decided to notify Song of their decision to remove him as president, "allow him to recuperate with a settled heart."[88] In his stead, the board appointed Yang Tianshou, who had been in banking and had served in a number of official positions under the Nationalists.[89]

Not fully comfortable with the position, Yang wanted more collective decision making at Dongya. He made a motion that the board "meet every two weeks to facilitate discussion of company matters and take collective responsibility for solutions" and that the company charter be revised such that "all of the company's operations will gradually move toward a system of responsibility by the board." The board as a whole preferred to let Yang shoulder the burden of responsibility for a capitalist enterprise under socialism and failed to meet him even halfway. They only reluctantly agreed to meet once a month and "continue to discuss the idea of revising the charter to move toward a system of board management."[90]

In any case, there was little to do except fulfill government production targets and allocate funds to government needs. In its public announcement about Song Feiqing's replacement, the board performed the expected self-criticism and resolved to do better. "Starting today the board of directors will face toward production and take responsibility. In observing land reform and seeing the increase in grain production, gunnysack production will also increase accordingly."[91] Management later reported to the board the need to meet government-set production targets as a rationale for removing Song from his job.[92] Government directives drove personnel policies as well. In April 1951 Dongya's union demanded that the company's reserve fund be transferred to be used as a reserve fund for employee benefits. Management agreed because of newly announced regulations requiring benefit reserves at private companies. Further government interference came in a request for investment in another government firm. Dongya's directors meekly agreed. Five months later, Dongya also invested in the new government steel company.[93] Such donations to the construction of a state-owned industrial sector eliminated any possibility that Dongya could make significant investments itself. The second gunnysack factory and any other expansion plans quietly disappeared from company discussions.

Dongya had become fully enmeshed in socialist society governed by its own industrial vision imposed from outside of Dongya, rather than within, and it came without the presence of Song Feiqing or members of his immediate family. At the same time the People's New Democratic developmental state quickly evolved into a socialist developmental state—a command economy with little room for private business—long before the official announcement by the Communist Party about the conversion to socialism.

Song Feiqing in Hong Kong and Argentina

As employees in Tianjin adapted to the new political conditions of the People's Republic of China, Song Feiqing and his family tried to begin again in Hong Kong. They proved unable to leave the political changes in China behind, however. The Chinese Communist Party tried hard to get Song Feiqing to return to Tianjin. It even dispatched agents to watch him and his brother in Hong Kong. His brother later recalled that "it appeared that if we did not go back upon 'friendly persuasion' we might be kidnapped."[94] Nationalist agents from Taiwan were interested as well and in 1953, having already been labeled an enemy of the people by the Communists in mainland China, Nationalist officials labeled Song a traitor, noting that he had cooperated with the Communists and even served on several Communist commissions in 1949 and 1950. Thus, both the Communists and Nationalists considered him a traitor.[95] With both China and Taiwan cut off, Song and his family were left adrift in Hong Kong.

Shi Shandong recounted that during this time Song Feiqing was preoccupied with his dreams of an Industrial Eden. The Hong Kong business environment was not good in 1950 and 1951, and Song worried that he would be unable to support the employees who relied on him. Shi later recorded a conversation with Song from about that time in which they discussed Song's ideas for a "reliance camp" on one of the smaller Hong Kong islands where Dongya employees could live and work together in a kind of utopian communion. Song had come up with the idea during his last stint in Tianjin when "he had insomnia. During his insomnia he thought of all kinds of things. It was like being in a dreamland, but [he believed] the realization was possible and necessary."[96]

Such a camp only existed in the ideal, of course, and despite his preoccupation with such dreamy thinking, Song had to focus on Hong Kong Dongya as a means of rebuilding the family fortune. Song and his brother had begun planning to set up production in Hong Kong about two years before the Communists took Tianjin. Although the basic outlines of the story, and the eventual failure of the Hong Kong operation, are known, much of what transpired was not preserved in the documentary record. Little remains in the Hong Kong public records office, and later family disputes and political accusations have turned the history into a "he said, she said, the Chinese Communist Party said, and then the Chinese Communist Party said something completely different" situation where the truth is hard to see clearly. Nonetheless, the various versions of the story related here tell us much about the relationship between private enterprise and the ongoing Chinese Communist revolution.

From the standpoint of those Dongya directors and managers left in Tianjin, the Hong Kong operation was a wholly owned subsidiary that should obey orders, but distance, the political divide between the People's Republic of China and the British colony of Hong Kong, and the stature of Song Feiqing all discouraged active supervision. Reports from Hong Kong did filter in to Tianjin for a while between 1949 and 1951. Thus we know that Hong Kong Dongya began production of yarn in August 1949 before Song Feiqing's final departure from Tianjin. Song had dispatched his brother Song Yuhan, his cousin Song Xianmin, and the trusted Shi Shandong, who had run the agricultural research station under the Japanese occupation, to run the Hong Kong factory. In addition, one of Dongya Tianjin's directors, Du Zhishen, was from Guangdong Province next to Hong Kong and he had become instrumental in setting up the Hong Kong operation. Du had long represented Dongya products on China's southern coast and had even been in discussions to establish a branch factory there as early as 1935.[97]

The Hong Kong firm had assets of 1.5 million Hong Kong dollars.[98] According to discussions of the board of directors in Tianjin, these funds came from reserves of the Tianjin company, which had been covertly transferred for use in Hong Kong, though the transfer was not reported to the shareholders of the Tianjin company until early 1950. At that time, they explained to shareholders that the Hong Kong company planned to return the reserves to Tianjin by purchasing materials for shipment to Tianjin.[99] That return of funds never transpired and the Tianjin directors quickly lost any control over Hong Kong operations.

After Song Feiqing moved to Hong Kong, reports back to Tianjin became fewer. It was another year before the Tianjin board learned that sales of Hong Kong products had not been good because of a glut of wool yarn on the market, and that the subsidiary there had ceased production and laid off all but about ten workers. By July of 1951, on the eve of the "Three Antis" campaign in Tianjin (see Chapter 8), the Tianjin board was discussing the paucity of information on Hong Kong operations and it decided to write and ask for details to relay to the Tianjin company's shareholders. Hong Kong replied in September of 1951 with a few details. It reported total assets of HK$4,534,510.83 and liabilities of HK$1,539,491.80, but no news was forthcoming about revenues or profits. Hong Kong reported that both Song Feiqing and his brother had left Hong Kong to investigate further business opportunities since Hong Kong was in difficult economic straits and under threat of occupation by Chinese forces. The directors in Tianjin fumed impotently that they had not been consulted about this travel in advance.[100]

In fact, it turned out that Hong Kong Dongya was not a subsidiary of the Tianjin company at all, but an independent company in its own right, owned by a group of individuals including members of the Song family and several longtime Dongya directors, such as Du Zhishen who had helped set it up.[101] According to later recollections by Song Feiqing's brother, each remittance from Tianjin came with instructions about how much was to be entered in the name of the Tianjin company and how much under the names of certain individuals.[102] Thus from the standpoint of Song Feiqing and the other Hong Kong managers, they owed no obedience to Dongya Tianjin, even though much of the money had come from Tianjin initially.

The small group of insiders entrusted with ownership and management showed a turn to the safety of particularistic networks under the pressure of political crisis, but even the ownership structure of Hong Kong Dongya was something of a fiction. Song Feiqing himself was not a shareholder because his ties to the Chinese Communist Party during the time he had remained in China had now labeled him a "red" in the emerging Cold War world of the 1950s.[103] Instead his shares were held in name by intermediaries, but no one knows now who might have invested money (or at least liquidated their holdings in Tianjin through subterfuge and transferred that money to Hong Kong) or who was holding shares belonging to Feiqing as a favor to protect him. At the very least, Song family members held just over a third of the official registered stock of the Hong Kong company.[104] In the end, this particularistic network would not survive the strains of starting again outside of China.

When business turned sour in Hong Kong in 1951, Song Feiqing and his brother decided to immigrate to Argentina. When the Tianjin directors expressed concern about Song Feiqing's absence from Hong Kong, Song was in South America trying to find a location to which he could move the entire operation out of the way of a potential Communist takeover of Hong Kong.[105] At that time, Song Feiqing's immigration to the United States was not possible because of his reputation as a leftist. Unfortunately, there were many obstacles to obtaining legal residency in Argentina and the new Peronist government did not provide a welcoming environment for private businesspeople. Insult was added to injury when news filtered to Argentina via Hong Kong of attacks on Song Feiqing during the "Five Antis" campaign in Tianjin.[106] In Argentina, the Songs subsisted on money they brought with them and occasional remittances from Hong Kong.

Ever the idealist, Song spent time planning to build an industrial city in Brazil. Similar to his ideas for a "self-reliance" camp in Hong Kong, Song saw Brazil as an environment conducive to developing his Industrial Eden vision.[107] One of the few extant documents in Song's own hand from this period contains his notes for such a place. The small book is clearly labeled "private, do not touch," and inside are the rules and regulations for yet another attempt at Industrial Eden, ranging from the need to rent land and buildings, production of goods needed by the masses, a management committee with rotating membership, shareholding by the workers, and collective decision making.[108]

Eventually, the Hong Kong company said that the Songs had used up their share of company funds and cut off remittances to Argentina. Song Feiqing felt that he had been betrayed by his Cantonese business associate Du Zhishen. In a letter he wrote to Shi Shaodong in 1953, he stated, "What a shame it is to have not been able to know this person's [true nature], a shame that we trusted him who finally turned his back against us at this critical moment. I feel this as more disheartening than I did with the Chinese Communists' brutality. Killing, beating, and scorn from your enemies is imaginable, but betrayal by a close friend is like my heart being stabbed a thousand times."[109]

Without money or significant resources, Song and his brothers began to fight and suspect each other of having miss-appropriated money.[110] Song's brother later wrote that Song Feiqing "was badly hurt in his heart. Work of his whole life, gone. Life, aged. Wife, nagging. Children, not pleased. Brothers, disobeying. Friends, deserting. Money, used. Present situation, stranded in Argentina. Future, the Communists would persecute him; the Nationalists would persecute him. Health, heart, [illegible]. It's total darkness. It's the end. From despair developed hatred."[111] On 17 July 1955, Song Feiqing died in Argentina. His dreams of establishing an Industrial Eden died with him.[112]

After Song's death, Hong Kong Dongya continued to operate for another three years, though without direct oversight by Song Feiqing's immediate family. All accounts indicate that it was not a successful venture. Toward the end of its life, the Hong Kong factory employed workers only on a daily wage basis.[113] Gone was any pretense of the fabled Industrial Eden Dongya had worked so hard to develop in Tianjin in the 1930s and 1940s. Ironically, Hong Kong Dongya ended its life in a labor dispute. Because of economic difficulties, the Oriental Corporation Ltd. of Hong Kong closed down its spinning operations in May of 1958 when it laid off eighty workers and ceased dyeing and packaging in July when it tried to lay off its remaining fifty-five workers. The workers occupied the factory, refusing to leave and held the company's remaining inventory of products hostage until they received adequate severance.[114]

Failure in Hong Kong and Argentina showed the extent to which Song was exhausted by years of struggle and also points to how much of his earlier success had relied on support from developmental, and even extractive, states. Dongya as an overseas Chinese capitalist enterprise ceased to exist, but the company back in Tianjin continued to operate, and it became the center of attempts to control the narrative on the Song family legacy.

8 Industrial Eden's Legacy under Socialist Development

IN MANY WAYS the stories of Song Chuandian and Song Feiqing were larger than life from the beginning. Song Chuandian's rags to riches story, his involvement in warlord politics, and his fall from grace all seem worthy of a novel of archetypical rise and decline. He absorbed the gospel of development and ran with it in a direction and to a scale his British Baptist missionary mentors never imagined. Likewise, Song Feiqing's story of the eldest son rebuilding the family empire on a new model that combined May Fourth enlightenment, populism, notions of scientific modernity, consumer culture, and developmental help from the state took on a resonance in China that far outstripped the importance of the Dongya Corporation in economic terms. The mythology of Dongya, in particular, began almost as soon as Song Feiqing founded the company in 1932 and derived in part from his drive to present the company as something more than the average business firm, as a transformative vehicle for social change.

As time went on, Song Feiqing gradually lost control of the narrative of his own life as a businessperson. By the 1940s, he was responding testily to accusations that as a "capitalist" he was not working for the good of society. In 1949 and 1950, as part of his accommodation with the new Communist regime, he fought for his very survival as a capitalist in socialist China and worked to reshape his image so that it would be consistent with Communist policies.

After Song Feiqing left China in 1950, political actors, cultural critics, and even loyal employees took up his legacy and made claims about whether he was a good capitalist or a bad capitalist. The standards for those judgments changed with shifts in political direction and with the identities of the individuals involved. Proponents of the bad capitalist view focused on Song's relationship with his employees and with international markets. He was portrayed as an exploiter of the working classes and a coconspirator in the subjugation of China by imperialism. Supporters of the good capitalist image refuted those claims and pointed to his benevolence, innovative business practices, personnel policies, and patriotism.

Interestingly, when Song Feiqing's supporters lauded Dongya's business success, they rarely mentioned the firm's profits. Thus, in spite of the gulf that lay between the good capitalist and bad capitalist views, both shared an assumption that businesses—and the capitalists who ran businesses—should be judged by their impact on society and their morality rather than simply by profitability. The same assumption underlay much of the work of Song Feiqing and his managers in shaping Dongya's public image. As early as the 1930s, Dongya publicity tried to create a public narrative of a modern, scientific, socially responsible, patriotic, and moral business.

Good Capitalist, Song Feiqing's Own Mythmaking

From the beginning, Song Feiqing and the Dongya Corporation were astoundingly successful in generating and spreading a narrative that stressed the modernity of the company, its patriotic nature, and its role as symbol of scientific and compassionate business. This narrative appeared in the Tianjin press as early as October 1933, when *Dagong bao* profiled Dongya as part of its "national products investigation." In the article, the newspaper listed the major foreign brands of imported wool knitting yarn in China, and then said they will face a "competitive war to the death" with Dongya for China's market. As part of the profile, the article listed Dongya's modern mechanized equipment in exhaustive, and exhausting, detail.[1] That same year, rumors that Dongya's knitting yarn was not a national product allowed the company to grab the headlines once again when it offered a 10,000 yuan reward to anyone who could prove it.[2] In less than a year after its founding, Dongya had proved itself very successful in getting its name in the papers and at getting its narrative of industrial modernity into the public discourse.

In other instances, when Dongya sponsored a knitting competition in early 1934, not only did it advertise widely in the newspapers, but at the same time *Dagong bao* made the competition the subject of an editorial on the promotion of national products.[3] *Dagong bao* profiled Dongya again in 1936 lauding the company's progress and advanced labor policies.[4] Profiles of Dongya in the press followed one after the other after the war as well, even after Communist victory in 1949.[5] In addition to coverage in the press, the Dongya Corporation produced a constant stream of publications, especially its elaborate annual reports (which due to war were often less than annual) and the monthly magazine the *Ark*, both of which established Dongya's narrative of scientific and hygienic industrial modernity for the reading public. Most profiles in newspapers and magazines repeated the company's version of its development by largely following the narratives of company publications.

Dongya established its larger-than-life narrative by also hosting a constant stream of visitors. Shi Shaodong later recalled that unlike most factories, Dongya never turned away visitors. He wrote, "Feiqing did not see matters in the ordinary way. I have been all over the world and there are factories everywhere and at the gate is a notice 'visitors not allowed.' It is as if those who run factories are afraid of visitors and that visitors and stealing industrial secrets are tied together in a knot. Only on Dongya's gate you could not find such a sign that keeps people off at a distance." In fact, he noted, Song Feiqing welcomed people to copy his methods because by the time they had copied them, Dongya would already be moving on to something better.[6] The visits were, in part, an attempt by Song to spread the Dongya model of Industrial Eden throughout China, and even the world. In the 1934 annual report alone, photographs were printed showing visits by delegations from the North China Methodist Association, Beijing University's school of engineering, and Tianjin Zhongxi girls' high school.[7] In 1936's annual, the litany of visitors is much longer including eighteen groups, mostly school delegations.[8] Dongya gave each visitor copies of company publications that further reinforced the firm's own narrative.[9]

Dongya's footprint in Tianjin became relatively bigger when it seemed to be one of the only Chinese-owned textile firms that could survive China's economic crisis in the early 1930s. As Tianjin's large Chinese-owned cotton mills closed one after another in 1933 and 1934, Dongya's symbolic significance as a Chinese textile producer became more pronounced.[10] During the Japanese occupation, it became one of the few large companies that remained in private hands, and that was the period in which Industrial Eden policies reached their highest level and greatest reputation. In the postwar period, Dongya appeared frequently on a very short list of "large" or "representative" companies. For example, in 1946 an industrial advisory group for Yanjing University listed Dongya along with other iconic industries in North China such as Jiuda, Renli, Kailan Coal (Kailuan) and China Textile (Zhongsha); in 1947 *Dagong bao* enumerated the companies with which the Nationalist government's industry and commerce guidance commission had met as "Dongya, Renli, Zhongfang and other factories"; and again during the economic crisis of 1948, the government held a meeting where twenty factories sent representatives, and Dongya (along with Renli) was one of only four listed by name.[11] In May of 1948, when Tianjin established its own industrial association, Song Feiqing was elected one of twenty-five directors.[12] Likewise wage statistics on the textile industry in Tianjin compiled by the central government in Nanjing in 1947 included only three factories: China Cotton, Hengyuan (cotton), and Dongya.[13] The prominence of Dongya in these sources shows that the company's symbolic importance far outweighed its economic impact. According to a 1946 report by the Central Social Ministry, Dongya was only average sized among the twenty companies listed. Dongya had 976 workers, making it just larger than the average of 723 workers per factory. Dongya was one of seven textile factories, but it had only about one-tenth of the total textile workforce.[14]

Perhaps Dongya's greatest success in shaping its own narrative, though, was maintaining the fiction that it produced wool yarn as its main product. Dongya probably only produced significant amounts of wool yarn for ten of the twenty years from 1932 to 1952. Yet, company profiles and publications all trumpeted the fact that "the most famous product of the company is 'Butting Ram' wool yarn."[15] In truth, for most of the period after 1943, the company's main, and often only, product was gunnysacks. Nonetheless, the company's public identity was inextricably tied to knitting yarn as a modern consumer product.

After Japanese surrender, Dongya largely succeeded in rewriting history to represent the entire war period as a time of hardship and patriotic sacrifice.[16] Song Feiqing overcame public accusations of collaboration, and even outright spying, from longtime backer Sun Tongxuan, whose hyperbolic claims failed to gain traction, even during the supercharged witch-hunting of the postwar period. It is interesting to note that Sun bolstered his accusations against Song Feiqing by claiming that Song Chuandian too was a traitor who had provided information to the Japanese army at the time of the Jinan Incident in 1928.[17] Sun's strategy foreshadowed later Maoist period rhetoric when the Songs were condemned as a whole family. At the same time, Sun's accusations were predicated on widely accepted norms of patriotism and social good expected of businesspeople.

Another challenge to the Song image came in the mid-1940s when discussions of capitalism's negative role in society came to the fore. Song Feiqing responded with essays on the relationship between labor and capital. Most famously, he turned to the issue in a speech published in the Dongya Corporation newsletter in June of 1947 and titled "Labor and Capital Are on the Same Side." Song stated, "We often hear 'in industry there is labor and there is capital. Labor provides effort and capital provides money. The two sides are different and have conflicting interests.' " In contrast to this perception circulating in society at the time, Song argued that "this kind of thinking is incomplete and is harmful to both sides. In truth labor and capital are part of the same body and united [yitide, lianhede]. They also have the same goal and assist each other. Labor and capital are on the same side and have no distinction in terms of goals." Using a biological metaphor, Song said that "the limbs and organs of the body have different responsibilities and functions, but they must cooperate together for all to develop and only then can the body remain healthy."[18] It is not a coincidence that Song came up with this formulation after the labor unrest that practically tore Dongya apart. Clearly he was looking for a way of reconciling management and labor and restoring the ideal of Industrial Eden. A few months later, a published profile of Dongya in a government-related journal went to some lengths to prove that Song Feiqing was not a run-of-the-mill exploitative capitalist. That article stated, "Dongya does not have a 'big fish' shareholder and also no bureaucratic capital so it can develop as it has today. The development of a personnel system with everyone cooperating together provides special benefits which this reporter believes are quite good."[19] Thus Dongya was a company without a single owner and with personnel policies that created unity. By implication, then, Song Feiqing was not a capitalist at all. Song himself returned to this theme about a year later in the speech to his assembled employees in August 1948. In this speech he argued that a bicycle cart driver is just as much a capitalist as anyone, as were Dongya's employees who had all received shares in the company.[20] In his view, a capitalist was simply someone who received benefit from business. Industrialists were no different from bicycle cart drivers. Song Feiqing, who along with his family controlled about 5 percent of Dongya, was no different from one of his workers who owned one or two shares.

At the time Song Feiqing tried to take control of the discourse on capitalism, the Nationalist regime was already disintegrating in North China. The victory of the Communist Party brought a new regime that doomed to failure Song's attempt to redefine the relationship between capitalists and labor. The iconic status of the Dongya Corporation and Song Feiqing in Tianjin did not change, however, and both became symbolically central to defining the alliance between business and the Communist Party's New Democratic developmental state of the very early PRC period and the socialist developmental policies that took over shortly thereafter. Long after Song Feiqing's departure from China, his reputation and that of his father would be subject to waves of approbation and approval. Study of the course of the narrative about the Song family and Dongya, their legacy, thus tells us much about the relationship between the People's Republic of China's developmental state and private business.

Bad Capitalist, 1951–1952

Coverage of Dongya and Song Feiqing in the Tianjin press after the Communist revolution had been mixed, but their iconic status was undeniable. In the same article that suggested Song was "an unrepentant capitalist," the reporter recalled the birth of the Dongya Corporation amid foreign imperialism by describing the origin of the Butting Ram brand in poetic exaltation.

On top of a pile of stones, two rams go head to head. This [statue] is the three-dimensional emblem at the gates of the Dongya Corporation. . . . It also symbolizes this firm. On the coast of a colony [treaty-port Tianjin], the patriotic capitalist class was pinched between two "rams" (the East and the West) and ran into all kinds of obstacles. In order to strive for the broad domestic masses, [they] could only use the kung fu power of the cleverness of written Chinese characters. "Ram" [yang 羊] is also [a homophone] for "foreign" [yang 洋]. . . . Thus "Butting Ram [or 'oppose the foreigners'] brand" wool yarn appeared.[21]

Dongya achieved some success in the 1930s, but its position competing against much larger foreign competitors was highly tenuous. Nonetheless, even a Communist-run newspaper was willing to adopt the heroic Dongya narrative of patriotic import-substitution—replacing imports with domestically produced goods. In this version, though, Dongya stood alone and the article left out the assistance the company received from the developmental policies of the Communists' bitter enemies, the Nationalist state.

As the new Communist regime quickly and quietly instituted new controls on private business, as the New Democratic developmental state quickly shifted to the socialist developmental state, public proclamations of cooperation between the Communist Party and capitalists continued. That public narrative changed dramatically with the Three Antis campaign at the end of 1951. This campaign aimed at eliminating the "three harms" of corruption, waste, and bureaucratism. Although Tianjin's leadership announced that this campaign was directed at government officials and others who worked for the revolution, Mayor Huang Jing's speech launching the movement also pointed out that the source of most bribery was "business and industrial circles."[22] If that statement did not scare Tianjin businesspeople enough, a speech by Huang Huoqing, a party vice-secretary and head of the People's government union, a few months later in January 1952 refocused the Three Antis attack almost entirely at capitalists. After affirming the patriotic contributions of capitalists in opposing feudalism and imperialism and acknowledging their right to function in socialist society, Huang Huoqing reminded listeners that the weak points of capitalists needed to be criticized. Among these points, he included "exploitation of workers, eating without working, benefiting at the expense of others, only pursuing profit, using public to help private, speculation, waste, indulgence," and so on.[23]

Dongya's first major casualty from the campaign came less than a month later when the company fired its chairman of the board, Zi Yaohua. According to *Progressive Daily*, "Zi Yaohua repeatedly violated government orders and refused to come clean. He truly shamed the country and the people, this kind of person could certainly not represent the board of directors as chairman, so it was decided to rescind his appointment."[24] Although Zi's alleged crimes had more to do with his primary job as manager of the Tianjin branch of the Shanghai Commercial and Savings Bank, the message was clear. The public face of cooperation among the party, capitalists, and workers forged by Liu Shaoqi in Tianjin in the spring of 1949 was now over.

At the end of February 1952 the attack shifted to Dongya vice president Wang Xinsan. Wang had appeared clearly on the side of the Communist Party as recently as only four months before in October 1951 when he took charge of the Tianjin parade celebrating the "Resist America, Aid North Korea" campaign. Now he was criticized under the Three Antis movement for having committed "illegal behavior . . . to take over leadership of the Unified Jute Purchase Office . . . to steal property. . . . That office's loss is at the least more than 200 billion yuan and the loss in production is even more serious. This fact fully reveals a criminal wild attack of the capitalist class on the state and the people."[25] Wang Xinsan was sentenced to five years imprisonment.[26]

As the attack shifted from bureaucratism within the government to misdeeds in the business sector, the Three Antis movement morphed into the Five Antis attack on the five toxins: bribery, tax evasion, theft of industrial materials, theft of government wealth, and theft of economic information. At first, Dongya workers, accustomed to Three Antis activism, had no idea how to proceed with the Five Antis campaign. Company leaders had to hold intensive education sessions telling workers what they should do. As their first major target, campaign organizers chose another vice president, Chen Xisan. Workers hung a sign in Chen Xisan's office saying "the only way out is to come clean." Under this pressure, Chen made a tearful confession, which gave workers more confidence in finding other targets. Even then, an internal report regretted the fact that some workers took a passive attitude, saying that you could not eat the "Five Antis" and it was better to just stay at work than participate in the campaign.[27]

Nonetheless the Five Antis campaign picked up speed, and Song Feiqing became the primary target of attacks in spite of the fact that most employees still did not understand his crimes. An official from the local neighborhood committee gave a report thoroughly outlining his offenses. The report called him a comprador, a term used to refer to Chinese who worked for and helped foreign imperialists, and said he had a slavish (to foreigners) nature. The report also criticized his role as an evil businessperson, and his thieving and traitorous behavior toward the country. Even then, many employees said "Song may have been bad, but he was not bad to me," so the company organized a series of criticism meetings at which activists spoke up in detail about their own oppression. As small meetings gave way to bigger meetings, more and more activists spoke up. As the atmosphere heated up, worker activists began hunting for clues. Workers in the cafeteria investigated money spent to purchase food and factory workers pored over accounting records.[28]

As the investigation expanded, longtime Song family loyalists often bore the brunt of the attack, and their stories too became part of the legacy. You Baoshan had started out as an apprentice at Dechang back in Shandong and then worked for Song Chuandian both in the family bus company and as a secretary during Chuandian's tenure as president of the provincial assembly. When Song Feiqing founded Dongya in Tianjin, You Baoshan became the company's accountant. During one search for evidence of Song's crimes during the Five Antis campaign, Communist Party cadres came to You Baoshan's house, where he "initially refused and did not let them in his house. [Later] when the floor was littered with documents, he still shouted, 'Don't make a mess, when the president [Song Feiqing] comes back, you won't get off easy!'"[29] While it is true that this kind of heroic drama derived in part from the hypercharged political environment of the Maoist period, it also derived in part from the original, larger-than-life narrative promoted by the Songs themselves. You Baoshan was incarcerated and interrogated for two and a half years, but remained loyal to Song Feiqing.[30]

When the new details "uncovered" during the Five Antis campaign were added to the results of investigations of the Three Antis campaign, a final report concluded that investigation at Dongya had found twenty incidents of tax evasion, fifteen of bribery, six of stealing materials, sixteen of hiding enemy (Japanese) property, five of embezzling government property, and two of stealing foreign exchange.[31] The exhaustive detail and endless numbers in reports like this echoed Dongya's own publications of the 1930s and 1940s, which enumerated everything from worker height to number of letters received. Now in the 1950s the Communist regime used similar methods to bolster its own claims to scientific modernity.

During the Five Antis campaign, since most workers had very little contact directly with Song Feiqing, many of their early accusations focused on the activities of middle managers and foremen, Song's "dog legs" (*gou tuizi*), but campaign leaders urged them to "follow [these leads] to the top" so that the true target of the campaign, Song Feiqing, could be exposed. Once all of Song's crimes had been revealed, the campaign activists organized an exhibit to show the world. Among other things, the exhibit claimed to show that Song had secretly taken Dongya's blueprints and plans to Hong Kong to show the insurance company, with the idea of burning Dongya to the ground (to collect the insurance money?).[32]

A detailed description of the exhibit appeared in a national publication, *China Textile Worker*, in April 1952 (see Figure 8.1), claiming that the exhibition showed "the true reactionary character" of the capitalist class. The exhibit moved from critique of the personal habits of the Song family to the management of Dongya to the family's relationship with the state. The

FIGURE 8.1   Posters attacking Song Feiqing in the Five Antis campaign. *China Textile Worker* 7 (1 April 1952), cover.

first room of the exhibit showed the "dissolute and corrupt American-style" lifestyle, "from eating to defecating," of the Song family, including use of American cosmetics by Song Feiqing's wife, gold-handled brushes, and a children's toy from America that purportedly cost as much as a "worker's monthly salary." The exhibit claimed that the Song family had learned slavish admiration of America from American missionaries. Song Feiqing even smoked opium and frequented prostitutes, the posters proclaimed. The second room of the exhibition attacked Song's management style. It dismissed the Dongya Spirit training lectures, factory song, factory precept, and other techniques as a means of hiding the true exploitative nature of the company. But now, "the employees have awakened, especially with this 'Five-Antis' campaign." The third room of the exhibit claimed to show the emptiness of Dongya benefits. According to the narrative presented, workers' children could not get admitted to the primary school, dormitory fees had been deducted from wages, the employee cooperative was actually an opportunity for Song to speculate in commodities, and so on. Distributing shares of Dongya stock to employees was denounced as a way of trying to make them forget their class consciousness. The fourth exhibit room showed Song's collusion with the "bandit" Nationalists, his theft of money before fleeing the country, and his plan to burn down Dongya in Tianjin in order to rebuild in Hong Kong. It also included the litany of abuses that would be repeated over and over for the next two decades. Employees could only use the restroom with a pass, employees could not marry freely, women workers would be fired if they became pregnant, male and female workers had to stay separated, workers were prohibited from striking, and so forth. The exhibit's fifth room provided propaganda so that visitors could truly appreciate the crimes of Song Feiqing and Wang Xinsan, "awaken" and realize that they should never relax their vigilance toward "criminal capitalists."[33]

Most accusations were very general, but some were amazingly specific. In a pattern to be repeated, the subjugation and humiliation of women took a prominent place in the "bad capitalist" narrative. One woman worker had set her steamed buns aside to cool and was fired because it was believed she stole them. She subsequently committed suicide out of despair. In another instance, it was claimed that a woman worker's husband had died, but Song Feiqing refused to lend her money for the funeral. She jumped from a second-story building to kill herself.[34] This likely referred to the case of Liu Dezhong, but an oral history from a fellow worker said that a low-level Dongya manager, not Song Feiqing, had refused the loan. The pressure to follow crimes to the top during the Five Antis campaign, however, obscured such details.

The attacks during the Five Antis movement rewrote the narrative of the family's history with little regard to accuracy. For example, the fact that the Qingzhou missionaries actually were British, not American, was now an inconvenient truth, because Communist propaganda during the Korean War targeted the United States. Many of the accusations were based on the premise that anything that happened at Dongya before the era of Communist control was fair game. For example, movement of funds from Tianjin to Hong Kong before Communist control now became theft, and the implication was theft of state property. Likewise, everything that happened at Dongya became Song Feiqing's responsibility, even if it happened after he left Tianjin. One of the examples of his exploitative nature was the use of temporary workers in the period from 1951 to 1952, long after he had fled to Hong Kong.[35] Such details did not matter. In the hyperbolic rhetoric of the time, Song Feiqing and other Dongya managers targeted in the campaign were, in the words of a later report, "self-seeking by nature and have the repulsive nature of harming others in order to benefit themselves. In the five years since Liberation, the People's government has provided significant assistance, increased production, and developed operations, but the capitalists are ungrateful and attack the nation savagely.[36] Here we see the true nature of the socialist developmental state, which was now portrayed as carrying the burden of development and in which capitalists no longer had a role.

Although the Five Antis campaign at Dongya was directed at Song Feiqing as an enemy of the people, at the same time, it changed the relationships among the Dongya employees who took part. For example, it gave workers more power in relation to their supervisors. One staff member identified as a resister was "immediately arrested" and the unrepentant manager Ma Shouting was fired. Others, however, "lowered their heads," made a full confession of their mistakes, and stayed on at Dongya, though clearly diminished in the eyes of workers. Even workers were not immune to struggle. The Five Antis period account of the formation of the first union at Dongya after the end of World War II indicated that there were two "running dogs" among the union representatives.[37] They were not mentioned by name, but it was clear that the campaign caused rifts in the company from bottom to top.

In an internal report, Dongya's Communist Party general organization department summed up the monthlong Five Antis campaign at the company as a success, but also with a few problems. "In drawing a clear class line between themselves and Song Feiqing, 90 percent [of workers] were on the side of the union and the party, and the number of worker activists increased from ten plus to thirty-three." Although the writer of the report seemed to take pride in expanding the number of worker activists, thirty-three out of Dongya's approximately one thousand employees seems like a very small number on which to base a campaign that effectively eliminated the power of capitalists in a private corporation such as Dongya. In fact, the report on the Five Antis campaign at Dongya showed that many employees had not realized the extent of their exploitation. As examples of this lack of understanding, one report noted that most workers "believed that Song Feiqing was a model industrialist and philanthropist," and "democracy is not as good as Song Feiqingism." Only a few workers realized that Song Feiqing was "no good." During Five Antis discussions most workers believed that Dongya had paid its fair share of taxes and some even said that the relationship between the company and the workers was one of "water helping the fish and fish helping the water." Some workers even tended toward accepting Song Feiqing's admonition that male workers who go out are like "young masters" and women workers like "young misses." Clearly from the standpoint of the Communist Party, bourgeois thinking permeated Dongya's workforce. If nothing else, these complaints from Communists about the backward thinking of Dongya employees showed that some of them had indeed internalized and accepted the company's Industrial Eden ideology. At the same time, the Communists had a hard time getting their messages across to every worker, some of whom said, "there is no benefit to us for participating in the Five Antis [campaign]."[38]

Nonetheless, the party organization took satisfaction in the fact that "the masses through detailed study mastered the spirit of the political policy of combining punishment with leniency, and now understood that the 'government was truly the people's government' that 'workers were the masters of the nation.'" The recruitment of activists, the attacks on the power of capitalists and their managers, and the forging of a new mentality among workers all showed the political goals of the Five Antis campaign. The campaign had purported economic goals as well, but these were weakly summed up as "thoroughly showing the illegal behavior of capitalists."[39] Perhaps there was indeed reason for Communist Party leaders to believe cowing the capitalists and increasing economic control would contribute to the regime's developmental goals, but most of the evidence from Dongya showed a developmental state with the state firmly in command. For example, the idea of private property had quietly died in the furor. Alleged theft of company property was now by fiat a crime against the people and the state with the implication that the property already belonged to the state even though the formal handover would be some time away. Dongya would survive as a private company for two more years, but it was private in name only. By 1953, Dongya discontinued year-end bonuses to employees.[40] A year later in September 1954, negotiations to make Dongya a joint public-private enterprise concluded and state ownership became official.[41]

Bad Capitalist, 1958–1960

Under direct government control after 1954, Dongya continued to function and at some point even resumed production of knitting yarn and other wool products. Regularization under the bureaucracy of the Communist regime did not end the debates over the legacy of Song Feiqing and the Dongya company.

When the Communist regime launched the Great Leap Forward in 1958 to speed up China's industrialization, attention in Tianjin focused on Dongya once again. In 1960 a kind of popular novel-like "history" of Dongya appeared under apparent collective authorship. Called *Spring Returns to the Earth: The Story of the Workers' Struggles at the Dongya Woolen and Jute Mill* (*Dadihuichun: Dongya maomachang gongren douzheng de gushi*), it was part of a series dedicated to telling the story of Tianjin's businesses from the standpoint of labor struggles.[42] The plot of *Spring Returns to the Earth* takes place mostly in the years between Japanese surrender and a dramatic conclusion in the Five Antis campaign. The Great Leap Forward itself is covered only in an afterword, so it is possible that the book was written just after the Five Antis campaign, but did not appear until it was needed to bolster the party's credibility in the wake of the disastrous Great Leap Forward, which had caused food shortages in cities such as Tianjin.

So much of *Spring Returns to the Earth* included details and descriptions of real people that it indeed showed intimate knowledge of Dongya. It named names and even gave characters specific dialogue to advance the plot. According to the former Dongya manager (and relative of Song Feiqing's wife) Li Jingshan, the book resulted from information provided to Yuan Jing, listed as assisting editor of the book, by two Dongya staff members. After publication, all Dongya employees received a copy and Li later claimed that the book angered some who said they would use it to "wipe themselves after going to the bathroom."[43] Even so, this book became highly influential and some of its stories became part of the evolving legacy of the Song family and Dongya.

Spring Returns to the Earth has a preface that retells the narrative of the Song family beginning with "foreign devil" missionaries in Qingzhou who pushed wheelbarrows of cash around the countryside in order to bribe Chinese into listening to their message. Even then very few people listened except for the poverty-stricken Song Guangxu (Song Chuandian's father) who wanted the money and repeatedly came to listen. In this version of the story, Guangxu goes to work for the missionaries and only then does the missionary Couling notice Guangxu's son, Song Chuandian, whom he eventually takes as a godson. For the most part the capsule history of Dongya in the book's preface follows the revelations and accusations made public during the Five Antis campaign, including the idea that most Dongya workers never received any of the company's vaunted benefits.[44] The main part of *Spring Returns to the Earth* begins in 1945 with Japan's surrender and follows a story of union formation and labor activism. One of the heroes of the book is Zhang Guojun, a Communist Party labor organizer who participated in the first employee association of the Communist period and whose speech helped seal the deal in the spring of 1949, when, after Liu Shaoqi's visit, the union bowed to demands to promote production rather than worker rights and allow "exploitation" to make a contribution. In *Spring Returns to the Earth*, though, there is no thought of cooperation with the capitalist Song Feiqing.

In one chapter, Zhang organizes a theater club to perform the play *Song of Rejuvenation* (*Huichun zhi qu*, literally, "song of the return of the spring") by the leftist writer Tian Han. In this telling, Song Feiqing congratulates the workers on their performance and takes them to dinner to celebrate, but secretly wants to bribe them into being his allies and only performing plays he approves. As dinner continues, Zhang Guojun thinks to himself, "As soon as you [Song Feiqing] bare your ass, I know what kind of shit you plan to drop . . . you're trying to use [us]." There follows a cat-and-mouse game between Song and Zhang as the latter tries to insert political content into performances. At one point, Song tries to stop a performance, but the audience of workers claps and supports the actors until all chaos breaks loose. The last chapter of *Spring Returns to the Earth* recounts the Five Antis campaign at Dongya. With Zhang Guojun away participating in land reform, here the hero is a woman worker named Liu Enying who leads meetings and exposes the crimes of Dongya. This telling contains details not mentioned in the Five Antis work reports quoted above and which may or may not have happened. At one point, vice president Chen Xisan's child cries, "Papa, come clean! Every day you can't eat and can't sleep. . . . You are offending the nation and the people! I am a youth advanced brigade member and I want to take a firm stance and draw a clear line with the capitalist class. If you remain silent, what about Mama and me?"[45] Chen, of course, eventually comes clean under the persistent questioning of Liu Enying and the chapter ends happily in 1954 with the transformation of Dongya into a joint public-private enterprise.

In a brief afterword ecstatic workers at Dongya take part in the Great Leap Forward of 1958, realizing that they had become "masters of the company and the nation" who were working toward the era of Communism to "transform the face of the poor and empty motherland." Dongya is "both a factory and a school for the development of talent for the construction of socialism."[46] In this narrative, Dongya takes its place in the socialist developmental state under the leadership of its workers who had purged and tamed the company's capitalist managers.

Not Such a Bad Capitalist, 1962–1964

As the Chinese leadership came to realize the disastrous consequences of the Great Leap Forward, they reinstituted policies of careful bureaucratic economic planning in the early 1960s. At Dongya, this meant that in 1962 the gunnysack factory was separated and made into the Tianjin Gunnysack

Factory and Dongya became the Tianjin Municipal Joint Public and Private Dongya Woolen Mill (Tianjinshi gongsi heying dongya maofangchang). In 1965 yarn production reached 1.07 million pounds per year, along with 230,000 sweaters and 60,000 wool ropes (used for spinning thread).[47] At some point it became a wholly nationalized state-owned enterprise.

The period of the early 1960s brought moderation in the treatment of China's capitalist legacy. In 1962 Song Feiqing's widow, then living in the United States, wrote to her cousin Li Jingshan, a longtime Dongya employee, for the first time in ten years about the state of the family assets in Tianjin. Under the relatively moderate policies toward capitalists of the time, Li Jingshan made inquiries and assured his cousin that her furniture, savings, and accumulated dividends on Dongya shares could all be collected. He even went so far as to say if she had financial difficulties, she should move back to Tianjin, where "living conditions were good, and the government would care [for her and her family]."[48] It is impossible to know now what Li Jingshan was thinking when he made this proposal. Certainly he was concerned for the welfare of his cousin and perhaps he thought that she would truly be welcome under the relatively moderate policies of the early 1960s. Perhaps authorities had pressured him into making the suggestion. Either way, the idea that Song Feiqing's widow and youngest children could safely return to Tianjin only two years after the publication of *Spring Returns to the Earth* shows the continuing lack of resolution in the struggle in China to deal with the capitalist past. In any event, Song Feiqing's widow remained in the United States and the struggle over the family legacy in China developed without her immediate presence.

In 1964 Li Jingshan cooperated with then Dongya president Yang Tianshou to produce their version of the history of the Dongya Corporation, which was published in the all-China *Wenshi ziliao xuanji*.[49] They tell the story of Dongya with surprisingly little political content or analysis and none of the "labor hero versus evil capitalist" plotline of *Spring Returns to the Earth*. The original manuscript of their history was even more positive, but in publication the editors added sections to the original draft about the "comprador" background of Song Chuandian and other commentary such as a section about all of Dongya workers welcoming the arrival of the Communists in 1949. These added sections also indict the relationship between business and the prerevolutionary state by saying that "the capitalist class and the power of officials have always relied on each other."[50] All in all though, there was apparently space in the early 1960s for a moderate approach to China's capitalist past, and this narrative, as told by Li Jingshan and Yang Tianshou, focused on the innovative nature of Dongya management, marketing, and social policy. At the same time, unlike *Spring Returns to the Earth*, there is almost no mention of the work of underground party members.

At about the same time that this new history of Dongya appeared, in May and June of 1964 the investigation of the past of the Song family and the Dongya Corporation continued with at least six oral histories of longtime Song/Dongya employees, which I use throughout this book.[51] The immediate impetus for these histories is unknown, but their tone struck a balance between moderate policies toward capitalists and continued class struggle. Thus Li Jingshan, who had conducted a self-criticism during the Five Antis campaign, was listed as having a capitalist political aspect, but also a "currently pretty good attitude."[52] Four of the other interviewees were Communist Party members: the engineer Meng Guanglin, former workers Gao Xinzhai and Hao Guanyi, and former secretary and clerk Wei Yanying, the only woman with an oral history remaining from 1964. The sixth interviewee, Feng Naishen, was a former worker, but had no political aspect listed.[53] Three of the six, Li, Hao, and Feng, had begun working for Song Chuandian back in Shandong, showing the continuing interest in the entire Song legacy, not just that of Dongya's. The oral histories of the party members and former workers portrayed a relatively negative view of the Song family and Dongya. Wei Yanying, in particular, told the tragic story of having to undergo two abortions.

Bad Capitalist, 1965–1976

A year after these interviews, and likely drawing on them, a novel appeared in Tianjin telling the story of Song Feiqing and the Dongya Corporation yet again. Called *A Civilized Hell* (*Wenming diyu*), the novel by the writer Shi Ying tells the story of the fictional woolen mill the "Yadong Company," run by the fictional Sun family headed by Sun Peiqing. The bald attempt at disguise was meant to fool no one. "Yadong" is simply Dongya in reverse, and "Sun Peiqing" sounds much like "Song Feiqing" (the last character, *qing*, is even the same). The afterword of the book states explicitly that it concerns a "certain" woolen mill in Tianjin and draws from the true oral history accounts of veteran workers. In the novel, Shi tells the story from the standpoint of several workers, some of them Communist Party members and activists and others who become awakened under capitalist oppression. Unlike *Spring Returns to the Earth*, which has substantial coverage of the events of the early socialist period, *A Civilized Hell* confines itself to the politically much safer ground of prerevolutionary China. The novel starts in 1935 and culminates in the 1946 strike when workers' demands succeed with the provision of "three bags of flour and a bolt of cloth." According to the novel, success in the strike marked the beginning of the destruction of the civilized hell of Song Feiqing's Industrial Eden, and a year later workers prepared to welcome the revolution and see the final conclusion of capitalist exploitation.[54]

Humiliation of women workers features prominently in the novel and it retells the story of Liu Dezhong once again. In the oral history version of a coworker, Liu had tried to borrow money for her husband's funeral from a low-level manager. In the Five Antis exhibit of 1952 version, Liu had tried to borrow money directly from Song Feiqing. In *A Civilized Hell*, Liu, now renamed Lu Xiuyun, tries to borrow money from a personnel department manager at Dongya (Figure 8.2). The twist in the *Civilized Hell* version includes the added element that she wants to borrow money against the value of her Dongya shares. Dongya policies at the time required that workers complete three years of trouble-free work before actually taking possession of the shares. In the novel, her three-year probationary period is almost up and the shares would soon be hers, but the ruthless personnel manager refuses to lend her money and claims that she cursed him. This is a violation of rules and so she forfeits her right to the shares altogether. In despair, she jumps from the top of a building to kill herself.[55] In this telling, Liu Dezhong's story serves the purpose of discrediting Song Feiqing's practice of giving shares to employees, and the chapter that features the story is titled, "Shares with Blood on Them." Thus Liu's story not only shows the cold-heartedness of Dongya management, it also undermines Song Feiqing's idea that employee stock ownership put labor and capital on "the same side."

FIGURE 8.2 Illustration from *A Civilized Hell*, where a personnel department employee refuses to lend a woman worker money. Shi Ying, *Wenming diyu* (1965), opposite p. 90.

A Civilized Hell apparently captured the correct tone and zeitgeist of the Chinese Communist attitude toward capitalism at the time. Some chapters were reprinted in *People's Daily* and other newspapers such as the *Beijing Evening News*. The Central Broadcasting Network broadcast the novel in its entirety, and it was reviewed widely in publications such as *Literature Review* and *Guangming Daily*.[56] Publication of *A Civilized Hell* coincided with the end of the moderate policies toward capitalists of the early 1960s. Within a year of its publication, China, and the Dongya Corporation, would be embroiled in the Cultural Revolution. Many of the accusation brought against Song Feiqing, other members of the Song family, and Dongya managers during the Cultural Revolution would echo those of the Five Antis campaign, as well as the accounts in *Spring Returns to the Earth* and *A Civilized Hell*. This time, however, the attack would broaden and include party members who were now accused of having colluded with capitalists. Liu Shaoqi ranked first among the new targets of attack.

As the Cultural Revolution got under way in late 1966, Liu Shaoqi's 1949 visit to Tianjin became one of the major mistakes upon which his critics focused.[57] One Red Guard group in Beijing identified as the Education Ministry Guard Mao Zedong Thought Struggle Corps (Jiaoyubu baowei Mao Zedong sixiang zhandoutuan) listed Liu's Tianjin talks as one of his ten great crimes. A Red Guard group from Nankai University in Tianjin later published a detailed attack on Liu Shaoqi in a Beijing Qinghua University Red Guard publication. This piece specifically referred to Liu Shaoqi's crimes at the Dongya Corporation. According to this piece, the Nankai University Red Guards and a Dongya Company Red Guard group organized a large meeting at the Tianjin arena. At the meeting, revolutionary veteran workers revealed Liu's crimes. Chief among those crimes was Liu Shaoqi's speech to Dongya workers in which he said, according to this report, "Now your status has increased. In the past could you have met someone like me? If I am not the number one in China, I am number two." According to the Red Guards, this revealed Liu's wolflike ambition to take control of China from Mao Zedong, the real number one. In addition, Liu told Dongya's workers to "listen to Song Feiqing" and, most famously, "under certain historical conditions, exploitation is advanced." He then told Song, "You must acknowledge exploitation. You are not forbidden to exploit, but don't exploit a small number to death. In this way you can exploit more people in the future, exploit more greatly." The Red Guards indicted Liu for promising Song Feiqing ten factories to manage and for letting him go freely to Hong Kong. As for Song, among other things, the Red Guards called him a "reactionary capitalist who was king of hell, of 'a civilized hell.' "[58] This publication was so influential that the accusations were eventually picked up and reprinted by overseas Chinese newspapers in San Francisco.[59]

In April 1967, *People's Daily* picked up the story as well. Its version emphasized Song's connections with the Nationalists in the 1930s, the Japanese during the war, and it declared that that Song had been swollen with reactionary arrogance when he heard that the "leading person taking the capitalist road in the Party (Liu Shaoqi)" was coming to visit capitalists in Tianjin in 1949.[60]

Although the Red Guards happily borrowed "civilized hell" from the title of Shi Ying's 1965 novel about Dongya, Shi was unable to enjoy his place in the sun as a critic of Dongya. As a veteran party member, he was soon labeled as one who "sang the same song as Liu Shaoqi," and one who "held up the placard of capitalism."[61] Veteran Communist Party cadres at Dongya suffered much the same fate. Zhang Guojun, who had joined the party in 1946, led the Dongya union at the time of the Communist takeover, and featured as hero in *Spring Returns to the Earth*, was working at another factory during the Cultural Revolution, but he could not escape Dongya's taint. He was "labeled a 'traitor,' 'big follower of Liu Shaoqi,' 'Song Feiqing's big favorite,' etc." Because he had shaken Liu Shaoqi's hand during the visit on 21 April 1949, Zhang was made the object of Maoist-style "struggle sessions," where accusations are made at a public meeting intended to humiliate, and sometimes harm, perceived public enemies. Shi Xiaodong, Shi Shaodong's brother, who had joined the Communist Party and had been sent to contact Song Feiqing on the eve of the Communist revolution "was called 'Liu Shaoqi's embodiment' and struggled against." Likewise, "Zhang Guoxun, Zhang Guojun's brother, who had transferred to run the Tianjin wool rope factory before the Cultural Revolution and who had done underground work before liberation was called a 'traitor,' and a member of the 'clique taking the capitalist road to power' and was struggled against."[62]

With such veteran cadres on the ropes, Song Feiqing loyalists fared even worse, including employees Li Jingshan and Yang Tianshou who had written the relatively moderate history of Song Feiqing and Dongya in 1963. Long-time employees and Song family retainers were called

loyalist "running dogs" and "ox ghosts and snake spirits." The factory director, Yang Tianshou (later vice-chairman of Tianjin zhengxie) and assistant manager, Li Jingshan, were both struggled against and put under supervised labor. The assistant factory director Chen Xisan who was recovering from a stroke at home was dragged by the "Red Guards" and "revolutionary corps" to the factory for struggle where he died after several days of conflict. Many in the factory were struggled against from the party secretary at the top to technicians, managers and veteran workers. Because veteran workers from before liberation all owned shares (Song Feiqing had given shares to employees), they were labeled as exploiting criminals during the Cultural Revolution. As many as one hundred people were struggled against creating a nationwide record.[63]

I am not sure "one hundred people" was truly a nationwide record, but for a factory Dongya's size it was a significant number. Once again, the company's symbolic and iconic status drew more than an average share of attention. At the same time, the ownership of shares by workers, which had been the subject of attack as "valueless" in *A Civilized Hell* only two years before, now appeared to have enough value to mark one as a capitalist. Ironically, this classification was consistent with Song Feiqing's 1940s definition of a capitalist.

Red Guards ran rampant on the factory grounds. "The statue of butting rams at the factory was destroyed by the Red Guards from the factory school and the 'Revolutionary Corps.' The trees in the Dongya courtyard were uprooted, the pond and the small manmade hill were seen as remnants of the old, pre-Communist society and leveled. 'Butting Ram' brand wool yarn stopped production, artisanal products were burned and the yarn completely looted." On 14 August 1966 the Dongya name finally disappeared as the factory became the Tianjin Municipal Number Three Wool Spinning Factory.[64]

Meanwhile activists at the Number Three Wool Spinning Factory (formerly Dongya) proved quick to capitalize on their unique situation in the evolving Cultural Revolution. *Tianjin Daily* devoted an entire page to articles from company activists on 6 November 1967. Many of the articles focused on Liu Shaoqi's relationship to Song Feiqing as evidence of his reactionary "capitalist roader" tendencies. Most articles repeated the accusations of the earlier Red Guard attacks. In the hyperbolic rhetoric of the time, articles screamed, "Liu Shaoqi threw himself into the arms of the reactionary capitalist Song Feiqing," "Liu Shaoqi turned his back on the party center and Chairman Mao to run hurriedly to our factory to promote the idea that 'exploitation can make a contribution,'" and "workers were told they should listen to Song Feiqing."[65] Two months later another full-page article thoroughly condemned Liu Shaoqi's Tianjin talks, repeating once again a version of Liu's words to Song Feiqing.[66] At the height of the Cultural Revolution, Song Feiqing, Dongya's prerevolutionary legacy, and capitalism itself had no redeeming characteristics.

Good Capitalist, 1976–Present

The high tide of political activism of the Cultural Revolution eventually faded, and with Mao's death in 1976, the socialist developmental state began to lumber away from political goals and back toward economic ones. A worker at Dongya, Chen Xiuwen, who had entered the company at thirteen, and who had been sent by the new regime to study textiles at college in 1958, had been criticized during the Cultural Revolution, but in 1976 she suggested to factory leaders and technicians the restoration of production of the Butting Ram brand and received support. After a quarter century of Maoist-style management, however, no one at the factory knew exactly how to reproduce the pre-1949 product. I suspect this was partly because Dongya had manufactured little knitting yarn during the last decade or so of Song Feiqing's administration. In order to reverse engineer what had been Dongya's most famous product, Chen brought in three pounds of Butting Ram yarn from her home and gave it to the factory as a standard for experimentation. As Chen Xiuwen later recounted, she "trained workers and established a system of procedures and rules which were posted on the factory floor. With struggle and hard work, production of Butting Ram wool yarn was restored in 1978."[67] For veteran employees, posted rules and procedures must have echoed Song Feiqing's management practices.

Subsequently, in 1979 Zhang Guoxun was brought back as factory director. In spite of all that had happened, early underground party workers at Dongya ended up running the machinery of the socialist developmental state. Zhang recommended restoration of the Dongya name to the Textile Bureau, which implemented the change in August 1980 when the factory became the Tianjin Municipal Dongya Woolen Mill (Tianjinshi Dongya Maofang Chang). As a commemoration of the name restoration, the factory commissioned a replacement for the Butting Ram statue that had been destroyed during the Cultural Revolution. The sculptor based the new work on a picture from the *Ark Monthly*, the Dongya women's magazine from the 1930s. "It was very close in appearance to the original which was destroyed during the Cultural Revolution, but a bit smaller."[68]

The period immediately after Mao's death witnessed confusing attitudes about China's capitalist past. Song Feiqing was still officially an enemy of the people as seen in a manuscript called "The Capitalist Exploitation of the Dongya Corporation," prepared by an unspecified Marxism-Leninism research institute in 1978. It is not known if this manuscript ever saw publication, but its tone echoed the accusations of the Five Antis campaign and the Cultural Revolution. For example, there is an entire section on Dongya's management methods called "The Spirit of Slavery."[69] In contrast to this Maoist-style portrayal, a number of Tianjin scholars and local historians began to revise their appraisal of the legacy of Dongya and the Song family. They received political cover in these actions by a decision of the Communist Party to reappraise Liu Shaoqi's Tianjin talks. In a full-page editorial explaining that Liu's ideas were consistent with Marxism-Leninism, the *Tianjin Daily* did not refer to Song Feiqing by name, but just said that Liu had spoken at a meeting with businesspeople and industrialists.[70] A small space appeared for Song Feiqing's rehabilitation in the public narrative.

One of the first relatively positive appraisals of Song Feiqing came in his biographical entry in a collection published by the Modern History Institute of the Chinese Academy of Sciences. This entry used the relatively moderate 1963 article by Yang Tianshou and Li Jingshan as one of its main sources. In this entry, Song Chuandian was still labeled a comprador, but Song Feiqing escaped without any explicit condemnation. The account of his patriotic competition with foreign companies in the 1930s was almost glowing and it said that during the Japanese occupation, the authorities "forced" Dongya to produce gunnysacks for the army." It also goes into some detail about the "Dongya spirit" and Song's management methods.[71]

In 1982, the same year that biographical entry appeared, the Tianjin People's Political Consultative Conference history and literature office convened a series of meetings among former Dongya managers and also collected a number of new oral and written histories from these individuals who had suffered under Maoist policies, but whose knowledge of the past now came to be valued.[72] These activities resulted in a lengthy piece in the office's *Wenshi ziliao*, a periodical that published articles about local history, called "Song Feiqing and the Tianjin Dongya Enterprise Corporation," under the authorship of the four former employees who participated in the discussions and edited by Fang Zhaolin, the Zhengxie official who organized the interviews and compiled them into this text.[73] This piece was a groundbreaking interpretation which portrayed Song, at least in part, in a positive manner. It provided a balanced account of Song's business affairs including the Japanese occupation and postwar periods. Like all publications in the post-Mao period, the authors devoted considerable space to discussion of Dongya's management methods.[74]

Subsequently, the 1980s witnessed a spate of publications based on the recollections of former Song family employees and acquaintances as well as on archives from the company itself. In 1984 the Tianjin Academy of Social Sciences also published a collection of documents about the Song family and Dongya, which had been in preparation since 1964, but publication had been impossible in the tumultuous political climate of the Cultural Revolution.[75] The capsule history in the introduction to the collection shows continued ambivalence about Song. It did not even mention the war with Japan, devoted about a third of its space to Dongya's innovative management, but still ended with a Marxist twist, saying that Song's innovative management served to increase exploitation of labor.[76] The new interest in China's capitalist past was not limited to Dongya and Song Feiqing, his father too received new attention. In 1982 and 1987, the Shandong People's Political Consultative Conference literature and history office published accounts of Song Chuandian and the family's origins in Shandong.[77] In 1989 the local Qingzhou People's Political Consultative Conference *wenshi ziliao* collection featured a history of Song written by a former employee.[78]

These early post-Mao publications from the 1980s have an inconsistent tone. The publications based on the input of former managers made a generally positive appraisal of Dongya and the Song family's legacy. Others such as the Tianjin Academy of Social Sciences collection took a more orthodox Marxist point of view calculating surplus value and critiquing capitalist methods. The Shandong articles about Song Chuandian were positively excoriating. Nonetheless, it was clear that the history of capitalism was on the rise. Perhaps in reaction to the new attention to capitalists, Shi

Ying's *A Civilized Hell* was republished in 1983. The timing coincided with the Communist Party's Anti-Spiritual Pollution Campaign of that year. It is interesting to note, however, that the cover of the new edition gave readers only the title, whereas the 1965 edition had used a drawing that proclaimed to all readers the revolutionary content of the novel (see Figure 8.3).

By the 1990s, appraisals of the Song family, especially Song Feiqing and to a lesser extent his father, and the Dongya Corporation became uniformly positive. In fact, in these publications, Song Feiqing became something of a model capitalist to be studied and emulated for his innovative management and patriotism. In these new narratives, his faults and mistakes faded into the background. For example, Fang Zhaolin's history of the Song family and Dongya stressed Song Feiqing's patriotism and innovative management methods.[79] A similar approach appeared in *Dongya's Corporate Culture*, written and published by the Dongya Corporation itself, as well as in Wang Weigang's account of Song Feiqing, published first in the series *China's Great Capitalists*.[80] Wang's account was the fullest to appear, yet he devoted sixty-five pages to history of the Song family and Dongya before 1938

FIGURE 8.3   Contrasting covers of *A Civilized Hell* from 1965 (*left*) and 1983 (*right*). Shi Ying, *Wenming diyu*, 1965 and 1983, author's collection.

and forty-seven pages to Song's management methods, but only forty pages to the entire period of war and revolution from 1938 to 1949. In a letter to Song Feiqing's son, he proudly proclaimed that his biography was part of a collection that was the first public celebration of the struggles, personalities, and contributions of capitalists in (Communist) China.[81] In 1997 a biography of Song Feiqing appeared in the multivolume *Century of Chinese Business Giants*. The capsule summary at the beginning repeated the accepted story of Song's life and accepted Song's own narrative that he founded the Dongya Corporation "to save the nation through industry and strengthen modern management methods." This author too left out the entire period from 1938 to 1949 and closed with the sentiment that Song's "management mentality and spirit of saving the nation deserve conscientious thought from people today."[82] Even the capsule history provided by the Dongya company itself at the time of a visit by Song Feiqing's children and myself in 2000 follows this line by focusing on the 1930s, skipping to nationalization in the 1950s, and then skipping again to the 1980s.[83] These 1990s positive portrayals reinforced the iconic, and now almost mythical, status of the Song family and Dongya. For example, in its list of the memorable dates of the twentieth century in Tianjin, the newspaper *Jinwan Bao* listed Song Feiqing's founding of Dongya as one of only two notable events of 1932.[84]

Since 2000, subsequent publications and two television documentaries— one for China's Central Television Channel Ten in 2005 and one for Xiamen Television—generally follow the line of Song Feiqing as a model capitalist, and very often new accounts simply copy parts of previous works.[85] In one odd exception to the "good capitalist" narrative that has dominated the public narrative in China for almost three decades, the Dongya Corporation has been used to teach calculation of surplus value (a Marxist concept) in several training classes.[86] One other major exception exists in an unproduced screenplay synopsis for a twenty-part television drama about Song Feiqing. Focusing on the drama of Song Chuandian's and Song Feiqing's lives, only half of the episodes cover the time from Song Chuandian's rise to the Japanese invasion in 1937. Events after the beginning of World War II make up the other half. Coverage of the Japanese occupation focuses on dramatic events such as the flood of 1939 and Song Feiqing's arrest. The last four episodes deal with the civil war period, the

Communist conquest of Tianjin, and Song Feiqing's death.[87] Perhaps the triumphant narrative of Song Feiqing as the model capitalist was simply not interesting enough for dramatic television. Although this screenplay was never produced, as this book goes to press, Chinese Central Television has commissioned a new screenplay for a multi-part fictionalized drama about Song Feiqing's life.

Narratives of Capitalism

In any case, study of the attempts to shape the narratives of Song Chuandian, Song Feiqing, and the Dongya Corporation tell us much about attitudes in China toward capitalists from the 1930s to today. Most important, these competing narratives tell us that capitalism was not a set of economic arrangements, it was a label, a way of organizing knowledge and understanding the world. The competing "good capitalist" and "bad capitalist" narratives have a common thread, which focused on the role of business in the polity and in society. Profits and balance sheets were often ignored while praise and condemnation both had a significant moral overtone. Capture of the moral high ground in narratives of capitalism, in turn, had real and important effects on the ability of Song Chuandian and Song Feiqing to run their business, as well as on the ability of authoritarian states to rule. For businesspeople and rulers alike in twentieth- and twenty-first-century China, control of the narrative was an important part of allocating and mobilizing material, financial, and human resources.

Conclusion

BY FOCUSING ON Song Feiqing and his father, Song Chuandian, I have shown the workings of four important phenomena: the uneven and arbitrary nature of imperialism, the diversity of Chinese business practices, the use of "capitalism" as a means of labeling enemies and constructing knowledge, and the increasing role for authoritarian governments in the economy matched by increasing expectations for government help from businesspeople. The nature of regime relations with the Song family businesses and Song Feiqing's utopian "Industrial Eden" capitalist vision have provided the two threads that weave this story together. In terms of the first of those threads, although the Songs' story is important, we should remember that there were certainly many firms that had different experiences with each of the authoritarian governments studied here. The impact of developmental and predatory states, like that of imperialism, was uneven, sometimes arbitrary, and varied from one regime to the next.

When Song Chuandian began making hairnets for export, he was in rural Shandong relatively far from central and provincial centers of power. His early business thrived in a kind of laissez-faire space of rural entrepreneurship during a time of transition between the fall of the Qing and the consolidation of warlord rule. Song Chuandian's initial business model, consistent with the gospel of development preached by his missionary mentors, ignored the Chinese state and connected directly with world markets formed by the system of European imperialism. Rather than remain distant from the state, however, Song used his newly gained wealth to enter into democratic politics, becoming head of the Shandong provincial assembly, likely by bribing himself into the position. As the warlord era progressed, Shandong's warlord rulers became more and more extractive, and they finally subdued or co-opted the democratic system and capitalist-politicians such as Song Chuandian himself.

When the new Nationalist state conquered Shandong's warlord in 1928, it declared Song Chuandian an enemy, issued an arrest warrant, and confiscated his property. In spite of this overt act of predation, his son Song Feiqing later managed to gain the patronage of the Nationalist military figure Han Fuju, who not only returned the family property but personally financed the launch of the Dongya Corporation. With this basis of ex officio support, Song Feiqing was in a good position to profit when the Nationalist state transformed itself into a friend of industry by implementing import-substitution policies such as tariffs and tax breaks, which allowed Dongya to be successful in the face of fierce foreign competition. Implementation of these policies, however, seemed arbitrary and confusing, so I call the Nationalist regime an "uncertain" developmental state, one with warlord characteristics and bouts of predatory behavior.

After 1937 Song Feiqing, developed even more symbiotic relations with the Japanese occupation government, which began with the announcement of grand developmental goals. That development was firmly centered on the interests of the Japanese military and Japanese business; however, what may have been developmental from the Japanese viewpoint was extractive from the Chinese point of view. Over the course of the war, the occupation regime became increasingly rapacious—threats of arrest and confiscation always loomed—but doled out favors, special treatment, and monopolies to companies such as Song Feiqing's Dongya Corporation, which could offer support for regime projects, which could corrupt venal regime agents, or which could carve out an advantageous position in the "economy of things" created by inflation and government incompetence.

In the period after the war, the central government of the renewed Nationalist regime proved completely unable to manage the toxic environment created in part by inflation. Song Feiqing retained high hopes for the state's visible hand, but ended up fuming helplessly in the face of the state's impotence. In the end, the regime was an unresponsive developmental state, but it did help Song by providing local coercive power to suppress restive workers.

Like the prewar Nationalists, the early period of the People's Republic of China was close to being a capitalist developmental state. Business had not been entirely nationalized or collectivized in this period, which Mao called "New Democracy" to refer to the alliance between the Communist Party and nonsocialist elements of society, including businesspeople such as Song Feiqing. Thus I call this period the People's "New Democratic" developmental state. The new regime reined in labor unrest and provided financing. In return, Song Feiqing promised cooperation in expanding production and employment. Although this accommodation appeared cooperative on the surface, neither the regime nor Song Feiqing was fully committed to establishing a symbiotic relationship. In reality, New Democracy was ephemeral and the Communists quickly shifted to policies more consistent with those of a socialist developmental state. They took control of finance, distribution, and supply, and although the Dongya Corporation remained technically private, it soon bent to the state's wishes in terms of production goals and "donations" to finance socialist construction.

After Song Feiqing left China in 1950, the regime quickly cast off the veneer of New Democracy and the Three Antis and Five Antis movements showed the true face of a socialist developmental state that rejected capitalism entirely. Living abroad, Song Feiqing no longer had any agency to influence the relationship between his legacy and the Communist state. In firm control of the discourse, the Communist state relied on its relationship with China's "capitalist" past, including the Song legacy, to justify its policies. Capitalists like Song Chuandian and especially Song Feiqing provided convenient enemies in political campaigns. When state policies changed after Mao's death, the state proved equally willing to rehabilitate the Song family legacy as a means to support its new economic policies.

In terms of the second narrative thread, Song Feiqing's Industrial Eden provided a vision of a particular kind of industrialization with moral and patriotic, as well as financial, goals. That vision and the "bad capitalist"–"good capitalist" dichotomy seen in the multiple tellings of Song Feiqing's story have obscured the reality and complexity of his life. A member of the May Fourth generation, Song Feiqing tried to position himself and the Dongya Corporation at the center of trends of modern urban consumerism and scientific management. To achieve these goals he drew eclectically from the Chinese, Christian, and Western influences that shaped his life and the world in which he lived. He engaged with the environment of international imperialism by copying foreign methods, using international markets, and cutting deals with various imperial powers, especially the Japanese. He summed up his flexible approach in advice given to his four oldest children when he sent them to the United States in 1949; he told them to obtain "new knowledge, but not to forget old morality."[1]

Thus in spite of his flexible pragmatism, Song Feiqing treated both business and life as a moral problem. He was sometimes sanctimonious, sometimes elitist, and sometimes lost in pursuit of unreachable dreams. It is impossible to doubt the depth of Song's idealism, his vision of an Industrial Eden where enlightened corporations transformed Chinese society and China's place in the world. The dashed off notes labeled "do not touch" from the broken and haunted Song Feiqing after leaving China show how he still dreamed of establishing a utopian community where labor and management lived together in harmony, either in a "self-sufficiency" community on a vacant island in Hong Kong or in a new industrial city in Brazil. His utopia, however, was an orderly society of modern consumers using scientific household management outside of the factory and a fully regulated hierarchy with Song firmly in control inside the factory.

Song's Industrial Eden was, in fact, exactly the opposite of the tumultuous times in which he lived. Nonetheless, Song achieved tremendous success in the rough-and-tumble world of business competition and potential predation from the agents of authoritarian states, and he looked to those same states for help in establishing and running his business. Although he was disappointed in governmental developmental policies more often than not, he never gave up. Perhaps he was motivated by his capitalist vision, or perhaps he and his father before him took consolation in the knowledge that most of those authoritarian states needed business as much as business needed them. The story of the Songs, however, shows that the balance in power in the mutual interdependence between authoritarian states and business was skewed in favor of the state. All of Song Chuandian's wealth and position could do little when faced with the voracious rule of the warlord Zhang Zongchang, and the new Nationalist Party confiscated the family's wealth with little thought and no hesitation. Likewise, when Liu Shaoqi arrived in Tianjin in 1949, he told Song Feiqing that the Communist state needed Song to even "exploit more workers," but when the Communist Party felt more secure in power, it cracked down on capitalists like Song Feiqing without mercy. Song Feiqing did not survive as a capitalist, but his vision did, and that vision has now become part of a conversation where capitalism, or market socialism, is still justified in moral terms.

Glossary

Notes

Bibliography

Acknowledgments

Index

Glossary of Chinese and Japanese Characters and Names

Note: Birth and death dates have been provided for individuals when available.

Ayama Ryūsuke 阿山隆介

Chen Luanshu 陳鸞書, 1891–1944; style Yunxuan 韵軒

da dongya gongrongquan (Chi.); *dai tōa kyōeiken* (Jap.) 大東亜共栄圈

da dongya xin zhixu (Chi.); *daitōa shin chitsujo* (Jap.) 大東亜新秩序

dai tōa kyōeiken (Jap.); *da dongya gongrongquan* (Chi.) 大東亜共栄圈

dai tōa shin chitsujo (Jap.); *da dongya xin zhixu* (Chi.) 大東亜新秩序

danwei 單位

Dechang huabian zhuang 德昌花邊莊

Dechang Yanghang 德昌洋行

diyang 抵洋

diyang 抵羊

Dongya 東亞

Dongya Maoni Fangzhi Gufen Youxian Gongsi 東亞毛呢紡織有限公司

Feiji 飛機

Gaoshepao 高射炮

gongyi 公益

gongzhu Dongya 功鑄東亞

guojia yuanqi 國家元氣

gou tuizi 狗腿子

Haijing 海京

Han Fuju 韓復榘, 1890–1938

Huabei machan gaijin hui 華北麻產改進會

Huang Jing 黃敬, 1912–1958

Huichun zhi qu 回春之曲

jiantao 檢討

Jiaoji 膠濟

Jiaoyubu baowei Mao Zedong sixiang zhandoutuan 教育部保衛毛澤東思想戰鬥團

jidu jingshen, junshi jilü 基督精神, 军事纪律

Jinpu 津浦

ji suo bu yu wu shi yu ren 己所不欲勿施于人

Kahoku asasan kaishinkai　華北麻産改進會

kenchi jikatsu chūi　見地自活注意

Kihara Sadamitsu　木原定光

kōa (Jap.); *xingya* (Chi.)　興亜

"Laofang jiushi zifang"　勞方就是資方

Maekawa　前川少將

minshengzhuyi de xiandao　民生主義的先導

Qingzhou　青州

sanyoutuan　三友團

seisen (Jap.); *shengzhan* (Chi.)　聖戰

shengzhan (Chi.); *seisen* (Jap.)　聖戰

Shi Shaodong　石少東

Song Chuandian　宋傳典, 1872 (perhaps 1875)–1929

Song Feiqing　宋棐卿, 1899–1955

Song Guangxu　宋光旭, 1852–1946

Song Yuhan　宋宇涵, 1910–?

Songwangzhuang　宋旺庄

Sun Peiqing　孫培卿

Tian Han　田漢, 1898–1968

Tian Zhongyu　田中玉, 1864–1945

Tianjin Dongya qiye gufen youxian gongsi　天津東亞企業股份有限公司

Tianjinshi Dongya Maofang Chang　天津市東亞毛紡廠

Tianjinshi gongsi heying dongya maofangchang　天津市公私合營東亞毛紡廠

tongji bu　統計部

Tsujihara Yafumi　辻原八二三

Wang Fuwu　王福五

Wang Guangying　王光英 1919–

weisheng yi　衛生衣

weisheng　衛生

Xianghe　祥和

xin　信

xing　行

xingya (Chi.); *kōa* (Jap.)　興亜

Xiong Bingqi　熊炳琦, 1885–1959

xiuyang　修養

Yidu　益都

yitide, lianhede　一體的, 聯合的

Yuanqi　元氣

zengjia shengchan, fanrong jingji, gongsi jiangu, laozi liangli　增加生產, 繁榮經濟, 公私兼顧, 勞資兩利

Zhang Boling　張伯苓 1876–1951

Zhang Guojun　張國鈞

Zhang Ting'e　張廷諤, 1890–1973

Zhao Zizhen　趙子貞, 1897–?

Zhenxing　振興

zhenzhu　真主

zhixu jingran　秩序井然

zimian, zilü, zizhi, zize　自勉, 自律, 自制, 自責

Notes

Introduction

1. The dates and years of schooling here rely on the Papers of Li Jingfang, the widow of Song Chuandian's son Song Feiqing.

2. For a good review of the arguments, see Bruce Scott, *Capitalism: Its Origins and Evolution as a System of Governance* (New York: Springer, 2011), chapter 2. For a thoughtful critique of historical explanations of the emergence of capitalism, see Immanuel Wallerstein, "The West, Capitalism, and the Modern World-System," in Timothy Brook and Gregory Blue, eds., *China and Historical Capitalism: Genealogies of Sinological Knowledge* (Cambridge: Cambridge University Press, 1999), 10–56.

3. For example, see Kellee S. Tsai, *Capitalism without Democracy: The Private Sector in Contemporary China* (Ithaca, NY: Cornell University Press, 2007). Tsai never defines capitalism, but treats it as synonymous with private business.

4. Victor Nee and Richard Swedberg, "Introduction," in Victor Nee and Richard Swedberg, eds., *On Capitalism* (Stanford, CA: Stanford University Press, 2007), 7.

5. Tsai, 5. Scott, 62, asserts that democracy is not necessary for capitalism, but undermines that assertion when he refers to the close relationship between capitalism and democracy throughout his book, and when he states that capitalist development in China was "handicapped by a succession of autocratic governments (the Ming and Qing dynasties), a brief interlude of oligarchy, and then communism, which combined to delay the delegation of power for centuries" (603).

6. Scott, 37, 39.

7. See the well-known exchange between Andrew J. Nathan and Joseph Esherick, in Andrew J. Nathan, "Imperialism's Effects on China," and Joseph Esherick, "Harvard on China: The Apologetics of Imperialism," *Bulletin of the Committee of Concerned Asian Scholars* [now known as *Critical Asian Studies*] 4, no. 4 (December 1972): 3–8 and 9–16 respectively. See also Robert F. Dernberger, "The Role of the Foreigner in China's Economic Development, 1840–1949," in Dwight Perkins, ed., *China's Modern Economy in Historical Perspectives* (Stanford, CA: Stanford University Press, 1975), 19–47; articles from the "Symposium on China's

Economic History, *Modern China* 4, no. 3 (July 1978); Thomas G. Rawski, *Economic Growth in Prewar China* (Berkeley: University of California Press, 1989); and Philip Richardson, *Economic Change in China, c. 1800–1950* (Cambridge: Cambridge University Press, 1999), chapter 4.

8. Sherman Cochran, *Chinese Medicine Men: Consumer Culture in China and Southeast Asia* (Cambridge, MA: Harvard University Press, 2006).

9. For a thoughtful consideration of the possible influence of Chinese culture on business institutions, see Mark W. Frazier, *The Making of the Chinese Industrial Workplace: State, Revolution, and Labor Management* (Cambridge: Cambridge University Press, 2002), 11–13.

10. Parks M. Coble, "Comments and Reflections on Chinese Business History," in Robert Gardella, Jane K. Leonard, and Andrea McElderry, eds., "Chinese Business History: Interpretive Trends and Priorities for the Future," special issue, *Chinese Studies in History* 31, nos. 3–4 (Spring–Summer 1998): 145. On the evolution of thinking about the Chinese economy, see R. Bin Wong, *China Transformed: Historical Change and the Limits of European Experience* (Ithaca, NY: Cornell University Press, 1997), 14–15.

11. On the debates about entrepreneurship, see Yen-P'ing Hao, "Themes and Issues in Chinese Business History," in Gardella, Leonard, and McElderry, 109; and Linsun Cheng, *Banking in Modern China: Entrepreneurs, Professional Bankers, and the Development of Chinese Banks, 1897–1937* (Cambridge: Cambridge University Press, 2003). For a recent study of an entrepreneur, see Kai Yiu Chan, *Business Expansion and Structural Change in Pre-War China: Liu Hongsheng and His Enterprises, 1920–1937* (Hong Kong: Hong Kong University Press, 2006). On undercapitalized firms, see Kang Chao, *The Development of Cotton Textile Production in China* (Cambridge, MA: Harvard University East Asian Center, 1997); and Tomoko Shiroyama, *China during the Great Depression: Market, State, and the World Economy, 1929–1937* (Cambridge, MA: Harvard University Asia Center, 2008), 81. On long-term investment versus quick returns, see William Goetzmann and Elisabeth Köll, "The History of Corporate Ownership in China: State Patronage, Company Legislation, and the Issue of Control," in Randall K. Morck, ed., *A History of Corporate Governance around the World: Family Business Groups to Professional Managers* (Chicago: University of Chicago Press, 2006), 168; and Madeleine Zelin, *Merchants of Zigong: Industrial Entrepreneurship in Early Modern China* (New York: Columbia University Press, 2005). On networks and the family-owned firm, see Hao, 112; Ming-Jer Chen, *Inside Chinese Business: A Guide for Managers Worldwide* (Boston: Harvard Business School Press, 2001), chapters 3 and 4; Wellington K. K. Chan, "Tradition and Change in the Chinese Business Enterprise: The Family Firm Past and Present," in Gardella, Leonard, and McElderry, 131.

12. Li Chun, quoted in William C. Kirby, "China Unincorporated: Company Law and Business Enterprise in Twentieth-Century China," *Journal of Asian Studies* 54, no. 1 (February 1995): 50. For a review of the literature on networks, see Morris L. Bian, "Interpreting Enterprise, State, and Society: A Critical Review of the Literature in Modern Chinese Business History, 1978–2008," *Frontiers of History in*

China 6, no. 3 (September 2011): 438–444. Even those who accept the stereotype of the family firm disagree on whether it was inimical or helpful to business success; see Hao, 110–111.

13. Siu-lun Wong, "The Chinese Family Firm: A Model," in R. Ampalavanar Brown, ed., *Chinese Business Enterprises: Critical Perspectives on Business and Management* (London: Routledge, 1996), 1:107–108, originally published in the *British Journal of Sociology* 36, no. 1 (1985): 58–72.

14. On networks, see Hao, 110, 112, 115; Mayfair Mei-hui Yang, *Gifts, Favors, and Banquets: The Art of Social Relationships in China* (Ithaca, NY: Cornell University Press, 1994); David L. Wank, *Commodifying Communism: Business, Trust, and Politics in a Chinese City* (Cambridge: Cambridge University Press, 1999); Zhongping Chen, *Modern China's Network Revolution: Chambers of Commerce and Sociopolitical Change in the Early Twentieth Century* (Stanford, CA: Stanford University Press, 2011); and Sherman Cochran, *Encountering Chinese Networks: Western, Japanese, and Chinese Corporations in China, 1880–1937* (Berkeley: University of California Press, 2000). On separation of management and control, see Man Houng Lin, "Interpretive Trends in Taiwan's Scholarship on Chinese Business History: 1600 to the Present," in Gardella, Leonard, and McElderry, 70–72; Kirby, "China Unincorporated," 45; Goetzmann and Köll, 151; and Stijn Claessens, Simeon Djankov, and Larry H. P. Lang, "The Separation of Ownership and Control in East Asian Corporations," *Journal of Financial Economics* 58 (2000): 81–112. On adoption of the joint-stock business form, see Christopher A. Reed, *Gutenberg in Shanghai: Chinese Print Capitalism, 1876–1937* (Vancouver: British Columbia Press, 2004); David Faure, *China and Capitalism: A History of Business Enterprise in Modern China* (Hong Kong: Hong Kong University Press, 2006), chapter 3; Zelin, chapter 4; Wellington K. K. Chan, "The Organizational Structure of the Traditional Chinese Firm and Its Modern Reform," *Business History Review* 56, no. 2 (Summer 1982): 218–235; and Ming-Jer Chen, chapter 2.

15. S. Gordon Redding, *The Spirit of Chinese Capitalism* (New York: Walter de Gruyter, 1990); Ming-Jer Chen, 10; and Souchou Yao, *Confucian Capitalism: Discourse, Practice and the Myth of Chinese Enterprise* (London: Routledge Curzon, 2002).

16. Arif Dirlik, "Critical Reflections on 'Chinese Capitalism' as a Paradigm," in Brown, 1:33.

17. Bian, "Interpreting," 460.

18. Quoted in Michael Hillard, "Labor at 'Mother Warren': Paternalism, Welfarism, and Dissent at S. D. Warren, 1854–1967," *Labor History* 45, no. 1 (February 2004): 39.

19. On the popularity of Frederick Taylor–style scientific management in China in the early decades of the twentieth century, see Frazier, 10.

20. Morris L. Bian, *The Making of the State Enterprise System in Modern China* (Cambridge, MA: Harvard University Press, 2005); Parks Coble, *Chinese Capitalists in Japan's New Order: The Occupied Lower Yangzi, 1937–1945* (Berkeley: University of California Press, 2003), chapter 5; and Frazier, 59–61.

21. These accounts are discussed in Chapters 6–7.

22. Wen-hsin Yeh shows a commitment to disciplined time at the Bank of China in "Corporate Space, Communal Time: Everyday Life in Shanghai's Bank of China," *American Historical Review* 100, no. 1 (1995): 97–122.

23. On the similar regimented nature of Chinese management in official enterprises during the war, see Frazier, 66.

24. Karl Gerth, *China Made: Consumer Culture and the Creation of the Nation* (Cambridge, MA: Harvard University Asia Center, 2003), 333.

25. On Chinese views of capitalism, see Timothy Brook, "Capitalism and the Writing of Modern History in China," in Brook and Blue, 110–157.

26. Juan J. Linz, "Authoritarianism," in Seymour Martin Lipset, ed., *Political Philosophy: Theories, Thinkers, Concepts* (Washington, DC: CQ Press, 2001), 3.

27. On the dominant state thesis, see Hao, 114; and Albert Feuerwerker, *China's Early Industrialization: Sheng Hsuan-huai (1844–1916) and Mandarin Enterprise* (New York: Atheneum, 1970; originally published in 1958). On the symbiotic relationship, see Hao, 114; and Susan Mann, *Local Merchants and the Chinese Bureaucracy, 1750–1950* (Stanford, CA: Stanford University Press, 1987). On a business sector separate from and wary of the state, see Faure; and Hill Gates, *China's Motor: A Thousand Years of Petty Capitalism* (Ithaca, NY: Cornell University Press, 1996), 7. Kirby, "China Unincorporated," echoes the idea of wariness. Albert Feuerwerker seems to argue for a combination of a dominant state and a private business sector separate from the state in "Doing Business in China over Three Centuries," in Gardella, Leonard, and McElderry, 16–34.

28. Man Bun Kwan, *The Salt Merchants of Tianjin: State-Making and Civil Society in Late Imperial China* (Honolulu: University of Hawaii Press, 2001); Zelin; Cynthia Brokaw, *Commerce in Culture: The Sibao Book Trade in the Qing and Republican Periods* (Cambridge, MA: Harvard East Asian Center, 2007); Goetzmann and Köll; and Elisabeth Köll, *From Cotton Mill to Business Empire: The Emergence of Regional Enterprise in Modern China* (Cambridge, MA: Harvard East Asian Center, 2004).

29. Marie-Claire Bergère, *The Golden Age of the Chinese Bourgeoisie, 1911–1937*, trans. Janet Lloyd (Cambridge: Cambridge University Press, 1989), 8.

30. Parks Coble, *The Shanghai Capitalists and the Nationalist Government, 1927–1937* (Cambridge, MA: Council on East Asian Studies, Harvard University, 1980).

31. Brett Sheehan, *Trust in Troubled Times: Money, Banking, and State-Society Relations in Republican Tianjin* (Cambridge, MA: Harvard University Press, 2003).

32. Bian, *Making.*

33. Sherman Cochran, "Capitalists Choosing Communist China: The Liu Family of Shanghai, 1948–56," in Jeremy Brown and Paul Pickowicz, eds., *Dilemmas of Victory: The Early Years of the People's Republic of China* (Cambridge, MA: Harvard University Press, 2010), 359–385; and Sherman Cochran, ed. *The Capitalist Dilemma in China's Communist Revolution: Stay, Leave, or Return?* (Ithaca, NY: Cornell University East Asian Series, forthcoming).

34. Frazier, 14, chapter 2, and on the movement to increase state ownership of business in Guangzhou, 50–52; Bian, *Making*, chapters 1–2; William C. Kirby, *Ger-*

many and Republican China (Stanford, CA: Stanford University Press, 1984), 77, 85–100, 206–217.

35. Song Yunzhang and Wang Weigang, *Tade meng: Song Feiqing* [His dream: Song Feiqing] (Hong Kong: Wenming, 2006), 80. Here and throughout this book, all translations are mine unless otherwise noted.

36. Peter Evans, *Embedded Autonomy: States and Industrial Transformation* (Princeton, NJ: Princeton University Press, 1995), 10. On the term "visible hand," see Alfred D. Chandler, *The Visible Hand: The Managerial Revolution in American Business* (Cambridge, MA: Belknap Press, 1977), especially chapter 1; and Richard R. John, "Elaborations, Revisions, Dissents: *The Visible Hand* after Twenty Years," *Business History Review* 71, no. 2 (Summer 1977): 153–156. On the visible hand of the state, see Lars Magnusson, *Nation, State and the Industrial Revolution: The Visible Hand* (London: Routledge, 2009); and Scott.

37. Chalmers Johnson, "The Developmental State: Odyssey of a Concept," in Meredith Woo-Cumings, ed., *The Developmental State*, 32–60 (Ithaca, NY: Cornell University Press, 1999).

38. Hugo Radice, "The Developmental State under Global Neoliberalism," *Third World Quarterly* 29, no. 6 (2008): 1154.

39. Yu-shan Wu, "Taiwan's Developmental State: After the Economic and Political Turmoil," *Asian Survey* 47, no. 6 (November/December 2007): 980; see also Victor Nee, Sonja Opper, and Sonia Wong, "Developmental State and Corporate Governance in China," *Management and Organization Review* 3, no. 1 (2007): 20.

40. Evans, 12.

41. Dietrich Rueschemeyer, "Capitalism," in Lipset, 15.

42. Bruce Cumings, "Webs with No Spiders, Spiders with No Webs," in Meredith Woo-Cumings, ed., *The Developmental State* (Ithaca, NY: Cornell University Press, 1999), 65.

43. Tsai, 6–10.

44. For a discussion of business under uncertainty, see Naomi R. Lamoreaux, "Reframing the Past: Thoughts about Business Leadership and Decision Making under Uncertainty," *Enterprise and Society* 2 (December 2001): 632–659.

1. The Warlord State and the Capitalist-Politician

1. Song Chuandian's birth year is listed as 1872 in some sources and 1875 in others. Li Jingfang's notes refer to both dates.

2. In comparison with activists in late Qing dynasty politics, Song Chuandian was roughly the same age as Sun Yat-sen, Qiu Jin, and Liang Qichao.

3. Bergère; and Rawski.

4. Lin Xiuzhu, *Shandong gexian xiangtu diaocha lu* [Record of investigation of localities in Shandong Province's counties] (place of publication not given, 1919), 109.

5. Ma Shouting, in Zhengxie interview with Qie Xinyuan, Ma Shouting, Li Jingshan, Chen Yadong, and Meng Guanglin, 22 October 1982.

6. For example, see the map in *Qingzhou shizhi* [Qingzhou County gazetteer] (Tianjin: Nankai daxue chubanshe, 1989), unpaged front matter.

7. Timothy Richard, *Forty-Five Years in China* (New York: Frederick A. Stokes, 1916), 176–177.

8. Alfred Jones, a British Baptist missionary in Qingzhou, to Alfred Henry Baynes, Secretary of the Baptist Missionary Society (London), 1 May 1885, Archives of the British Baptist Missionary Society (hereafter BMS), reel 55.

9. Kenneth Pomeranz, *The Making of a Hinterland: State, Society, and Economy in Inland North China, 1853–1937* (Berkeley: University of California Press, 1993).

10. Jones (in England) to J. S. Whitewright, a British Baptist missionary in Qingzhou, November 1891, BMS, reel 55.

11. On gentry opposition to Western missionaries living in Jinan, see Jones to Baynes, 1 March 1888, BMS, reel 55.

12. There were also Catholic missionaries in Qingzhou, but they do not concern us here.

13. Medhurst to Baynes, 10 May 1886, reprinted in *Baptist Missionary Work in North-China (Province of Shantung: Letters Written by the Missionaries on the Field, Relative to Its Consolidation and Development)*, for private circulation only (Shanghai: Kelly & Walsh, 1886), 27, BMS, reel 56.

14. Brian Stanley, *The History of the Baptist Missionary Society, 1792–1992* (Edinburgh: T & T Clark, 1992), 182.

15. Richard, 110.

16. Jane Hunter, *The Gospel of Gentility: American Women Missionaries in Turn-of-the-Century China* (New Haven, CT: Yale University Press, 1984), 229.

17. Jones to Baynes, 9 February 1880 and 30 November 1877, BMS, reel 55.

18. Jones to Baynes, 25 July 1881 and 8 September 1881, BMS, reel 55.

19. Jones to Baynes, 26 October 1885, BMS, reel 55, emphasis his.

20. On the firewood, see Ma Shouting, in Zhengxie interview, 22 October 1982.

21. Papers of Li Jingfang. Other stories about Song Guangxu have circulated among family and friends and many of them are recounted in Song Yunzhang and Wang Weigang. Li Jingfang's notes strongly imply that Song Guangxu's wife was already a Christian when they married.

22. Medhurst to Baynes, 10 May 1886, reprinted in *Baptist Missionary Work in North-China;* on the number of Christians and Christian schools in Qingzhou, see also H. R. Williamson, *British Baptists in China, 1845–1952* (London: Carey Kingsgate Press, 1957), 45.

23. Whitewright and Couling to Baynes, May 1886, reprinted in *Baptist Missionary Work in North-China.*

24. Jones to Baynes, 10 May 1879, BMS, reel 55, emphasis his.

25. Jones (in England) to Baynes, 17 June 1883, BMS, reel 55.

26. Jones (in England) to Baynes, 25 September 1884, BMS, reel 55.

27. Whitewright and Couling to Baynes, May 1886, reprinted in *Baptist Missionary Work in North-China.* On the number of missionaries, see Jones to Baynes, 1 May 1885, BMS, reel 55; on the Whitewright museum, see Williamson, 48; and Stanley, 306.

28. Samuel Couling, "The Ideal Missionary," *Chinese Recorder* 47, no. 10 (October 1916): 665–673; Charles Hodge Corbett, *Shantung Christian University (Cheloo)* (New York: United Board for Christian Colleges in China, 1955), 40; and Williamson, 260.

29. Jones to Baynes, 16 March 1886, BMS, reel 56.

30. Jones to Baynes, 11 May 1886, BMS, reel 56.

31. Jones to Baynes, 3 March 1886, BMS; Whitewright and Couling to Baynes, May 1886, reprinted in *Baptist Missionary Work in North-China*.

32. Papers of Li Jingfang. A slightly different version of Song Chuandian's journey to the Qingzhou school is given in Song Yunzhang and Wang Weigang, 6–10. Xu Hualu and Ming Shaohua claim that Song Guangxu first went to work for another household in the county seat before going to work for the BMS; see their "Guanliao maiban zibenjia Song Chuandian de choue yisheng" [The evil life of the bureaucratic comprador capitalist Song Chuandian], *Shandong wenshi ziliao xuanji* 4 (1982): 71–85. Where accounts differ, I rely on Li Jingfang's recollections.

33. Alfred Jones, "Report on the Position & Prayers of the Church at Tsingchou Fu [Qingzhou Fu] for this year [1887]," 9 March 1888, BMS, reel 56.

34. Jones to Baynes, 19 May 1886, BMS, reel 56.

35. Couling (Scotland) to Jones (England), 6 December 1891, BMS, reel 56, emphasis his.

36. Jones (England) to Williams, November 1891, BMS, reel 56.

37. Alfred Jones, "The Social Question in the North China Mission Field," 3 February 1892, BMS, reel 56.

38. Couling (Scotland) to Jones, 6 December 1891, BMS, reel 56.

39. Hunter, 222.

40. Corbett, 210.

41. Mrs. James McMullan, "Report of the Chefoo [Chifu] Industrial Work," *Chinese Recorder* 30, no. 4 (April 1899): 183–184.

42. On the close circle formed by Protestant missionaries in Shandong, see Corbett, vii. For the reports published by the McMullans, see Mrs. James McMullan; James McMullan, "Report Read at the Opening Service of the Chefoo Industrial Mission, September 26th, 1902," *Chinese Recorder* 33, no. 11 (November 1902): 550–554; and James McMullan, "The Value of Industrial Training and Enterprise from a Missionary Standpoint," *Chinese Recorder* 45, no. 3 (March 1914): 144–145.

43. James McMullan, "Value of Industrial Training," 144.

44. Jones (England) to Baynes, 23 January 1892, BMS, reel 56.

45. Jones (England) to Baynes, 1 February 1892, BMS, reel 56.

46. Williamson, 265.

47. Jones to Baynes, 16 January 1893 and 10 June 1895, BMS, reel 56.

48. Jones to Baynes, 29 August 1900 and 10 September 1900, BMS, reel 56. On the cooperative attitude of Chinese officials in making good BMS losses, see Williamson, 75–76. There is no record to tell us how Song Chuandian and his family survived the Boxer violence, but survive they did.

49. Shandong Christian University (Qilu University), which grew out of an amalgamation of the Coulings' school and a Presbyterian school, did not begin to

teach English regularly until 1908, and only then in response to striking students who demanded foreign-language training; see Corbett, 77, 81.

50. Wang Juntang and Feng Baoguang, "Wo suo zhidao de Song Chuandian" [The Song Chuandian that we know], *Shandong wenshi ziliao xuanji* 5 (1987): 68.

51. Papers of Li Jingfang.

52. *Qingzhou shizhi*, 1028.

53. Corbett, 39.

54. Wang Juntang and Feng Baoguang, 68; see also Papers of Li Jingfang.

55. Corbett, 68; and Papers of Li Jingfang.

56. Zhou Chuanming, *Jinan kuailan* [Jinan at a glance] (Jinan: Shijie shuju, 1927), 71–73.

57. James McMullan, "Report Read," 554.

58. Corbett, 69.

59. Papers of Li Jingfang.

60. Xu Hualu and Ming Shaohua, 75.

61. Katherine Morris Lester, Bess Viola Oerke, and Helen Westermann, *Accessories of Dress: An Illustrated Encyclopedia* (Mineola, NY: Dover Publications, 2004; reprint of 1940 work), 130.

62. On McMullan's involvement with hairnets, see Corbett, 210–211. Corbett even quotes one Chinese Christian convert who called James McMullan the "inventor of hairnets," 211.

63. Wang Juntang and Feng Baoguang, 70.

64. Qie Xinyuan, oral history, 27 December 1964, Tianjin zhengxie.

65. Wang Juntang and Feng Baoguang, 70. For an account that attributes the innovation to Song Feiqing, see Song Xingcun, written materials, in Cui Shuju and Jin Yanshi, eds., "Tianjin Dongya maofang gongsi shiliao" [Historical materials on the Tianjin Dongya Woolen Mill], *Tianjin lishi ziliao* [Tianjin historical materials] 20 (8 February 1984): 2.

66. Many of the oral histories of Dechang in this period were taken in the 1960s when authorities in China encouraged criticism of capitalism and pre-Communist China so these accounts should be read with caution.

67. Xu Hualu and Ming Shaohua, 76.

68. Feng Naishen, oral history, 21 May 1964, Tianjin History Museum.

69. Wang Juntang and Feng Baoguang, 70.

70. Ma Shouting, Zhengxie interview, 22 October 1982. Recollections also differ regarding the number of copper coins equal to a silver dollar. Ma says eight to thirteen strings of cash were 1.4 or 1.5 yuan, and the former female worker quoted in Wang and Feng estimated that two strings equal something less than one yuan. They could be dealing with separate periods or even separate locations since the copper-silver exchange ratio was always changing and new copper coins of different value circulated at different times. Another former employee, Gao Xinzhai, says that two strings of cash were equal to one yuan; see Gao Xinzhai, oral history, 21 May 1964, Tianjin History Museum.

71. A. G. Parker, *Social Glimpses of Tsinan* [Jinan] (Tsinan [Jinan]: Department of Sociology, Shantung [Shandong] Christian University, 1924), 19.

72. Parker, 19.

73. Clarence E. Gauss, "Economic Development of Shantung [Shandong] Province, China, 1912–1921," United States Department of Commerce, *Supplement to Commerce Reports Trade Information Bulletin* no. 70 (Far Eastern Division), 9 October 1922, 19.

74. Ma Shouting, Zhengxie interview, 22 October 1982.

75. Feng Naishen, oral history.

76. Gao Xinzhai, oral history.

77. Qie Xinyuan, oral history, 27 December 1964.

78. David D. Buck, *Urban Change in China: Politics and Development in Tsinan, Shantung, 1890–1949* (Madison: Wisconsin University Press, 1978), 140.

79. Gao Xinzhai, oral history.

80. Feng Naishen, oral history; Gao Xinzhai, oral history.

81. Gao Xinzhai, oral history. Even Li Jingshan, a firm supporter of the Song family, confirms the length of the workday; see Li Jingshan, written materials, in Cui Shuju and Jin Yanshi, 5.

82. Feng Naishen, oral history.

83. Qie Xinyuan, oral history, 27 December 1964; and Yidu Gongshanglian, in Cui Shuju and Jin Yanshi, 3. The low estimate from Qie Xinyuan's oral history comes from his interview with Sun Zhuxuan (孙竹轩), a descendant of one of Song Chuandian's original partners. At the time the Sun family claimed that Song Chuandian had cheated his family out of much of the profits earned from hairnets, so Sun had no reason to understate profits. In fact, he went to great lengths to paint Song Chuandian as a profiteer. Thus, using the 0.5 yuan profit per gross is likely to be as accurate as we will get. Zhou Chuanming, the only available source from the 1920s to calculate income on hairnets, estimates profits as high as 0.6 yuan per hairnet (an unlikely 86.4 yuan per gross). I suspect the author mistook profits per gross for profits per hairnet. See Zhou Chuanming, 9–10.

84. Qie Xinyuan, oral history, 27 December 1964.

85. Zhang Wenxing, "Song Chuandian shilue" [A brief account of Song Chuandian's life], *Qingzhou wenshi ziliao* 5 (1987): 133; Yidu Gongshanglian, in Cui Shuju and Jin Yanshi; Qie Xinyuan, oral history, 27 December 1964.

86. Lin Xiuzhu, 112.

87. Qie Xinyuan, oral history, 27 December 1964.

88. Gao Xinzhai, oral history, 27 December 1964.

89. Blaming Song Chuandian for cheating his partners out of their share of the business became a minor industry in writings about Song Chuandian from the 1960s through the 1980s, especially in writings by or related to interviews with the descendants of those partners. See Qie Xinyuan, oral history, 27 December 1964.

90. Wang Juntang and Feng Baoguang, 70–71.

91. Williamson, 265.

92. Harvey C. Sung (Song Yuhan) to Mr. C. B. Currie, 12 October 1957, Sung Family Papers.

93. On Qingzhou's population and the large size of its tax base, see Lin Xiuzhu, 2–3, 108–109.

94. Corbett, 65.

95. On move of the museum and founding of the university, see Williamson, 76.

96. Lin Xiuzhu, 2.

97. Parker, 3–5.

98. Lin Xiuzhu, 4.

99. Buck, 133.

100. Zhou Chuanming, 79.

101. Buck, 130.

102. Parker, 18; Vice Consul Milbourne to Steinberg and Son, Inc., 20 May 1925, U.S. Consulate, Jinan.

103. Buck, 131.

104. Consul to Hobart Brothers, 30 November 1920, U.S. Consulate, Jinan; for similar language five years later, see Vice Consul Milbourne to Steinberg and Son, Inc., 20 May 1925, U.S. Consulate, Jinan.

105. Parker, 4.

106. Buck, 131; see also Parker, 4; and Vice Consul Milbourne to Steinberg and Son, Inc., 20 May 1925, U.S. Consulate, Jinan.

107. Lin Xiuzhu, 3; and Parker, 5.

108. Parker, 5, 18.

109. Papers of Li Jingshan 2. Li Jingshan's daughter edited and published her father's manuscripts in his name, but here I rely on the original papers in the family's possession. For the published version, see Li Jingshan, "Yi jindai fangzhi shiyejia Song Feiqing he Dongya gongsi," [Memories of the modern textile industrialist Song Feiqing and the Dongya Corporation], *Tianjin wenshi ziliao* 101 (January 2004): 81–102.

110. Papers of Li Jingshan 2; see also Qie Xinyuan, oral history, 27 December 1964. Businesses in Jinan commonly provided dormitories for male workers; see Parker, 19–20.

111. Vice Consul Milbourne to Steinberg and Son, Inc., 20 May 1925, U.S. Consulate, Jinan; Milbourne seems to be quoting Parker (see Parker, 18).

112. Advertisement for Sung Chuan Tien & Co., in the *Comacrib Commercial Directory of China*, vol. 2, 1926 (Shanghai: Commercial Credit and Information Bureau, 1926), J1. On the Qingdao operations, see Qie Xinyuan, oral history.

113. Qie Xinyuan, oral history 27 December 1964. See also Qie's oral history from nineteen years later, Qie Xinyuan, Zhengxie notes, 21 April 1983.

114. Vice Consul Milbourne to Steinberg and Son, Inc., 20 May 1925, U.S. Consulate, Jinan.

115. Parker, 9.

116. Xu Hualu and Ming Shaohua, 81, quotes a former female worker named Zhou Jingxuan.

117. Xu Hualu and Ming Shaohua, 79.

118. Gao Xinzhai, oral history.

119. Ma Shouting, in Zhengxie interview, 22 October 1982.

120. Papers of Li Jingshan 2. On the rudimentary nature of housing, see Feng Naishen, oral history.

121. Gao Xinzhai, oral history; Feng Naishen, oral history.

122. Gao Xinzhai, oral history.

123. Xu Hualu and Ming Shaohua, 79.

124. Li Jingshan et al., "Song Feiqing yu Tianjin Dongya qiye gongsi" [Song Feiqing and the Tianjin Dongya Corporation], *Tianjin wenshi ziliao xuanji* 29 (1984): 88.

125. Papers of Li Jingshan 4.

126. Liu Wentian, written materials, in Cui Shuju and Jin Yanshi, 1.

127. Buck, 124.

128. Parker, 7.

129. Buck, 108–112, quote from 108–109; on those parts of loans that went to Shandong, see Buck, 108; on the May Fourth Movement in Jinan, see Buck, 114–117.

130. Buck, 105–106.

131. Buck, 120.

132. Buck, 124–125; and *Jinan shizhi dashiji* [Jinan municipal gazetteer, chronicle of events], http://www.jinan.gov.cn/col/col40/index.html (2005), 17 January 1922 (accessed 31 July 2008). Zhang Wenxing, 134, claims that this disruption was aimed at preventing Song Chuandian's election.

133. *Jinan shizhi dashiji*, 19 March 1922.

134. Buck, 103, indicates that Xiong Bingqi exercised critical power from September 1922 to November 1924.

135. *Jinan shizhi dashiji*, 8 January 1923.

136. Zhang Wenxing, 133–134.

137. Xu Hualu and Ming Shaohua, 82–83; Buck, 125, also notes that the different factions tended to break down along regional lines with members of each faction coming from different places in Shandong.

138. Biographical information on Chen Luanshu is scarce. The Weifang municipal government has a short biography at http://www.wfsq.gov.cn/rwview .asp?id=497 (accessed 31 July 2008). In addition, Chen's grandson-in-law includes a short biography of his wife's grandfather in the author's forward to his book; see Ma Hanfang, *Jinluandian: Lütou qian* [Hall of the golden bell: Green bamboo slip] (Beijing: Zuojia chubanshe, 2008), http://www.exvv.com/mall/detail.jsp? proID=683147 (accessed 31 July 2008).

139. Buck, 125.

140. Qie Xinyuan,who worked for Song at the time, gives the figure as 200,000; see Qie Xinyuan, oral history, 27 December 1964. According to Xu Hualu and Ming Shaohua, 82, "Song's general bookkeeper says it was 288,800 yuan (Zhang Gongzhi says it was 180,000, and other people say it was 200,000 yuan)." Li Jingfang quotes a figure of 360,000 (Papers of Li Jingfang). Separately, David Buck portrays Song as a compromise candidate, though most histories of Shandong do not take that interpretation; see Buck, 124–125.

141. Archives of the Interior Ministry (Neiwu Bu), Number Two Historical Archives, Nanjing, 1001–1229.

142. Buck, 124.

143. Xu Hualu and Ming Shaohua, 83; see also Qie Xinyuan, oral history, 27 December 1964.

144. Song Xingcun, written materials, in Cui Shuju and Jin Yanshi, 1.

145. Buck, 138.

146. Zhou Chuanming, 79; Wang Juntang and Feng Baoguang, 72. Wang Juntang managed the bus company for a number of years.

147. Wang Juntang and Feng Baoguang, 72.

148. The newspaper was called *Qilu Xinwen* 齊魯新聞 [Shandong News], see *Jinan shizhi, Wenhua, xinwen, jiefangqian de baozhi, minguo shiqi de baozhi*[Jinan municipal gazetteer, culture section, news, pre-liberation newspapers, republican-period newspapers], http://sd.infobase.gov.cn/bin/mse.exe?seachword=%u5B8B%u4F20%u5178&K=bl&A=18&rec=57&list=1&page=20&run=13 (accessed 31 July 2008).

149. Unfortunately, this cable is not extant, but Tian Zhongyu's 23 January 1923 response can be found in Tian Zhongyu to president, cabinet, and Ministry of the Army, 23 January 1923, Archives of the Army Ministry (Lujun Bu), Number Two Historical Archives, Nanjing, 1011-609-01.

150. Zheng Shiqi, commander of the Jinan garrison, mentioned in his response to Song's accusations that newspapers published the telegram; see Zheng Shiqi to the president, cabinet, and army ministry, 23 January 1923, Archives of the Army Ministry, 1011-609-02.

151. Tian Zhongyu to president, cabinet, and Ministry of the Army, 23 January 1923, Archives of the Army Ministry, 1011-609-01.

152. *Jinan shizhi dashiji*, 3 April 1923.

153. Song Chuandian, Chen Luanshu, and Du Shang to the cabinet and the Treasury Department, 4 September 1923, Archives of the Interior Ministry, 1001-3640-01.

154. *Neiwu Bu gonghan* (Public announcement of the Interior Ministry), 16 September 1923, Archives of the Interior Ministry, 1001-3640-02.

155. Shandong Provincial Assembly to cabinet, Foreign Ministry, and Treasury, 19 September 1923, Archives of the Interior Ministry, 1001-3640-03.

156. Interior Ministry to Governor Xiong, 6 October 1923, Archives of the Interior Ministry, 1001-3640-04.

157. Buck, 124–125, quote from 125.

158. Tian's departure is mentioned in the telegram from Zhang Yinglin et al. to the president, cabinet, Foreign Ministry, Army Ministry, Wu Peifu, and Feng Yuxiang, 15 October 1923, Archives of the Army Ministry, 1011-609-03.

159. Zhang Wenxing, 134.

160. Buck, 125.

161. Buck, 126.

162. Buck, 131, 126–127.

163. Wang Juntang and Feng Baoguang, 72.

164. Buck, 127.

165. *Jinan shizhi dashiji*, 4 October 1925 and January 1927 (no day of the month given).

166. Xu Hualu and Ming Shaohua, 83.

167. In all there were seven classes of criminals with Zhang Zongchang and seven other military commanders in the first class. The second class consisted of twenty-eight individuals with Song Chuandian listed first; see Chen Diaoyuan to Chiang Kai-shek, 18 October 1929, Guomin Zhengfu, "Funi renyuan tongqi an (ba)"[Cases of arrest warrants of traitors (8)], Archives of the Nationalist Government (Academia Historica, Taipei), 001000006448A, 19290408~19430527.

168. Wang Juntang and Feng Baoguang, 73; and Yang Tianshou and Li Jingshan, "Jiefang qian de Dongya gongsi (xianming: Tianjinshi Dongya maoma fangzhichang)" [The Dongya Corporation before liberation (now called: the Tianjin Municipal Dongya Wool and Jute Mill)] (unpublished manuscript, 30 June 1963), 2. In an alternative version of the story, Song led the delegation to Manchuria; see Xu Hualu and Ming Shaohua, 84.

169. Price to State Department, "Political Report for October 1928," 6 November 1928, U.S. Consulate, Jinan.

170. Michael G. Murdoch, "The Politics of Exclusion: Revolutionary and Christian Competition over China's National Identity during the Northern Expedition Period, 1923–27" (Ph.D. diss., University of Michigan, 1999).

171. Stanley, 309, 314, quote from 309.

172. For details on the family's trials and tribulations, see Song Yunzhang and Wang Weigang, chapter 6; and Papers of Li Jingfang.

173. Stanley, 309.

174. Buck, 107.

175. Buck, 149.

2. The Prewar Nationalists' Uncertain Developmental State

1. On the autonomy of the Nationalist movement, see Lloyd Eastman, *The Abortive Revolution: China under Nationalist Rule, 1927–1937* (Cambridge, MA: Harvard University Asia Center, 1990); and Coble, *Shanghai Capitalists*. On despotism, see Frederic Wakeman Jr., *Policing Shanghai, 1927–1937* (Berkeley: University of California Press, 1996). On factions, see Kirby, *Germany*; and Frederic Wakeman Jr., *Dai Li and the Chinese Secret Service* (Berkeley: University of California Press, 2003). On economic control, see Margherita Zanasi, *Saving the Nation: Economic Modernity in Republican China* (Chicago: Chicago University Press, 2006), 7.

2. Zanasi, 4.

3. Coble, *Shanghai Capitalists*, 84.

4. Gerth.

5. Papers of Li Jingfang.

6. Song Feiqing, "Jidu jiaotu: Song jingli jiangdao" 基督教徒:宋經理講道 [Protestants: Song Feiqing gives a sermon], *Dongya Sheng* 6 (16 August 1947): 5.

7. Many biographies of Song Feiqing vary in details, but I rely here on the written recollections of his widow, Papers of Li Jingfang.

8. Chow Tse-tsung, *The May Fourth Movement: Intellectual Revolution in Modern China* (Cambridge, MA: Harvard University Press, 1960), 176–182.

9. Vera Schwarcz, *The Chinese Enlightenment: Intellectuals and the Legacy of the May Fourth Movement of 1919* (Berkeley: University of California Press, 1986).

10. Papers of Li Jingfang.

11. Cui Shuju and Jin Yanshi, 6–7.

12. Papers of Li Jingfang.

13. Song Yunzhang and Wang Weigang, 194–207.

14. Qie Xinyuan and Li Jingshan, oral history, in Cui Shuju and Jin Yanshi, 3.

15. Qie Xinyuan and Li Jingshan, oral history.

16. Zhengxie interview with Ma Shouting, Li Jingshan, and Chen Yadong, 5 November 1982.

17. Ma Shouting, in Zhengxie interview, 5 November 1982. All of Dechang's local advertising in Tianjin focused on automobiles and automobile products; see *Dagong bao*, 1, 5, 17, and 24 January and 30 March 1930. Federal Motor Trucks was an independent producer of trucks that kept its models simple and its prices low; see Rolland Jerry, "A Flashback on Federal," *Old Cars Weekly*, 20 November 1980, 8ff., http://www.federalmotortrucks.com/company%20history/index_history.htm (accessed 23 March 2014).

18. *Dagong bao*, 24 and 28 January and 12, 14, 15, and 17 February 1930. The movement continued well beyond the winter; see for example *Dagong bao*, 18 December 1930, 2.

19. "Yiyuan fushi, wanxiang gengxin, shehui wenming, yushi jujin" 一元復始, 萬象更新, 社會文明, 與時俱進 [Another year is upon us; everything is new; civilized society; always advancing]. *Dagong bao*, 1 January 1930, sect. 3, p. 9.

20. *Dagong bao*, 29 June 1930, 3. On Wu Dingchang, see Sheehan, *Trust*, 103–104.

21. Ji Hua, "Changlu yanwu de liang da anjian" [Two big incidents of the Tianjin salt merchants], *Tianjin wenshi ziliao* 26 (1984): 131–133. On predations against capitalists in Shanghai, see also Coble, *Shanghai Capitalists*.

22. For biographical information on Han, see Diana Lary, "Treachery, Disgrace and Death: Han Fuju and China's Resistance to Japan," *War in History* 1 (2006): 65–90.

23. Song Yunzhang and Wang Weigang, 75; Dongya Corporation, annual report, *Tianjin Dongya maoni fangzhi gufen youxian gongsi niankan* [Tianjin Dongya Woolen Limited Liability Corporation Annual Report] (Tianjin: Dongya Corporation, ca. 1933), unpaged, hereafter Dongya Corporation, *Annual Report*, 1933.

24. Zhao Zizhen, "Tianjin Dongya Maoni Gongsi chuangban qianhou" [Before and after the founding of the Dongya Woolen Mill], *Tianjin wenshi ziliao* 95 (March 2002): 104.

25. Zhao Zizhen, 104. According to his widow, Song Feiqing was held for about ten days; see Papers of Li Jingfang. For a slightly different version of the story, see Zhengxie interview with Qie Xinyuan, Li Jingshan, Meng Guanglin, and Chen Yadong, 12 November 1982.

26. Han Fuju to Chiang Kai-shek, 27 December 1930, Guomin Zhengfu, "Funi renyuan tongqi an (ba)" [Cases of arrest warrants of traitors (8)], Archives of the Nationalist Government (Academia Historica, Taipei), 19301230~19310615. Zhao

Zizhen is strangely silent about this event. It is possible that the Song family had built other ties with Han separate from Zhao's mediation; see Zhao Zizhen, 102–115.

27. Papers of Li Jingfang. The timing here is imprecise because Li may have remembered the dates based on the Chinese lunar calendar, whereas the government documents base days and months on the Western calendar. The oft-repeated story that Song Chuandian suffered a fatal heart attack upon hearing the news of his exoneration seems to be a legend. For versions of that story, see Wang Juntang and Feng Baoguang, 73–74; and Xu Hualu and Ming Shaohua, 84.

28. Song Yunzhang and Wang Weigang, 88–90; Xu Hualu and Ming Shaohua, 84.

29. Gauss to State Department, "Political Report for January 1929," 6 February 1929, U.S. Consulate, Tianjin. On Han Fuju, see Lary.

30. Gauss to State Department, "Political Reports" for April and May 1930, 4 May 1930 and 4 June 1930, U.S. Consulate, Tianjin.

31. Gauss to State Department, "Political Report for September and October 1930," 11 November 1930, U.S. Consulate, Tianjin.

32. Gauss to State Department, "Political Report for March 1931," 1 April 1931, U.S. Consulate, Tianjin.

33. Gauss to State Department, "Political Report for March 1931," 1 April 1931, U.S. Consulate, Tianjin. For the makeup of the Nationalist Party Committee, see the Sûreté information bulletin, 11 July 1931, French Foreign Ministry, Archives of the Tianjin Consulate (Nantes), Box 97.

34. Lary.

35. *Dagong bao*, 2 November 1930, sect. 3, p. 1.

36. *Dagong bao*, 9 November 1930, sect. 4, p. 1.

37. *Shanghai minzu mao fangzhi gongye* [The Shanghai domestic spinning and weaving industry], ed. Shanghai gongshang xingzheng guanli ju [Shanghai Business and Industry Management Bureau], Shanghaishi maoma fangzhi gongye gongsi [Shanghai Municipal Wool Spinning Company], and Maofang shiliao zu [Wool Historical Materials Group] (Beijing: Zhonghua shuju, 1963), 2–66; Gao Yuetian, *Zhongguo fangzhi shi* [A history of spinning and weaving in China] (Taipei: Gongshang yuekan she, 1953), 83–84; Chen Zhen, ed., *Zhongguo jindai gongyeshi ziliao, di si ji, Zhongguo gongye de tedian, ziben, jiegou he gongye zhong ge hangye gaikuang, shang juan* [Historical materials on industry in modern China, vol. 4, Characteristics, capital, and structure of private industry and general industrial conditions, first section] (Beijing: Shenghuo, Dushu, Xinzhi Sanlian shudian, 1961), 339–345; and Yoshida Miyuki, "Tenshin no keori kōgyō" [Tianjin's wool industry], *Mantetsu chōsa geppō* [South Manchurian Railway Investigation Monthly] 19, no. 8 (August 1939): 139, 144. A good summary of the nature of early official-sponsor industrial enterprises can be found in Goetzmann and Köll, 149–181. On the growth of a modern sector of the economy in the republican period, see Rawski, xix.

38. Papers of Li Jingshan 2; see also Ma Shouting, in Zhengxie interview, 22 October 1982.

39. Zhao Zizhen claims that the idea of manufacturing knitting yarn was his; see Zhao Zizhen, 105. He may have had a similar idea, but Song Feiqing's experience in Shandong shows that he had been thinking along these lines much earlier.

40. On limited liability corporations in modern China, see Kirby, "China Unincorporated," 43–63. Thomas Rawski's study of the republican-period economy used "cotton textile factories, rail or steamship transport, and western-style commercial banking" as examples; see Rawski, xix.

41. Chen Xiuwen, Song Yuzan, and Zhang Guoxun, "Dongya de 'diyang' pai maoxian he diyang bei" [Dongya's "Butting Ram" brand and statue], *Tianjin wenshi ziliao* 81 (January 1999): 140–141; Zhao Zizhen, 106; and Liu Wentian, written materials, in Cui Shuju and Jin Yanshi, 8.

42. General information on the early history of the Dongya Corporation is drawn from Li Jingshan et al., "Song Feiqing yu Tianjin dongya qiye gongsi," 86–114; *Maozhi gongye baogao shu* [Report on the wool goods industry], Quanguo jingji weiyuanhui jingji zhuankan [All-China Economic Commission Economic Monograph Series], no. 2 (1935), 89–150; Dongya Corporation, *Tianjin Dongya maoni fangzhi gufen youxian gongsi niankan* [Tianjin Dongya Woolen Limited Liability Corporation Annual Report] (Tianjin: Dongya Corporation, ca. 1934), hereafter *Annual Report*, 1934; Fang Zhaolin, "'Diyang' lingxiu Song Feiqing" [The "Butting Ram" leader Song Feiqing], in Zhongguo renmin zhengzhi xieshang huiyi Tianjinshi weiyuanhui wenshi ziliao weiyuanhui, ed., *Jindai Tianjin shi da shiyejia* [Ten great industrialists of Tianjin] (Tianjin: Tianjin renmin chubanshe, 1999), 176–206; and Cui Shuju and Jin Yanshi.

43. Although founded as a joint-stock, limited liability corporation, in its early years, Dongya followed the traditional Chinese custom of listing shareholders under hall (*tang* 堂) names. Unless otherwise relevant, I have dropped hall names in favor the individuals behind the halls.

44. There are inconsistent versions of the value of Song Chuandian's estate and how it was divided. See Papers of Li Jingfang; Qie Xinyuan, oral history; and Song Yunzhang and Wang Weigang, 68–69. On the use of equipment as part of the Song family investment in Dongya, see Yang Tianshou and Li Jingshan, "Tianjin Dongya Gongsi yu Song Feiqing" [Tianjin's Dongya Corporation and Song Feiqing], *Gongshang shiliao* 2 (1981): 106; and Cui Shuju and Jin Yanshi, 9.

45. Conventional accounts treat Zhang Huizhong's share as part of Han's investment, and indeed both used the same address in Shandong, but subsequent events will show that with shifts in the political environment, Sun Tongxuan and his wife Zhang Huizhong came to operate separately from Han, see Cui Shuju and Jin Yanshi, 9–10; and Zhao Zizhen, 104. Fang Zhaolin, "'Diyang' lingxiu," is more careful and treats them as two investors.

46. For the first version, see Li Jingshan, written materials, in Cui Shuju and Jin Yanshi, 9; the account in Song Yunzhang and Wang Weigang, 94–96, is similar in tone. For the second, see Gao Xinzhai, oral history; and Board of Directors Minutes, 5 January 1933, Dongya Archives, 1-3-5-06. For the third, see Zhao Zizhen, 104. To make matters even more confusing, Dongya reported its shareholders to the Tianjin Chamber of Commerce in September of 1932 and included Zhao Zizhen

as well as Zhao Shuzhen (a brother?) in the list along with three Songs, Han Fu-ju's son, and another associate of Han Fuju; see Dongya to Tianjin Chamber of Commerce, September 1932, reprinted in Tianjinshi Dang'anguan et al., eds., *Tianjin Shanghui dangan huibian, 1928–1937*, 1928–1937 [Collection of materials from the Tianjin Chamber of Commerce Archives, 1928–1937] (Tianjin: Renmin, 1996), 1563–1565.

47. Record of the First Shareholders' Meeting, 15 August 1931, Dongya Archives, 1-1-1-02.

48. Li Jingshan, written materials, in Cui Shuju and Jin Yanshi, 9. Zhao Zizhen's own recollections remain silent on a key point and do not refer to his own stock ownership at this time; see Zhao Zizhen, 104.

49. Board of Directors Minutes, 5 January 1933, and Record of the 1933 Share-holders' Meeting, 5 January 1933, Dongya Archives, 1-3-5-06 and 1-5-3-01/02.

50. Board of Directors Minutes, 3 January 1934, Dongya Archives, 1-3-5-09. Cui Shuju and Jin Yanshi worked off of the no longer extant 1935 shareholders' list, but by then Zhao Zizhen was indeed owner of account.

51. Zhao was still owner of record of 30,000 yuan in capital in 1940; see share-holders' list, Dongya Archives, 2-132-9-02.

52. Record of the First Shareholders' Meeting, 15 August 1931, Dongya Archives, 1-1-1-02.

53. On Xu's relationship with Song Chuandian, see Zhengxie interview with Ma Shouting, Li Jingshan, and Chen Yadong, 5 November 1982. Han Fuju's place on the board is taken over by someone else at that time; see Dongya to directors, December 1933, and Board of Directors Minutes, Dongya Archives, 1-3-5-08, 1-3-5-09. But Cui Shuju and Jin Yanshi, 10, cite a 1935 shareholder list no longer ex-tant that listed Han as still holding shares; and Han's son will reappear on the board later in the 1940s (see Chapter 6).

54. Hao, 114; Faure; Gates; Kirby, "China Unincorporated." Feuerwerker, "Doing Business," 16–34. seems to argue for a combination of a dominant state and a private business sector separate from the state.

55. On the symbiotic relationship, see Hao, 114; and Susan Mann, *Local Merchants*.

56. Gary G. Hamilton, *Commerce and Capitalism in Chinese Societies* (London: Routledge, 2006).

57. Board of Directors Minutes, 5 January 1933, Dongya Archives, 1-3-5-06.

58. Liu Huizhai 劉惠齋, "Fanlun maozhiye" 泛論毛織業 [A general theory of the wool textile industry], in Dongya Corporation, *Annual Report*, 1933, unpaged.

59. Dongya Corporation, *Annual Report*, 1934, unpaged.

60. Dongya Corporation, *Tianjin Dongya maoni fangzhi gufen youxian gongsi niankan* [Tianjin Dongya Woolen Limited Liability Corporation Annual Report] (Tianjin: Dongya Corporation, ca. 1936) (hereafter *Annual Report*, 1936), "Short History," unpaged.

61. Dongya Corporation, *Annual Report*, 1934.

62. Charters of the Dongya Corporation, August 1932 and 6 January 1933, Dongya Archives, 1-2-1-01 and 1-4-2-02. The main difference between the two

charters was the amount of authorized capital, 250,000 yuan in 1932 and 800,000 yuan in 1933.

63. Board of Directors Minutes, 3 January 1934, Dongya Archives, 1-3-5-09.

64. Board of Directors Minutes, 1 March 1937, Dongya Archives, 1-17-1-01.

65. Former executive Chu Jitiang 儲輯唐 confirmed that this strategy was intentional (written materials, in Cui Shuju and Jin Yanshi, 23).

66. On the history of the National Products Movement, see Gerth.

67. It is highly possible that Zhao Zizhen confuses this trip with some of the many others he took over the years. Dongya did not begin producing underwear until 1936; see Dongya Corporation, *Annual Report*, 1936, "The New Weaving and Knitting Departments," unpaged. Also, here Zhao incorrectly identifies Kong Xiangxi as minister of finance, a post he later held for many years. Kong was first minister of commerce and industry (Gongshang bu 工商部) from 1928 through 4 December 1930, then of the renamed Ministry of Industry (Shiye bu 實業部) from 4 December 1930 to 20 December 1931; see Zhang Pengyuan and Shen Huaiyu, eds., *Guomin Zhengfu zhiguan nianbiao (1925–1949) di yi ce* [Yearly record of officials of the Nationalist government, vol. 1, 1925–1949] (Taipei: Zhongyang yanjiu Yuan jindai shi yanjiu suo shiliao congkan (6), 1989), 222–225.

68. Zhao Zizhen, 104; see also Cui Shuju and Jin Yanshi, 15–18.

69. Zhao Zizhen, 109; see also Archives of the Tianjin Finance Bureau, Tianjin Municipal Archives (Tianjin), 54-1-0840, 54-2-3759; Yoshida, 145; and Cui Shuju and Jin Yanshi, 15–18.

70. Dongya Corporation, *Annual Report*, 1934, unpaged.

71. Board of Directors Minutes, 10 July 1934, Dongya Archives, 1-3-5-10.

72. Cited in Bank of Communications to Dongya, 24 March 1936, Archives of the Bank of Communications (Shanghai), Q55-2-566-06.

73. Toru Kubo, "The Tariff Policy of the Nationalist Government, 1929–36: A Historical Assessment," in Kaoru Sugihara, ed., *Japan, China, and the Growth of the Asian International Economy, 1850–1949* (Oxford: Oxford University Press, 2005), 145–176.

74. Minami manshū tetsudō kabushiki gaisha hokushi chōsajo [South Manchurian Railway Corporation North China Research Office], *Kita Shina kōjō jittai chōsa hō* [Report on the status of factories in North China] (Tianjin, 1939), 9.

75. Yoshida, 145.

76. Yoshida, 144. On reduced imports due to low silver prices, see Lockhart to Johnson, "Political Report for March 1932," 1 April 1932, U.S. Consulate, Tianjin, 13, 14,; on declining wool prices in Tianjin see *Dagong bao*, 10 April 1933, sect. 7, p. 2.

77. For example, see Minami manshū tetsudō kabushiki gaisha hokushi chōsajo, 9.

78. Board of Directors Minutes, 19 June 1935, quoted in Cui Shuju and Jin Yanshi, 15.

79. Coble, *Shanghai Capitalists*, 172–192.

80. Central Bank to Bank of Communications, 8 October 1935 (actual report on Dongya dated 14 August), Archive of the Bank of Communications (Shanghai), Q55-2-566-01.

81. Finance Ministry to Bank of Communications, 17 October 1935, Archives of the Bank of Communications (Shanghai), Q55-2-566-02.

82. Finance Ministry to Bank of Communications, 26 October 1935, Archives of the Bank of Communications (Shanghai), Q55-2-566-05.

83. Zhonghua quanguo maofangzhichang lianhe hui 中華全國毛紡織廠聯合會 [Wool Producers' Association] to the Shiye bu 實業不 [Ministry of Industry], 30 June 1936, Archives of the Ministry of Industry, Number Two Historical Archive (Nanjing), 422(3)-470-01.

3. Building Eden outside the Firm with National Products and Urban Consumerism

1. Gerth, chapter 7, quote from 289.

2. Gao Yuetian, 83; *Shanghai minzu*, 1–2; Shanghaishi fangzhi kexue yanjiu yuan [Shanghai Municipal Textile Scientific Research Istitute], ed., *Fangzhi shihua* [Historical stories about textiles] (Shanghai: Shanghai kexue jishu chubanshe, 1978), 26–32, 104–118; and Chen Zhen, 337. Proving that something did not exist is impossible, but the fact that the Chinese did not knit is taken as accepted fact by most scholars; see Chao, 179; and Richard Rutt, *A History of Hand Knitting* (Loveland, CO: Interweave Press, 1987), 223.

3. Jones to Baynes, 30 November 1877, BMS, reel 55.

4. Mrs. James McMullan, 183–184; and James McMullan, "Report Read," 551.

5. Ruiqiu [clearly a penname], "Weisheng yi" [Hygiene clothing], *Funü zazhi* 5, no. 1 (January 1919), unpaged. The article uses the Spanish term *medias* (tights or stockings) as well as the English term "stockings," but adds in Chinese that the category also includes undershirts (*hanshan* 汗衫, literally "sweat shirts") and hygiene shirts (*weisheng shan* 衛生衫). On the concept of hygiene (*weisheng* in Chinese), see Ruth Rogaski, *Hygienic Modernity: Meanings of Health and Disease in Treaty-Port China* (Berkeley: University of California Press, 2004); and Angela Ki Che Leung and Charlotte Furth, eds., *Health and Hygiene in Chinese East Asia: Policies and Publics in the Long Twentieth Century* (Durham, NC: Duke University Press, 2010).

6. Yoshida, 139.

7. *Guowen zhoubao* 2, no. 13 (26 October 1924), cited in Antonia Finnane, *Changing Clothes in China: Fashion, History, Nation* (New York: Columbia University Press, 2008), 122.

8. Finnane, 123.

9. *Dagong Bao*, 15 October 1933, sect. 3, p. 11.

10. Rutt, 139–161; Anne L. Macdonald, *No Idle Hands: The Social History of American Knitting* (New York: Ballantine Books, 1988), 225–288; and Heather Nicholson, *The Loving Stitch: A History of Knitting and Spinning in New Zealand* (Auckland: Auckland University Press, 1998), 77–116.

11. Yoshida, 139.

12. *Liangyou*, nos. 53 and 83 (December 1930 and December 1933), unpaged.

13. On Japanese encroachment in North China, see Marjorie Dryburgh, *North China and Japanese Expansion, 1933–1937: Regional Power and the National Interest* (Richmond, UK: Curzon, 2000).

14. Li Jingneng et al., *Tianjin renkou shi* (Tianjin: Nankai daxue chubanshe, 1990), 309. It is unclear if the number of residents includes members of the Japanese garrison in Tianjin, but I think it unlikely.

15. Brett Sheehan, "Boycotts and Bombs: The Failure of Economic Sanctions in the Sino-Japanese Conflict, Tianjin, China 1928–1932," *Management and Organizational History* 5, no. 2 (May 2010): 197–220; Lin Kaiming and Li Shuying, "Tianjin fanri hui yu dizhi rihuo yundong" [Tianjin's anti-Japanese society and the anti-Japanese goods boycott], *Tianjin wenshi ziliao*, no. 78 (1998): 87–92.

16. Brett Sheehan, "An Awkward but Potent Fit: Photographs and Political Narratives of the Tianjin Incidents During the Sino-Japanese Conflict, November 1931," *European Journal of East Asian Studies* 7, no. 2 (2008): 193–227; Donald Jordan, *Chinese Boycotts versus Japanese Bombs: The Failure of China's Revolutionary Diplomacy, 1931–32* (Ann Arbor: University of Michigan Press, 1991), chapter 3.

17. Record of the First Shareholders' Meeting, 15 August 1931, Dongya Archives, 1-1-1-02. Yang Tianshou and Li Jingshan claim that the idea for Dongya came during the Nationalist fervor following the seizure of Manchuria, but the date of this shareholders' meeting shows that plans were well under way before September. See Yang Tianshou and Li Jingshan, "Tianjin Dongya Gongsi yu Song Feiqing," 106.

18. Song Xianyong, "Jue ji bu wang women tong Riben de zhanzheng" [Our unforgotten war with Japan], *Nankai chunqiu* (1995): 74.

19. Sheehan, "Awkward."

20. Dongya to Tianjin Chamber of Commerce, 8 December 1933, in Tianjinshi Dang'anguan et al., 1565–1566.

21. Chen Xiuwen, Song Yuzan, and Zhang Guoxun, 141.

22. Liu Huaizhai 劉惠齋, "Diyangpai maoxian zai Shanghai biaoyan de yi my xiju" 抵羊牌毛線在上海表演的一幕戲劇 [A comedy performed in Shanghai by Butting Ram Yarn], Dongya Corporation, *Annual Report*, ca. 1933, unpaged.

23. Dongya Corporation, *Annual Report*, 1934, unpaged; and Cui Shuju and Jin Yanshi, 50. The North China region accounted for 100 percent of sales in 1932 (the first year of production), 42 percent in 1933, and 44 percent in 1934. Regional sales figures are not available for later years. Documents on the background of the Tianjin National Products Sales Office are collected in "Tianjin guohuo shoupinsuo 'zongwubu gongbu liudi' zhailu" [Selection of file copies of the General Affairs Office of the Tianjin National Products Sales Office], *Tianjin wenshi ziliao* 47 (July 1989): 66–123.

24. *Dagong bao*, 16 March 1933, sect. 3, p. 9.

25. The Butting Ram brand registration documents are in the Archives of the Ministry of Industry (Nanjing), 422(4)-3755 and 422(4)-2273. This claim is repeated in the profile of Dongya in *Dagong bao*, 15 October 1933, sect. 3, p. 11.

26. Song Feiqing, "Juantou yu" 卷頭語 [Opening words], Dongya Corporation, *Annual Report*, 1933, unpaged.

27. Zhao Zizhen, 108. On the Australian wool industry, see H. Munz, *The Australian Wool Industry* (Melbourne: F. W. Cheshire, 1964).

28. *Dagong bao*, 13 and 14 February 1933, sect. 2, p. 5 and sect. 1, p. 2.

29. Gao Xinzhai, oral history; I. Clunies Ross, *A Survey of the Sheep and Wool Industry in North-Eastern Asia, with Special Reference to Manchukuo, Korea, and Japan* (Melbourne: Commonwealth of Australia Council for Scientific and Industrial Research, 1936), 41; S. Y. Shah, "A Survey of the Wool Industry of China," *Chinese Economic Journal* 20, no. 6 (June 1937): 662.

30. Board of Directors Minutes, 20 April 1937, Dongya Archives, 1-17-1-02.

31. Dongya Corporation, *Annual Report*, 1936, "Short History," unpaged.

32. Dongya Corporation, *Annual Report*, 1934, unpaged.

33. Dongya used the term "modern ladies" for the first time in November 1933; see *Dagong bao*, 4 November 1933, sect. 7, p. 2.

34. Dongya Corporation, *Annual Report*, 1936, unpaged.

35. Finnane, 118.

36. *Dagong bao*, 2 November 1934, sect. 2, p. 8.

37. For an advertisement for the *Ark Monthly*, see *Dagong bao*, 9 September 1934, sect. 2, p. 8.

38. Song Feiqing, "Wode meng," in Cui Shuju and Jin Yanshi, 131.

39. Anonymous, *Fangzhou yuekan* [Ark Monthly], no. 1 (June 1934): 1.

40. Hunter, 168.

41. Alfred Jones, "The Social Question in the North China Mission Field," 3 February 1892, BMS, reel 56.

42. On the use of American knitting magazines, see Dongya Corporation, *Annual Report*, 1934, unpaged.

43. Ada S. Ballin died in 1906. For this and other biographical details, see entry in *Who Was Who, 1897–1915: A Companion to Who's Who Containing the Biographies of Those Who Died during the Period 1897–1915* (London: A & C Black, 1988), 27.

44. Ada S. Ballin, "Yinger yifu kexuehua de zhunbei" [Preparation for making infant clothes scientific], trans. Shao Qiu, speech given at the London Society of Mothers, *Ark Monthly* 1 (June 1934): 13–14.

45. The first ad using the word "scientific" appeared in *Dagong bao*, 28 October 1934, sect. 2, p. 7.

46. *Ark Monthly*, nos. 1 (June 1934): 17–19; 3 (August 1934): 24–26; 4 (September 1934): 24–27; 8 (January 1935): 29–34; 31 (December 1936): 22–25; and 39 (August 1937): 11–14.

47. Dongya Corporation, *Annual Report*, 1934, unpaged.

48. Minutes from the 1935 shareholders' meeting, as quoted in Cui Shuju and Jin Yanshi, 60, 61.

49. *Dagong bao*, 4 May 1935, sect. 2, p. 6.

50. "Canguan Dongya maoni fangzhi gongsi baogao" [Report on the visit to the Dongya Woolen Mill], *Shishi zhoukan*, 24 February 1936, 27.

51. Ding Xiuyun 丁秀雲, "Shidai de nüxing, renren dou hui bianzhi" 時代的女性,人人都會編織 [Women of the times can all knit], *Ark Monthly* 37 (June 1937): 45.

52. *Ark Monthly* 9 (February 1935): 20–21. Publication of this article coincided exactly with the New Life Movement in Tianjin where a mass rally was held on 19 February; see Lockhart to Trusler, "Political Report for February 1935," 4 March 1935, U.S. Consulate, Tianjin.

53. See discussions in Francesca Bray, *Technology and Gender: Fabrics of Power in Late Imperial China* (Berkeley: University of California Press, 1997), chapter 4; and Susan Mann, *Precious Records: Women in China's Long Eighteenth Century* (Stanford, CA: Stanford University Press, 1997), chapter 6.

54. Susan Glosser, "The Contest for Family and Nation in Republican China" (Ph.D. diss., University of California, Berkeley, 1995), 206.

55. Carleton Benson, "Story-Telling and Radio Shanghai," *Republican China* (April 1995): 117–146.

56. *Maozhi gongye baogao shu*, 105. According to the recollections of Zhu Jisheng, president of the Renli Corporation, Renli had planned to produce knitting yarn, but Song Feiqing and Zhu came to an agreement that the two woolen mills would produce separate products and not compete directly; recounted in Song Yunzhang and Wang Weigang, 100–101.

57. Minami manshū tetsudō kabushiki gaisha hokushi chōsajo, 231; Yoshida, 155, has similar statistics, but for 1934 to 1935.

58. Dongya Corporation, *Dongya Annual*, 1936, unpaged.

59. Papers of Li Jingshan 7; Ross, 41–41; Zhengxie interview with Ma Shouting, Li Jingshan, and Chen Yadong, 5 November 1982.

60. For a Xianghe ad, see *Dagong bao*, 22 June 1934, sect. 1, p. 2, and for Haijing, 26 August 1934, sect. 1, p. 1.

61. Yoshida, 146, counts three Chinese companies other than Dongya; see also *Shanghai minzu*, 68–83.

62. Dongya Archives, 1-10-4-01.

63. Dongya Archives, 1-10-4-01.

64. On the general history of Patons and Baldwins, see Michael Harvey, *Patons: A Story of Handknitting* (St. Peters, Australia and Rugby, England: Little Hill Press, 1985).

65. Patons and Baldwins, Fourteenth Report and Balance Sheet, 30 April 1933, and Report of Proceedings at the Fifteenth and Sixteenth Annual Meeting of Stockholders, 18 July 1934 and 17 July 1935, Archives of the Patons and Baldwins Company, Alloa, Scotland; quote from the former.

66. Board of Directors Minutes, 10 July 1934, Dongya Archives, 1-3-5-10; *Dagong bao*, 11 July 1936, sect. 1, p. 1.

67. *Maozhi gongye baogao shu*, 93, 98. The strength and technological sophistication of Patons is reminiscent of British American Tobacco in relation to the Chinese Nanyang Co. as studied by Sherman Cochran, *Big Business in China: Sino-Foreign Rivalry in the Cigarette Industry, 1890–1930* (Cambridge, MA: Harvard University Press, 1980).

68. On the merger negotiations, see Fang Zhaolin, "'Diyang' lingxiu," 191–192.

69. *Dagong bao*, 20 February and 23 and 27 March 1935, all sect. 1, p. 2.

70. *Dagong bao*, 25 March 1935, sect. 1, p. 1.

71. Zhao Zizhen, 113.

72. On plans to increase Dongya's national reach, see Board of Directors Minutes, 7 June 1936, Dongya Archives, 1-13-2-06.

73. Dongya Archives, 1-17-1-01.

74. Dongya Archives, 1-10-4-01.

75. Shi Shaodong 1, but must be based on Li Jingfang; Gao Xinzhai, oral history.

76. For profiles of many of these employees, see Gao Xinzhai, Feng Naishen, oral histories; Zhengxie interview with Qie Xinyuan, Li Jingshan, Meng Guanglin, and Chen Yadong, 12 November 1982; Papers of Li Jingshan 4; Shi Shaodong 2; and *Dongya Sheng* 8 (16 September 1947): 2, and 19 (1 March 1948): 5.

77. Central Bank to Bank of Communications, 8 October 1935 (actual report on Dongya dated 14 August), Archive of the Bank of Communications (Shanghai), Q55-2-566-01. For ads selling these sweaters, see *Dagong bao*, 16 and 19 November, 1935, both sect. 3, p. 10, and 16 December 1935, sect. 2, p. 5.

78. Report to the Shareholders' Meeting, 5 January 1933, Dongya Archives, 1-5-3-02. The Japanese planned to use Manchuria as a source of raw wool for Japan and as a destination for exports of Japanese wool products; see Minami manshū tetsudō keizai chōsakai dainibu daiyonhan [South Manchurian Railway Economics Research Office, Bureau Two, Team Four], *Yōmō kōgyō tai sakuan* [Wool industry policy], June 1933.

79. Lockhart to State Department, "Political Reports" for March and April 1933, 7 April and 8 May 1933, U.S. Consulate, Tianjin.

80. Dongya to board members, 31 March 1933, Dongya Archives, 1-3-5-07.

81. Lockhart to State Department, "Political Report for May 1933," 2 June 1933, U.S. Consulate, Tianjin.

82. Lockhart to Gauss, "Political Report for November 1934," 7 December 1934, U.S. Consulate, Tianjin. On Zhang Ting'e, see *Tianjin tongzhi, zhengquan zhi, zhengfu juan* [Tianjin gazetteer, politics, government volume] (Tianjin: Tianjin shehui kexue chubanshe, 2000), 393.

83. Caldwell to Trusler, "Political Report for December 1935," 14 January 1936, U.S. Consulate, Tianjin.

84. Dryburgh.

85. Board of Directors Minutes, 7 June 1936, Dongya Archives, 1-13-2-06. Patons and Baldwins, Report of Proceedings at the Seventeenth Annual Meeting of Stockholders, 16 June 1936, Archives of the Patons and Baldwins Company.

86. For an example, see *Dagong bao*, 16 February 1933, sect. 2, p. 5.

87. Sheehan, "Boycotts and Bombs"; Lin Kaiming and Li Shuying.

88. Lockhart to Johnson, "Political Report for December 1933," 4 January 1934, U.S. Consulate Tianjin.

89. Song Xianyong, 74.

90. *Maozhi gongye baogao shu*, 126–127.

91. On distribution networks in China, see Cochran, *Encountering Chinese Networks*.

92. Minutes of the 5 March 1935 meeting of the standing committee of the Dongya Corporation board of directors, as quoted in Cui Shuju and Jin Yanshi, 59.

93. *Maozhi gongye baogao shu*, 126.

94. Board of Directors Minutes, 3 January 1934, Dongya Archives, 1-3-5-09; Report to the Shareholders' Meeting, 5 January 1933, Dongya Archives, 1-5-3-02.

95. *Dagong bao*, 23 January 1934, sect. 3, p. 9.

96. *Dagong bao*, 15 and 31 December 1934, sect. 3, p. 10 and sect. 3, p. 11.

97. *Dagong bao* 15 August, 1934, sect. 3, p. 10.

98. *Dagong bao*, 3 January 1936, sect. 2, p. 6.

99. "Weishenme yao shunlian" [Why train?], Archives of the Dongya Corporation.

100. Shah, 665.

101. Gail Hershatter, *The Workers of Tianjin, 1900–1949* (Stanford, CA: Stanford University Press, 1993).

102. Berger to State Department, "Political Report for July 1935," 15 August 1935, U.S. Consulate, Tianjin.

103. Quoted in Dryburgh, 65.

104. Shina chūton gun shirei bu [Commander of China Garrison], "Tenshin bōseki jigyō ni kan suru hōsakuan (kimitsu)" [Policy for the fibers industry in Tianjin (secret)], February 1936.

105. Lepissier to the Foreign Minister, "Political Situation in Tianjin," 5 August 1936, 5, French Foreign Ministry, Asie-Oceanie 1930–1940 (Paris), file 616.

106. Lepissier to Naggiar, 20 January 1937 and 13 June 1937, French Foreign Ministry, Archives of the Tianjin Consulate (Nantes), Box 99.

107. On *Dagong bao*, see Caldwell to Trusler, "Political Report for December 1935," 14 January 1936, U.S. Consulate, Tianjin. On the departure of Chinese bank headquarters, see Brett Sheehan, "Urban Identity and Urban Networks in Cosmopolitan Cities: Banks and Bankers in Tianjin, 1900–1937," in Joseph W. Esherick, ed., *Remaking the Chinese City: Modernity and National Identity, 1900–1950* (Honolulu: University of Hawaii Press, 2000), 47–64. See also minutes of the standing committee of the shareholders, 7 March 1936, Dongya Archives, quoted in Cui Shuju and Jin Yanshi, 14.

108. Minutes of the meeting of the shareholders, 5 March 1937, Dongya Archives, 1-15-4-01.

109. Zhengxie interview with Chen Yadong, December 1982.

110. On lack of sales for Dongya in 1937, see letter from Tianjin Branch of the Bank of China, 16 October 1937, Archives of the Bank of Communications (Shanghai Archive), Q55-2-566-09.

4. Japanese Occupation and the "Economy of Things"

1. Zhang Xianwen et al., *Zhongguo kangri zhanzheng shi* [A history of China's anti-Japanese war] (Tianjin: Nanjing University Press, 2001), 256–258; and Liu Jingyue, "Tianjin lunxian qian de zui hou yi zhan [The last battle before the occupation of Tianjin], in Tianjin wenshi zhiliao yanjiu weiyuanhui, ed., *Lunxian shiqi*

de Tianjin [Tianjin in the era of occupation] (Tianjin: Tianjin Zhengxie Hui, 1992), 1–8.

2. Board of Directors Minutes, 20 April 1937, Dongya Archives, 1-17-1-02.

3. *Ark Monthly* 38 (July 1937) and 39 (August 1937), unpaged advertisements, mention of price from the latter; see also advertisement in *Dagong bao*, 16 July 1937, sect. 2, p. 6.

4. Board of Directors Minutes, 30 August 1937, Dongya Archives, 1-17-1-03.

5. Tianjin Branch of the Bank of China to head office, 16 October 1937, Archives of the Bank of Communications (Shanghai), Q55-2-566-09.

6. Song Yunzhang and Wang Weigang, 191.

7. Song Xianyong, 75–76.

8. Robert Boyce, "Economics," in Robert Boyce and Joseph A. Maiolo, eds., *The Origins of World War Two: The Debate Continues* (Basingstoke: Palgrave Macmillan, 2003), 254.

9. Asia Renaissance (Jap., *kōa*; Chi., *xingya*); New Order in East Asia (Jap., *daitōa shin chitsujo*; Chi., *da dongya xin zhixu*); Greater East Asia Co-Prosperity Sphere (Jap., *dai tōa kyōeiken*; Chi., *da dongya gongrongquan*); and Sacred War (Jap., *seisen*; Chi., *shengzhan*). On "total empire," see Louise Young, *Japan's Total Empire: Manchuria and the Culture of Wartime Imperialism* (Berkeley: University of California Press, 1999), 13. See also Coble, *Chinese Capitalists in Japan's New Order*, 34. In fact there was a Russian-language newspaper in Tianjin in the early years of the occupation called *Asian Renaissance*; see Lepissier to Naggiar "General Military and Political Situation," 5 August 1938, French Foreign Ministry, Archives of the Tianjin Consulate (Nantes), Box 99.

10. Shanghai Commercial and Savings Bank, "Report on Tianjin's Business and Industry for 1938" (internal), Archives of the Shanghai Commercial and Savings Bank (Shanghai), Q275-1-1801-01.

11. Figures are not available for the full year in 1937, but interim reports as of 30 September indicated that Dongya had been able to ship almost 500,000 pounds of yarn on orders of almost 658,000 pounds; see Board of Director Minutes, 1 October 1938, Dongya Archives, 1-23-2-02.

12. Board of Director Minutes, 1 October 1938, Dongya Archives, 1-23-2-02.

13. Patons and Baldwins, Ltd., Report of Proceedings at the Twentieth Annual Meeting of Stockholders, 19 July 1939, Archives of the Patons and Baldwins Company (Alloa).

14. Board of Directors Minutes, 1 March 1937 and 3 July 1939, Dongya Archives, 1-17-1-01 and 1-23-2-03. Yoshida, 152, says as much as 80 percent was sold in South China before the war, but this is belied by internal company documents.

15. Yoshida, 147, 149, 143.

16. Parks M. Coble, "Japan's New Order and the Shanghai Capitalists: Conflict and Collaboration, in David P. Barrett and Larry N. Shyu, eds., *Chinese Collaboration with Japan, 1932–1945* (Stanford, CA: Stanford University Press, 2001), 144.

17. Minami manshū tetsudō kabushiki gaisha hokushi chōsajo, 4; and Takeo Ito, *Problems in the Japanese Occupied Areas in China* (Tokyo: Japanese Council of the Institute of Pacific Relations, 1941), 28.

18. George Taylor, *Japanese Sponsored Regime in North China* (New York: International Secretariat, Institute of Pacific Relations, 1939; reprinted, New York: Garland, 1980), 35; and Kurt Bloch, "The Basic Conflict over Foreign Concessions in China," *Far Eastern Survey* 8, no. 10 (10 May 1939): 115.

19. Asada Kyōji, *Nihon teikokushugika no Chūgoku* [China under Japanese imperialism] (Tokyo: Rakuyū Shobō, 1981), 189.

20. Lepissier to Naggiar, "Report on the General Political Situation," 8 November 1937, 11; see also Lepissier to Foreign Minister (Paris), "Report on the General Political Situation in North China," 9 December 1937, 8; both in French Foreign Ministry, Archives of the Tianjin Consulate (Nantes), Box 99.

21. Lepissier to Naggiar, "On the New Government," 18 December 1937, 4, French Foreign Ministry, Archives of the Tianjin Consolate (Nantes), Box 99; see also Taylor, 67.

22. "Note on the Political and Economic Situation," 15 July 1938, 49; on activities of the private sector early in the occupation, see Lepissier to Naggiar, "Report on the General Political Situation," 8 November 1937, 12; both in French Foreign Ministry, Archives of the Tianjin Consulate (Nantes), Box 99; Taylor, 105; Coble, *Chinese Capitalists in Japan's New Order*, 49–53.

23. On the Koa Institute, see Kubo Toru, "The Koa-in," in Stephen R. MacKinnon, Diana Lary, and Ezra Vogel, eds., *China at War: Regions of China, 1937–45* (Stanford, CA: Stanford University Press, 2007), 44–64; Tien-wei Wu, "Contending Political Forces during the War of Resistance," in James C. Hsiung and Steven I. Levine, eds., *China's Bitter Victory: The War with Japan, 1937–1945* (Armonk, NY: M. E. Sharpe, 1992), 70; and Imura Tetsuo, ed., *Kōain kankō tosho zasshi mokuroku* [Catalog of Kōain periodicals, books, and magazines], Jyūgo-nen sensō jyūyō bunken shirīzu 17 [Documents from Fifteen Years' War series 17] (Tokyo: Fuji, 1994), 1–12.

24. Kubo, "The Koa-in," 57–58, quote at 58.

25. Kubo, "The Koa-in," 56; see also Ito, 52.

26. On tensions between the South Manchurian Railway and the Japanese military regarding the development of both Manchuria and North China, see Sherman Cochran, "Business, Governments, and War in China, 1931–1949," in Akira Iriye and Warren Cohen, eds., *American, Chinese and Japanese Perspectives on Wartime Asia, 1931–1949* (Wilmington, DE: SR Books, 1990), 127.

27. Antony Best, "Imperial Japan," in Boyce and Maiolo, *Origins of World War Two*, 55.

28. Cochran, "Business, Governments, and War in China," 131–132.

29. Best, 55.

30. Taylor, 3.

31. Lepissier to Naggiar, "Political Report," 5 September 1938, 18–19, French Foreign Ministry, Archives of the Tianjin Consulate (Nantes), Box 99. An American writer attributed some of the export restrictions to an attempt to "divert raw materials to the 'former' axis partners (as in the case of wool) or restrict them to Japanese use (as in the case of raw cotton, furs, hides, and skins, etc.)"; see John R. Stewart, "North China Restrictions and Exports to the U.S.," *Far Eastern*

Survey 8, no. 20 (11 October 1939): 240. On control of foreign exchange, see Bloch, 115.

32. Lacoste to Naggiar, 5 September 1938, French Foreign Ministry, Asie-Oceanie 1930–1940 and 1944–1955 (Paris), file 829.

33. "Economic and Political Situation for the Last Half of 1938," French Foreign Ministry, Archives of the Tianjin Consulate (Nantes), Box 99; on the trade deficit with Japan, see also J. K. Caldwell, U.S. Consul General Tianjin, to Nelson Trusler Johnson, U.S. Ambassador to China, "Political Report for December 1939," 9 January 1940, 12, U.S. Consulate, Tianjin.

34. Quoted in Lepissier to French Ambassador, "General Military and Political Situation," 3 December 1938, 18–19, French Foreign Ministry, Archives of the Tianjin Consulate (Nantes), Box 99.

35. De Boissezon, secretary for the French ambassador Beiping, to Cosme, French Ambassador to China in Shanghai, "Provisioning of North China," 12 May 1939, 2–4, French Foreign Ministry, Archives of the Tianjin Consulate (Nantes), Box 99.

36. Caldwell to Peck, "Political Report for April 1939," 3 May 1939, 4, U.S. Consulate, Tianjin.

37. Lepissier to Naggiar, "Political Report," 5 September 1938, 6–7; see also Lepissier to Foreign Minister, "General Military and Political Situation," 2 February 1939; both in French Foreign Ministry, Archives of the Tianjin Consulate (Nantes), Box 99.

38. Bloch, 115; Sebastian P. Swann, "The Tientsin Incident (1939): A Case Study of Japan's Imperial Dilemma in China" (Ph.D. diss., University of London, 1998); Lin Meili, *Kangzhan shiqi de huobi zhanzheng* [The currency war at the time of the anti-Japanese war] (Taipei: Guoli Taiwan Shifan Daxue Lishi Yanjiusuo, 1996), 406–409. For example of reporting on exchange rates, see Tenshin Rikugun Tokumu Kikan, "Tenki Geppoo" [Tianjin Army Intelligence, "Tianjin Unit Monthly Report], January 1940, National Archives of Japan, Japan Center for Asian Historical Records, JACAR C04121985000; Caldwell to Johnson, "Political Report for January 1940," 12 February 1940, 13; and "Political Report for August 1939," 15 September 1939, iv, U.S. Consulate, Tianjin.

39. Reported in Board of Directors Minutes, 3 July 1939, Dongya Archives, 1-23-3-03.

40. On the porous borders of occupied China in other regions, see Lloyd E. Eastman, "Nationalist China during the Sino-Japanese War, 1937–1945," in John K. Fairbank and Albert Feuerwerker, eds., *The Cambridge History of China*, vol. 13: *Republican China, 1912–1949* (Cambridge: Cambridge University Press, 1886), 567.

41. E. G. Jamieson, Consul General Tianjin, to Clark Kerr, Ambassador to China, "Political Report for the Quarter Ended 31 March 1940," 1 April 1940, 6, British Foreign Office, National Archives, FO 371-24657.

42. Dongya Archives, 1-17-1-01 (1935) and 1-27-3-01 (1939).

43. Likewise, the wool, paper, and silk industries in Shanghai also thrived during this period; see Coble, *Chinese Capitalists in Japan's New Order*, 29.

44. Yoshida, 147–149.

45. Board of Directors Minutes, 23 May 1940, Dongya Archives, 1-27-3-02. I am grateful to Kwan Man Bun for sharing his information on the Yongli connection with me; see "Yongli changshi gao" 永利廠史稿 [A draft history of the Yongli Company] (unpublished manuscript from the Archives of the Yongli Corporation). Hashimoto incorrectly states that Dongya began gunnysack production before the outbreak of the China "incident"; see Hashimoto Masayasu, *Hokushi ni okeru asabukuro gaisetsu* [Gunnysacks in North China] (Mantetsu Research Department, 1940), 22.

46. Details of the accord can be found in Fletcher to Johnson, "Political Report for June 1940," 8 July 1940, 6–7, U.S. Consulate, Tianjin.

47. Apparently Dongya kept its books in *fabi* until 1941, and even then only used occupation government currency for new accounts; see Board of Director Minutes, 23 December 1945, Dongya Archives, 1-59-12-02.

48. Samuel J. Fletcher, U.S. Consul General Tianjin, to Johnson, "Political Report for April 1940," 8 May 1940, 1, U.S. Consulate, Tianjin.

49. Fletcher to Johnson, "Political Report for May 1940," 6 June 1940, 3–4, U.S. Consulate, Tianjin.

50. "Economic and Political Situation for the Last Half of 1938," French Foreign Ministry, Archives of the Tianjin Consulate (Nantes), Box 99.

51. Jamieson to Clark Kerr, "Intelligence Report for Six Months Ending 30 September 1939," 14 October 1939, 13, British Foreign Office, National Archives, FO371-24657.

52. A. E. Tipper, President of British Council Tianjin, to Oswald White, British Consul General Tianjin, 2 February 1940; and "Compte rendu succinct d'une reunion tenue au Consulat d'Angleterre [Brief Minutes of a Meeting at the British Consulate]," 26 February 1940, French Foreign Ministry, Archives of the Tianjin Consulate (Nantes), Box 21.

53. Caldwell to Johnson, "Political Report for February 1940," 7 March 1940, 9, U.S. Consulate, Tianjin.

54. Fletcher to Johnson, "Political Report for May 1940," 6 June 1940, 9; "Political Report for August 1940," 7 September 1940, 13–14, U.S. Consulate, Tianjin; and "Intelligence Report for the Six Months Ended 30 September, 1940," 8, British Foreign Office, National Archives, FO371-24657.

55. Ito, 48.

56. The company purchased 1.5 million pounds of wool in 1939, approximately 0.5 million pounds in 1940 (approximate because only a nine-month report not a full year report is available), 0.25 million pounds in 1941, and 0.1 million pounds in 1942; see Dongya Archives, 1-23-2-03, 1-27-3-05, 1-38-5-01, 1-42-3-01.

57. Dongya Archives, 1-27-3-05, 1-38-5-01.

58. Dongya Corporation, *Tianjin dongya maoni fangzhi youxian gongsi tekan, 1941* [Tianjin Dongya Woolen Corporation special report for 1941] (Tianjin: Dongya Corporation, 1941), unpaged, section on wool yarn discontinuation (hereafter cited as *Annual Report*, 1941).

59. Report compiled by the Beijing Social Bureau (Beipingshi zhengfu shehui lei), in the Beijing Municipal Archives, J2-7-198. General inflation levels from

Nankai indexes, as quoted in Cui Shuju and Jin Yanshi. Financial information for the Dongya Corporation during the war is very spotty. The income statement for 1940, however, shows record profits and record profit margins, Dongya Corporation, *Annual Report of Financial Statements*, 1940, Dongya Archives, 1-25-1-03. Although British exports to Tianjin generally grew from 1937 to 1938, wool exports shrank; see Irving S. Friedman, "Britain's Large, Tangible Stake in Tientsin [Tianjin]," *Far Eastern Survey* 8, no. 14 (5 July 1939): 166–167.

60. Dongya Corporation, *Annual Report*, 1941, unpaged, section on wool yarn discontinuation.

61. "Monthly Report on Tianjin's Business and Industry," May 1941, Archives of the Shanghai Commercial and Savings Bank (Shanghai), Q275-1-391-01.

62. Board of Directors Minutes, 2 January 1941, quoted in Cui Shuju and Jin Yanshi, 13.

63. A. G. N. Ogden, Acting Consul General Tianjin, to Clark Kerr, 25 May 1941, British Foreign Office, National Archives, FO371-27667.

64. Caldwell to C. E. Gauss, U.S. Consul General Tianjin, "Political Report for September 1941," 14 October 1941, 13–14, U.S. Consulate, Tianjin.

65. Announcement regarding price controls, 10 June 1942, French Foreign Ministry, Archives of the Tianjin Consulate (Nantes), Box 20.

66. Saburo Kato, Japanese Consul General Tianjin, to L. Colin, French Consul General Tianjin, 23 January 1942, French Foreign Ministry, Archives of the Tianjin Consulate (Nantes), Box 44.

67. "Hokushi bukka seisaku to taichūshi kōeki" [North China price policy effect on Central China trade), *Kōain seimubu jōhō* [Koa Institute Politics Department intelligence reports], no. 76 (October 1942): 27–28; Tianjin branch to main office, 7 December 1942, Archives of the Shanghai Commercial and Savings Bank (Shanghai), Q275-1-440-06.

68. Board of Directors Minutes, 2 January 1942, Dongya Archives, 1-38-5-01.

69. Caldwell to Gauss, "Political Report for September 1941," 14 October 1941, 14, U.S. Consulate, Tianjin; report indicates information came directly from Dongya.

70. Hashimoto, 13, 15, 22.

71. Dongya Archives, 1-38-5-01, 1-42-3-01.

72. Board of Directors Minutes, 20 September 1942, Dongya Archives, 1-38-5-03; see also Dongya Corporation, *Annual Report*, 1941, unpaged, section on gunnysack production.

73. "Monthly Report on Tianjin's Business and Industry," March 1942, Archives of the Shanghai Commercial and Savings Bank (Shanghai), Q275-1-394-01.

74. Kikakubu [Planning Bureau], "Asakōgyō tōsei un'ei yōkō kaisetsu" [Flax [jute] industry: Explanation of the outline for control of operations], *Kahoku bōshoku kōgyōkai geppō* [North China Textile Industry Association Monthly] 3 (March 1944): 45, 49.

75. On wartime profits of firms, see Kubo, "The Koa-in," 60–61.

76. Nakamura Kanichi, "Peikin, Tenshin, Sainan, I ken oyobi Aoshima ni okeru seiyaku shō chōsa" [Investigation of medicine factories in Beijing, Tianjin, Jinan,

Wei County and Qingdao], *Kōain chōsa geppō* [Koa Institute Investigation Monthly] 2, vol. 6 (1941): 296–299, 301.

77. Board of Directors Minutes, 9 March 1943, Dongya Archives, 1-42-3-04.

78. Dongya Corporation, *Fushe huaxue chang gongzuo gaikuang* [General situation of the subsidiary chemical factory] (Tianjin: Dongya Corporation, 1944).

79. Board of Directors Minutes, 15 September 1944, Dongya Archives, 1-30-3-04.

80. Personal communication from Jennifer Chang, Academia Sinica.

81. Shi 1.

82. Dongya advertised its willingness to purchase cotton husks and stalks; see *Yong bao*, 15 September 1942, 7.

83. "Report on Tianjin Market Conditions," 12 June 1944, Archives of the Shanghai Commercial and Savings Bank (Shanghai), Q275-1-440-02.

84. Li Jingshan in Zhengxie interview with Qie Xinyuan et al., 26 November 1982. On Tiger brand balm, see Cochran, *Chinese Medicine Men*.

85. Gao Xinzhai, oral history.

86. Board of Director Minutes, 5 November 1937, Dongya Archives, 1-17-1.

87. Board of Director Minutes, 3 July 1939, Dongya Archives, 1-23-2-03.

88. Gao Xinzhai, oral history.

89. Board of Director Minutes, 23 May 1940, Dongya Archives, 1-27-3-02.

90. Board of Director Minutes, 6 January 1944, Dongya Archives, 1-30-3-03; and Dongya Archives, 1-30-3-04; see also Gao Xinzhai, oral history.

91. Board of Directors Minutes, 7 June 1942 and 20 September 1942, Dongya Archives, 1-38-5-02, 1-38-5-03.

92. Board of Directors Minutes, 7 June 1942, Dongya Archives, 1-38-5-02. Planning for the bank became quite involved, but its eventual demise remains undocumented.

93. Board of Directors Minutes, 28 October 1942, Dongya Archives, 1-38-5-04.

94. Board of Directors Minutes, 20 September 1942, Dongya Archives, 1-38-5-03.

95. Board of Directors Minutes, 4 June 1943, Dongya Archives, 1-42-3-05.

96. "Monthly Report on Tianjin's Business and Industry," March 1944, Archives of the Shanghai Commercial and Savings Bank (Shanghai), Q275-1-400-01; Board of Directors Minutes, 3 March 1944, Dongya Archives, 1-30-3-01; "Chuangzhi madai yanzhi xinyao, kuxin jingying gongye baoguo: Dongya maoni fangzhi gongsi fangwen ji" [Manufacturing gunnysacks and researching the manufacture of new medicine, working hard to manage industry for the nation: Record of a visit to the Dongya Corporation], *Huabei Xinbao*, 13 May 1944, 3; and 29 October 1944.

97. Board of Directors Minutes, 30 August 1937, Dongya Archives, 1-17-1-03.

98. Board of Directors Minutes, 1 October 1938, Dongya Archives, 2-23-2-02.

99. Tenshin Nihon shōkō kaigisho [Tianjin Japanese Chamber of Commerce and Industry], *Tenshin keizai jijō* [Tianjin's economy] (Tianjin, 1939), 42.

100. Yoshida, 147; for the purchase price, see Dongya Archives, 1-17-1-03.

101. Archives of the Dongya Corporation, 1-17-1-03, 1-38-5-01, 1-38-5-03, 1-42-3-01, 1-42-3-05.

102. Board of Directors Minutes, 1 October 1938, Dongya Archives, 2-23-2-02.

103. Board of Directors Minutes, 3 July 1939, Dongya Archives, 1-23-2-03.

104. Board of Directors Minutes, 28 December 1944, Dongya Archives, 1-30-3-05.

105. Shi 2.

106. Board of Directors Minutes, 25 December 1942 and 3 March 1944, Dongya Archives, 1-38-5-05 and 1-30-3-01; "Monthly Report on Tianjin's Business and Industry," March 1944, Archives of the Shanghai Commercial and Savings Bank (Shanghai), Q275-1-400-01; "Chuangzhi madai."

107. Board of Directors Minutes, 9 March 1943, Dongya Archives, 1-42-3-04.

108. Board of Directors Minutes, 15 September 1944, Dongya Archives, 1-30-3-04; "Monthly Report on Tianjin's Business and Industry," September 1944, Archives of the Shanghai Commercial and Savings Bank (Shanghai), Q275-1-400-02.

109. Board of Directors Minutes, 28 December 1944, Dongya Archives, 1-30-3-05.

110. Board of Directors Minutes, 16 March 1945, Dongya Archives, 1-59-12-01.

111. Song Yuzhan, second interview, Tianjin, 2000.

112. Dongya Archives, 1-25-1-03.

113. On the scarcity of supplies, see Board of Directors Minutes, 28 October 1942, Dongya Archives, 1-38-5-04.

114. On South American wool, see Board of Directors Minutes, 2 January 1941, Dongya Archives 1-38-5-01; on sugar, see Board of Directors Minutes, 16 March 1945, Dongya Archives, 1-59-12-01.

115. Dongya Corporation, *Annual Report*, 1941, unpaged, section on Christmas program for poor children.

116. Asada, 189.

117. Caldwell to Johnson, "Political Report for October 1939," 6 November 1939, 3, U.S. Consulate, Tianjin; White to Clark Kerr, "Political Report for the Quarter Ended 31 March 1940," 1 April 1940, 1, British Foreign Office, National Archives, FO371-24657; Caldwell to Johnson, "Political Report for April 1941," 10 May 1941, 4, U.S. Consulate, Tianjin; Caldwell to Gauss, "Political Report for May 1941," 11 June 1941, 1–2, U.S. Consulate, Tianjin.

118. Hashimoto, 2.

119. See summary of protest from both the German and American consuls in Tianjin, archives of the Provisional Government Executive Committee, 2014–752.

120. Hashimoto, 3.

121. Beijing army intelligence chief Yoshida Kitoku to Beijing mayor Yu Jinhe, "Military Requirements and Regulation for the Control of Linen (Jute) and Leather," Archives of the Beijing [Beiping] Police, Beipingshi zhengfu jingwu lei, Beijing Municipal Archives, J1-2-135.

122. Board of Directors Minutes, 3 July 1939, Dongya Archives, 1-23-2-03.

123. Except where otherwise noted by citation, the following account relies primarily on Shi 1.

124. Board of Directors Minutes, 7 June 1942, Dongya Archives, 1-38-5-02.

125. Song Yuzhan, first and second interviews, Tianjin, 2000.

126. Taylor, 102.

127. *Huabei nongshi shiyanchang yaolan* [Survey of experimental farms in North China], Archives of the Agriculture Department of the North China Political Affairs Council, Huabei zhengwu weiyuanhui nongwu zongshu, Beijing Municipal Archives, J25-1-156.

128. On the agricultural research station, see Brett Sheehan, "When Urban Met Rural in the Japanese Occupation: Life on an Agricultural Research Station in North China," in Wen-hsin Yeh and Brett Sheehan, eds., "Chinese Experiences of Total War" (unpublished manuscript).

129. Quoted in Cui Shuju and Jin Yanshi, 19.

130. Shi 1; Cui Shuju and Jin Yanshi, 18; Song Yuzhan, second interview, Tianjin, 2000.

131. Board of Directors Minutes, 15 September 1944, Dongya Archives, 1-30-3-04.

132. Lary, 65–66.

133. Board of Directors Minutes, 28 October 1942, Dongya Archives, 1-38-5-04.

134. Liu Wentian, written materials, in Cui Shuju and Jin Yanshi, 19.

135. Tsujihara was likely the author of a two-volume textbook on the Chinese language published in 1935 and 1936 called *Kago kyōhon* 華語教本. For romanization of Tsujihara's name, I follow the catalog entry for this textbook in the foreign studies library of Osaka University, http://webcatplus-equal.nii.ac.jp/libportal/DocDetail?txt_docid=NCID%3ABA65214772 (accessed 9/28/2009). Thanks to Michelle Damien for finding this entry for me.

136. Shi 1.

137. Details on these plans can be found in a series of articles in the North China Textile Board's periodical *Kahoku bōshoku kōgyōkai geppō* [North China Textile Industry Association Monthly], under the authorship of the Kikakubu [Planning Bureau]: "Huabei qianwei tongzhi guicheng" [Regulations for the control of North China fiber]," "Mōbōshoku kōgyō: Tōsei un'ei yōkō kaisetsu" [Wool spinning industry: Explanation of the outline for control of operations], "Kahoku sen'i kōgyō kanri yōkō ni tsuite" [Outline for the management of North China fiber industries], and "Mōbōshoku kōgyō: Tōsei yōkō" [Outline for the control of the wool spinning industry] 1 (January 1944): 71, 36, 39, and 71–73; and "Asakōgyō tōsei un'ei yōkō kaisetsu" [Flax [jute] industry: Explanation of the outline for control of operations] and "Asakōgyō tōsei un'ei yōkō" [Flax [jute] industry: Outline for control of operations] 3 (March 1944): 45–50 and 63–64.

138. Kikakubu, "Asakōgyō tōsei un'ei yōkō kaisetsu," 45.

139. Board of Directors Minutes, 7 June 1942 and 6 January 1944, Dongya Archives, 1-38-5-02, 1-30-3-03.

140. Asada, 189.

141. Kahoku bōshoku kōgyōkai [North China Textile Industry Association], *Mōbōshoku kōshō jitai chōsa ichiranhyō* [Woolen mills at a glance], 1 September 1943; and *Asa kōshō jitai chōsa ichiranhyō* [Jute mills at a glance], 1 November 1943, Ar-

chives of the Japan Spinners' Association (Osaka University) II-1-61-253 and II-1-68-218.

142. Board of Directors Minutes, 28 December 1944, Dongya Archives, 1-30-3-05.

143. Kikakubu, "Asakōgyō tōsei un'ei yōkō kaisetsu," 49.

144. Yang Tianshou and Li Jingshan, "Tianjin Dongya Gongsi yu Song Feiqing" 124.

145. North China Political Affairs Council to North China Jute Promotion Board, Archives of the North China Political Affairs Council (Nanjing), 2005(1)-331.

146. "Shōwa jūkyū nendo honkai gyōmu hōkoku" [Report on operations of this association for the year 1944], *Kahoku bōshoku kōgyōkai geppō* [North China Textile Industry Association Monthly], no. 7 (March 1945): 27.

147. "Malei zengchan shiye yusuan shu" 麻類增産事業預算書 [Budget for increase in jute production in 1945], Archives of the Agriculture Department of the North China Political Affairs Council (Beijing), J25-1-113.

148. Kahoku asasan kaishinkai [North China Jute Promotion Board], "Jūku nendo gyōmu seiseki hōkokusho" [Report on jute achievements in 1944], Archives of the Agriculture Department of the North China Political Council (Beijing), J25-1-127.

149. Shi 1.

150. Dates of Song Feiqing's incarceration come from notes made by his widow, Papers of Li Jingfang; and Cui Shuju and Jin Yanshi, 18.

151. Papers of Li Jingshan 7.

152. Shi 1.

153. Shi 1.

154. On prices, see "Report on Tianjin Market Conditions," 26 June 1944, Archives of the Shanghai Commercial and Savings Bank (Shanghai), Q275-1-440-01; and on rationing, see Tianjin Mayor to French Consulate, 29 June 1944, French Foreign Ministry, Archives of the Tianjin Consulate (Nantes), Box 21.

155. Dongya Archives, 1-57-10-01.

156. Dongya Archives, 1-57-10-02.

157. Dongya Archives, Sung family collection.

158. Japanese Consulate to French Consulate, transcription of verbal note, 10 March 1945, French Foreign Ministry, Archives of the Tianjin Consulate (Nantes), Box 100; and depositions of French consular officials, 13 March 1945, Box 102.

159. This reinforces Parks Coble's conclusions about the lower Yangzi that different industries faced different conditions; see Coble, *Chinese Capitalists in Japan's New Order*, 106–107.

160. Ding Jiyou, written materials, in Cui Shuju and Jin Yanshi, 132.

161. Shi 1.

162. Li Jingfang, Song Feiqing's widow, places the trip in October of 1939 (Papers of Li Jingfang); Liu Wentian simply says it happened in 1939 (written materials, in Cui Shuju and Jin Yanshi, 19).

5. Building Eden inside the Firm

1. Bian, *Making*, 213.

2. Shi 2. On the clinic, see Minami manshū tetsudō kabushiki gaisha hokushi chōsajo, 285; and Dongya Corporation, *Annual Report*, 1941, unpaged.

3. Bian, *Making*, 128. The YMCA played an important role in advocating for worker welfare in the republican period; see Robin Porter, *Industrial Reformers in Republican China* (Armonk, NY: M. E. Sharpe, 1994).

4. Frazier, 9.

5. Dongya Corporation, *Annual Report*, 1941, unpaged.

6. Yoshida, 147, 148.

7. "Tianjin Dongya maozhi gongsi gaikuang" [The general situation of the Dongya Wool Company], *Huabei laodong* [North China Labor] 1 (15 November 1946): 16.

8. Shi 2.

9. Dongya Corporation, *Annual Report*, 1941, unpaged.

10. Yeh, "Corporate Space," 108–111.

11. Quoted in Frazier, 58.

12. Shi 2.

13. Shi 1.

14. Shi 1. On the precedents for the precept, see Confucius, *The Analects*, book 12, chapter 2; and the Bible, Mark 7:12. In later years, Dongya rephrased the slogan with more vernacular wording: "Ni yuan ren zenyang dai ni, ni jiu xian zenyang dairen" 你願人怎樣待您, 你就先怎樣待人; see "Machang qiangbi juxing geyan yi zhuangjun" 麻廠牆壁巨型格言已裝俊 [The huge slogan on the wall of the gunny-sack factory completed], *Dongya sheng* 11 (16 November 1947): 5. According to the article in the newsletter, this slogan derived from the Bible, "Do unto others as you would have them do unto you" (*ji suo bu yu, wu shi yu ren* 己所不欲, 勿施於人).

15. Gao Xinzhai, oral history.

16. Li Jingshan in Zhengxie interview, 26 November 1982; on the importance of discipline, see also Ding Xiuzhu, oral history, undated, but likely early 1980s, Tianjin zhengxie.

17. Yeh, "Corporate Space," 105–106.

18. *Er shi san niandu guizhang* 二十三年度規章 [1934 regulations], Dongya Archives, 1-4-2-01.

19. *Dagong bao* 9 September 1936, sect. 2, p. 7.

20. Shi 1.

21. Interview with Song Yuzhan, Tianjin, 2000.

22. "Huanying Tianjin ge gongcheng xueshu tuanti" 歡迎天津各工程學術團體 [Welcome to Tianjin's engineering academic groups], *Dongya sheng* 10 (16 October 1947): 6–7.

23. On pay at textile mills, see *Dagong bao*, 14, 21, and 28 December 1930 and 12 and 19 January 1931.

24. Dongya Corporation, *Annual Report*, 1936, "Short History," unpaged.

25. "Dongya maozhi gongsi gongyou renshike guicheng" 東亞毛織公司工友人事科規程 [Rules for the personnel department for workers [as opposed to staff] for the Dongya Woolen Corporation], undated but in a file with other documents dated 1946, Dongya Archives, 1-63-4-01 (hereafter cited as "Worker Rules").

26. Shi 2.

27. "Worker Rules."

28. Interview with Chen Xiuwen, Tianjin, 2000.

29. "Worker Rules."

30. "Worker Rules."

31. Gao Xinzhai, oral history.

32. Jamieson to Clark Kerr, "Intelligence Report for Six Months Ending 30 September 1939," 23.

33. Taylor, 3, 79; Jamieson to Clark Kerr, "Intelligence Report for Six Months Ending 30 September 1939," 24.

34. Hao Guanyi, oral history, taken 22 May 1964, Tianjin History Museum.

35. Feng Naishen, oral history.

36. Interview with Song Yuzhan, Tianjin, 2000.

37. Board of Directors Minutes, 28 October 1942, Dongya Archives, 1-38-5-04.

38. Shi 2.

39. "Worker Rules."

40. Qie Xinyuan in Zhengxie interview, 26 November 1982.

41. Julia Strauss, "The Evolution of Republican Government," *China Quarterly* 150 (June 1997): 345.

42. "Worker Rules."

43. "Gongyou tong guanli de guanxi, shunlian jiangyi di san hao" 工友同管理的關係,順練講義第三號 [Training lecture number three: Relations between workers and managers], Dongya Archives, 1-18-2-15.

44. "He Qingru boshi jiangdao" 何清儒博士講道 [Dr. He Qingru gives a sermon], *Dongya sheng* 9 (1 October 1947): 6.

45. Kevin Landdeck, "Under the Gun: Nationalist Military Service and Society in Wartime Sichuan, 1938–1945" (Ph.D. diss., University of California, Berkeley, 2011), 365.

46. "Worker Rules."

47. Qie Xinyuan in Zhengxie interview, 26 November 1982.

48. *Dagong bao*, 15 October 1933, sect. 3, p. 11; see also, *Dongya Annual*, 1936, unpaged.

49. Hao Guanyi, oral history; the use of the phrase "thought training" probably represents a later vocabulary from the Maoist period.

50. Many of the documents about worker training are undated, but evidence from the file indicates the earliest were dated in the late 1930s; see Dongya Archives, 1-18-2-02 and 1-18-2-12.

51. "Weishenme you shunlian yishi? Shunlian jiangyi di ershiwu hao" 為什麼有順練儀式? 順練講義第二十五號 [Training lecture no. 25: Why is there a ceremony at training lectures?], Dongya Archives, 1-18-2-03.

52. "Weishenme you shunlian yishi?"

53. Hao Guanyi, oral history.

54. Dongya Corporation, *Annual Report*, 1936, unpaged.

55. Dongya Archives, 1-18-2.

56. "Weishenme yao shunlian? Gongren tong guanli de guanxi, shulian jiangyi di liu hao" 為什麼要順練? 工友同管理的關係, 順練講義第六號 [Training lecture no. 6: Why train? Relations between workers and managers], Dongya Archives, 1-18-2-18.

57. Hao Guanyi, oral history.

58. Feng Naishen, oral history.

59. "Weishenme yao zhuyi limao? Shunlian jiangyi di shijiu hao" 為什麼要注意禮貌? 順練講義第十九號 [Training lecture no. 19: Why pay attention to courtesy?], Dongya Archives, 1-18-2-32.

60. Shi 2.

61. "Buyao tong ren zhengchao dajia, shunlian jiangyi di shisan hao" 不要同人爭吵打架, 順練講義第三十號 [Training lecture no. 30: Don't fight and argue with others], Dongya Archives, 1-18-2-08.

62. "Zenyang qingqiu weisheng, shunlian jiangyi di shisanhao" 怎樣請求衛生, 順練講義第十三號 [Training lecture no. 13: How to strive for hygiene), Dongya Archives, 1-18-2-26.

63. Shi 1.

64. *Dongya jingshen* [Dongya spirit] (Tianjin: Dongya Corporation, 1945); Meng Guanglin, oral history, 19 May 1964, Tianjin History Museum.

65. Employee training lecture handbook and text document preserved at the Tianjin History Museum.

66. "Rending mubiao jihua qianjin" 認定目標計劃前進 [Set your mind on a goal and plan for advance], *Dongya sheng* 18 (16 February 1948): 2.

67. "Yeyu zixiu shi jinqu de jiben" 業餘自修是進取的基本 [Self-cultivation outside of work is the basis for advancement], *Dongya sheng* 14 (16 December 1947): 2.

68. Wen-hsin Yeh, "Progressive Journalism and Shanghai's Petty Urbanites: Zou Taofen and the *Shenghuo Weekly*, 1926–1945," in Frederic Wakeman Jr. and Wen-hsin Yeh, eds., *Shanghai Sojourners* (Berkeley: Institute of East Asian Studies, University of California, 1992), 203.

69. Dongya Corporation, *Annual Report*, 1941, unpaged.

70. Zhengxie interview with Chen Yadong, December 1982.

71. Shi 2.

72. Dongya Corporation, *Annual Report*, 1941, unpaged, section on establishing the primary school; see also Shi 2.

73. *Dongya jingshen*, unpaged.

74. Shi 1.

75. Dongya Corporation, *Annual Report*, 1941. Shi says he wrote the lyrics in 1942, but it is possible he misremembered the year.

76. Taylor, 81.

77. Shi 1.

78. Song Yuzhan, interview, 2000.

79. Shi 1.

80. "Huanying Tianjin ge gongcheng xueshu tuanti," 6, 7.

81. Dongya Corporation, *Annual Report*, 1941, section on employee benefits; see also the 1936 *Annual Report* for a very similar outline.

82. Shi 1.

83. Song Yunzhang and Wang Weigang, 122.

84. "Dongya maozhi gongsi changgui (ji guanli gongren guize)" 東亞毛織公司廠規 (即管理工人規則) [Dongya Woolen Factory rules (regulations for managing workers)], undated but other documents in the same file come from 1946, Dongya Archives, 1-63-4-02.

85. Hao Guanyi, oral history.

86. Feng Naishen, oral history.

87. Cui Shuju and Jin Yanshi, 113–114.

88. Cui Shuju and Jin Yanshi, 114–116. Feng Naishen also refers to the Liu Dezhong incident in his oral history.

89. Interview with Chen Yadong, December 1982.

90. Dongya Corporation, *Annual Report*, 1933, unpaged.

91. Interview with Chen Yadong, December 1982.

92. Li Jingshan in Zhengxie interview, 26 November 1982.

93. Feng Naishen, oral history.

94. Gao Xinzhai, oral history; see also Meng Guanglin, oral history.

95. Meng Guanglin, oral history.

96. Feng Naishen, oral history.

97. Feng Naishen, oral history.

98. Dongya Archives, 1-18-2-01, 1-34-1-01.

99. Hao Guanyi, oral history.

100. "Canjia tongren jucanhui guize" 參加同仁聚餐會規則 [Rules for employee dinner meetings], Dongya Archives, 1-75-9-01.

101. Dongya Archives, 1-55-8-02.

102. Dongya Archives, 1-42-3-06.

103. Feng Naishen, oral history.

104. Gao Xinzhai, oral history.

105. Wei Yanying, oral history, 22 May 1964, Tianjin History Museum.

106. Wei Yanying, oral history; Shi 2.

107. "Gongyou gebie tanhua zonghe baogao" [General report on individual talks with workers], Tianjin History Museum, undated, but internal evidence indicates the 1940s.

108. "Dui gongyou xunhua xuyao jieshi zhi wenti" 對工友訓話須要解釋之問題 [Problems that need to be explained to workers in training lectures], Dongya Archives (Tianjin History Museum), undated but most likely in the mid to late 1940s.

109. Kikakubu [Planning Bureau], "Bōseki kōshō ni okeru rōkō kakuho taisaku ni tsuite [Policies for the guarantee of labor for spinning factories]," *Kahoku bōshoku kōgyōkai geppō* [North China Textile Industry Association Monthly] 7 (10 March 1945): 29–31.

110. *Dagong bao*, 15 October 1933, sect. 3, p. 11.

111. Dongya Corporation, *Annual Report*, 1936, unpaged.

112. Bo Dianyuan, statistical materials provided in 1965," in Cui Shuju and Jin Yanshi, 101.

113. Frazier. For another example from Tianjin, see Liu Yanchen, ed., "Tianjin guohuo shoupin suo 'zongwubu gongbu liudi' zhailu" [Selections recorded from the 'General Affairs Office Announcements' of the Tianjin National Products Bureau], *Tianjin wenshi ziliao xuanji* 47 (July 1989): 66–123. On scientific management in Japan, see William M. Tsutsui, *Manufacturing Ideology: Scientific Management in Twentieth-Century Japan* (Princeton, NJ: Princeton University Press, 1998).

114. Barbara Weinstein, *For Social Peace in Brazil: Industrialists and the Remaking of the Working Class in São Paulo, 1920–1964* (Chapel Hill: University of North Carolina Press, 1996), 4–7.

115. Qie Xinyuan in Zhengxie interview, 26 November 1982; Song Yunzhang and Wang Weigang, 46.

116. Frazier, 12. For a review of the literature on early welfare capitalism in the United States, see, Michael Hillard, "Labor at 'Mother Warren': Paternalism, Welfarism, and Dissent at S. D. Warren, 1854–1967," *Labor History* 45, no. 1 (February 2004): 39–40.

117. Howard R. Stanger, "From Factory to Family: The Creation of a Corporate Culture in the Larkin Company of Buffalo, New York," *Business History Review* 74 (Autumn 2000): 423, 426.

118. Frazier, 15.

119. Wen-hsin Yeh, "Republican Origins of the *Danwei*: The Case of Shanghai's Bank of China," in Xiaobo Lü and Elizabeth Perry, eds., *Danwei: The Changing Chinese Workplace in Historical and Comparative Perspective* (Armonk, NY: M. E. Sharpe, 1997), 61; and Elizabeth Perry, "From Native Place to Workplace: Labor Origins and Outcomes of China's *Danwei* System," in Lü and Perry, 43 and 54–55. Xiaobo Lü traces the welfare and social functions of the *danwei* to the free supply system the Chinese Communist Party used in rural areas during the pre-1949 period, but that is of less relevance in understanding economic organization in urban areas before 1949; see Xiaobo Lü, "Minor Public Economy: The Revolutionary Origins of the Danwei," in Lü and Perry, 21–41.

120. On the *danwei*, see Xiaobo Lü and Elizabeth Perry, "Introduction," in Lü and Perry, 5–6.

6. The Postwar Nationalists' Unresponsive Developmental State

1. Interview with Song Yuzhan. Zhang had served as mayor of Tianjin in the 1930s (see Chapter 3).

2. Zhengxie interview with Qie Xinyuan, Li Jingshan, Meng Guanglin, and Chen Yadong, 3 December 1982.

3. Dongya Archives, 1-57-10-05.

4. Shi 1.

5. *Dagong bao*, 1 December 1945, sect. 1, p. 1.

6. Board of Directors Minutes, Dongya Archives, 23 December 1945, 1-59-12-2.

7. Dongya Archives 1-55-8-01, undated, but internal evidence indicates late 1945 or early 1946.

8. Minutes of the meeting of the board of directors, 29 July 1945, in Cui Shuju and Jin Yanshi, 52.

9. Dongya Archives, 1-55-8-01.

10. Shi 2.

11. Feng Feifan, department head (*chuzhang*), to Health Ministry head, 29 January 1946; and Tianjin Health Bureau to Health Ministry, 8 March 1946, Archives of the Health Ministry (Weisheng ju) (Nanjing), 372–572; and correspondence between the Tianjin City Health Bureau and Dongya, Archives of the Tianjin Health Bureau (Tianjin), 116-1-633.

12. Yang Tianshou and Li Jingshan, "Jiefang qian de Dongya gongsi," 55–56.

13. Wang Weigang, "Dongya fangzhi dawang Song Feiqing" [Dongya's textile king Song Feiqing], in Zhao Yunsheng, ed., *Zhongguo da ziben jia*, vol. 7, *Jingjin dagu juan* [China's great capitalists, vol. 7, Great businesspeople of Beijing and Tianjin] (Changchun: Shidai wenyi chubanshe, 1994), 88.

14. Tianjin Election Commission to National Election Commission, 26 March 1946; and Interior Ministry to National Election Commission, 1 May 1946, quoting original letter from Sun Tongxuan 孫桐萱 to his commander, Archives of the National Assembly (Nanjing), 451-18.

15. *Dagong bao*, 13 June 1946, sect. 1, p. 1; Board of Directors Minutes, Dongya Archives, 23 December 1945, 1-59-12-2; *Dagong bao*, 8 February 1946, sect. 1, p. 1.

16. *Dagong bao*, 6 July 1946, sect. 1, p. 1; see also name change announcements in *Dagong bao*, 25, 27, and 29 June and 1 and 2 July 1947.

17. "Tianjin Dongya maozhi gongsi gaikuang," 15.

18. Charter of the Dongya Corporation, 30 June 1946, Dongya Archives, 1-63-4-03.

19. Yoshida, 148; Minami manshū tetsudō kabushiki gaisha hokushi chōsajo, 285.

20. *Tianjinshi chanye gongren gongzi diaocha zhengli biao* 天津市產業工人工資調查整理表 [Sorted chart of production worker wages in Tianjin], May 1946, Archives of the Central Social Ministry (Nanjing), 11-2-257-02. On actual wage rates at Dongya, see also Zhao Xingguo, "Tianjin Dongya maozhi gongsi niaokan" [A bird's-eye view of Tianjin Dongya Company], *Hebei sheng yinghang jingji ban yuekan* [Hebei Provincial Bank Economic Bimonthly] 1, no. 10 (last half of May 1946): 28.

21. On the relationship between inflation and worker unrest, see Shi 1.

22. Zhengxie interview with Chen Yadong, December 1982.

23. Report of the Tianjin Police Department, 11 January 1946, in Cui Shuju and Jin Yanshi, 118; and report of the Tianjin Social Bureau, 12 January 1946, in Cui Shuju and Jin Yanshi, 116.

24. Minutes of the Board of Directors of the Dongya Corporation, 10 January 1946, in Cui Shuju and Jin Yanshi, 116–117.

25. Report of the Tianjin Police Department, 13 January 1946, in Cui Shuju and Jin Yanshi, 117–118; see also Shi 1.

26. Minutes of the Board of Directors of the Dongya Corporation, 13 January 1946, in Cui Shuju and Jin Yanshi, 117.

27. Report of the Tianjin Police Department, 16 February 1946, in Cui Shuju and Jin Yanshi, 118; Cui notes that the original document was damaged so much that it was illegible.

28. Minutes of the Board of irectors of the Dongya Corporation, 14 February 1946, in Cui Shuju and Jin Yanshi, 118.

29. Union announcement, 1 March 1946, Dongya Archives, 1-61-2-01.

30. Announcement, 24 May 1946, Dongya Archives, 1-61-2-02.

31. Chart of daily production attached to Dongya to Mayor Zhang, 29 July 1946, and forwarded to Social Department, 30 July 1946, Archives of the Tianjin Municipal Government, 2-2-1-537-01.

32. *Dagong bao*, 14 July 1946, sect. 1, p. 3.

33. Dongya union to Social Bureau, 19 June 1946; and report of the Social Bureau, 20 June 1948, in Cui Shuju and Jin Yanshi, 118 and 120 respectively.

34. Report of the Social Bureau, 30 June 1946, in Cui Shuju and Jin Yanshi, 119.

35. Dongya to Mayor Zhang, 29 July 1946, and forwarded to Social Department, 30 July 1946, Archives of the Tianjin Municipal Government, 2-2-1-537-01.

36. "Announcement (26) no. 51," 5 July 1946, Dongya Archives, 1-61-2-03.

37. "Announcement (26) no. 53," 8 July 1946, Dongya Archives, 1-57-10-03.

38. The date of his visit is noted on the chart in the attachment to Dongya to Mayor Zhang, 29 July 1946, and forwarded to Social Department, 30 July 1946, Archives of the Tianjin Municipal Government, 2-2-1-537-01.

39. Report of the Social Bureau, 21 July 1946, in Cui Shuju and Jin Yanshi, 119–120.

40. "Announcement (26) no. 58," 24 July 1948, Dongya Archives, 1-61-2-04.

41. Dongya to Mayor Zhang, 29 July 1946, and forwarded to Social Department, 30 July 1946, Archives of the Tianjin Municipal Government, 2-2-1-537-01.

42. Interview with Song Yuzhan.

43. Zhengxie interview with Chen Yadong, December 1982.

44. *Dagong bao*, 8 August 1946, sect. 2, p. 5.

45. Frazier, 14.

46. *Dagong bao*, 21 August 1946, sect. 1, p. 3.

47. Dongya to Central Trust (Zhongyang Xintuo Ju, Tianjin Fenju 中央信託局天津分局), 15 August 1946, and Central Trust to Dongya, 30 August 1946, Archives of the Central Trust (Tianjin), 20-2-2-1346-01.

48. *Dagong bao*, 21, 23, and 25 August 1946, sect. 1, p. 1, sect. 1, p. 4, and sect. 1, p. 4, respectively.

49. "Tianjin Dongya maozhi gongsi gaikuang," 15–16.

50. Zhao Xingguo, 29.

51. Likewise in Shanghai, many labor disputes in private factories centered on the demand to match benefits supplied at state-owned enterprises; see Frazier, 85.

52. Yuan Zemin, "Dongya maozhi gongchang laozi jiufen tiaojie jingguo" [Process of resolution of the labor-capital dispute at Dongya Wool] *Gongren zhoukan* [Worker Weekly], no. 1 (1 October 1946): 7. Yuan Zemin was one of the mediators.

53. Hao Guanyi, oral history. Hao's account is in general agreement with the 13 September 1946 police report; see Cui Shuju and Jin Yanshi, 120–121.

54. Dongya to Tianjin Police Command (Tianjin jingbei silingbu 天津警備司令部), 18 September 1946, Dongya Archives, 1-64-5-01; and Yuan Zemin, 7.

55. Dongya union to the Tianjin Social Bureau, 12 September 1946, in Cui Shuju and Jin Yanshi, 121.

56. Three People's Principles Youth League, Tianjin Branch Preparation Office (Sanminzhuyi Qingniantuan Tianjin zhituanbu choubeichu 三民主義青年團天津支團部籌備處) to Mayor, 12 September 1946, Archives of the Tianjin Municipal Government (Tianjin), 2-2-1-537-04.

57. "Announcement (26) no. 71," 13 September 1946, Dongya Archives, 1-64-5-01.

58. Tianjin Police Command (Tianjin jingbei silingbu 天津警備司令部), "announcement no. 620," 14 September 1946, Dongya Archives, 1-64-5-01.

59. Dongya to Tianjin Police Command, 18 September 1946, Dongya Archives, 1-64-5-01.

60. At the end of the war, Beijing was again renamed Beiping to reflect the fact that the Nationalist capital was in Nanjing in the South.

61. Shi 1.

62. Interview with Song Yuzhan.

63. Three People's Principles Youth League to Mayor, 12 September 1946.

64. Zhonggong Dongya maoma fangzhi chang dang zhongzhi youguan "san wu fan" yundong zhuanjuan, 中共東亞毛麻紡織廠黨部總支有關 "三五反" 運動專卷材料 [General Office of the Dongya Wool and Jute Factory Communist Party Committee, special file on the "Five Anti and Three Anti" campaigns], "Guanyu Dongya gongsi yufan yundong gongren zhengzhi jiaoyu wenti yixie qingkuang" 關於東亞公司五反運動工人, 政治教育問題一些情況 [Workers in the Five Anti's Movement at the Dongya Company, some matters of the question of education], 22 May 1952, Dongya Archives, holdings of the Tianjin History Museum. On such mutual-help groups, see Emily Honig, *Sisters and Strangers: Women in the Shanghai Cotton Mills, 1919–1949* (Stanford, CA: Stanford University Press, 1992).

65. Liu Wentian, written materials, in Cui Shuju and Jin Yanshi, 101.

66. *Dagong bao*, 21 September 1946, sect. 2, p. 6.

67. Advertisement, *Dagong bao*, 26, 28, and 29 November, 1 December 1946, sect. 2, p. 4, sect. 2, p. 6, sect. 2, p. 6, and sect. 2, p. 5, respectively. Dongya will continue to offer this product in the early PRC period; see Chapter 7.

68. *Dagong bao*, 11 December 1946, sect. 1, p. 2.

69. C. E. Whitamore, British Consul General Tianjin, to British Embassy Nanjing, "December Report," 15 January 1947, British Foreign Office, British National Archives (London) FO371-63432.

70. *Dagong bao*, 22 December 1946, sect. 1, p. 3.

71. Copies of the correspondence regarding Dongya's registration for the Shanghai subsidiary can be found in the Archives of the Shanghai Commercial and Savings Bank (Shanghai), Q6-1-1251.

72. Archives of the Central Social Ministry (Nanjing), 11-2-257-01.

73. Dongya Archives, 1-71-5-01, 1-71-5-02, 1-71-5-03.

74. Shi 2. The golden millet dream refers to a Chinese story about the fleeting nature of wealth and fame.

75. Dongya to Central Trust, 1 January 1947, and "Loan Agreement," 9 February 1947, Archives of the Central Trust (Tianjin), 20-2-2-1346.

76. Archives of the Tax Office (Shuiwu shu), Nanjing, 14 January 1947, 340(9)-286.

77. Dongya Corporation, *Dongya gequ ji* [Collection of Dongya songs], July 1947, Sung [Song] Family Papers. An early version of the song appeared in Dongya Corporation, *Annual Report*, 1934, unpaged.

78. Dongya Corporation, *Qingzhu chengli shi wu zhounian ji geng ming jinian tekan* [Special publication commemorating the celebration of the fifteenth anniversary and the name change], 1947, unpaged (hereafter *Annual*, 1947).

79. Dongya Corporation, *Annual*, 1947.

80. Dongya Corporation, *Dongya gequ ji*.

81. Shi 2.

82. Whitamore to embassy, "January Report," "February Report," and "March Report," 20 February 1947, 19 March 1947, and 3 April 1947, British Foreign Office, British National Archives (London) FO371-63432; and *Dagong bao*, 17 February 1947, sect. 1, p. 2.

83. Whitamore to embassy, 20 February 1947, "January Report," British Foreign Office, British National Archives (London) FO371-63432.

84. Tianjin Municipal Social Bureau Order 291 to Dongya, 21 February 1947, Dongya Archives, 1-74-8-01.

85. Dongya to Tianjin Municipal Social Bureau, undated draft, Dongya Archives, 1-74-8-01.

86. C. S. Whitamore to embassy, "April Report," 17 May 1947, and "May Report," 10 June 1947, British Foreign Office, British National Archives (London) FO371-63432.

87. Cited in Siguret to Sivan, 13 and 17 June 1947, French National Archives, Tianjin Consulate (Nantes), Box 100.

88. Tianjin Grain Merchants Guild to Post-War Welfare Office, Hebei, Rehe, Beiping, Tianjin Branch, 10 June 1947, Archives of the Executive Yuan (Nanjing), 21-7005-01.

89. "Banyue tan: Jiajin gongzuo sudu" 半月談: 加緊工作速度 [Bimonthly talk: Increasing work speed] and "Huanying Tianjin ge gongcheng xueshu tuanti," *Dongya sheng* 1 (1 June 1947): 2, 6–7.

90. Cui Shuju and Jin Yanshi, 81–82. For a full discussion of this essay, see Chapter 8.

91. "Ben gongsi zhuban di yi jie jituan jiehun xili" 本公司主辦第一屆集團結婚喜禮 [The first group wedding by this company], *Dongya sheng* 1 (1 June 1947): 6.

92. "Kexue yu zongjiao zuotan" 科學與宗教座談 [A conversation about science and religion], *Dongya sheng* 8 (16 September 1947): 8; "Shuangshi jie youyihui jisheng" 雙十節遊藝會 [Glories of the Double Ten holiday cultural performance], *Dongya sheng* 10 (16 October 1947): 5.

93. *Dagong bao*, 2 July 1947, sect. 2, p. 5; see also "Zhigong xianqi dianli" 職工 獻旗典禮 [Employee flag presentation ceremony], *Dongya sheng* 4 (16 July 1947): 6.

94. On worker compensation, see "Huanying Tianjin ge gongcheng xueshu tu-anti," 6–7; and "Chanye gongren gongzi zhengli biao" 產業工人工資整理表 [Production workers wages table], March, June, September, and December 1947, Archives of the Central Social Ministry (Nanjing), 11-2-125. On distribution, see "Gaobai" 告白 [Announcement (26) no. 36], *Dongya sheng* 4 (16 July 1947), 3; and "Gaobai" 告白 [Announcement (26) no. 64], *Dongya sheng* 9 (1 October 1947): 2.

95. "Zuzhi yue da guilü yue yan" 組織越大規律越嚴 [The larger the organization, the stricter the rules], *Dongya sheng* 3 (1 July 1947): 4; "Shoufa shi meide" 守 法是美德 [Obeying the law is a virtue], *Dongya sheng* 5 (1 August 1947): 2.

96. "Yao xiang minzhu bi xian zizhi" 要想民主必先自治 [If you want democracy, it is necessary to first govern yourself], *Dongya sheng* 4 (16 July 1947): 2.

97. Interview with Song Yuzhan.

98. "Ben gongsi peigei gudong wupin" 本公司配給股東物品 [The distribution of goods to shareholders by this company], *Dongya sheng* 4 (16 July 1947): 3; and "Gaobai" 告白 [Announcement], *Dongya sheng* 5 (1 August 1947): 3.

99. "Hezuoshe menshi bu bayue yiri kaimui" 合作社門市部八月一日開幕 [The cooperative store opened 1 August], *Dongya sheng* 5 (1 August 1947): 9.

100. Cui Shuju and Jin Yanshi, 51.

101. For example, see the advertisements in *Dagong bao*, 17, 19, 21, and 23 November and 25 and 28 December 1947.

102. Liu Wentian, written materials, in Cui Shuju and Jin Yanshi, 132.

103. Cui Shuju and Jin Yanshi, 51.

104. Report to the Woolen Producers Association, 1 April 1948, in Cui Shuju and Jin Yanshi, 54.

105. Dongya to Tianjin Customs, 1947 investigation by the Tianjin Customs Administration, in Cui Shuju and Jin Yanshi, 52–53.

106. *Dagong bao*, 5 July 1947, sect. 2, p. 5.

107. *Dagong bao*, 6 September 1947, sect. 2, p. 5.

108. Whitamore to embassy, "June Report," 7 July 1947, "July Report," 11 August 1947, and "August Report," 9 September 1947, all British Foreign Office, British National Archives (London) FO371-63432.

109. "Jidu jiaotu: Song jingli jiangdao" 基督教徒:宋經理講道 [Protestants: Song Feiqing sermon], *Dongya Sheng* 6 (16 August 1947): 5.

110. "Machang qiangbi juxing geyan yi zhuangjun" 麻廠牆壁巨型格言已裝俊 [The huge slogan on the wall of the gunnysack factory completed], *Dongya sheng* 11 (16 November 1947): 5.

111. Rui Fu, "Tianjin Dongya qiye gufen youxian gongsi jianxie" [A brief account of the Dongya Corporation], *Gongye yuekan* 4, no. 10 (October 1947): 21–22, quote from 22.

112. "Shieryue wuri qi peishou gudong er bai hao maoxian" 十二月五日起配售股 東二百號毛線 [Distribution of no. 200 wool yarn to shareholders begins 5 December], *Dongya sheng* 11 (16 November 1947): 6.

113. *Dagong bao*, 27 November 1947, sect. 1, p. 3.

114. Minutes of the meeting of the board of directors, 1947 [exact date not given], in Cui Shuju and Jin Yanshi, 52.

115. "Chanye gongren gongzi zhengli biao" 產業工人工資整理表 [Production workers wages table], March, June, September, and December 1947, Archives of the Central Social Ministry (Nanjing), 11-2-125.

116. "Renshi dongtai" 人事動態 [Personnel situation], *Dongya sheng* 11 (1 November 1947): 5.

117. Lianhe zhengxin suo 聯合徵信所 [United Credit Bureau], "Gongshang ye diaocha, Dongya qiye gufen youxian gongsi" 工商事業調查,東亞企業股份有限公司 [Credit investigation, Dongya Enterprise Limited Liability Corporation], undated, likely mid-1947, Archives of the Shanghai Commercial and Savings Bank (Shanghai), Q78-2-13710.

118. Internal memo, 7 July 1947, Public Records Office, Hong Kong Records Service, HKRS no. 41.

119. You Baoshan, written materials, and Liu Wentian, written materials, in Cui Shuju and Jin Yanshi, 132.

120. Song Yunzhang and Wang Weigang, 306, 307.

121. *Dagong bao*, 27 November 1947, sect. 1, p. 3.

122. Song Yunzhang and Wang Weigang, 304.

123. *Dagong bao*, 4 November 1947, sect. 2, p. 5.

124. *Dagong bao*, 27 November 1947, sect. 1, p. 3.

125. "Chanye gongren gongzi zhengli biao" 產業工人工資整理表 [Production workers wages table], March, June, September, and December 1947, Archives of the Central Social Ministry (Nanjing), 11-2-125.

126. Dongya Archives, 1-71-5-06, 1-80-5-01.

127. Whitamore to embassy, "October/November Report," 9 December 1947, British Foreign Office, British National Archives (London) FO371-63432; and *Dagong bao*, 12 December 1947, sect. 2, p. 5.

128. *Dagong bao*, 18 December 1947, sect. 2, p. 5.

129. *Dagong bao*, 7 January 1948, sect. 1, p. 2; 13 January 1948, sect. 2, p. 5; and 27 January 1948, sect. 1, p. 2.

130. Tianjin Mayor's Office Bureau of Foreign Affairs to French Consul, Tianjin, 21 January 1948 (French translation of original Chinese missive), French National Archives, Tianjin Consulate (Nantes), Box 100.

131. *Dagong bao*, 16 March 1948, sect. 2, p. 6.

132. *Dagong bao*, 13 January 1948, sect. 2, p. 5.

133. *Dagong bao*, 6 March 1948, sect. 1, p. 1.

134. *Dagong bao*, 17 March 1948, sect. 2, p. 5.

135. "Huanying Song jingli huiguo chahui zhisheng" 歡迎宋經理回國茶會志盛 [Record of the welcome back party for President Song], *Dongya sheng* 21 (1 April 1948): 3–4.

136. "Huanying Song jingli huiguo chahui zhisheng," 3–4.

137. "Zong jingli de hua" 總經理的話 [The president's words], *Dongya sheng* 22 (16 April 1948): 2.

138. "Ben gongsi saliu niandu di shiliu jie gudong hui linzhao" 本公司卅六年度第十六屆股東會臨爪 [Fragments from the 1947 sixteenth shareholders' meeting], *Dongya sheng* 21 (1 April 1948): 5.

139. "Dui gudong qishi" 對股東啟事 [A notice for shareholders], *Dongya sheng* 23 (1 May 1948): 4.

140. "Ben gongsi saliu niandu di shiliu jie gudong hui linzhao," 5.

141. "Sushe fantuan xingjiang mianmu yixin" 宿舍飯團行將面目一新 [A new face for the dormitories and the group meal plan], *Dongya sheng* 23 (1 May 1948): 5.

142. "Dongya niusi: Zhigong sushe zhixu anjing" 東亞紐斯:職工宿舍秩序安警 [Dongya news: The employee dormitory is orderly and quiet], *Dongya sheng* 25 (1 June 1948): 13.

143. "Zong jingli zhaoji gebu guanli: Yantao ruhe lingdao nuli gongzuo wenti" 總經理召集各部管理:研討如何領導努力工作問題 [The president gathers department heads: Discusses the problem of leading hard work], *Dongya sheng* 24 (16 May 1948): 3; and "Weishenme zuzhi fudao weiyuanhui" 為甚麼組織輔導委員會 [Why organize the guidance committees], *Dongya sheng* 25 (1 June 1948): 7.

144. "Dongya zhigong fuwu fudao weiyuanhui fuwu tuanti jiben tuanyuan xuanshi dianli" 東亞職工服務輔導委員會服務團體基本團員宣誓典禮 [Ceremony for the swearing in of the base members for the Dongya Employee Guidance Service Committee], *Dongya sheng* 27 (1 July 1948): 9.

145. Dongya Archives, untitled photo album.

146. Interview with Song Yuzhan.

147. Dongya Archives, 1-74-8-02-05; "Ben gongsi gonghui gaizu junshi" 本公司工會改組竣事 [Completion of the reelection of officers of this company's union], *Dongya sheng* 29 (1 August 1948): 2.

148. Dongya Archives, 1-56-9-03; and Archives of the Tianjin Municipal Government, 2-2-1-537.

149. "Gonghui lijianshi yejian zong jingli tanhua cuoyao" 工會理監事謁見總經理談話撮要 [Important items from the talk between union officers and the president], *Dongya sheng* 29 (1 August 1948): 3.

150. My estimates of average age and time at Dongya are likely to be conservative since they derive from union representatives, profiles of "longtime employees" in the company newsletter, and memberships in religious clubs in 1948. These employees are more likely to have longer and deeper ties to Dongya. See Dongya Archives, 1-56-9-01, 1-56-9-02, 1-56-9-03; *Dongya sheng*, nos. 3, 13, 18, 19, 28, and 29 (1947–1948).

151. Worker status is listed in the chart of living expense subsidies found in Dongya Archives, 1-79-4-01.

152. *Dagong bao*, 21 May 1948, sect. 1, p. 1.

153. "Ben gongsi jiang dui gudong peishou yibaihao maoxian" 本公司將對股東配售一百號毛線 [This company will sell no. 100 wool yarn to shareholders], *Dongya sheng* 28 (16 July 1948): 5; "Dongya niusi: Gongsi zeng tongren maoxian" 東亞紐斯:公司贈同仁毛線 [Dongya news: The company gives wool yarn to employees], *Dongya sheng* 29 (1 August 1948); and Dongya Archives, 1-78-3-01.

154. "Dongya niusi" 東亞紐斯 [Dongya news], *Dongya sheng* 28 (16 July 1948): 6.

155. "Dongya niusi: Fanweihui peishou zhi manshou" 東亞紐斯:飯委會配售之饅首 [Dongya news: Steamed buns sold by the food plan committee], *Dongya sheng* 23 (16 August 1948): 4.

156. *Dagong bao*, 17 May 1948, sect. 2, p. 5.

157. "Zong jingli dui quanti zhigong tanhua" 總經理對全體職工談話 [The president's talk to all the employees], *Dongya sheng* 30 (16 August 1948): 3–4.

158. "Ben gongsi peishou maoxian 'datong' 'maorongshe'" 本公司配售毛線 "大通" "毛絨社," [Sale of this company's wool yarn, "Datong," "Maorongshe"], *Dongya sheng* 32 (16 September 1948): 4.

159. "Benkan qishi" 本刊啟事 [Publication notice], *Dongya sheng* 31 (1 September 1948): 2.

160. "Dongya niusi: Lianjia peiyu zhigong mianfen" 東亞紐斯:廉價配預職工麵粉 [Dongya news: Flour sold to employees at cheap price], *Dongya sheng* 33 (1 October 1948): 2.

161. "Dongya niusi: Kaishi peishou gudong dayi ni" 東亞紐斯:開始配售股東大衣呢 [Dongya news: Start of sale at preferential price of overcoat wool cloth to shareholders], *Dongya sheng* 33 (1 October 1948): 2.

162. "Dongya niusi: 'Datong' 'Maorongshe' zanting" 東亞紐斯: "大通"毛絨社暫停 [Dongya news: The "Datong" and "Maorongshe" sales outlets temporarily suspend operations], *Dongya sheng* 33 (1 October 1948): 2.

163. *Dagong bao*, 7 October 1948, sect. 2, p. 5.

164. Report to Dongya Shareholders, 26 March 1950, Dongya Archives, Tianjin History Museum (03).

165. "Wei zengjin gongzuo xiaoneng ji juxing fenbu jiantao zuotanhui" 為增進工作效能即舉行分部檢討座談會 [Self-criticism discussions to be held to increase work effectiveness], *Dongya sheng* 34 (16 October 1948): 4.

166. "Zong jingli dui quanti zhigong tanhua" 總經理對全體職工談話 [The president's talk to all the employees], *Dongya sheng* 35 (1 November 1948): 3.

167. *Dagong bao*, 28 October 1948, sect. 2, p. 6.

168. "Ben gongsi chupin zan cai yihuoyihuo banfa" 本公司出品暫採以貨易貨辦法 [The company temporarily adopts a barter method for its products], *Dongya sheng* 35 (1 November 1948): 2.

169. "Hezuoshe zhaokai lilianshi huiyi" 合作社召開理監事會議 [Officers of the cooperative hold a meeting], *Dongya sheng* 35 (1 November 1948): 4.

170. "Zong jingli dui tongren kaiqie zhishi fuwu taidu" 總經理對同仁剴切指示服務態度 [The president instructs the employees on the proper service attitude], *Dongya sheng* 36 (16 November 1948): cover.

171. Siguret to Foreign Ministry, 23 November 1948, French Foreign Ministry, Asie-Oceanie 1930–1940 and 1944–1955, French National Archives (Paris), file 172.

172. *Dongya sheng* 37 (1 December 1948).

173. Siguret to Meyrier, 8 November 1948, "Situation in North China," 2, French Foreign Ministry, Asie-Oceanie 1930–1940 and 1944–1955, French National Archives (Paris), file 172.

174. Jobez to Meyrier, 12 April 1949, 1, French Foreign Ministry, Asie-Oceanie 1930–1940 and 1944–1955, French National Archives (Paris), file 172.

7. The People's "New Democratic" Developmental State

1. Cochran, "Capitalists Choosing Communist China," 359–385.

2. Report to Dongya Shareholders, 26 March 1950, Dongya Archives, Tianjin History Museum (03).

3. Siguret to Foreign Ministry, in French National Archives, Asie-Oceanie 1944–1955 (Paris), file 172.

4. Tianjin Consulate to Foreign Ministry, 14 December 1948, in French National Archives, Asie-Oceanie 1944–1955 (Paris), file 172.

5. Report to Dongya Shareholders, 26 March 1950, Dongya Archives, Tianjin History Museum (03).

6. This account is based on the recollections of Song family and friends, including Shi Xiaodong, Song Yunzhang, 323–326. See also Papers of Li Jingshan 7.

7. "Announcement (27) no. 93," 18 December 1948, Dongya Archives, 1-77-2-09; and "Committee for Facing the Political Change, Notice 18-83-quan-37," 20 December 1948, and various documents related to the work of the Committee for Facing the Political Change, 23 December 1948, Dongya Archives, 1-84-9-01.

8. Reuters dispatch, 30 December 1938, in J. Siguret, French Consul General Tianjin, to J. Meyrier, French Ambassador to China, 31 December 1948, French National Archives, Tianjin Consulate (Nantes), Box 100.

9. Siguret to Foreign Ministry, 3 January 1949 and 7 January 1949, French National Archives, Asie-Oceanie 1944–1955 (Paris), file 172.

10. Liu Wentian, written materials, in Cui Shuju and Jin Yanshi, 132.

11. Zhou Qilun, "Jiefang qian Tianjin wujia feizhang min buliao sheng jishi" [A true record of soaring prices and people unable to live in pre-liberation Tianjin], in Yang Daxin and Fang Zhaolin, eds., *Tianjin lishi de zhuanzhe, yuan guomindang junzheng renyuan de huiyi* [Tianjin's historical turning point, memories of Nationalist military and political officials] (Tianjin: Tianjinshi zhengxie wenshi ziliao yanjiu weiyuanhui, 1988), 281–282.

12. Papers of Li Jingshan 7.

13. Jobez (Hong Kong) to Meyrier (Nanjing), "Situation in Tianjin," 12 April 1949, French National Archives, Asie-Oceanie 1944–1955 (Paris), file 172.

14. U.S. Economic Cooperation Administration Mission to China, Tianjin Regional Office, "General Situation Report, 10–31 January 1949," 5, Papers of R. Allen Griffin, Box 4, Hoover Institution Archives, Stanford University, Stanford, CA.

15. Liu Wentian, recounted by his daughter Liu Yuying, interview, Tianjin, 28 July 1999.

16. U.S. Economic Cooperation Administration, "Situation Report. 10–31 January 1949," 6.

17. Song Yunzhang and Wang Weigang, 330.

18. Dongya Archives, 2-86-2-01.

19. Huang Xiaotong and Li Wenfang, *Liu Shaoqi yu Tianjin jianghua* [Liu Shaoqi and the Tianjin talks] (Kaifeng: Henan University Press, 1998), 56.

20. Song Yunzhang and Wang Weigang, 332.

21. "Huang Huoqing tongzhi zai siying qiye weiyuanhui huiyi shang de tan hua" 黃火青同志在私營企業委員會會議上的談話 [Comrade Huang Huoqing's speech at the meeting of the Private Enterprise Commission], in Zhonggong Tianjin shiwei dangshi ziliao zhengji weiyuan hui [Historical Records Committee of the Tianjin Chinese Communist Party Committee], Zhonggong Tianjin shiwei tongzhan bu [United Front Work Office of the Tianjin Chinese Party Committee], and Tianjinshi Dang'anguan [Tianjin Municipal Archives], eds., *Zhongguo ziben-zhuyi gongshangye de shehuizhuyi gaizao, Tianjin juan* [The socialist transformation of China's capitalist business and industry, Tianjin volume] (Tianjin: Zhonggong dangshi chubanshe, 1991), 26.

22. Board of Directors Minutes, 20 February 1949, Dongya Archives, 2-91-7-02.

23. *Jinbu ribao*, 27 and 28 February and 2 March 1949.

24. U.S. Economic Cooperation Administration, China, Tianjin Regional Office, "General Situation Report of Tientsin [Tianjin] for 1 February–19 March 1949," 1, Papers of R. Allen Griffin, Box 4, Hoover Institution Archives.

25. Report to Dongya Shareholders, 26 March 1950, Dongya Archives, Tianjin History Museum (03).

26. Board of Directors Minutes, 20 February 1949, Dongya Archives, 2-91-7-02.

27. Song Yunzhang and Wang Weigang, 332; and Huang Xiaotong and Li Wenfang, 54.

28. Huang Xiaotong and Li Wenfang, 27–28.

29. U.S. Economic Cooperation Administration Mission to China, "Situation Report, 10–31 January 1949," 2–3.

30. Huang Xiaotong and Li Wenfang, 34; see also Frederic Wakeman, "'Cleanup': The New Order in Shanghai," in Jeremy Brown and Paul G. Picko-wicz, eds. *Dilemmas of Victory: The Early Years of the People's Republic of China* (Cambridge, MA: Harvard University Press, 2007), 25.

31. *Jinbu ribao*, 27 March 1949 and 28 March 1949, both sect. 1, p. 3.

32. *Jinbu ribao*, 27 March 1949 and 28 March 1949, both sect. 1, p. 3. The idea that the party could decide whether or not individual capitalists were good or bad echoes Zhou Enlai's conversation with Liu Hongsheng; see Cochran, "Capitalists Choosing Communist China," 370.

33. These recollections are recorded in Huang Xiaotong and Li Wenfang, 36–37; and almost word for word in Chen Yingci (apparently the party historian who actually visited Liu Shaoqi's wife, Wang Guangmei), "Guanyu jiefang chu Liu Shaoqi de Tianjin zhi xing" [Liu Shaoqi's trip to Tianjin in the early period of liberation] *Yahuang chunqiu*, no. 4 (1996): 2–8.

34. Huang Xiaotong and Li Wenfang, 37–38.

35. "Tianjinshi gongshangju guanyu fugong fuye wenti de zongjie" 天津市工商局關於復工復業問題的總結 [General conclusion by the Tianjin Municipal In-

dustry and Commerce Bureau on the problem of restarting industry and employ-ment], in Tianjinshi Dang'anguan, ed., *Jiefang chuqi Tianjin chengshi jingji hong-guan guanli* [Macro-management of Tianjin's economy in the early liberation period] (Tianjin: Tianjinshi Dang'anguan, 1995), 25–26.

36. Nationwide, the Nationalist government owned about one-third of indus-trial production; see Frazier, 96.

37. Huang Xiaotong and Li Wenfang, 47. The other private company was the wool carpet company Renli.

38. Huang Xiaotong and Li Wenfang, 54–56.

39. The text of Song's opinion paper is reprinted in Huang Xiaotong and Li Wenfang, 134–139; and is reprinted in Cui Shuju and Jin Yanshi as well, 133–136.

40. "Liu Shaoqi tongzhi zai zhonggong Tianjinshi weiyuanhui shang de ji-anghua" 劉少奇同志在中共天津市委員會上的講話 [Comrade Liu Shaoqi's talk to the Tianjin party committee], 18 April 1949, in Tianjinshi Dang'anguan, 47, 54, 48.

41. "Liu Shaoqi tongzhi zai zhonggong Tianjinshi weiyuanhui shang de jian-ghua," 50.

42. Huang Xiaotong and Li Wenfang, 141.

43. Zhang Boyang, "Huiyi Liu Shaoqi huijian 'Dongya' zhigong daibiao" [Re-membering Liu Shaoqi's meeting with Dongya employee representatives], *Tianjin wenshi ziliao* 79 (1998): 107.

44. Zhao Runnian, "Yi Liu Shaoqi jianghua" [Remembering Liu Shaoqi's talk] *Tianjin wenshi ziliao* 79 (1998): 108. For alternative but largely similar tellings of Liu Shaoqi's visit to Dongya, see also Ding Xiuzhu, "Yi Liu Shaoqi, Wang Guangmei shicha 'Dongya' "[Remembering Liu Shaoqi and Wang Guangmei's tour of Dongya]; Song Yuzan, "Liu Shaoqi zai 'Dongya' "[Liu Shaoqi at Dongya]; Zhang Guojun, "Huiyi Liu Shaoqi shicha 'Dongya' "[Remembering Liu Shaoqi's tour of Dongya]; and Zhang Guoxun, "Yi Liu Shaoqi 'Dongya' zhi xing" [Remembering Liu Shaoqi's trip to Dongya]. All of these recollections by former Dongya employees are published in *Tianjin wenshi ziliao* 79 (1998): 103–104, 104–105, 109–110, and 111 respectively. In addition the Papers of Li Jingshan 2 contains an account later ex-panded by Li Jingshan's daughter and two other authors and published as Liu Sha-ochun, Sun Jian, and Li Yulian, "Huiyi Liu Shaoqi tongzhi shicha Dongya Gongsi" [Remembering Comrade Liu Shaoqi's visit to the Dongya Company], *Tianjin dangshi* 4 (1999): 50–52.

45. Papers of Li Jingshan 2. The original version presented to the Commu-nists complete with a drawing of hands clasping as a symbol of management and labor working together was at the Tianjin History Museum in 2000.

46. *Jinbu ribao*, 6 May 1949, sect. 1, p. 3; the letters are also reproduced in Huang Xiaotong and Li Wenfang, 143–144.

47. "Liu Shaoqi tongzhi zai Tianjinshi ganbu hui shang de jianghua" 劉少奇同志在天津市幹部會上的講話 [Comrade Liu Shaoqi's talk to the Tianjin cadre meeting], 24 April 1949, Tianjin Dang'anguan, 55–73, quote from 69.

48. *Jinbu ribao*, 12 May 1949, sect. 1, p. 3.

49. *Renmin ribao* [People's Daily], 14 May 1949.

50. Memo dated 5 August 1949, Dongya Archives, 2-86-2-02. For the company's response, see memo dated 12 September 1949, Dongya Archives, 2-86-2-04; and "Dongya Corporation Proposal" (draft with handwritten corrections), Dongya Archives, 2-86-2-03.

51. *Jinbu ribao*, 12 May 1949, sect. 1, p. 3; *Renmin ribao*, 14 May 1949.

52. *Jinbu ribao*, 15 April 1949, sect. 1, p. 1; 1 May 1949, sect. 2, p. 8; 4 May 1949, sect. 2, p. 5; and 19 July 1949, sect. 1, p. 1.

53. *Jinbu ribao*, 7 August 1949, sect. 3, p. 1.

54. *Jinbu ribao*, 17 September 1949, sect. 3, p. 1.

55. Board of Directors Minutes, 18 September 1949 (provisional), Dongya Archives, 2-92-08-01. On the market price of the yarn, see financial statements in the Dongya Archives, 2-96-2-01.

56. Board of Directors Minutes, 31 October 1949, Dongya Archives, 2-91-7-03.

57. Board of Directors Minutes, 28 December 1949, Dongya Archives, 2-91-7-04.

58. *Jinbu ribao*, 27 January 1950, sect. 2, p. 1; on such labor-capital committees elsewhere in China, see Frazier, 110–111.

59. Report to Dongya Shareholders, 26 March 1950, Dongya Archives, Tianjin History Museum (03).

60. *Jinbu ribao*, 27 January 1950, sect. 2, p. 1; Report to Dongya Shareholders, 26 March 1950, Dongya Archives, Tianjin History Museum (03).

61. Tianjinshi Dang'anguan, 70; and "Liu Shaoqi tongzhi zai Tianjinshi gongshangyejia zuotanhui shang de jianghua" 劉少奇同志在天津市工商業家座談會上的講話 [Comrade Liu Shaoqi's talk at the Tianjin industrialists and businesspersons' discussion meeting], 2 May 1949, in Tianjinshi Dang'anguan, 85–97, citation from 89–91.

62. Board of Directors Minutes, 26 January 1950, 28 December 1949, and 18 September 1949 (provisional), Dongya Archives, 2-91-7-05, 2-91-7-04, and 2-92-08-01.

63. Board of Directors Minutes, 28 December 1949 and 26 January 1950, Dongya Archives, 2-91-7-04 and 2-91-7-05.

64. *Jinbu ribao*, 7 August 1949, sect. 3, p. 1. In this report, the unification of purchase is dated to the previous autumn; see Shareholders' Meeting, 29 July 1951, Dongya Archives, 2-99-5-01; see also Shareholders' Meeting, 30 October 1950, Dongya Archives, 2-91-7-09.

65. Report to Dongya Shareholders, 26 March 1950, Dongya Archives, Tianjin History Museum (03).

66. Reports discussed in Board of Directors Minutes, Dongya Archives, 2-91-7-20 and 2-91-7-17.

67. Report to Dongya Shareholders, 26 March 1950, Dongya Archives, Tianjin History Museum (03).

68. Board of Directors Minutes, 21 March 1950, Dongya Archives, 2-91-7-06.

69. Report to Dongya Shareholders, 26 March 1950, Dongya Archives, Tianjin History Museum (03).

70. Board of Directors Minutes, 21 March 1950 and 9 March 1950, Dongya Archives, 2-91-7-06 and 2-91-7-07.

71. Dongya Archives, 2-96-2-02.

72. Board of Directors Minutes, 30 October 1950, Dongya Archives, 2-91-7-09.

73. Papers of Li Jingshan 2.

74. Song Yunzhang and Wang Weigang, 348–358.

75. Board of Directors Minutes, 23 July 1950 and 30 October 1950, Dongya Archives, 2-91-7-08 and 2-91-7-09.

76. Production reports discussed at board of directors meetings, Dongya Archives, 2-91-7-04, 2-91-7-10, and 2-91-7-17.

77. Press clipping from the English-language "English Intelligence," French National Archives, Asie-Oceanie 1944–1955 (Paris), file 172.

78. Meffreys to Royere, 11 December 1950, French National Archives, Asie-Oceanie 1944–1955 (Paris), file 172.

79. Board of Directors Minutes, 20 October 1951, Dongya Archives, 2-91-7-16.

80. Shareholders' Meeting, 29 July 1951, Dongya Archives, 2-99-5-01.

81. Board of Directors Minutes, 20 November 1951, Dongya Archives, 2-91-7-17.

82. Board of Directors Minutes, 14 January 1951, Dongya Archives, 2-91-7-12.

83. Shareholders' Meeting, 29 July 1951, Dongya Archives, 2-99-5-01.

84. Board of Directors Minutes, 19 May 1951, Dongya Archives, 2-91-7-20.

85. Shareholders' Meeting, 29 July 1951, Dongya Archives, 2-99-5-01.

86. Meffreys to Royere, 21 November 1950, French Foreign Ministry, Tianjin Consulate (Nantes), Box 100.

87. Board of Directors Minutes, 20 October 1951 and 20 November 1951, Dongya Archives, 2-91-7-16 and 2-91-7-17.

88. Board of Directors Minutes, 11 April 1951, Dongya Archives, 2-91-7-19.

89. Papers of Li Jingshan 7.

90. Board of Directors Minutes, 11 April 1951, Dongya Archives, 2-91-7-19.

91. *Jinbu ribao*, 13 April 1951, sect. 2, p. 1.

92. Shareholders' Meeting, 29 July 1951, Dongya Archives, 2-99-5-01.

93. Board of Directors Minutes, 6 April 1951 and 26 September 1951, Dongya Archives, 2-91-7-11 and 2-91-7-15.

94. Harvey C. Sung [Song Yuhan] to Mr. C. B. Currie, 12 October 1957, Sung Family Papers.

95. "Renshi diaocha biao / feiwei renwu zhi" 人事調查表 /匪偽人物誌 [Personal investigation form/Traitor's record], Archives of the Junshi weiyuanhui shicong shi 軍事委員會侍從室 [Military Affairs Commission, Service Room], 10 September 1953, Academia Historica, 129000062088A.

96. Shi 1.

97. Board of Directors Minutes, 1 March 1935, Dongya Archives, 1-9-3-03.

98. Board of Directors Minutes, 18 September 1949 (provisional), Dongya Archives, 2-92-08-01.

99. "Report on Dongya's Condition in 1949 to the 1950 Shareholders' Meeting," Dongya Archives, Tianjin History Museum.

100. Board of Directors Minutes, 6 April 1951, 19 May 1951, July 1951, 26 September 1951, and 20 October 1951, Dongya Archives, 2-91-7-11 and 2-91-7-20, 2-91-7-13, 2-91-7-15, and 2-91-7-16.

101. Papers of Li Jingfang. Based on internal evidence, it is clear that this document was prepared either by Li Jingfang herself, or perhaps one of her sons; see Harvey C. Sung to Mr. C. B. Currie, 12 October 1957, Sung Family Papers.

102. Sung to Currie, 12 October 1957.

103. Sung to Currie, 12 October 1957.

104. Papers of Li Jingfang.

105. Papers of Li Jingfang.

106. Sung to Currie, 12 October 1957.

107. In some ways Song's plan echoed Henry Ford's ideas a couple of decades earlier; see Greg Grandin, *Fordlandia: The Rise and Fall of Henry Ford's Forgotten Jungle City* (New York: Metropolitan Books, 2009).

108. Sung Family Papers. This ideal was not without precedent: a Shenxin manager in Wuxi tried something very similar in the 1930s; see Frazier, 57.

109. Song Feiqing to Shi Shaodong, 19 [no month stated] 1953, Sung Family Papers.

110. Harvey C. Sung to Mr. C. B. Currie, 12 October 1957, Sung Family Papers.

111. Sung to Currie, 12 October 1957.

112. Some sources place the date of Song's death in 1956, but I rely here on the notes of his widow, Li Jingfang, and other family sources.

113. H. F. G. Chauvin, Director of Social Welfare, to Commissioner of Labour, 23 July 1958, Hong Kong Records Service 939-1-178.

114. Chauvin to Commissioner of Labour, 23 July 1958; and T. F. Tsui to Director of Social Welfare, 28 July 1958, Hong Kong Records Service 939-1-178.

8. Industrial Eden's Legacy under Socialist Development

1. *Dagong bao*, 15 October 1933, sect. 3, p. 11.

2. See discussion in Chapter 3; and Song Yunzhang and Wang Weigang, 129.

3. See Chapter 3; and *Dagong bao*, 7 January 1934, sect. 3, p. 11.

4. *Dagong bao*, 9, 10, and 11 September 1936, all sect. 2, p. 7.

5. Zhao Xingguo, 29; *Dagong bBao*, 2 July 1947, sect. 2, p. 5; Rui Fu, 21–22; *Jinbu ribao*, 28 March 1949, sect. 1, p. 3.

6. Shi 2.

7. Dongya Corporation, *Annual Report*, 1934, unpaged.

8. Dongya Corporation, *Annual Report*, 1936, unpaged.

9. "Canguan Dongya maoni fangzhi gongsi baogao," 27–38.

10. On the crisis in cotton spinning and weaving, see Sun Dechang and Zhou Zuchang, eds., *Tianjin jindai jingji shi* [Economic history of modern Tianjin] (Tianjin: Tianjin shehui kexue chubanshe, 1990), 237–238.

11. *Dagong bao*, 19 August 1946, sect. 1, p. 3; 5 July 1947, sect. 2, p. 5; and 13 January 1948, sect. 2, p. 5.

12. *Dagong bao*, 17 May 1948, sect. 2, p. 5.

13. "Chanye gongren gongzi zhengli biao" 產業工人工資整理表 [Production workers wages table], March, June, September, and December 1947, Archives of the Central Social Ministry (Nanjing), 11-2-125.

14. "Chanye gongren gaikuang diaochabiao" 產業工人概況調查表 [Production workers situation table], Archives of the Central Social Ministry (Nanjing), 11-2-174-01.

15. "Tianjin Dongya Maozhi Gongsi Gaikuang," 16.

16. See Chapter 6. For a version of this history from the company newsletter, see Liu Wentian 劉文田, "Zai zhi shiwunian" 在職十五年 [Fifteen years on duty], *Dongya sheng* 3 (1 July 1947): 3.

17. Interior Ministry to National Election Commission, 1 May 1946, quoting original letter from Sun Tongxuan 孫桐萱 to his commander, Archives of the National Assembly (Nanjing), 451-18.

18. Song Feiqing, "Laofang jiu shi zifang" 勞方就是資方 [Labor and capital are on the same side], *Dongya sheng* 2 (16 June 1947), quoted in Cui Shuju and Jin Yanshi, 81–82.

19. Rui Fu.

20. Song Feiqing, "Zong jingli dui quanti zhigong tanhua" 總經理對全體職工談話 [The president's talk to all the employees], *Dongya sheng* 30 (16 August 1948): 3, 4.

21. *Jinbu ribao*, 27 March 1949, sect. 1, p. 3.

22. "Huang Jing tongzhi zai quanshi ganbu, gejie daibiao dongyuan dahui shang de baogao 'Fandui tanwu, fandui langfei, fandui guanliaozhuyi,'" 黃敬同志在全市幹部，各界代表動員大會上的報告 '反對貪污，反對浪費，反對官僚主義' [Comrade Huang Jing's report to the mobilization meeting for all municipal cadres and representatives of each circle to "oppose corruption, oppose waste, and oppose bureaucratism"] in Tianjinshi Dang'anguan, 375–385, citation from 378.

23. "Huang Huoqing tongzhi 1952 nian 1 yue 16 ri zai ge jie renmin fan tanwu, fan langfei, fan guanliaozhuyi tanbai jianju dahui shang de bao gao" 黃火青同志1952年1月16日在各界人民反貪污，反浪費，反官僚主義坦白檢舉大會上的報告 [The report of Comrade Huang Huoqing to the 16 January 1952 frank admissions meeting of all circles of the people against corruption, waste and bureaucratism], in Tianjinshi Dang'an Guan, 385–389, citation from 386.

24. *Jinbu ribao*, 8 February 1952, sect. 1, p. 11. Zi Yaohua completely skips over this episode in his autobiography; see Zi Yaohua, *Shiji zuyin: Yiwei jindai jinrongxue jia de zishu* [A century's footsteps: The autobiography of a modern financial expert] (Hunan: Hunan wenyi chubanshe, 2005), chapter 38.

25. *Jinbu ribao*, 27 February 1952, sect. 1, p. 1.

26. Song Yunzhang and Wang Weigang, 385.

27. "Guanyu Dongya Gongsi wufan yundong gongren zhengzhi, jiaoyu wenti yixie qingkuang" 關於東亞公司五反運動工人：政治, 教育問題一些情況 [In regard to some political and educational matters for workers in the Five Antis campaign at

the Dongya Corporation], 22 May 1952, Dongya Archives, Tianjin History Museum (hereafter "Five Antis Report").

28. "Five Antis Report."

29. Shi 2.

30. Song Yunzhang and Wang Weigang, 307.

31. "Dongya zibenjia feifa xingwei zongjie" [Final summation of the criminal behavior of the Dongya capitalist], April 1952, Tianjin History Museum. Li Jingshan believed that Song Feiqing never accepted the state's offer of foreign exchange for the Hong Kong factory, but Dongya records from both Tianjin and Hong Kong seem to belie this belief; see Papers of Li Jingshan 2.

32. "Five Antis Report."

33. Zhongguo fangzhi gonghui Tianjin Dongya qiye gongsi weiyuan hui [The Tianjin Dongya Enterprise Corporation Committee of the Chinese Textile Union], "'Song Feiqing zuixing zhanlan hui' jieloule zichan jieji de fandong xing" [The 'Crimes of Song Feiqing Exhibit' reveals the reactionary nature of the capitalist class], *Zhongguo fangzhi gongren* [China Textile Worker] 7 (1 April 1952): cover and 12–15, citation from 12.

34. Zhongguo fangzhi gonghui, 14.

35. "Five Antis Report."

36. "Dongya gongsi zibenjia xian guojia changkuang jingong de zuixing" 東亞公司資本家向國家猖狂進攻的罪行 [The furious criminal attack against the nation by the Dongya Corporation capitalist], Tianjin History Museum, undated, but accompanying documents dated to the spring and summer of 1952.

37. "Five Antis Report."

38. "Five Antis Report."

39. "Five Antis Report."

40. Interview with Song Yuzhan, Tianjin, 2000.

41. *Jinbu ribao*, 2 September 1954, sect. 2, p. 1.

42. Yuan Jing, ed., *Dadihuichun: Dongya maomachang gongren douzheng de gushi* [Spring returns to the earth: The story of the workers' struggles at the Dongya Woolen and Jute Mill], Tianjin gongshangshi congshu [Tianjin business history series] (Tianjin: Baihua wenyi chubanshe, 1960).

43. Papers of Li Jingshan 8. Li's notes meticulously document areas where he thought *Spring Returns to the Earth* was inaccurate.

44. Yuan Jing, 1–2, 7.

45. Yuan Jing, 163, 272.

46. Yuan Jing, both quotes from 284.

47. Chen Xiuwen, Song Yuzan, and Zhang Guoxun, 142.

48. Li Jingshan to Li Jingfang, 28 October 1962; see also letter of 19 August 1962, Papers of Li Jingfang.

49. Yang Tianshou and Li Jingshan, "Song Feiqing yu Dongya gongsi" [Song Feiqing and the Dongya Corporation]. *Wenshi ziliao xuanji* 49 (1964): 161–182.

50. Yang Tianshou and Li Jingshan, "Jiefang qian de Dongya gongsi," 1.

51. Cui Shuju and Jin Yanshi cite a number of other oral histories and manuscripts listed here in the bibliography, but I was not able to locate them and Cui Shuju and Jin Yanshi leave them undated.

52. Li Jingshan, oral history, 10 June 1964, Tianjin History Museum.

53. Meng Guanglin, Gao Xinzhai, Hao Guanyi, Wei Yanying, Feng Naishen, oral histories, Tianjin History Museum.

54. Shi Ying, *Wenming diyu* [A civilized hell] (Beijing: Zuojia chubanshe, 1965), quotes from 112, 113.

55. Shi Ying, *Wenming diyu* (1965), 86–98.

56. Shi Ying, "Zaiban houji" [Afterword of the new edition], *Wenming diyu* [A civilized hell] (Beijing: Renmin wenxue chubanshe, 1983), 144.

57. On the history of the "Tianjin Talks," see Kenneth G. Lieberthal, *Revolution and Tradition in Tientsin, 1949–1952* (Stanford, CA: Stanford University Press, 1980), 42, starred footnote; and a variety of Chinese publications that appeared at the time of Liu Shaoqi's posthumous rehabilitation in 1980, such as Huang Xiaotong and Li Wenfang; Ye Wuxi and Shao Yunrui, "Chongping 'Tianjin Jianghua'"[A new evaluation of the Tianjin talks], *Lishi yanjiu* 2 (1980): 47–58.

58. Zhonggong zazhi she [Chinese Communist Party Research Agency], *Liu Shaoqi wenti ziliao zhuanji* [Collection of materials on Liu Shaoqi's problems] (Taipei: Zhonggong yanjiu zazhi she, 1970), 373–401.

59. See, for example, *Xingdao ribao*, 23 March 1967.

60. *Renmin ribao*, 15 April 1967, http://www.cssn.cn/news/190899.htm (accessed 4 March 2012).

61. Shi Ying, "Zaiban houji," 144.

62. Chen Xiuwen, Song Yuzan, and Zhang Guoxun, 142–143.

63. Chen Xiuwen, Song Yuzan, and Zhang Guoxun, 142.

64. Chen Xiuwen, Song Yuzan, and Zhang Guoxun, 142.

65. *Tianjin ribao*, 6 November 1968, 3.

66. *Tianjin ribao*, 22 January 1969, 3.

67. Chen Xiuwen, Song Yuzan, and Zhang Guoxun, 143.

68. Chen Xiuwen, Song Yuzan, and Zhang Guoxun, 143–144.

69. Sanxiao maliezhuyi jiaoyanshi, zhengzhi jingji xue zu [Three-School Marxism-Leninism Research Institute, Political Economy Group], "Dongya maofangchang de zibenzhuyi boxue" [The capitalist exploitation of Dongya], mimeograph manuscript, 1978, Tianjin History Museum.

70. *Tianjin ribao*, 4 March 1980, 2.

71. "Song Feiqing," in Zhongguo shehui kexueyuan jindaishi yanjiusuo zhonghua minguoshi yanjiushi [Republican Period Research Office of the Modern History Institute of the Chinese Academy of Social Sciences], ed., *Zhonghua minguo shi ziliao conggao, renwu zhuanji, di shiwu ji* [Collection of materials on the history of Republican China, Biography, vol. 15] (Beijing: Zhonghua shuju, 1982).

72. Zhengxie interview with Qie Xinyuan et al., 26 November 1982; Zhengxie interview with Chen Yadong, December 1982.

73. Fang Zhaolin, ed., "Song Feiqing yu Tianjin Dongya qiye gongsi" [Song Feiqing and the Tianjin Enterprise Corporation], by Li Jingshan et al., *Tianjin wenshi ziliao* 29 (October 1984): 87–114.

74. Fang, ed., "Song Feiqing yu Tianjin Dongya qiye gongsi," 104–111.

75. Cui Shuju and Jin Yanshi.

76. Cui Shuju and Jin Yanshi, 1–3.

77. Wang Juntang and Feng Baoguang, 73–74; and Xu Hualu and Ming Shaohua, 84.

78. Ma Xiafu, "Song Feiqing he Dongya Gongsi" [Song Feiqing and the Dongya Corporation], *Qingzhou wenshi ziliao* 7 (December 1989): 86–103.

79. Fang Zhaolin, "'Diyang' lingxiu Song Feiqing," 176–206.

80. Deng Weisheng and Liu Zhiman, *Dongya Qiye wenhua* [Dongya's corporate culture] (Tianjin: Tianjin shehui kexue chubanshe, 1995), Wang Weigang, "Dongya fangzhi dawang Song Feiqing," 3–160. See also letter from Wang Weigang to Albert Sung [Song Feiqing's son], 25 June 1994, Sung Family Papers.

81. Wang Weigang to Albert Sung, 25 June 1994.

82. Xiao Fang, "Song Feiqing he Dongya maofangzhi gufan youxian gongsi" [Song Feiqing and the Dongya Corporation], in Liu Yu, ed., *Zhongguo bainian shangye juzi, xia* [A century of Chinese business giants, vol. 2] (Changchun: Dongbei shifan daxue chubanshe, 1997), 42, 58.

83. Dongya Corporation, "Dongya Maofangchang Jituan Youxian Gongsi lishi jianjie" [A brief introduction on the history of the Dongya Woolen Mill Group, Limited Liability Corporation], unpublished, 22 October 2000.

84. *Jinwan Bao, Tekan*, 31 December 1999, 29.

85. Chen Kai, "Song Feiqing: 'Diyangpai' maoxian zhi fu" [Song Feiqing: The father of "Butting Ram Brand" wool yarn], *Xinmin wanbao, Jiatingzhoukan* 家庭周刊, 11 June 2010, B8; Wang Hao, "Lun Song Feiqing dui Tianjin Dongya gongsi de qiye linian" [On Song Feiqing's concept of the firm in regard to the Dongya Corporation] (Senior thesis, Nankai University, May 2005); see also evaluation of Liu Shaoqi's' Tianjin talks, http://news.qq.com/a/20111116/000902_3.htm, page dated 18 November 2011 (accessed 4 March 2012). The Xiamen Television documentary is available at http://www.taihaitv.cn/20111226/113717.shtml (accessed 4 March 4, 2012). See also biographical entries at Baidu and a history buff's blog, http://baike.baidu.com/view/1091799.htm and http://sd.infobase.gov.cn/bin/mse.exe?seachword=&K=a&A=84&rec=1189&run=13 (accessed 4 March 2012).

86. It is hard to know the source of this item of curriculum, but I found three different sources that use Dongya in 1936 to demonstrate the calculation of surplus value. For the Shandong Economics and Trade Practical Training Institute (Shandong jingmao shishun xueyuan 山東經貿實順學院), see http://www.jingmaoshixun.com/newsdetail1.asp?newsid=2647 (accessed 4 March 2012). For the Henan Province Sanmenxia City Middle and Primary School Teacher's Distance Learning Training (Sanmenxia shi zhong xiao xue jiaoshi yuancheng peixun 三門峡市中小學教師遠程培訓), see http://sanmenxia.henan.teacher.com.cn/GuoPeiAdmin/TeachingIntrospection/TeachingIntrospectionView.aspx?TiID=22635&cfName=2011100822635 (accessed 4 March 2012). For a syllabus for an uniden-

tified training class in 2001–2002, see http://www.google.com/url?sa=t&rct=j&q
=&esrc=s&source=web&cd=8&cts=1330891646112&ved=0CGAQFjAH&url=http
%3A%2F%2Fwww.tjyz.org%2Ftjyz%2Fzybk%2Fjdja%2FLib%2Fzz%2FC3%2F
c3zzz11.doc&ei=yslTT9OxCoiRiQKK1-W0Bg&usg=AFQjCNFtfKnBlb9qx0C
G42SWvzPuPEBasQ (accessed 4 March 2012).

87. Jiang Zilong 蔣子龍, "Wode Meng" 我的夢 [My dream], unpublished
screenplay, Sung Family Papers.

Conclusion

1. Song Yunzhang and Wang Weigang, 208.

Bibliography

Archival, Manuscript, and Interview Sources

Personal Papers

Sung [Song] Family Papers (Courtesy of the Sung family, Berkeley, California)

Papers of Li Jingfang (Song Feiqing's widow).

Recollections of Shi Shaodong [1970s?]. There are two different manuscripts in the Sung family possession, and I have arbitrarily labeled
them Shi 1 and Shi 2. There is some evidence that Shi compiled the
notes along with Song Feiqing's widow, Li Jingfang, though for
convenience I refer to them as the Shi manuscripts. The flow of the
manuscripts is often interrupted and picked up again at a later point,
blanks have been left in many places, which were never filled in and the
pages are not in any coherent order. As a result, I have not cited page
numbers.

Other miscellaneous notes and correspondence.

Papers of Li Jingshan (Courtesy of the Li family, Tianjin)

The papers of Li Jingshan, a longtime employee of the Song family, an
executive at the Dongya Corporation, and a loyal defender of Song
Feiqing throughout his life, were provided to me courtesy of his family.
For bibliographic control, I arbitrarily numbered the key documents
from 1 to 8, though not all are cited in this text.

*Papers of R. Allen Griffin, Box 4, Hoover Institution Archives, Stanford University,
Stanford, CA.*

Oral Histories, Interview Transcripts, and Personal Testimonies

Zhengxie interviews (transcripts held at the Tianjin Zhengxie Hui, Tianjin)

Chen Yadong 陳亞東, December 1982.

Ding Xiuzhu 丁修竹, written testimony, undated, but likely early 1980s.

Ma Shouting 馬壽亭, Li Jingshan 李靜山, and Chen Yadong陳亞東,
    5 November 1982.
Qie Xinyuan 郄心源, oral history, 27 December 1964.
Qie Xinyuan 郄心源, oral history, 21 April 1983.
Qie Xinyuan 郄心源, Li Jingshan 李靜山, Meng Guanglin 孟廣林, and Chen
    Yadong 陳亞東, 12 November 1982; 26 November 1982; 3 December
    1982.
Qie Xinyuan 郄心源, Ma Shouting 馬壽亭, Li Jingshan 李靜山, Chen
    Yadong 陳亞東, and Meng Guanglin 孟廣林, 22 October 1982.

Oral history transcripts held at the Tianjin History Museum

Feng Naishen 馮乃申, 21 May 1964.
Gao Xinzhai 高馨斋, 21 May 1964.
Hao Guanyi 郝貫一, 22 May 1964.
Li Jingshan 李靜山, 10 June 1964.
Meng Guanglin 孟廣林, 19 May 1964.
Wei Yanying 魏燕英, 22 May 1964.

*Oral histories and testimonies of Song family members and employees published as
    undated selections in Cui Shuju* 崔樹菊 *and Jin Yanshi* 金岩石, *eds., "Tianjin
    Dongya maofang gongsi shiliao"* 天津東亞毛紡公司史料 *[Historical materials on
    the Tianjin Dongya Woolen Mill], Tianjin lishi ziliao* 天津歷史資料 *[Tianjin
    historical materials] 20 (8 February 1984).*

Bo Dianyuan 薄殿元, "statistical materials provided in 1965."
Chu Jitang 儲輯唐, "written materials," multiple pages.
Ding Jiyou 丁濟佑, "written materials," multiple pages.
Jiang Yurong 姜玉榮, Jiang Jinbiao 姜金標, and Chu Liying 儲利英, oral
    histories, 116.
Li Jingshan, "written materials," multiple pages.
Liu Wentian 劉文田, "written materials," multiple pages.
Qie Xinyuan 郄心源, "written materials," multiple pages.
Qie Xinyuan 郄心源 and Li Jingshan 李靜山, oral history, multiple pages.
Song Xingcun 宋杏村 [Song Feiqing's cousin], "written materials," multiple
    pages.
Su Yueqin 蘇月琴 and Han Guizhen 韓貴珍, oral histories, 114–115.
You Baoshan 有寶山, written materials, multiple pages.

Interviews conducted by the author

Chen Xiuwen, Tianjin, 2000.
Liu Yuying, Tianjin, 28 July 1999.
Song Yuzhan, Tianjin, 2000.

Archives

Beijing Municipal Archives

Agriculture Department of the North China Political Affairs Council
(Huabei zhengwu weiyuanhui nongwu zongshu 華北政務委員會農務總
署).
Beijing Police Department (Beipingshi zhengfu jingwu lei 北平市政府警務
類).
Beijing Social Bureau (Beipingshi zhengfu shehui lei 北平市政府社會類).
North China Political Affairs Council (Huabei zhengwu weiyuanhui 華北
政務委員會).

Corporate archives

Bank of Communications (Jiaotong yinhang zonghang 交通銀行總行,
Shanghai Municipal Archive).
Dongya Corporation holdings at the Dongya Corporation (Dongya gongsi
東亞公司, Tianjin).
Dongya Corporation holdings at the Tianjin History Museum (Tianjin
lishi bowuguan 天津歷史博物館, Tianjin). Uncataloged hand-copied
records made from the Dongya Corporation archives sometime in the
1960s. I have numbered them arbitrarily for ease of reference.
Japan Spinners' Association (Nihon bōseki kyōkai 日本紡績協会, Osaka
University).
Patons and Baldwins Company (Clackmannanshire Archives, Alloa,
Scotland).
Shanghai Commercial and Savings Bank (Shanghai shangye chuxu yinhang
上海商業儲蓄銀行, Shanghai Municipal Archive).

Diplomatic archives

British Foreign Office, British National Archives, London.
French Foreign Ministry, Archives of the Tianjin Consulate, French
National Archives, Nantes.
French Foreign Ministry, Asie-Oceanie 1930–1940 and 1944–1955, French
National Archives, Paris.
Japanese Foreign Ministry, JACAR, National Archives of Japan, Japan
Center for Asian and Historical Records, http://www.jacar.go.jp/
english/. Accessed on various dates.
U.S. Consulate, Jinan, Records of the U.S. Department of State Relating to
the Internal Affairs of China, 1910–1929, Decimal File 329, Reel 84.
U.S. Consulate, Tianjin, Records of the U.S. Department of State Relating to
the Internal Affairs of China, 1910–1929, Decimal File 893, Reels 39–41.

Japanese Government

JACAR. National Archives of Japan. Japan Center for Asian and Historical
Records. http://www.jacar.go.jp/english. Accessed on various dates.

Japanese Occupation Government of North China

Provisional Government Executive Committee (Linshi zhengfu xingzheng weiyuanhui 臨時政府行政委員會, Number Two Historical Archives, Nanjing).

North China Political Affairs Council (Huabei zhengwu weiyuanhui 華北政務委員會, Number Two Historical Archives, Nanjing).

Nationalist Government

Central Social Ministry, Number Two Historical Archives (Zhongyang shehuibu 中央社會部, Number Two Historical Archives, Nanjing).

Central Trust (Zhongyang xintuo she 中央信託設, Tianjin Municipal Archives, Tianjin).

Executive Yuan (Xingzheng yuan 行政院, Number Two Historical Archives, Nanjing)

Health Ministry (Weisheng bu 衛生部, Number Two Historical Archives, Nanjing).

Military Affairs Commission, Service Room (Junshi weiyuanhui shicong shi 軍事委員會侍從室, Academia Historica, Taipei).

Ministry of Industry, Number Two Historical Archives (Shiyu bu 實業部, Number Two Historical Archive, Nanjing).

National Assembly, Number Two Historical Archives (Guomin dahui 國民大會, Nanjing).

Nationalist Government (Guomin zhengfu 國民政府, Academia Historica, Taipei).

Tax Office (Shuiwu shu 稅務署, Number Two Historical Archives, Nanjing).

Tianjin Municipal Government

Tianjin Municipal Government, Tianjin Municipal Archives (Tianjinshi zhengfu or Tianjin tebieshi zhengfu 天津市政府 or 天津特別市政府, Tianjin).

Tianjin Finance Bureau, Tianjin Municipal Archives (Tianjinshi caizhengju 天津市財政局, Tianjin).

Tianjin Health Bureau, Tianjin Municipal Archives (Tianjinshi weishengju 天津市衛生局, Tianjin).

Warlord-period Beiyang Government

Army Ministry (Lujun bu 陸軍部, Number Two Historical Archives, Nanjing).

Interior Ministry (Neiwu bu 內務部, Number Two Historical Archives, Nanjing).

Other

British Baptist Missionary Society (Wheaton College, Wheaton, IL), on microfilm, reels 55 and 56 (BMS).

Hong Kong Records Service (Hong Kong).

Published Sources

Newspapers and Periodicals Cited as Primary Sources

Chinese Recorder

Dagong bao 大公報 (Tianjin), later *Jinbu ribao* 進步日報 [*Progressive Daily*] (Tianjin)

Dongya sheng 東亞聲 [*Voice of Dongya*] (Archives of the Dongya Corporation, Tianjin)

Fangzhou yuekan 方舟月刊 [*Ark Monthly*] (Dongya Corporation, Tianjin)

Funü zazhi 婦女雜誌 [Ladies' Journal]

Gongren zhoukan 工人週刊 [Worker Weekly]

Gongye yuekan 工業月刊 [Industry Monthly]

Hebei sheng yinghang jingji ban yuekan 河北省銀行經濟半月刊 [Hebei Provincial Bank Economic Bimonthly]

Huabei laodong 華北勞動 [North China Labor]

Huabei xinbao 華北新報 [New North China News]

Jinwan bao, tekan 今晚報, 特刊 [Evening News, Special Edition] (Tianjin)

Kahoku bōshoku kōgyōkai geppō 華北紡織工業會月報 [North China Textile Industry Association Monthly]

Liangyou 良友 [Good Companion]

Renmin ribao 人民日報 [People's Daily]

Shishi zhoukan 市師周刊 [Tianjin Normal Weekly]

Tianjin dangshi 天津黨史 [Tianjin Party History]

Tianjin ribao 天津日報 [Tianjin Daily]

Xingdao ribao 星島日報 [Xingdao Daily]

Xinmin wanbao 新民晚報, Jiating zhoukan 家庭周刊 [New People's Evening News, Family Weekly Supplement] (Shanghai)

Yahuang chunqiu 炎黃春秋

Yong bao 庸報

Zhongguo fangzhi gongren 中國紡織工人 [China Textile Worker]

Other Published Sources

Asada Kyōji 浅田喬二. *Nihon teikokushugika no Chūgoku* 日本帝国主義下の中国 [China under Japanese imperialism]. Tokyo: Rakuyū Shobō, 1981.

Baptist Missionary Work in North-China (Province of Shantung: Letters Written by the Missionaries on the Field, Relative to Its Consolidation and Development). For private circulation only. Shanghai: Kelly & Walsh, 1886.

Benson, Carleton. "Story-Telling and Radio Shanghai." *Republican China* (April 1995): 117–146.

Bergère, Marie-Claire. *The Golden Age of the Chinese Bourgeoisie, 1911–1937*. Trans. Janet Lloyd. Cambridge: Cambridge University Press, 1989.

Best, Antony. "Imperial Japan." In Robert Boyce and Joseph A. Maiolo, eds., *The Origins of World War Two: The Debate Continues*, 52–69. Basingstoke: Palgrave Macmillan, 2003.

Bian, Morris L. "Interpreting Enterprise, State, and Society: A Critical Review of the Literature in Modern Chinese Business History, 1978–2008." *Frontiers of History in China* 6, no.3 (September 2011): 423–462.

———. *The Making of the State Enterprise System in Modern China.* Cambridge, MA: Harvard University Press, 2005.

Bloch, Kurt. "The Basic Conflict over Foreign Concessions in China." *Far Eastern Survey* 8, no. 10 (10 May 1939): 111–116.

Boyce, Robert. "Economics." In Robert Boyce and Joseph A. Maiolo, eds., *The Origins of World War Two: The Debate Continues*, 249–272. Basingstoke: Palgrave Macmillan, 2003.

Bray, Francesca. *Technology and Gender: Fabrics of Power in Late Imperial China.* Berkeley: University of California Press, 1997.

Brokaw, Cynthia. *Commerce in Culture: The Sibao Book Trade in the Qing and Republican Periods.* Cambridge, MA: Harvard East Asian Center, 2007.

Brook, Timothy. "Capitalism and the Writing of Modern History in China." In Timothy Brook and Gregory Blue, eds., *China and Historical Capitalism: Genealogies of Sinological Knowledge*, 110–157. Cambridge: Cambridge University Press, 1999.

Brook, Timothy, and Gregory Blue, eds. *China and Historical Capitalism: Genealogies of Sinological Knowledge.* Cambridge: Cambridge University Press, 1999.

Brown, R. Ampalavanar, ed. *Chinese Business Enterprise: Critical Perspectives on Business and Management.* 4 vols. London: Routledge, 1996.

Buck, David D. *Urban Change in China: Politics and Development in Tsinan, Shantung, 1890–1949.* Madison: University of Wisconsin Press, 1978.

"Canguan Dongya maoni fangzhi gongsi baogao" 參觀東亞毛呢紡織公司 [Report on the visit to the Dongya Woolen Mill]. *Shishi zhoukan* 市師周刊, 24 February 1936, 27–38.

Chan, Kai Yiu. *Business Expansion and Structural Change in Pre-War China: Liu Hongsheng and His Enterprises, 1920–1937.* Hong Kong: Hong Kong University Press, 2006.

Chan, Wellington K. K. "The Organizational Structure of the Traditional Chinese Firm and Its Modern Reform." *Business History Review* 56, no. 2 (Summer 1982): 218–235.

———. "Tradition and Change in the Chinese Business Enterprise: The Family Firm Past and Present." In Robert Gardella, Jane K. Leonard, and Andrea McElderry, eds., "Chinese Business History: Interpretive Trends and Priorities for the Future," special issue, *Chinese Studies in History* 31, nos. 3–4 (Spring–Summer 1998): 127–144.

Chandler, Alfred D. *The Visible Hand: The Managerial Revolution in American Business.* Cambridge, MA: Belknap Press, 1977.

Chao, Kang. *The Development of Cotton Textile Production in China.* Cambridge, MA: Harvard University East Asian Center, 1997.

Chen Kai 陳凱. "Song Feiqing: 'Diyangpai' maoxian zhi fu" 宋棐卿: '抵羊牌' 毛線之父 [Song Feiqing: The father of "Butting Ram Brand" wool yarn]. *Xinmin wanbao* 新民晚報, *Jiating zhoukan* 家庭周刊, 11 June 2010, B8.

Chen, Ming-Jer. *Inside Chinese Business: A Guide for Managers Worldwide*. Boston: Harvard Business School Press, 2001.

Chen Xiuwen 陳秀文, Song Yuzan 宋毓瓚, Zhang Guoxun 張國勛. "Dongya de 'diyang' pai maoxian he diyang bei" 東亞的 '抵羊' 牌毛線和抵羊碑 [Dongya's "Butting Ram" brand and statue]. *Tianjin wenshi ziliao* 81 (January 1999): 140–144.

Chen Yingci 陳英苃. "Guanyu jiefang chu Liu Shaoqi de Tianjin zhi xing" 關與解放初劉少奇的天津之行 [Liu Shaoqi's trip to Tianjin in the early period of liberation]. *Yanhuang chunqiu* 炎黃春秋 4 (1996): 2–8.

Chen Zhen 陳真, ed. *Zhongguo jindai gongyeshi ziliao, di si ji, Zhongguo gongye de tedian, ziben, jiegou he gongye zhong ge hangye gaikuang, shang juan* 中國近代工業史資料, 第四輯, 中國工業的特點, 資本, 結構和工業中各行業概況, 上卷 [Historical materials on industry in Modern China, vol. 4, Characteristics, capital, and structure of private industry and general industrial conditions, first section]. Beijing: Shenghuo, Dushu, Xinzhi Sanlian shudian, 1961.

Chen, Zhongping. *Modern China's Network Revolution: Chambers of Commerce and Sociopolitical Change in the Early Twentieth Century*. Stanford, CA: Stanford University Press, 2011.

Cheng, Linsun. *Banking in Modern China: Entrepreneurs, Professional Bankers, and the Development of Chinese Banks, 1897–1937*. Cambridge: Cambridge University Press, 2003.

Chow Tse-tsung. *The May Fourth Movement: Intellectual Revolution in Modern China*. Cambridge, MA: Harvard University Press, 1960.

"Chuangzhi madai yanzhi xinyao, kuxin jingying gongye baoguo: Dongya maoni fangzhi gongsi fangwen ji" 創織麻袋研製新藥, 苦心經營工業報國: 東亞毛呢紡織公司訪問記 [Manufacturing gunnysacks and researching the manufacture of new medicine, working hard to manage industry for the nation: Record of a visit to the Dongya Corporation]. *Huabei xinbao* 華北信報 13 May 1944, 3.

Claessens, Stijn, Simeon Djankov, and Larry H. P. Lang. "The Separation of Ownership and Control in East Asian Corporations." *Journal of Financial Economics* 58 (2000): 81–112.

Coble, Parks. *Chinese Capitalists in Japan's New Order: The Occupied Lower Yangzi, 1937–1945*. Berkeley: University of California Press, 2003.

———. "Comments and Reflections on Chinese Business History." In Robert Gardella, Jane K. Leonard, and Andrea McElderry, eds., "Chinese Business History: Interpretive Trends and Priorities for the Future," special issue, *Chinese Studies in History* 31, nos. 3–4 (Spring–Summer 1998): 145–150.

———. "Japan's New Order and the Shanghai Capitalists: Conflict and Collaboration." In David P. Barrett and Larry N. Shyu, eds., *Chinese Collaboration with Japan, 1932–1945*, 135–155 Stanford, CA: Stanford University Press, 2001.

———. *The Shanghai Capitalists and the Nationalist Government, 1927–1937*. Cambridge, MA: Council on East Asian Studies, Harvard University, 1986.

Cochran, Sherman. *Big Business in China: Sino-Foreign Rivalry in the Cigarette Industry, 1890–1930*. Cambridge, MA: Harvard University Press, 1980.

———. "Business, Governments, and War in China, 1931–1949." In Akira Iriye and Warren Cohen, eds., *American, Chinese and Japanese Perspectives on Wartime Asia, 1931–1949*, 117–145. Wilmington, DE: SR Books, 1990.

———. *The Capitalist Dilemma in China's Communist Revolution: Stay, Leave, or Return?* Ithaca, NY: Cornell University East Asian Series, forthcoming.

———. "Capitalists Choosing Communist China: The Liu Family of Shanghai, 1948–56." In Jeremy Brown and Paul Pickowicz, eds., *Dilemmas of Victory: The Early Years of the People's Republic of China*, 359–385. Cambridge, MA: Harvard University Press, 2010.

———. *Chinese Medicine Men: Consumer Culture in China and Southeast Asia.* Cambridge, MA: Harvard University Press, 2006.

———. *Encountering Chinese Networks: Western, Japanese, and Chinese Companies in China, 1880–1937.* Berkeley: University of California Press, 2000.

Comacrib Commercial Directory of China. Vol. 2, *1926*. Shanghai: Commercial Credit and Information Bureau, 1926.

Corbett, Charles Hodge. *Shantung Christian University (Cheloo).* New York: United Board for Christian Colleges in China, 1955.

Couling, Samuel. "The Ideal Missionary." *Chinese Recorder* 47, no. 10 (October 1916): 665–673.

Cui Shuju 崔樹菊 and Jin Yanshi 金岩石, eds. "Tianjin Dongya maozhi gongsi shiliao" 天津東亞毛織公司史料 [Historical materials on the Tianjin Dongya Woolen Mill]. *Tianjin lishi ziliao* 天津歷史資料 [Tianjin historical materials] 20 (8 February 1984).

Cumings, Bruce. "Webs with No Spiders, Spiders with No Webs." In Meredith Woo-Cumings, ed., *The Developmental State*, 61–92. Ithaca, NY: Cornell University Press, 1999.

Deng Weisheng 鄧衛生 and Liu Zhiman 劉志滿. *Dongya Qiye wenhua* 東亞企業文化 [Dongya's corporate culture]. Tianjin: Tianjin shehui kexue chubanshe, 1995.

Dernberger, Robert F. "The Role of the Foreigner in China's Economic Development, 1840–1949." In Dwight Perkins, ed., *China's Modern Economy in Historical Perspective*, 19–47. Stanford, CA: Stanford University Press, 1975.

Ding Xiuzhu 丁修竹. "Yi Liu Shaoqi, Wang Guangmei shicha 'Dongya'" 憶劉少奇, 王光美視察 '東亞' [Remembering Liu Shaoqi and Wang Guangmei's tour of Dongya]. *Tianjin wenshi ziliao* 79 (1998): 103–104.

Dirlik, Arif. "Critical Reflections on 'Chinese Capitalism' as a Paradigm." In R. Ampalavanar Brown, ed., *Chinese Business Enterprise: Critical Perspectives on Business and Management*, 1:17–34. London: Routledge, 1996.

Dongya Corporation. *Annual Reports.* Titles varied from year to year and there was not a report every year due to wartime conditions. A complete list of full bibliographical citations follows:

   Tianjin Dongya maoni fangzhi gufen youxian gongsi niankan 天津東亞毛呢紡織股份有限公司年刊 [Tianjin Dongya Woolen Limited Liability Corporation Annual Report]. Tianjin: Dongya Corporation, ca. 1933.

Tianjin Dongya maoni fangzhi gufen youxian gongsi niankan 天津東亞毛呢紡織股份有限公司年刊 [Tianjin Dongya Woolen Limited Liability Corporation Annual Report]. Tianjin: Dongya Corporation, ca. 1934.

Tianjin Dongya maoni fangzhi gufen youxian gongsi niankan 天津東亞毛呢紡織股份有限公司年刊 [Tianjin Dongya Woolen Limited Liability Corporation Annual Report]. Tianjin: Dongya Corporation, ca. 1936.

Tianjin Dongya maoni fangzhi youxian gongsi tekan, 1941 天津東亞毛呢紡織有限公司特刊, 1941 [Tianjin Dongya Woolen Corporation Special Report for 1941]. Tianjin: Dongya Corporation, 1941.

Tianjin Dongya qiye gufen youxian gongsi 天津東亞企業股份有限公司, *Qingzhu chengli shi wu zhounian ji geng ming jinian tekan* 慶祝成立十五周年及更名紀念特刊 [Tianjin Dongya Enterprise Limited Liability Company, special publication commemorating the celebration of the fifteenth anniversary and the name change]. Tianjin: Dongya Corporation, 1947.

———. *Dongya gequ ji* 東亞歌曲集 [Collection of Dongya songs]. July 1947. Sung Family Papers.

———. *Dongya jingshen* 東亞精神 [Dongya spirit]. Tianjin: Dongya Corporation, 1945.

———. "Dongya Maofangchang Jituan Youxian Gongsi lishi jianjie" 東亞毛紡廠集團有限公司歷史簡介 [A brief introduction on the history of the Dongya Woolen Mill Group, Limited Liability Corporation]. Dongya Corporation, unpublished work presented to the author, 22 October 2000, Tianjin.

———. *Fushe huaxue chang gongzuo gaikuang* 附設化學廠工作概況 [General situation of the subsidiary chemical factory]. Tianjin: Dongya Corporation, 1944.

———. "Gongyou gebie tanhua zonghe baogao" 工友個別談話綜合報告 [General report on individual talks with workers]. Tianjin History Museum, undated, but internal evidence indicates the 1940s.

"Dongya zibenjia feifa xingwei zongjie" 東亞資本家非法行為總結 [Final summation of the criminal behavior of the Dongya capitalist], unpublished manuscript. April 1952. Tianjin History Museum, Tianjin.

Dryburgh, Marjorie. *North China and Japanese Expansion, 1933–1937: Regional Power and the National Interest.* Richmond, UK: Curzon, 2000.

Eastman, Lloyd E. *The Abortive Revolution: China under Nationalist Rule, 1927–1937.* Cambridge, MA: Harvard University Asia Center, 1990.

———. "Nationalist China during the Sino-Japanese War, 1937–1945." In John K. Fairbank and Albert Feuerwerker, eds., *The Cambridge History of China*, vol. 13, *Republican China, 1912–1949*, 547–608. Cambridge: Cambridge University Press, 1886.

Esherick, Joseph. "Harvard on China: The Apologetics of Imperialism." *Bulletin of the Committee of Concerned Asian Scholars* [now known as *Critical Asian Studies*] 4, no. 4 (December 1972): 9–16.

Evans, Peter. *Embedded Autonomy: States and Industrial Transformation.* Princeton, NJ: Princeton University Press, 1995.

Fang Zhaolin 方兆麟. "'Diyang' lingxiu Song Feiqing" 抵羊領袖宋棐卿 [The "Butting Ram" leader Song Feiqing]. In Zhongguo renmin zhengzhi xieshang huiyi Tianjinshi weiyuanhui wenshi ziliao weiyuanhui 中國人民政治協商會議天津市委員會文史資料委員會, ed., *Jindai Tianjin shi da shiyejia* 近代天津十大實業家 [Ten great industrialists of Tianjin], 176–206. Tianjin: Tianjin renmin chubanshe, 1999.

————, ed. "Song Feiqing yu Tianjin Dongya qiye gongsi" 宋棐卿與天津東亞企業公司 [Song Feiqing and the Tianjin Enterprise Corporation], by Li Jingshan 李靜山, Qie Xinyuan 郄心源 [printed as Xiyuan 希源 in this publication, but the original documents provided to Zhengxie were signed Xinyuan], Chen Yadong 陳亞東, and Meng Guanglin 孟廣林. *Tianjin wenshi ziliao* 29 (October 1984): 87–114.

Faure, David. *China and Capitalism: A History of Business Enterprise in Modern China.* Hong Kong: Hong Kong University Press, 2006.

Feuerwerker, Albert. *China's Early Industrialization: Sheng Hsuan-huai (1844–1916) and Mandarin Enterprise.* New York: Atheneum, 1970; originally published in 1958.

————. "Doing Business in China over Three Centuries." In Robert Gardella, Jane K. Leonard, and Andrea McElderry, eds., "Chinese Business History: Interpretive Trends and Priorities for the Future," special issue, *Chinese Studies in History* 31, nos. 3–4 (Spring–Summer 1998): 16–34.

Finnane, Antonia. *Changing Clothes in China: Fashion, History, Nation.* New York: Columbia University Press, 2008.

Frazier, Mark W. *The Making of the Chinese Industrial Workplace: State, Revolution, and Labor Management.* Cambridge: Cambridge University Press, 2002.

Friedman, Irving S. "Britain's Large, Tangible Stake in Tientsin [Tianjin]." *Far Eastern Survey* 8, no. 14 (5 July 1939): 166–167.

Gao Yuetian 高越天. *Zhongguo fangzhi shi* 中國紡織史 [A history of spinning and weaving in China]. Taipei: Gongshang yuekan she 工商月刊社, 1953.

Gardella, Robert, Jane K. Leonard, and Andrea McElderry, eds. "Chinese Business History: Interpretive Trends and Priorities for the Future." Special issue, *Chinese Studies in History* 31, nos. 3–4 (Spring–Summer 1998).

Gates, Hill. *China's Motor: A Thousand Years of Petty Capitalism.* Ithaca, NY: Cornell University Press, 1996.

Gauss, Clarence E. "Economic Development of Shantung [Shandong] Province, China, 1912–1921." United States Department of Commerce, *Supplement to Commerce Reports Trade Information Bulletin* no. 70 (Far Eastern Division), 9 October 1922.

Gerth, Karl. *China Made: Consumer Culture and the Creation of the Nation.* Cambridge, MA: Harvard University Asia Center, 2003.

Glosser, Susan. "The Contest for Family and Nation in Republican China." Ph.D. dissertation, University of California, Berkeley, 1995.

Goetzmann, William, and Elisabeth Köll. "The History of Corporate Ownership in China: State Patronage, Company Legislation, and the Issue of Control." In Randall K. Morck, ed., *A History of Corporate Governance around the World:*

Family Business Groups to Professional Managers, 149–181. Chicago: University of Chicago Press, 2005.

Grandin, Greg. *Fordlandia: The Rise and Fall of Henry Ford's Forgotten Jungle City*. New York: Metropolitan Books, 2009.

Hamilton, Gary G. *Commerce and Capitalism in Chinese Societies*. London: Routledge, 2006.

Hao, Yen-P'ing. "Themes and Issues in Chinese Business History." In Robert Gardella, Jane K. Leonard, and Andrea McElderry, eds., "Chinese Business History: Interpretive Trends and Priorities for the Future," special issue, *Chinese Studies in History* 31, nos. 3–4 (Spring–Summer 1998): 106–126.

Harvey, Michael. *Patons: A Story of Handknitting*. St. Peters, Australia: Little Hill Press, 1985.

Hashimoto Masayasu 橋本正保. *Hokushi ni okeru asabukuro gaisetsu* 北支に於ける麻袋概説 [Gunnyaacks in North China]. Mantetsu Research Department, 1940.

Hershatter, Gail. *The Workers of Tianjin, 1900–1949*. Stanford, CA: Stanford University Press, 1993.

Hillard, Michael. "Labor at 'Mother Warren': Paternalism, Welfarism, and Dissent at S. D. Warren, 1854–1967." *Labor History* 45, no. 1 (February 2004): 37–60.

"Hokushi bukka seisaku to taichūshi kōeki" 北支物価政策と対中支交易 [North China price policy effect on central China trade]. *Kōain seimubu jōhō* 興亜院政務部情報 [Koa Institute Politics Department intelligence reports], no. 76 (October 1942).

Honig, Emily. *Sisters and Strangers: Women in the Shanghai Cotton Mills, 1919–1949*. Stanford, CA: Stanford University Press, 1992.

Huabei nongshi shiyanchang yaolan 華北農事試驗場要覽 [Survey of experimental farms in North China]. Archives of the Agricultural Department of the North China Political Affairs Council, Beijing Municipal Archives, J25-1-156.

Huang Xiaotong 黃小同 and Li Wenfang 李文芳. *Liu Shaoqi yu Tianjin jianghua* 劉少奇與天津講話 [Liu Shaoqi and the Tianjin talks]. Kaifeng: Henan University Press, 1998.

Hunter, Jane. *The Gospel of Gentility: American Women Missionaries in Turn-of-the-Century China*. New Haven, CT: Yale University Press, 1984.

Imura Tetsuo 井村哲郎, ed. *Kōain kankō tosho zasshi mokuroku* 興亜院刊行図書雑誌目録 [Catalog of Kōain periodicals, books, and, magazines]. Jyūgo-nen sensō jyūyō bunken shirīzu 17 十五年戦争重要文献シリーズ17 [Documents from Fifteen Years' War series 17]. Tokyo: Fuji, 1994.

Ito, Takeo. *Problems in the Japanese Occupied Areas in China*. Tokyo: Japanese Council of the Institute of Pacific Relations, 1941.

Ji Hua 季華. "Changlu yanwu de liang da anjian" 長盧鹽務的兩大案件 [Two big incidents of the Tianjin salt merchants]. *Tianjin wenshi ziliao* 26 (1984): 131–133.

Jinan shizhi dashiji 濟南市大事記 [Jinan municipal gazetteer, chronicle of events]. http://www.jinan.gov.cn/col/col40/index.html, 2005. Accessed 31 July 2008.

Jinan shizhi, Wenhua, xinwen, jiefangqian de baozhi, minguo shiqi de baozhi. 濟南市
誌, 文化, 新聞, 解放前的報紙, 民國時期的報紙 [Jinan municipal gazetteer, cul-
ture section, news, pre-liberation newspapers, republican-period newspapers].
http://sd.infobase.gov.cn/bin/mse.exe?seachword=%u5B8B%u4F20%u5178
&K=b1&A=18&rec=57&list=1&page=20&run=13. Accessed 31 July 2008.

John, Richard R. "Elaborations, Revisions, Dissents: *The Visible Hand* after Twenty
Years." *Business History Review* 71, no. 2 (Summer 1977): 151–200.

Johnson, Chalmers. "The Developmental State: Odyssey of a Concept." In Meredith Woo-Cumings, ed., *The Developmental State*, 32–60. Ithaca, NY: Cornell University Press, 1999.

———. *MITI and the Japanese Miracle: The Growth of Industrial Policy, 1925–1975.*
Stanford, CA: Stanford University Press, 1982.

Jordan, Donald. *Chinese Boycotts versus Japanese Bombs: The Failure of China's Revolutionary Diplomacy, 1931–32.* Ann Arbor: University of Michigan Press, 1991.

Kahoku asasan kaishinkai 華北麻産改進会 [North China Jute Promotion Board].
"Jūku nendo gyōmu seiseki hōkokusho" 十九年度業務成績報告書 [Report on
jute achievements in 1944]. Archives of the North China Political Council (Beijing), J25-1-127.

Kahoku bōshoku kōgyōkai 華北紡織工業會 [North China Textile Industry Asso-
ciation]. *Asa kōshō jitai chōsa ichiranhyō* 麻工廠事態調査一覽表 [Jute mills at a
glance], 1 November 1943. Held in archives of the Japan Spinners' Association (Osaka University), II-1-68-218.

———. *Mōbōshoku kōshō jitai chōsa ichiranhyō* 毛紡織工廠事態調査一覽表 [Woolen
mills at a glance], 1 September 1943. Held in archives of the Japan Spinners'
Association (Osaka University), II-1-61-253.

Kikakubu 企画部 [Planning Bureau]. "Asakōgyō tōsei un'ei yōkō" 麻工業統制運営
要綱 [Flax [jute] industry: Outline for control of operations]. *Kahoku bōshoku
kōgyōkai geppō* 華北紡織工業會月報 [North China Textile Industry Association Monthly] 3 (March 1944): 63–64.

———. "Asakōgyō tōsei un'ei yōkō kaisetsu" 麻工業統制運営要綱解説 [Flax [jute]
industry: Explanation of the outline for control of operations]. *Kahoku
bōshoku kōgyōkai geppō* 華北紡織工業會月報 [North China Textile Industry Association Monthly] 3 (March 1944): 45–50.

———. "Bōseki kōshō ni okeru rōkō kakuho taisaku ni tsuite" 紡績工廠における 労
工確保対策について [Policies for the guarantee of labor for spinning facto-
ries]. *Kahoku bōshoku kōgyōkai geppō* 華北紡織工業會月報 [North China Textile
Industry Association Monthly] 7 (March 1945): 29–31.

———. "Huabei qianwei tongzhi guicheng" 華北繊維統制規程 [Regulations for
the control of North China fiber]. *Kahoku bōshoku kōgyōkai geppō* 華北紡織工
業會月報 [North China Textile Industry Association Monthly] 1 (January
1944): 71.

———. "Kahoku sen'i kōgyō kanri yōkō ni tsuite" 華北繊維工業管理要綱に就いて
[Outline for the management of North China fiber industries]. *Kahoku
bōshoku kōgyōkai geppō* 華北紡織工業會月報 [North China Textile Industry Association Monthly] 1 (January 1944): 39.

————. "Mōbōshoku kōgyō: Tōsei un'ei yōkō kaisetsu" 毛紡織工業: 統制運営要綱解説 [Wool spinning industry: Explanation of the outline for control of operations]. *Kahoku bōshoku kōgyōkai geppō* 華北紡織工業會月報 [North China Textile Industry Association Monthly] 1 (January 1944): 36, 39.

————. "Mōbōshoku kōgyō: Tōsei yōkō" 毛紡織工業: 統制要綱 [Outline for the control of the wool spinning industry]. *Kahoku bōshoku kōgyōkai geppō* 華北紡織工業會月報 [North China Textile Industry Association Monthly] 1 (January 1944): 71–73.

Kim, Wonik. "Rethinking Colonialism and the Origins of the Developmental State in East Asia." *Journal of Contemporary Asia* 39, no. 3 (August 2009): 382–399.

Kirby, William C. "China Unincorporated: Company Law and Business Enterprise in Twentieth-Century China." *Journal of Asian Studies* 54, no. 1 (February 1995): 43–63.

————. *Germany and Republican China*. Stanford, CA: Stanford University Press, 1984.

Köll, Elisabeth. *From Cotton Mill to Business Empire: The Emergence of Regional Enterprise in Modern China*. Cambridge, MA: Harvard East Asian Center, 2004.

Kubo Toru. "The Koa-in." In Stephen R. MacKinnon, Diana Lary, and Ezra Vogel, eds., *China at War: Regions of China, 1937–45*, 44–64. Stanford, CA: Stanford University Press, 2007.

————"The Tariff Policy of the Nationalist Government, 1929–36: A Historical Assessment." In Kaoru Sugihara, ed., *Japan, China, and the Growth of the Asian International Economy, 1850–1949*, 145–176. Oxford: Oxford University Press, 2005.

Kwan, Man Bun. *The Salt Merchants of Tianjin: State-Making and Civil Society in Late Imperial China*. Honolulu: University of Hawaii Press, 2001.

Lamoreaux, Naomi R. "Reframing the Past: Thoughts about Business Leadership and Decision Making under Uncertainty." *Enterprise and Society* 2 (December 2001): 632–659.

Landdeck, Kevin. "Under the Gun: Nationalist Military Service and Society in Wartime Sichuan, 1938–1945." Ph.D. dissertation, University of California, Berkeley, 2011.

Lary, Diana. "Treachery, Disgrace and Death: Han Fuju and China's Resistance to Japan." *War in History* 13, no. 1 (2006): 65–90.

Lester, Katherine Morris, Bess Viola Oerke, and Helen Westermann. *Accessories of Dress: An Illustrated Encyclopedia*. Mineola, NY: Dover Publications, 2004; reprint of 1940 work.

Leung, Angela Ki Che, and Charlotte Furth, eds. *Health and Hygiene in Chinese East Asia: Policies and Publics in the Long Twentieth Century*. Durham, NC: Duke University Press, 2010.

Li Jingneng et al. *Tianjin renkou shi*. Tianjin: Nankai daxue chubanshe, 1990.

Li Jingshan李静山. "Yi jindai fangzhi shiyejia Song Feiqing he Dongya gongsi" 憶近代紡織事業家宋棐卿和東亞公司 [Memories of the modern textile industrialist Song Feiqing and the Dongya Corporation]. *Tianjin wenshi ziliao* 101 (January 2004): 81–102.

Li Jingshan 李静山, Qie Xiyuan 郄希源, Chen Yadong 陳亞東, and Meng Guan-glin 孟廣林. "Song Feiqing yu Tianjin dongya qiye gongsi" 宋棐卿與天津東亞企業公司 [Song Feiqing and the Tianjin Dongya Corporation]. *Tianjin wenshi ziliao* 29 (1984): 86–114.

Lieberthal, Kenneth G. *Revolution and Tradition in Tientsin, 1949–1952.* Stanford, CA: Stanford University Press, 1980.

Lin Kaiming 林開明 and Li Shuying 李淑英. "Tianjin fanri hui yu dizhi rihuo yundong" 天津反日會與抵制日貨運動 [Tianjin's anti-Japanese society and the anti-Japanese goods boycott]. *Tianjin wenshi ziliao* 78 (1998): 87–92.

Lin, Man Houng. "Interpretive Trends in Taiwan's Scholarship on Chinese Busi-ness History: 1600 to the Present." In Robert Gardella, Jane K. Leonard, and Andrea McElderry, eds., "Chinese Business History: Interpretive Trends and Priorities for the Future," special issue, *Chinese Studies in History* 31, nos. 3–4 (Spring–Summer 1998): 65–94.

Lin Meili 林美莉. *Kangzhan shiqi de huobi zhanzheng* 抗戰時期的貨幣戰爭 [The currency war at the time of the anti-Japanese war]. Taipei: Guoli Taiwan Shifan Daxue Lishi Yanjiusuo, 1996.

Lin Xiuzhu 林修竹. *Shandong gexian xiangtu diaocha lu* 山東省個縣鄉土調查祿 [Re-cord of investigation of localities in Shandong Province's counties]. Place of publication not given, 1919.

Linz, Juan J. "Authoritarianism." In Seymour Martin Lipset, ed., *Political Philos-ophy: Theories, Thinkers, Concepts,* 3–7. Washington, DC: CQ Press, 2001.

Lipset, Seymour Martin, ed. *Political Philosophy: Theories, Thinkers, Concepts.* Wash-ington, DC: CQ Press, 2001.

Liu Jingyue 劉景岳. "Tianjin lunxian qian de zui hou yi zhan" 天津淪陷前的最後一戰 [The last battle before the occupation of Tianjin]. In Tianjin wenshi ziliao yanjiu weiyuanhui, ed., *Lunxian shiqi de Tianjin* 淪陷時期的天津 [Tianjin in the era of occupation], 1–8. Tianjin: Tianjin Zhengxie Hui, 1992.

Liu Shaochun 劉紹春, Sun Jian 孫健, and Li Yulian 李玉璉. "Huiyi Liu Shaoqi tongzhi shicha Dongya Gongsi" 回憶劉少奇同志視察東亞公司 [Remembering Comrade Liu Shaoqi's visit to the Dongya Company]. *Tianjin dangshi* 4 (1999): 50–52.

Liu Yanchen 劉炎臣, ed. "Tianjin guohuo shoupin suo 'zongwubu gongbu liudi' zhailu" 天津國貨售品所 '總務部公布留底' 摘錄 [Selections recorded from the "General Affairs Office Announcements" of the Tianjin National Products Bureau]. *Tianjin wenshi ziliao* 47 (July 1989): 66–123.

Lü, Xiaobo. "Minor Public Economy: The Revolutionary Origins of the Danwei." In Xiaobo Lü and Elizabeth Perry, eds., *Danwei: The Changing Chinese Work-place in Historical and Comparative Perspective,* 21–41. Armonk, NY: M. E. Sharpe, 1997.

Lü, Xiaobo, and Elizabeth Perry, eds. *Danwei: The Changing Chinese Workplace in Historical and Comparative Perspective.* Armonk, NY: M. E. Sharpe, 1997.

Ma Hanfang 馬含芳. *Jinluandian: Lütou qian* 金鑾殿:綠頭簽 [Hall of the golden bell: Green bamboo slip]. Beijing: Zuojia chubanshe, 2008. http://www.exvv.com/mall/detail.jsp?proID=683147. Accessed 31 July 2008.

Ma Xiafu 馬俠夫. "Song Feiqing he Dongya Gongsi" 宋棐卿和東亞公司 [Song Feiqing and the Dongya Corporation]. *Qingzhou wenshi ziliao* 7 (December 1989): 86–103.

Macdonald, Anne L. *No Idle Hands: The Social History of American Knitting.* New York: Ballantine Books, 1988.

Magnusson, Lars. *Nation, State and the Industrial Revolution: The Visible Hand.* London: Routledge, 2009.

Mann, Susan. *Local Merchants and the Chinese Bureaucracy, 1750–1950.* Stanford, CA: Stanford University Press, 1987.

———. *Precious Records: Women in China's Long Eighteenth Century.* Stanford, CA: Stanford University Press, 1997.

Maozhi gongye baogao shu 毛織工業報告書 [Report on the wool goods industry]. Quanguo jingji weiyuanhui jingji zhuankan 全國經濟委員會經濟專刊 [All-China Economic Commission Economic Monograph Series], no. 2 (1935).

McMullan, James. "Report Read at the Opening Service of the Chefoo Industrial Mission, September 26th, 1902." *Chinese Recorder* 33, no. 11 (November 1902): 550–554.

———. "The Value of Industrial Training and Enterprise from a Missionary Standpoint." *Chinese Recorder* 45, no. 3 (March 1914): 144–145.

McMullan, Mrs. James. "Report of the Chefoo Industrial Work." *Chinese Recorder* 30, no. 4 (April 1899): 182–185.

Minami manshū tetsudō kabushiki gaisha hokushi chōsajo 南満州鉄道株式会社北支調査所 [South Manchurian Railway Corporation North China Research Office]. *Kita Shina kōjō jittai chōsa hō* 北支那工場実態調査報 [Report on the status of factories in North China]. Tianjin, 1939.

Minami manshū tetsudō keizai chōsakai dainibu daiyonhan 南満州鉄道経済調査会第二部第四班 [South Manchurian Railway Economics Research Office, Bureau Two, Team Four]. *Yōmō kōgyō tai sakuan* 羊毛工業対策案 [Wool industry policy]. June 1933.

Munz, H. *The Australian Wool Industry.* Melbourne: F. W. Cheshire, 1964.

Murdoch, Michael G. "The Politics of Exclusion: Revolutionary and Christian Competition over China's National Identity during the Northern Expedition Period, 1923–27." Ph.D. dissertation, University of Michigan, 1999.

Nakamura Kanichi 中村一之 "Peikin, Tenshin, Sainan, I ken oyobi Aoshima ni okeru seiyaku shō chōsa" 北京, 天津, 済南濰県及び青島に於ける製薬廠調査 [Investigation of medicine factories in Beijing, Tianjin, Jinan, Wei County and Qingdao]. *Kōain chōsa geppō* 興亜院調査月報 [Koa Institute Investigation Monthly] 2, no. 6 (1941): 294–306.

Nathan, Andrew J. "Imperialism's Effects on China." *Bulletin of the Committee of Concerned Asian Scholars* [now known as *Critical Asian Studies*] 4, no. 4 (December 1972): 3–8.

Nee, Victor, Sonja Opper, and Sonia Wong. "Developmental State and Corporate Governance in China." *Management and Organization Review* 3, no. 1 (2007): 19–53.

Nee, Victor, and Richard Swedberg. "Introduction." In Victor Nee and Richard Swedberg, eds., *On Capitalism*, 1–18. Stanford, CA: Stanford University Press, 2007.

Nicholson, Heather. *The Loving Stitch: A History of Knitting and Spinning in New Zealand*. Auckland: Auckland University Press, 1998.

Parker, A. G. *Social Glimpses of Tsinan*. Tsinan [Jinan]: Department of Sociology, Shantung [Shandong] Christian University, 1924.

Perry, Elizabeth. "From Native Place to Workplace: Labor Origins and Outcomes of China's *Danwei* System." In Xiaobo Lü and Elizabeth Perry, eds., *Danwei: The Changing Chinese Workplace in Historical and Comparative Perspective*. 42–59. Armonk, NY: M. E. Sharpe, 1997.

Pomeranz, Kenneth. *The Making of a Hinterland: State, Society, and Economy in Inland North China, 1853–1937*. Berkeley: University of California Press, 1993.

Porter, Robin. *Industrial Reformers in Republican China*. Armonk, NY: M. E. Sharpe, 1994.

Qingzhou shizhi 青州市誌 [Qingzhou County gazetteer]. Tianjin: Nankai daxue chubanshe, 1989.

Radice, Hugo. "The Developmental State under Global Neoliberalism." *Third World Quarterly* 29, no. 6 (2008): 1153–1174.

Rawski, Thomas G. *Economic Growth in Prewar China*. Berkeley: University of California Press, 1989.

Redding, S. Gordon. *The Spirit of Chinese Capitalism*. New York: Walter de Gruyter, 1990.

Reed, Christopher A. *Gutenberg in Shanghai: Chinese Print Capitalism, 1876–1937*. Vancouver: British Columbia Press, 2004.

Richard, Timothy. *Forty-Five Years in China*. New York: Frederick A. Stokes, 1916.

Richardson, Philip. *Economic Change in China, c. 1800–1950*. Cambridge: Cambridge University Press, 1999.

Rogaski, Ruth. *Hygienic Modernity: Meanings of Health and Disease in Treaty-Port China*. Berkeley: University of California Press, 2004.

Ross, I. Clunies. *A Survey of the Sheep and Wool Industry in North-Eastern Asia, with Special Reference to Manchukuo, Korea, and Japan*. Melbourne: Commonwealth of Australia Council for Scientific and Industrial Research, 1936.

Rueschemeyer, Dietrich. "Capitalism." In Seymour Martin Lipset, ed., *Political Philosophy: Theories, Thinkers, Concepts*, 12–19. Washington, DC: CQ Press, 2001

Rui Fu 瑞甫. "Tianjin Dongya qiye gufen youxian gongsi jianxie" 天津東亞企業股份有限公司簡寫 [A brief account of the Dongya Corporation]. *Gongye yuekan* 4, no. 10 (October 1947): 21–22.

Ruiqiu 瑞秋. "Weisheng yi" 衛生衣 [Hygiene clothing]. *Funü zazhi* 婦女雜誌 5, no. 1 (January 1919).

Rutt, Richard. *A History of Hand Knitting*. Loveland, CO: Interweave Press, 1987.

Sanxiao maliezhuyi jiaoyanshi, zhengzhi jingji xue zu 三校馬列主義教研室政治經濟學組 [Three-School Marxism-Leninism Research Institute, Political Economy Group]. "Dongya maofangchang de zibenzhuyi boxue" 東亞毛紡廠

的資本主義剝削 [The capitalist exploitation of Dongya]. Mimeograph manuscript, 1978, Tianjin History Museum.

Schwarcz, Vera. *The Chinese Enlightenment: Intellectuals and the Legacy of the May Fourth Movement of 1919.* Berkeley: University of California Press, 1986.

Scott, Bruce. *Capitalism: Its Origins and Evolution as a System of Governance.* New York: Springer, 2011.

Shah, S. Y. "A Survey of the Wool Industry of China." *Chinese Economic Journal* 20, no. 6 (June 1937): 656–666.

Shanghai minzu mao fangzhi gongye 上海民族毛紡織工業 [The Shanghai domestic spinning and weaving industry]. Ed. Shanghai gongshang xingzheng guanli ju 上海工商行政管理局 [Shanghai Business and Industry Management Bureau], Shanghaishi maoma fangzhi gongye gongsi 上海市毛麻紡織工業公司 [Shanghai Municipal Wool Spinning Company], and Maofang shiliao zu 毛紡史料組 [Wool Historical Materials Group]. Beijing: Zhonghua shuju 中華書局, 1963.

Shanghaishi fangzhi kexue yanjiu yuan 上海市紡織科學研究院 [Shanghai Municipal Textile Scientific Research Institute], ed. *Fangzhi shihua* [Historical stories about textiles)]. Shanghai: Shanghai kexue jishu chubanshe, 1978.

Sheehan, Brett. "An Awkward but Potent Fit: Photographs and Political Narratives of the Tianjin Incidents during the Sino-Japanese Conflict, November 1931." *European Journal of East Asian Studies* 7, no. 2 (2008): 193–227.

———. "Boycotts and Bombs: The Failure of Economic Sanctions in the Sino-Japanese Conflict, Tianjin, China, 1928–1932." *Management and Organizational History* 5, no. 2 (May 2010): 197–220.

———. "Shotgun Wedding: The Dongya Corporation and the Early Communist Regime." In Sherman Cochran, ed., *The Capitalist Dilemma in China's Communist Revolution: Stay, Leave, or Return?* Ithaca, NY: Cornell University East Asian Series, forthcoming.

———. *Trust in Troubled Times: Money, Banking, and State-Society Relations in Republican Tianjin.* Cambridge, MA: Harvard University Press, 2003.

———. "Urban Identity and Urban Networks in Cosmopolitan Cities: Banks and Bankers in Tianjin, 1900–1937." In Joseph Esherick, ed., *Remaking the Chinese City: Modernity and National Identity, 1900–1950*, 47–64. Honolulu: University of Hawaii Press, 2000.

———. "When Urban Met Rural in the Japanese Occupation: Life on an Agricultural Research Station in North China." In Wen-hsin Yeh and Brett Sheehan, eds., "Chinese Experiences of Total War." Unpublished manuscript.

Shi Ying 石英. *Wenming diyu* 文明地獄 [A civilized hell]. Beijing: Zuojia chubanshe, 1965.

———. "Zaiban houji" 再版後記 [Afterword of the new edition]. *Wenming diyu* 文明地獄 [A civilized hell], 144. Beijing: Renmin wenxue chubanshe, 1983.

Shina chūton gun shirei bu 支那駐屯軍司令部 [Commander of China Garrison]. "Tenshin bōseki jigyō ni kan suru hōsakuan (kimitsu)" 天津紡績事業ニ関スル

方策案 (機密) [Policy for the fibers industry in Tianjin (secret)], February 1936.

Shiroyama, Tomoko. *China during the Great Depression: Market, State, and the World Economy, 1929–1937.* Cambridge, MA: Harvard University Asia Center, 2008.

"Shōwa jūkyū nendo honkai gyōmu hōkoku" 昭和十九年度本会業務報告 [Report on operations of this association for the year 1944]. *Kahoku bōshoku kōgyōkai geppō* 華北紡織工業會月報 [North China Textile Industry Association Monthly] 7 (March 1945): 26–28.

Song Xianyong. "Jue ji bu wang women tong Riben de zhanzheng" 絕記不忘我們同日本的戰爭 [Our unforgotten war with Japan]. *Nankai chunqiu* 南開春秋 (1995): 74–76.

Song Yunzhang and Wang Weigang 宋允璋 王維剛. *Tade meng: Song Feiqing* 他的夢: 宋棐卿 [His dream: Song Feiqing]. Hong Kong: Wenming, 2006.

Song Yuzan 宋毓瓚. "Liu Shaoqi zai 'Dongya'" 劉少奇在 '東亞' [Liu Shaoqi at Dongya]. *Tianjin wenshi ziliao* 79 (1998): 104–105.

Stanger, Howard R. "From Factory to Family: The Creation of a Corporate Culture in the Larkin Company of Buffalo, New York." *Business History Review* 74 (Autumn 2000): 407–433.

Stanley, Brian. *The History of the Baptist Missionary Society, 1792–1992.* Edinburgh: T & T Clark, 1992.

Stewart, John R. "North China Restrictions and Exports to the U.S." *Far Eastern Survey* 8, no. 20 (11 October 1939): 240–241.

Strauss, Julia. "The Evolution of Republican Government." *China Quarterly* 150 (June 1997): 329–351.

Sun Dechang 孫德常 and Zhou Zuchang 周組常, eds. *Tianjin jindai jingji shi* 天津近代經濟史 [Economic history of modern Tianjin]. Tianjin: Tianjin shehui kexue chubanshe, 1990.

Swann, Sebastian P. "The Tientsin Incident (1939): A Case Study of Japan's Imperial Dilemma in China." Ph.D. dissertation, University of London, 1998.

"Symposium on China's Economic History." *Modern China* 4, no. 3 (July 1978).

Taylor, George. *Japanese Sponsored Regime in North China.* New York: International Secretariat, Institute of Pacific Relations, 1939; reprinted, New York: Garland, 1980.

Tenshin Nihon shōkō kaigisho 天津日本商工会議所 [Tianjin Japanese Chamber of Commerce and Industry]. *Tenshin keizai jijō* 天津経済事情 [Tianjin's economy]. Tianjin, 1939.

"Tianjin Dongya maozhi gongsi gaikuang" 天津東亞毛織公司概況 [The general situation of the Dongya Wool Company]. *Huabei laodong* 華北勞動 [North China Labor] 1 (15 November 1946): 15–16.

"Tianjin guohuo shoupinsuo 'zongwubu gongbu liudi' zhailu" 天津國貨售品所 '總務部公布留底' 摘錄 [Selection of file copies of the General Affairs Office of the Tianjin National Products Sales Office]. *Tianjin wenshi ziliao* 47 (July 1989): 66–123.

Tianjin tongzhi, zhengquan zhi, zhengfu juan 天津通志, 政權志, 政府卷 [Tianjin gazetteer, politics, government volume]. Tianjin: Tianjin shehui kexue chubanshe, 2000.

Tianjinshi Dang'anguan 天津市檔案管 [Tianjin Municipal Archive], ed. *Jiefang chuqi Tianjin chengshi jingji hongguan guanli* 解放初期天津城市經濟宏觀管理 [Macro-management of Tianjin's economy in the early liberation period]. Tianjin: Tianjinshi Dang'anguan, 1995.

Tianjinshi Dang'anguan 天津市檔案館 et al., eds. *Tianjin Shanghui dangan huibian, 1928–1937* 天津商會檔案匯編, 1928–1937 [Collection of materials from the Tianjin Chamber of Commerce Archives, 1928–1937]. Tianjin: Renmin, 1996.

Tsai, Kellee S. *Capitalism without Democracy: The Private Sector in Contemporary China.* Ithaca, NY: Cornell University Press, 2007.

Tsutsui, William M. *Manufacturing Ideology: Scientific Management in Twentieth-Century Japan.* Princeton, NJ: Princeton University Press, 1998.

Wakeman, Frederic, Jr. "'Cleanup': The New Order in Shanghai." In Jeremy Brown and Paul G. Pickowicz, eds., *Dilemmas of Victory: The Early Years of the People's Republic of China,* 21–58. Cambridge, MA: Harvard University Press, 2007).

———. *Dai Li and the Chinese Secret Service.* Berkeley: University of California Press, 2003.

———. *Policing Shanghai, 1927–1937.* Berkeley: University of California Press, 1996.

Wallerstein, Immanuel. "The West, Capitalism, and the Modern World-System." In Timothy Brook and Gregory Blue, eds., *China and Historical Capitalism: Genealogies of Sinological Knowledge,* 10–56. Cambridge: Cambridge University Press, 1999.

Wang Hao 王昊. "Lun Song Feiqing dui Tianjin Dongya gongsi de qiye linian" 論宋棐卿對天津東亞公司的企業理念 [On Song Feiqing's concept of the firm in regard to the Dongya Corporation]. Senior thesis, Nankai University, May 2005.

Wang Juntang 王鈞堂 and Feng Baoguang 馮寶光. "Wo suo zhidao de Song Chuandian" 我所知道的宋傳典 [The Song Chuandian that we know]. *Shandong wenshi ziliao xuanji* 5 (1987): 67–74.

Wang Weigang 王維剛. "Dongya fangzhi dawang Song Feiqing" 東亞紡織大王宋棐卿 [Dongya's textile king Song Feiqing]. In Zhao Yunsheng 趙云聲, ed., *Zhongguo da ziben jia,* vol. 7, *Jingjin dagu juan* 中國大資本家, 7 京津大賈卷 [China's great capitalists, vol. 7, Great businesspeople of Beijing and Tianjin], 3–160. Changchun: Shidai wenyi chubanshe, 1994.

Wank, David L. *Commodifying Communism: Business, Trust, and Politics in a Chinese City.* Cambridge: Cambridge University Press, 1999.

Weifang municipal government. http://www.wfsq.gov.cn/rwview.asp?id=497. Accessed 31 July 2008.

Weinstein, Barbara. *For Social Peace in Brazil: Industrialists and the Remaking of the Working Class in São Paulo, 1920–1964.* Chapel Hill: University of North Carolina Press, 1996.

Williamson, H. R. *British Baptists in China, 1845–1952.* London: Carey Kingsgate Press, 1957.

Wong, R. Bin. *China Transformed: Historical Change and the Limits of European Experience.* Ithaca, NY: Cornell University Press, 1997.

Wong, Siu-lun. "The Chinese Family Firm: A Model." In R. Ampalavanar Brown, ed., *Chinese Business Enterprise: Critical Perspectives on Business and Management,*

1:107–121. London: Routledge, 1996. Originally published in the *British Journal of Sociology* 36, no. 1 (1985): 58–72.

Wu, Tien-wei. "Contending Political Forces during the War of Resistance." In James C. Hsiung and Steven I. Levine, eds., *China's Bitter Victory: The War with Japan, 1937–1945,* 51–78. Armonk, NY: M. E. Sharpe, 1992.

Wu, Yu-shan. "Taiwan's Developmental State: After the Economic and Political Turmoil." *Asian Survey* 47, no. 6 (November/December 2007): 977–1001.

Xiao Fang 肖舫. "Song Feiqing he Dongya maofangzhi gufan youxian gongsi" 宋棐卿和東亞毛紡織股份有限公司 [Song Feiqing and the Dongya Corporation]. In Liu Yu 柳渝, ed., *Zhongguo bainian shangye juzi, xia* 中國百年商業巨子,下 [A century of Chinese business giants, vol. 2], 2–58. Changchun: Dongbei shifan daxue chubanshe, 1997.

Xu Hualu 徐化魯 and Ming Shaohua 明少華. "Guanliao maiban zibenjia Song Chuandian de choue yisheng" 官僚賣辦資本家宋傳典的丑惡一生 [The evil life of the bureaucratic comprador capitalist Song Chuandian]. *Shandong wenshi ziliao xuanji* 4 (1982): 71–85.

Yang, Mayfair Mei-hui. *Gifts, Favors, and Banquets: The Art of Social Relationships in China.* Ithaca, NY: Cornell University Press, 1994.

Yang Tianshou 楊天受 and Li Jingshan 李靜山. "Jiefang qian de Dongya gongsi (xianming: Tianjinshi Dongya maoma fangzhichang)" 解放前的東亞公司 (現名: 天津市東亞毛麻紡織廠) [The Dongya Company before liberation (now called: Tianjin Municipal Dongya Wool and Jute Mill)]. Unpublished manuscript, 30 June 1963.

———. "Song Feiqing yu Dongya gongsi" 宋棐卿與東亞公司 [Song Feiqing and the Dongya Corporation]. *Wenshi ziliao xuanji* 49 (1964): 161–182.

———. "Tianjin Dongya Gongsi yu Song Feiqing" 天津 東亞公司與宋棐卿 [Tianjin's Dongya Corporation and Song Feiqing]. *Gongshang shiliao* 2 (1981): 105–127.

Yao, Souchou. *Confucian Capitalism: Discourse, Practice and the Myth of Chinese Enterprise.* London: Routledge Curzon, 2002.

Ye Wuxi 葉梧西 and Shao Yunrui 邵雲瑞. "Chongping 'Tianjin Jianghua'" 重評 '天津講話' [A new evaluation of the Tianjin talks]. *Lishi yanjiu* 2 (1980): 47–58.

Yeh, Wen-hsin. "Corporate Space, Communal Time: Everyday Life in Shanghai's Bank of China." *American Historical Review* 100, no. 1 (1995): 97–122.

———. "Progressive Journalism and Shanghai's Petty Urbanites: Zou Taofen and the *Shenghuo Weekly,* 1926–1945." In Frederic Wakeman Jr. and Wen-hsin Yeh, eds., *Shanghai Sojourners,* 186–238. Berkeley: Institute of East Asian Studies, University of California, 1992.

———. "Republican Origins of the *Danwei:* The Case of Shanghai's Bank of China." In Xiaobo Lü and Elizabeth Perry, eds., *Danwei: The Changing Chinese Workplace in Historical and Comparative Perspective,* 60–88. Armonk, NY: M. E. Sharpe, 1997.

Yoshida Miyuki 吉田美之. "Tenshin no keori kōgyō" 天津の毛織工業 [Tianjin's wool industry]. *Mantetsu chōsa geppō* 满铁调查月报 [South Manchurian Railway Investigation Monthly] 19, no. 8 (August 1939): 137–175.

Young, Louise. *Japan's Total Empire: Manchuria and the Culture of Wartime Imperialism*. Berkeley: University of California Press, 1999.

Yuan Jing 遠靜, ed. *Dadihuichun: Dongya maomachang gongren douzheng de gushi* 大地回春:東亞毛麻廠工人鬥爭的故事 [Spring returns to the earth: The story of the workers' struggles at the Dongya Woolen and Jute Mill]. 天津工商史叢書 [Tianjin business history series]. Tianjin: Baihua wenyi chubanshe, 1960.

Yuan Zemin 袁澤民 "Dongya maozhi gongchang laozi jiufen tiaojie jingguo" 東亞毛織工廠勞資糾紛調解經過 [Process of resolution of the labor-capital dispute at Dongya Wool]. *Gongren zhoukan* 工人週刊 [Worker Weekly], no. 1 (1 October 1948): 7.

Zanasi, Margherita. *Saving the Nation: Economic Modernity in Republican China*. Chicago: Chicago University Press, 2006.

Zelin, Madeleine. *The Merchants of Zigong: Industrial Entrepreneurship in Early Modern China*. New York: Columbia University Press, 2005.

Zhang Boyang 張伯揚. "Huiyi Liu Shaoqi huijian 'Dongya' zhigong daibiao" 回憶劉少奇會見 '東亞' 職工代表 [Remembering Liu Shaoqi's meeting with Dongya employee representatives]. *Tianjin wenshi ziliao* 79 (1998): 106–107.

Zhang Guojun 張國鈞. "Huiyi Liu Shaoqi shicha 'Dongya'" 回憶劉少奇視察 '東亞' [Remembering Liu Shaoqi's tour of Dongya]. *Tianjin wenshi ziliao* 79 (1998): 109–110.

Zhang Guoxun 張國熏. "Yi Liu Shaoqi 'Dongya' zhi xing" 憶劉少奇 '東亞' 之行 [Remembering Liu Shaoqi's trip to Dongya]. *Tianjin wenshi ziliao* 79 (1998): 111.

Zhang Pengyuan 張朋園 and Shen Huaiyu 沈懷玉, eds. *Guomin Zhengfu zhiguan nianbiao (1925–1949) di yi ce* 國民政府職官年表 (1925–1949) 第一冊 [Yearly record of officials of the Nationalist government, vol. 1, 1925–1949]. Taipei: Zhongyang yanjiu Yuan jindai shi yanjiu suo shiliao congkan (6), 1989.

Zhang Wenxing 張文星. "Song Chuandian shilue" 宋傳典略 [A brief account of Song Chuandian's life]. *Qingzhou wenshi ziliao* 5 (1987): 133–135.

Zhang Xianwen 張憲文 et al. *Zhongguo kangri zhanzheng shi* 中國抗日戰爭史 [A history of China's anti-Japanese war]. Tianjin: Nanjing University Press, 2001.

Zhao Runnian. "Yi Liu Shaoqi Jianghua" 憶劉少奇講話 [Remembering Liu Shaoqi's talk]. *Tianjin wenshi ziliao* 79 (1998): 108.

Zhao Xingguo 趙興國. "Tianjin Dongya maozhi gongsi niaokan" 天津東亞毛織公司鳥瞰 [A bird's-eye view of Tianjin Dongya Company]. *Hebei sheng yinghang jingji ban yuekan* 河北省銀行經濟半月刊 [Hebei Provincial Bank Economic Bimonthly] 1, no. 10 (last half of May 1946): 26–29.

Zhao Zizhen 趙子貞. "Tianjin Dongya Maoni Gongsi chuangban qianhou" 天津東亞毛呢公司創辦前後 [Before and after the founding of the Dongya Woolen Mill]. *Tianjin wenshi ziliao* 95 (March 2002): 102–115.

Zhonggong Tianjin shiwei dangshi ziliao zhengji weiyuan hui 中共天津市委黨史資料委員會 [Historical Records Committee of the Tianjin Chinese Communist Party Committee], Zhonggong Tianjin shiwei tongzhan bu 中共天津市委統戰部 [United Front Work Office of the Tianjin Chinese Party Committee], and Tianjinshi Dang'anguan 天津市檔案管 [Tianjin Municipal Archives], eds. *Zhongguo zibenzhuyi gongshangye de shehuizhuyi gaizao, Tianjin juan*

中國資本主義工商業的社會主義改造, 天津卷 [The socialist transformation of China's capitalist business and industry, Tianjin volume]. Tianjin: Zhonggong dangshi chubanshe, 1991.

Zhonggong zazhi she 中共雜誌社 [Chinese Communist Party Research Agency]. *Liu Shaoqi wenti ziliao zhuanji* 劉少奇問題資料專輯 [Collection of materials on Liu Shaoqi's problems]. Taipei: Zhonggong yanjiu zazhi she, 1970.

Zhongguo fangzhi gonghui Tianjin Dongya qiye gongsi weiyuan hui 中國紡織工會天津東亞企業公司委員會 [The Tianjin Dongya Enterprise Corporation Committee of the Chinese Textile Union]. "'Song Feiqing zuixing zhanlan hui' jieloule zichan jieji de fandong xing" '宋棐卿罪行展覽會' 揭露了資產階級的反動性 [The "Crimes of Song Feiqing Exhibit" reveals the reactionary nature of the capitalist class]. *Zhongguo fangzhi gongren* 中國紡織工人 [China Textile Worker] 7 (1 April 1952): cover and 12–15.

Zhongguo shehui kexueyuan jindaishi yanjiusuo zhonghua minguoshi yanjiushi 中國社會科學院近代史研究所, 中華民國史研究室 [Republican Period Research Office of the Modern History Institute of the Chinese Academy of Social Sciences], ed. *Zhonghua minguo shi ziliao conggao, renwu zhuanji, di shiwu ji* 中華民國史資料叢稿, 人物傳記, 第十五輯 [Collection of materials on the history of Republican China, Biography, vol. 15]. Beijing: Zhonghua shuju, 1982.

Zhou Chuanming 周傳銘. *Jinan kuailan* 濟南快覽 [Jinan at a glance]. Jinan: Shijie shuju, 1927.

Zhou Qilun. 周啟綸. "Jiefang qian Tianjin wujia feizhang min buliao sheng jishi" 解放前天津物價飛漲民不聊生紀事 [A true record of soaring prices and people unable to live in pre-liberation Tianjin]. In Yang Daxin and Fang Zhaolin, eds., *Tianjin lishi de zhuanzhe, yuan guomindang junzheng renyuan de huiyi* 天津歷史的轉折,原國民黨軍政人員的回憶 [Tianjin's historical turning point, memories of Nationalist military and political officials], 281–282. Tianjin: Tianjinshi zhengxie wenshi ziliao yanjiu weiyuanhui, 1988.

Zi Yaohua 資耀華. *Shiji zuyin: Yiwei jindai jinrongxue jia de zishu* 世紀足音:一位近代金融學家的自述 [A century's footsteps: The autobiography of a modern financial expert]. Hunan: Hunan wenyi chubanshe, 2005.

Acknowledgments

First and foremost, I want to thank Roberta Sung whose enthusiasm to find out more about the father she hardly knew inspired me to learn more as well. She was generous with her time and with family documents and she made it possible to conduct my first preliminary-research trip to gather materials for this book. I know she has despaired of ever seeing this volume in print and I thank her and the rest of the Sung family for their patience. Rebecca Sung hosted me on a trip to New Jersey to speak with Shi Shaodong's family and provided good-humored help on many occasions, as did Albert Sung, Rachel Sung, Rhoda Sung, and David Lee.

In the fourteen years I have worked on this book, I have traveled to eight countries to collect research materials. Countless people and institutions have generously provided their help in this process.

Multiple trips to Tianjin would not have been possible without the help of many. I would particularly like to thank the Work Department of the Dongya Corporation Party Committee, especially Ma Laoshi, who hosted me while I perused the Dongya archives and who provided me with many memories, including an unforgettable and impromptu Thanksgiving lunch. In addition, the staffs at the Tianjin Library, the Tianjin Municipal Archive, the Tianjin History Museum, the Tianjin Academy of Social Sciences, and the Tianjin Zhengxie Hui all made my various trips to Tianjin productive and pleasant. Luo Shuwei, Zhang Limin, and Liu Haiyan all gave help and advice. Special thanks to Fang Zhaolin who has been a good friend and adviser over the years and who pioneered the study of the Dongya Corporation. Song Meiyun was an invaluable research colleague whose humor always put me in a good mood and who has generously invited me to dinner at her house more times than I can remember. Thanks, too, to Li Yulian and Liu Yuying for their help; Li Yulian was particularly gracious in making her father's papers available to me. Chen Xiuwen and Song Yuzhan gave their time and an insider's view of Dongya.

Outside of Tianjin I would like to thank the staffs of the National Library in Beijing, the Beijing Municipal Archives, Shandong University Library, the city of Qingzhou, the Number Two Historical Archives in Nanjing, the Shanghai Municipal Archive, the Hong Kong Public Records Office, the National Diet Library and Toyo Bunko in Tokyo, the library of Osaka University, Academia Historica in Taiwan, the Alloa Historical Society and Clackmannanshire Archives in Scotland, the British National Archives, the French Foreign Ministry archives at both the Quai d'Orsay, Paris, and in Nantes, the Billy Graham Center at Wheaton College, and the libraries of the University of Wisconsin, Madison, the University of California, Berkeley, Stanford University, the Hoover Institution at Stanford, the University of California, San Diego, the University of California, Los Angeles, and the University of Southern California. A memorable trip to the Song Family Village in 2000 was hosted by a cast of dozens and included a banquet the likes of which I have not seen since. Chen Teh-chih, Liu Jiang, Adeel Mohammadi, Go Oyagi, Sha Qingqing, Wu Shijin, and Ben Uchiyama all provided able research assistance. Thanks too to Luman Wang for providing advice and support. No teacher could ask for a more filial student.

Funding for this long period of research was provided by the Fulbright Foundation, the University of Wisconsin Graduate School, the Chiang Ching-kuo Foundation, and the University of Southern California.

Many people have commented on conference presentations, drafts, and partial drafts of the manuscript. I would like to thank the participants in a manuscript review seminar at the Center for East Asian Studies at the University of Southern California. Grace Ryu, Eva Luc, and Sarah Johnson made the seminar possible. David Kang hosted the event and his advice saved me from an embarrassing mistake. Parks Coble and Sherman Cochran read the manuscript in minute detail, led the discussion, and made thoughtful and useful comments, as did Brian Bernards, Betinne Birge, Maura Dykstra, Charlotte Furth, Josh Goldstein, Liu Haiwei, and Ben Uchiyama. Georgia Mickey provided advice during that seminar and in many other conversations. In addition, I have received helpful comments from Nan Enstadt, Fran Hirsch, and Ramzi Rouighi. Tommy Pan read multiple drafts and his disdain for cliché improved the manuscript immensely. Pui-tak Lee helped with materials from the Hong Kong Public Records Office, and he provided much advice from his encyclopedic knowledge of the sources. Man Bun Kwan has heard many conference papers related to this book and has shared important insights with me. Two readers for Harvard University Press, Karl Gerth and David Strand, read the manuscript with thoroughness, acuity, and generosity.

Kathleen McDermott and the staff at Harvard University Press have provided professional, efficient, and patient support. Brian Ostrander and Westchester Publishing Services handled the manuscript with care that I can only describe as old-fashioned and now rare. Jennifer Shenk copyedited with thoroughness and an eye for inconsistency which is truly remarkable. William Keegan prepared the maps with good humor.

As always, none of these people is responsible for my obtuseness in ignoring their advice, and any remaining errors are my own.

My family has also supported this volume in more ways than I can count. My mother- and father-in-law, Zhang Peiwen and Jiang Xiling, decoded Shi Shaodong's indecipherable scribbles; Tian Yuan typed notes; Shelly and George helped make my academic career possible; Alexis, Chris, Sara, Lindsay, and Hillary unknowingly provided moral support as well; my sons Kevin and Angel listened sympathetically and provided much-needed diversions; and my wife, Yiyu Jiang, provided love, support, and endless patience throughout the long years of work.

Index